Discovering William of Malmesbury

Discovering William of Malmesbury

EDITED BY

Rodney M. Thomson

Emily Dolmans

AND

Emily A. Winkler

THE BOYDELL PRESS

© Contributors 2017

All Rights Reserved. Except as permitted under current legislation no part of this work may be photocopied, stored in a retrieval system, published, performed in public, adapted, broadcast, transmitted, recorded or reproduced in any form or by any means, without the prior permission of the copyright owner

First published 2017
The Boydell Press, Woodbridge
Paperback edition 2020

ISBN 978 1 78327 136 8 hardback
ISBN 978 1 78327 536 6 paperback

The Boydell Press is an imprint of Boydell & Brewer Ltd
PO Box 9, Woodbridge, Suffolk IP12 3DF, UK
and of Boydell & Brewer Inc.
668 Mount Hope Ave, Rochester, NY 14620–2731, USA
website: www.boydellandbrewer.com

A catalogue record for this book is available
from the British Library

The publisher has no responsibility for the continued existence or accuracy of URLs for external or third-party internet websites referred to in this book, and does not guarantee that any content on such websites is, or will remain, accurate or appropriate

Typeset in Arno by Word and Page, Chester, UK

CONTENTS

Preface and Acknowledgements — vii

Abbreviations — ix

1. Discovering William of Malmesbury: The Man and his Works
   Emily A. Winkler and *Emily Dolmans* — 1

2. *Gesta Pontificum Anglorum*: History or Hagiography?
   Anne E. Bailey — 13

3. William of Malmesbury and Civic Virtue
   Daniel Gerrard — 27

4. The Ironies of History: William of Malmesbury's Views of William II and Henry I
   John Gillingham — 37

5. William of Malmesbury and the Jews
   Kati Ihnat — 49

6. Advising the King: Kingship, Bishops and Saints in the Works of William of Malmesbury
   Ryan Kemp — 65

7. Roman Identity in William of Malmesbury's Historical Writings
   William Kynan-Wilson — 81

8. William of Malmesbury and the Chronological Controversy
   Anne Lawrence-Mathers — 93

9. William of Malmesbury and Durham: The Circulation of Historical Knowledge in Early Twelfth-Century England
   Stanislav Mereminskiy — 107

10. William of Malmesbury as Librarian: The Evidence of his Autographs
    Samu Niskanen — 117

11. William of Malmesbury: Medical Historian of the Crusades
    Joanna Phillips — 129

12. German Emperors as Exemplary Rulers in William of Malmesbury and Otto of Freising
    Alheydis Plassmann   139

13. *Lector amice*: Reading as Friendship in William of Malmesbury
    Sigbjørn Sønnesyn   153

14. William of Malmesbury's Historical Vision
    Rodney M. Thomson   165

15. *Verax historicus Beda*: William of Malmesbury, Bede and *historia*
    Emily Joan Ward   175

16. William of Malmesbury and the Britons
    Emily A. Winkler   189

17. Words, Words, Words …
    Michael Winterbottom   203

Epilogue: The Rediscovery of William of Malmesbury
    Rodney M. Thomson   219

Index   225

PREFACE AND ACKNOWLEDGEMENTS

Around the turn of 2013–14 Rodney Thomson began to think about a conference with William of Malmesbury as its theme. He did so for at least three reasons: firstly, there had never been a conference devoted solely to William, and the time seemed ripe for one; secondly, Michael Winterbottom would turn 80 on 21 September 2014, and a conference seemed an appropriate way of honouring his long and fundamental service to William studies; and finally, Rodney and Michael had in hand a new edition and translation of William's *Miracles of the Virgin*; its completion would mean that all of William's original works were now available in critical editions with accompanying translation. Publication was scheduled for the middle of 2015, and it seemed possible that it could be made to coincide with an appropriate date for a conference – in the event it appeared a little later.

Because Rodney Thomson and Michael Winterbottom were both long retired, their access to funding and other forms of institutional support was limited. RMT therefore contacted the Medieval Chronicle Society early in 2014, who quickly put him in touch with Ilya Afanasyev, then a graduate student at Hertford College, Oxford. Ilya had been responsible for organising a conference of the Society held in Oxford in 2012, in which Rodney Thomson had played a marginal role. Ilya was willing to put together a team, and the conference began to take shape. From the ground in Oxford, Ilya, Emily Dolmans and Emily Winkler organised and managed the programme on the theme of 'William of Malmesbury and his Legacy', held on 3–5 July 2015. What the conference revealed is that the true extent of William's legacy is still beyond our grasp. There is much more to learn, and to discover.

The conference was an impetus for the volume, but this book is also an endeavour in its own right. It includes papers not delivered at the conference, and covers a wider range of material. It does not purport to represent the full range of scholarship on William of Malmesbury, but rather to show that such efforts are very much alive. It is our express hope that the volume will be as inspiring to others as the conference and papers were to us.

This volume would not have been possible without all of the conference delegates: their stimulating papers, lively discussion, and mutual fascination with William and his works inspired us to discover William of Malmesbury in more depth. We wish to thank the Ioannou Centre for Classical and Byzantine Studies, Corpus Christi College and the Oxford Research Centre for the Humanities for their support. Although Ilya did not join the editorial team, his efforts have made a significant contribution to the volume, for which we are immensely grateful.

Discovering William of Malmesbury

Lastly, we wish to thank our contributors for their illuminating ideas and hard work, with special thanks to Michael Winterbottom for his editorial advice.

Rodney Thomson   Emily Dolmans   Emily A. Winkler

ABBREVIATIONS

ANS	*Anglo-Norman Studies*
ASC	*Anglo-Saxon Chronicle*
ASE	*Anglo-Saxon England*
Aspects	*Aspects of the Language of Latin Prose*, ed. T. Reinhardt, M. Lapidge and J. N. Adams (Oxford, 2005)
BAV	Biblioteca Apostolica Vaticana
Bede, *HE*	Bede, *Historia Ecclesiastica Gentis Anglorum*, ed. and trans. B. Colgrave and R. A. B. Mynors (OMT 1969)
BL	London, British Library
BnF	Paris, Bibliothèque nationale Française
Bodl. Libr.	Oxford, The Bodleian Library
CBMLC	Corpus of British Medieval Library Catalogues (London, 1989–)
CCCC	Cambridge, Corpus Christi College
CCCM	Corpus Christianorum, Continuatio Mediaevalis
CCSL	Corpus Christianorum, Series Latina
CUL	Cambridge University Library
DML	*Dictionary of Medieval Latin from British Sources*, ed. R. D. Latham et al. (17 vols, Oxford, 1975–2013)
Eadmer, *Historia Novorum*	Eadmer, *Historia Novorum in Anglia*, ed. M. Rule (RS 1884), trans. G. Bosanquet (London, 1964)
EHR	*English Historical Review*
EME	*Early Medieval Europe*
Geoffrey of Monmouth	Geoffrey of Monmouth, *The History of the Kings of Britain*, ed. M. D. Reeve, trans. N. Wright (Woodbridge, 2007)
Gildas	Gildas, *The Ruin of Britain*, ed. and trans. M. Winterbottom (London, 1978)
Henry of Huntingdon	Henry of Huntingdon, *Historia Anglorum*, ed. and trans. D. Greenway (OMT 1996)
JEH	*Journal of Ecclesiastical History*
JMH	*Journal of Medieval History*
JML	*Journal of Medieval Latin*
Lambeth	London, Lambeth Palace Library

Lewis and Short	C. T. Lewis and C. Short, *A Latin Dictionary* (Oxford, 1880, frequently reprinted)
Med. St.	*Medieval Studies*
MGH	Monumenta Germaniae Historica
fontes	fontes iuris Germanici antiqui
SS	scriptores (in folio)
srg	scriptores rerum Germanicarum
OMT	Oxford Medieval Texts
Orderic	Orderic Vitalis, *Historia Ecclesiastica*, ed. and trans. M. Chibnall (6 vols, OMT 1968–80)
RB	*Revue bénédictine*
Rhetoric and Renewal	*Rhetoric and Renewal in the Latin West 1100–1540: Essays in Honour of John O. Ward*, ed. C. J. Mews, C. J. Nederman and R. M. Thomson (Turnhout, 2003)
RMS	*Reading Medieval Studies*
RS	Rolls Series
Sønnesyn, *Ethics*	S. Sønnesyn, *William of Malmesbury and the Ethics of History* (Woodbridge, 2012)
Symeon of Durham, *LDE*	Symeon of Durham: *Libellus de Exordio atque Procursu istius hoc est Dunhelmensis Ecclesie*, ed. D. Rollason (OMT 2000)
The Long Twelfth-Century View	*The Long Twelfth-Century View of the Anglo-Saxon Past*, ed. D. A. Woodman and M. Brett (Farnham, 2015)
Thomson, *William of Malmesbury*	R. M. Thomson, *William of Malmesbury* (2nd edn, Woodbridge, 2003)
TRHS	*Transactions of the Royal Historical Society*

Works of William of Malmesbury

AG	*De Antiquitate Glastonie Ecclesie*, ed. and trans. J. Scott (Woodbridge, 1981)
Comm. Lam.	*Willelmi Meldunensis Monachi Liber super Explanationem Lamentationum Ieremiae Prophetae*, ed. M. Winterbottom and R. M. Thomson (CCCM 244, 2011), referred to by book and line-number.
GP	*Gesta Pontificum Anglorum*, ed. and trans. M. Winterbottom and R. M. Thomson (2 vols, OMT 2007). Text and trans. cited by chapter and subsection (00. 00), notes and commentary by vol. and page (I/II, p. 00)

Abbreviations

GR	*Gesta Regum Anglorum*, ed. and trans. R. A. B. Mynors, R. M. Thomson and M. Winterbottom (2 vols, OMT 1998–9). Text and trans. cited by chapter and subsection (00. 00), notes and commentary by vol. and page (I/II, p. 00)
GR (Stubbs)	*Gesta Regum Anglorum*, ed. W. Stubbs (2 vols, RS 1887)
HN	*Historia Nouella*, ed. and trans. E. King and K. Potter (OMT 1998). Text and trans. cited by book and chapter.
Lam.	William of Malmesbury, *On Lamentations*, trans. M. Winterbottom (Corpus Christianorum in Translation: Turnhout, 2013)
MBVM	*The Miracles of the Blessed Virgin Mary*, ed. and trans. R. M. Thomson and M. Winterbottom (Boydell Medieval Texts, Woodbridge, 2015). Cited by number of miracle and subsection (0. 00).
Polyhistor	*Polyhistor Deflorationum*, ed. H. Testroet Ouellette (Binghamton, 1982)
Saints' Lives	William of Malmesbury, *Saints' Lives*, ed. and trans. M. Winterbottom and R. M. Thomson (OMT 2002)
VD	*Vita Dunstani*, in *Saints' Lives*, pp. 166–303. Cited by book and chapter.
VW	*Vita Wulfstani*, in *Saints' Lives*, pp. 8–155. Cited by book and chapter.

→ 1 ←

Discovering William of Malmesbury: The Man and his Works

Emily A. Winkler and Emily Dolmans

Describing William of Malmesbury, scholars have often found it appropriate to draw upon superlatives: he was one of medieval England's finest men of letters, among the most learned historians of twelfth-century Europe, and, some would argue, the greatest historian of England since Bede.[1] In examining William's own words, however, it becomes clear that he was not a man of extremes; careful, measured, considered and erudite, William's life was devoted to grappling with the complexities of history, and reconciling his own interests and personal relationships with his quest for truth and objectivity, both historical and religious. The present volume is a celebration of his achievements, and an attempt to become acquainted with the man and his works that allows us to enjoy a glimpse into the multifaceted world of twelfth-century England. It is, however, also a celebration of a more immediate achievement: it marks the release of the edition of *The Miracles of the Virgin* by Rodney Thomson and Michael Winterbottom, the last of William's works to be edited and translated into modern English.

William's humble biography belies his cultural importance and the scholarly ambitions that underpinned his career. What little precise information we have has been gleaned from his own writings. Born in Somerset or Wiltshire in the last decade of the eleventh century, William was well educated and entered the Benedictine abbey of Malmesbury as a youth. At the time, Malmesbury was under the abbacy of Godfrey of Jumièges, a man committed to the education

---

[1] For opinions about William of Malmesbury, see Thomson, *William of Malmesbury*, p. 40; S. N. Vaughn, *Archbishop Anselm 1093–1109* (Farnham, 2012), p. 18; D. R. Howlett, 'The literary context of Geoffrey of Monmouth: an essay on the fabrication of sources', *Arthuriana* 5 (1995), 25–69, at p. 26; J. Campbell, 'Some twelfth-century views of the Anglo-Saxon past', *Peritia* 3 (1984), 131–50, at p. 136, repr. in his *Essays in Anglo-Saxon History* (London and Ronceverte, 1986), pp. 209–28, at 214. The latter two are cited in D. Rollo, 'William of Malmesbury, Gerbert of Aurillac and the excavation of the Campus Martius', in *Translatio Studii: Essays by his Students in Honour of Karl D. Uitti*, ed. R. Blumenfeld-Kosinski et al. (Amsterdam, 2000), pp. 261–86, at 282, n.1.

of his monks, and who established Malmesbury as a centre of learning.[2] From around 1120, William was precentor, or cantor, of the abbey, a role which involved acting as librarian as well as the director of the liturgy; during this time, William undertook an expansion of Malmesbury's library, partially achieved through contributions of his own works. These texts ranged from the popular and ambitious *Gesta Regum Anglorum*, written for Queen Matilda, which details the history of England from the time of Bede to the twelfth century, and the *Gesta Pontificum Anglorum*, which reflected on the history of the English Church, to local histories of Glastonbury and Lives of local saints. He also produced remarkable works of religious reflection and accounts of miracles. For William, the study of history was important for its ability to convey morals in an accessible manner: it 'adds flavour to moral instruction by imparting a pleasurable knowledge of past events, spurring the reader by the accumulation of examples to follow the good and shun the bad'.[3] These three elements – moral instruction, pleasure and historical knowledge – provide the primary reasons why William's works have retained their importance into the twenty-first century.

Because the complete corpus of William's works now exists in critical editions, the horizons of possible scholarship have expanded dramatically. Concordances, word-frequency, borrowings, will all be easier to compare and to trace; scholars of all language levels will be able to engage with William's works. But most important of all, we can now study two whole entities: William the individual, and William's corpus of writing. The challenge is of course greater, as there is more to learn; but the potential for insights into both the specific and the broad is much greater. The present volume is designed to be a handlist of approaches to William and his works: an introduction to the man and his writing, and an opportunity to find the kinds of connections between themes and ideas for which William spent a lifetime searching.

In his description of the role of the historian, Orosius uses the metaphor of a watchtower ('specula'), a high vantage point from which he can observe the world around him.[4] From this position, the historian is able to see connections between periods and conflicts between peoples, and to contemplate the sins of the world. For Orosius, the world was an object of meditation, one that had to be seen from a distance.[5] William uses the same metaphor in his prologue to the *Gesta Pontificum*:

---

[2] Thomson, *William of Malmesbury*, p. 5. See also R. M. Thomson, 'Malmesbury, William of (b. c. 1090, d. in or after 1142)', in *Oxford Dictionary of National Biography*, ed. C. Morris and B. Harrison (Oxford, 2004), 36. 348–61.

[3] GR bk 2 prol. 1: 'iocunda quadam gestorum notitia mores condiens, ad bona sequenda uel mala cauenda legentes exemplis irritat'.

[4] Paulus Orosius, *Historiarum aduersus Paganos Libri Septem*, 2. 18. 5; 3. 12. 11.

[5] See N. Lozovsky, *'The Earth is Our Book': Geographical Knowledge in the Latin West ca. 400–1000* (Ann Arbor, 2000), pp. 39, 71.

> I do not here have the advantage of the same bountiful supply of information as in the *History of the Kings*. There, I could borrow something from the Chronicle I had by me; it was as though a beacon were shining bright from some high vantage point ('specula') to keep my course from straying. But *here* I am devoid of almost all help. I grope my way through a dense fog of ignorance, and no lantern of history goes before me to direct my path.[6]

While Orosius placed himself on the watchtower of history, William envisages himself below it; history guides him in his understanding of the past and of the world around him. This rhetorically elegant way of illustrating the challenges of history writing is a testament to William's humility and signals the degree to which he broke new ground in all of his works, not only the *Gesta Pontificum*. Through this image, William places himself within the landscape of the past; for him, history is not a distant scene ripe for observation, but a world to be engaged with, grappled with and involved in. His was not an 'ivory tower' erudition: the depth of his rhetoric attached him more closely to the ideas, events and people of the world he lived in and of bygone ages.

Yet, in the creation of his *Gesta Pontificum*, among his other works, William also illuminates the paths of his successors. As both the follower and the holder of the 'lantern of history', William allows us to see the world as he sees it, to understand the world as if we, too, stand on the tower alongside him as he shines a light on twelfth-century England, its history, attitudes, culture, politics, beliefs, concerns and stories.

The aim of this volume is to present an image of William as both subject and object, as we see the world through his eyes, and as we turn the spotlight onto William himself, as a man, a monk, a historian and a writer. Because of William's ambitious writings, his eloquence and his insights, his works are an ideal lens through which to understand the world in which he lived, and to learn about others by examining his relationships with them. William, however, presents something of a paradox: he provides a window into the lives and thoughts of those living in twelfth-century England, and yet by virtue of providing that window, he marks himself as exceptional.[7] William allows us to view the twelfth century, and the history he recounts, through a new lens, which accentuates the vibrancy and complexity of his thoughts and experience.

The essays in this volume offer insights into English politics, the roles and inner workings of monastic houses and their scriptoria, and, ultimately, the psychology of an individual who struggled to reconcile his own beliefs with the world he

---

[6] *GP* prol. 4: 'non hic affligat eadem copia scientiae quae in Gestis Regum. Siquidem ibi, aliquid de Cronicis quae pre me habebam mutuatus, uelut e sullimi specula fulgente facula, qua gressum sine errore tenderem, ammonebar. Hic autem, pene omni destitutus solatio, crassas ignorantiae tenebras palpo, nec ulla lucerna historiae preuia semitam dirigo.'

[7] V. H. Galbraith wrote in 1951 '[William's] ability to see the wood for the trees is, in that age, extraordinary; but for expressing it he is nearly unique'. V. H. Galbraith, *Historical Research in Medieval England* (London, 1951), p. 15.

read about and observed around him. Now that all of his works have been edited and translated, we are able to stand on the watchtower of history with William. Given this privileged view, it becomes clear that much work on the man and his works remains to be conducted. Each essay serves as a spotlight that focuses on an aspect of the world illuminated by William's texts. He knew about medicine[8] and mathematics;[9] libraries[10] and the 'law of history';[11] regions of England[12] and the far reaches of the known world[13] – and, as our contributors show, he wrote about them in a lively and engaging way.

Taken together, these papers reveal a man who was eager to make connections between disparate ideas, and who took nothing for granted. He was neither dogmatic nor driven by doctrine. There was no political view, religious belief or approach to his career which he accepted as a matter of course without questioning or considering it. He had that ability to regard matters from the outside: to step aside from a line of thinking, and to consider and to evaluate it as an observer.

What is remarkable about the range of subjects covered here in relation to William is that the insights of all the papers have validity, because William truly was a 'Renaissance man' who was able to look at a wide variety of subjects from a number of angles, and to make connections between them. The collected papers show the futility of asking 'either–or' questions about William's life and works: did he favour the English or the Normans? Was he writing history or hagiography? Did he think ancient Britain civilised or uncivilised? Were his loyalties local or national? The conclusions of every paper show that William's works were, ultimately, both complex beyond the scope of any binary question, and coherent in a way only possible as the result of a highly sophisticated and erudite mind. With William, any binary question ends up with an answer that far exceeds the question's remit: such questions are really only rhetorical ways forward of getting at *a man who was both individual and universal*.

It is clear that William was interested in fostering a network of scholarship among his peers and his readers, and he was a vital node in the centre of twelfth-century learning. This is articulated through his erudition and his relationships with his patrons, his friends and other men of letters, both precursors and contemporaries. William valued interpersonal relationships – between kings and

---

[8] Joanna Phillips, 'William of Malmesbury: Medical Historian of the Crusades', in this volume, pp. 129–38.

[9] Anne Lawrence-Mathers. 'William of Malmesbury and the Chronological Controversy', in this volume, pp. 93–105.

[10] Samu Niskanen, 'William of Malmesbury as Librarian: The Evidence of his Autographs', in this volume, pp. 117–27.

[11] Emily Joan Ward, '*Uerax historicus Beda*: William of Malmesbury, Bede and *historia*', in this volume, pp. 175–87.

[12] Daniel Gerrard, 'William of Malmesbury and Civic Virtue', in this volume, pp. 27–36; Stanislav Mereminskiy, 'William of Malmesbury and Durham: The Circulation of Historical Knowledge in Early Twelfth-Century England', in this volume, pp. 107–16.

[13] Kati Ihnat, 'William of Malmesbury and the Jews', in this volume, pp. 49–63.

clerics, between writer and reader, between a scriptorium director and his scribes; his works reconciled, acknowledged and appreciated opposing ideas and diverse traditions of thought. Fascinated by classical texts and an avid scholar of late antique and contemporary literatures, he read widely and was keen to draw connections between a variety of ideas, events and traditions.[14] As he states himself, he wished to draw together logic, physic, ethics and history, and to illuminate the forgotten parts of the past. Yet he also concedes that, in spite of attempts to read as widely as possible, there is yet more to know: William implores the reader of the *Gesta Regum*, if a piece of information is found to be lacking, 'let him not be angry with me for not including it. Rather, let him share his information with me, while I yet live, so that my pen can at least add in the margin details that did not find a place in the text.'[15] In this spirit of collaboration and networking, he also had many friends among his contemporaries, whose works he drew on and reframed within his own writings. William knew how to use the resources he had, whether personal or scholarly. He was a free thinker, engaged in an attempt to make sense of the past and the world around him.

Scholarship on medieval historians tends to treat the writer and his works as one and the same – what he wrote is who he is. But in order to discover William of Malmesbury, it is worth distinguishing between the man and his works in order to get to know him, and to appreciate the personality of his writing.

Discovering William the man

Unlike many scholarly clerics of twelfth-century England, such as John of Salisbury or Gerald of Wales, William was not career-driven as we would understand it; he turned down the abbacy of Malmesbury and appears to have had few aspirations toward political influence beyond his literary career.[16] Nevertheless, William did display the kind of leadership, practicality and entrepreneurial spirit that we might attribute to a modern businessman, with the hope of scholarly and spiritual, rather than financial, profit. As Samu Niskanen's paper discusses, in his capacity as precentor William managed a team of scribes engaged in the task of expanding Malmesbury's library.[17] Self-driven and ambitious in his endeavours, William engaged in his enterprise with abandon, and was effective at delegating responsibilities amongst his peers. This illustrates his ability to make the most effective use of the resources he had, from the texts – both classical and religious – that he

---

[14] For example, M. Winterbottom, 'The language of William of Malmesbury', in *Rhetoric and Renewal*, pp. 129–47; N. Wright, 'Twelfth-century receptions of a text: Anglo-Norman historians and Hegesippus', *ANS* 31 (2009), 177–95; idem, 'William of Malmesbury and Latin poetry: further evidence for a Benedictine's reading', *RB* 101 (1993), 122–53; Thomson, *William of Malmesbury*; idem, 'William of Malmesbury's Historical Vision', in this volume, pp. 165–73.

[15] *GR* bk 2. prol. 3.

[16] Thomson, *William of Malmesbury*, p. 6. *GR* I, pp. xxxviii–ix; *HN*, pp. 29–34.

[17] Niskanen below, pp. 117 and 122–7.

had studied, to those he sought out in England's other abbeys and the works of his fellow historians, both his antecessors (Bede) and his contemporaries (such as Eadmer and John of Worcester).[18] William used his relationships to their full potential, whether by acquiring patronage, working with his friends, or even, as Sigbjørn Sønnesyn argues, by developing a relationship with his readers.[19] He was conscious of his own abilities and knowledge, as demonstrated by his apparent insistence that he copy those texts that required interpretation or abbreviation himself, and was innovative with language.[20] His economy of resources and time is evidenced by his – occasionally faulty – abbreviations and expansions of texts. Just as his expansions can show us how he interpreted the texts he was presented with, his abbreviations can equally give us insight into his assumptions: they can show us what he took for granted, and also indicate how he valued expediency.

Collaboration and supervision were principles that William valued, both in his own life as he directed the copying of manuscripts, and when it came to the lives of those he wrote about. William emphasised the Crown's reliance on clerical advice, on the text's dependence on the efforts and charity of its readers, and on his own engagement with his sources as he judged which writers were granted the honour of being called 'uerax historicus', a truthful historian.[21] Partly because of his confidence in his own abilities and his admiration for successful historical figures,[22] he did not suffer fools gladly. These standards of morality, quality and work ethic are evident in his management style, in his decisiveness about copying, cutting and reframing, and doing work for himself, and in his attitudes to England's kings or princes such as Harold, Æthelred II and Edgar the Ætheling.[23]

But his high expectations of others reflect his even higher expectations for himself. William was aware of his limitations and exercised caution when it came to controversy: while he was interested in parsing out the intricacies of computus, he did not pursue it beyond a certain point for fear of political repercussions and because he may not have found a receptive audience for his findings.[24] He also knew that his predilection for classical texts and the excitement he derived from

---

[18] Ward below, pp. 175–87. Martin Brett has argued that John of Worcester and William worked together; see M. Brett, 'John of Worcester and his contemporaries', in *The Writing of History in the Middle Ages*, ed. R. H. C. Davis and M. Wallace-Hadrill (Oxford, 1981), pp. 113–17.

[19] S. Sønnesyn, '*Lector amice*: Reading as Friendship in William of Malmesbury', in this volume, pp. 153–63.

[20] See Niskanen below, pp. 122–3; M. Winterbottom, 'Words, Words, Words…', in this volume, pp. 203–18.

[21] Ryan Kemp, 'Advising the King: Kingship, Bishops and Saints in the Works of William of Malmesbury', in this volume, pp. 65–79; Sønnesyn below, pp. 153–63; Ward below, pp. 175–87.

[22] J. Gillingham, 'The Ironies of History: William of Malmesbury's Views of William II and Henry I', in this volume, pp. 37–48; Alheydis Plassmann, 'German Emperors as Exemplary Rulers in William of Malmesbury and Otto of Freising', in this volume, pp. 139–52.

[23] Niskanen below, pp. 122–3; Lawrence-Mathers below, pp. 97–105; Emily A. Winkler, 'England's defending kings in twelfth-century historical writing', *Haskins Society Journal* 25 (2013), 147–63; idem, '1074 in the twelfth century', *ANS* 36 (2014), 241–58.

[24] Lawrence-Mathers below, pp. 96–8.

history did not befit a monk, and in his texts we witness a struggle between his delights and his obligations.

It is clear that his self-prescribed task was not merely to expand his monastic library, but also to understand the problems of history and scholarship for himself. Through these essays we constantly see William grappling with difficult ideas and attempting to make sense of them: the care and thoughtfulness we see in his attempts to engage with the 'chronological controversy' in Anne Lawrence-Mathers's paper on computus; Alheydis Plassmann's discussion of his attempt to reconcile historical patterns with the actions of monarchs; Michael Winterbottom's detailed explanation of the linguistic intricacies of William's Latin. He was both opinionated and open-minded, and could take the long view of history as well as one keenly rooted in contemporary concerns. For instance, he had fierce regional loyalties,[25] but he recognised that the *patria* he loved had belonged to a number of different peoples over time, including the English, the Normans and the native Britons.[26]

A fascinating benefit of the editions of William's works is that we can see clearly the personal growth of the man over the course of his life, and it is a growth which we can set firmly in the historical context of the Anglo-Norman world in which he lived. William changed his mind about how harshly to write about certain individuals in different versions of the *Gesta Regum*, perhaps in response to new research or concerns about patrons' reception.[27] Rodney Thomson, Michael Winterbottom and Sigbjørn Sønnesyn have suggested that William's relationship with the Bible changed over time: over the course of his life, his interests tended towards the more neglected parts of the Bible, as demonstrated by his *Commentary on Lamentations*. His view of the Norman Conquest changed too: he appears to have become far less sanguine about it when he reached old age than he had been when writing about it in the *Gesta Regum*, when he was perhaps in his late twenties.[28]

But it would be a mistake to ascribe these changes to the character of a man growing jaded, closed up in a monastery, losing touch with the world. He remained keenly aware of and involved in both local and national politics throughout his life. His changing ideas about the Normans probably related to direct experience with Norman patrons who were putting the future of Malmesbury at risk with the threat of withdrawing support; his biblical studies reflect the refinement and sophistication of a mind improved over decades of study. William may have changed his mind,[29] but he did not change his energy or spirit of enquiry. William's journey in writing his works was ultimately one of self-discovery.

---

[25] Gerrard below, pp. 31–6.
[26] Emily A. Winkler, 'William of Malmesbury and the Britons', in this volume, pp. 189–201.
[27] GR (Stubbs), I, pp. xxxiii–xxxvii; GP II, p. 24.
[28] M. Winterbottom, 'William of Malmesbury and the Normans', *JML* 20 (2010), 70–7.
[29] S. Bagge, 'The individual in medieval historiography', in *The Individual in Political Theory and Practice*, ed. J. Coleman (Oxford, 1996), pp. 36, 41.

Discovering William's works

William wrote for a wide range of literate audiences. He wrote to instruct princes,[30] to educate his fellow monks,[31] to share ideas with his contemporaries, to entertain his patrons and to record history for future readers. He would surely have considered himself as writing for anyone who wanted to know.

But it is essential to note that William of Malmesbury did not always write *for* an audience. At times he wrote, rewrote, copied and collected works simply for the sake of writing and for preserving knowledge. This is important to stress because modern scholars always ask the 'audience' question of their sources, usually for good reasons: whom were medieval readers trying to reach with their works? There is a problem with applying that question to William: the question presupposes that his writings are a means to an end, rather than an end in themselves, in which the audience are the means of giving life to the words contained therein. William was engaged in a process of self-expression.

William's efforts are often not really on behalf of the audience, but on behalf of the books. As an intellectual, he was generous in spirit: he was proud of his own work as a librarian, but his intention in curating a library was to be able to offer written works for future readers to cherish. He was not specific about the name or the demographic of any intended readership; rather, he hoped that the collection would be treasured by someone ('Vtinam sit qui labores nostros foueat!').[32] Let these books be known – let them not pass into oblivion – let them find friends, he seems to say. He treats books, whether his own or the works of others, as living creatures.

Although he was popular among readers in his own time and thereafter, this was not his primary aim: he hoped that his works would be discovered. Is there an intriguing irony here – does William's unconcern for his own popularity help to explain his enduring legacy? For it is his understanding, rather than any desperation to be understood, which has compelled and captivated subsequent generations of readers. An author who loves writing and knowing for its own sake is well positioned to write with a verve and a passion that withstands the passing of the centuries, and William's corpus is a testament to his hoped-for success in this regard.

Today, we are sometimes asked to reflect on the 'state of scholarship', but this is not a term which William would have accepted. For him, knowledge and ideas were meant to be constantly dynamic; they were never in stasis or unquestioningly accepted as true. As Sigbjørn Sønnesyn observes, William's values as a philosopher reflect the classical and patristic view of the highest good which humans can attain: that of *energeia*, or energy and movement. Simply to experience an impression, sensation or emotion, is not enough: whereas these are passive states, *energeia*

---

[30] Kemp below, pp. 65–79.
[31] Niskanen below, pp. 117–27, Lawrence-Mathers below, pp. 95 and 97–105.
[32] GP 271. 2; discussed by Niskanen below, p. 117.

requires activity; it requires the human individual to engage directly with his own environment and community.

William's life and views, as far his collected writings show, resonate with this view of being alive. His narratives and commentaries show that thinking, ideas and histories move, change and grow. He admitted that he had not always made up his own mind.[33] In this respect – his willingness to learn, to relearn and to revisit old conclusions – his works reflect the mind of a life-long scholar.

William's insights are incisive not only because of his vocabulary, but because of his depth of knowledge of Latin literature over several centuries. His particular skill was to create the medieval equivalent of a virtual reality: he used language with three-dimensional intelligence to capture and to convey as much of the experience of both earthly and spiritual realms as was possible. William's works embody the medieval interest in the affinity between creation of the world (Gen. 1: 1) and the speaking of the Word (John 1: 1),[34] perhaps as much as any set of collected works of any medieval author.

William tried to get as much meaning as possible out of every word he chose. In his prose style, then, William was an innovator in the use of the zeugma – a verb iterated once, but meant to connote several different meanings at the same time.[35] Michael Winterbottom offers an illuminating case study of William's use of the verb 'absoluere', in which William follows classical and medieval usage but also brings his own spark of originality in pushing the boundaries of definition. The word means to loose or unleash; to describe, to complete, as in a book or a building. William, in the act of writing, does all these things simultaneously: by describing the past – its people, its places, its events – he aims to complete stories, to complete pictures (as with his illustrating anecdotes),[36] and to complete the chain of England's history. In doing so, he looses or unleashes the experience of the past for his readers. He counters oblivion, one of the medieval historian's prime motivations, in a unified way that surpasses simple prose.

As Winterbottom observes, William's different, nuanced uses of words often puzzle the translator – which is perhaps precisely William's point. A reader who puzzles is one who reads with *energeia* – and William wanted his readers to engage with his work on just as deep a level as he did himself. With his extensive erudition and lively mind, William came closer than many of his contemporaries to crossing that line between language and reality. His very language, infused itself with *energeia*, seeks to transcend linguistic boundaries and to reflect on the nature of reality.

---

[33] GR 228. 3, 7, on the Norman Conquest.

[34] Cf. R. McKitterick, *Perceptions of the Past in the Early Middle Ages* (Notre Dame, 2006), esp. pp. 7–18.

[35] For example, Alexander Pope, *The Rape of the Lock*, Canto II (1712), for a famous use of the zeugma: 'Or lose her heart, or necklace, at a ball'.

[36] William sought to complete a picture of a place with words; even those places he himself never went: Mereminskiy below, pp. 107–16.

Discovering William of Malmesbury

William's affinity for metaphor and style made him more rather than less aware of the world around him. He realised that the power of an apt association was one of the best ways to communicate: a shared idea permitted him to forge a connection between his ideas and those of his readers. In communicating by connection, his abilities were wide-ranging and sophisticated. He articulated a connection between reading and friendship, affably reminding his readers that the two endeavours both involve commitment, care and an active intention.[37] In the *Gesta Regum* he created a relationship between the invading Romans and the defeated Britons in which mutual respect had a stronger claim than oppression and trauma, arguing that the history of human interactions on his home island began with an impressive chapter.[38] He linked Judaism and Christianity, contrasting what he considered the improper behaviour of Jews with the ideal form of veneration of the Virgin Mary, so as to offer a clear guide for Christian practice.[39] He challenged his readers to think about bishops and saints as men and miracle-workers by writing in a genre that transcended the conventional divide between hagiography and history. And, by quoting the Latin classics and biblical narratives, he associated the changes in present-day communities with similar changes in the ancient past, offering his readers the benefit of his insights into parallel events in history.[40]

This activity – communicating to an audience by relating ideas and concepts in a meaningful way – is an endeavour which permeates the corpus of William's works, from philosophy to humour,[41] and it helps to explain why there is so much to say about him. He understood how to convey not only meaning, but also something of human nature. The beauty of his similes, metaphors, allusions and connections is in their ability to entertain and to teach moral lessons with seamless elegance. To read William of Malmesbury's works is to find a friend – and to be educated.

As the title of this volume suggests, these papers together perform a 'discovering' of William of Malmesbury. This is both in the sense of finding something new, and also as an act of unveiling. Yet it is also a reminder that the act of discovery is ongoing, and one that has not yet afforded us a complete view of William. We are always in the act of discovering William, but as we hope William would agree, there can be no claims to have understood him fully. This volume is neither a beginning nor an end, but rather a glimpse of a man who lived in the past, and whose works and whose mind remain relevant today. Through this collection of

---

[37] Sønnesyn below, pp. 153–63.
[38] Winkler below, pp. 189–201.
[39] Ihnat below, pp. 49–63.
[40] Thomson below, pp. 165–73.
[41] On humour, see e.g. M. Otter, 'Functions of fiction in historical writing', in *Writing Medieval History*, ed. N. Partner (London, 2005), pp. 109–30; M. Otter, *Inventiones: Fiction and Referentiality in Twelfth-Century English Historical Writing* (Chapel Hill, 1996); N. F. Partner, *Serious Entertainments: The Writing of History in Twelfth-Century England* (Chicago, 1977); on philosophy, see e.g. Sønnesyn, *Ethics*.

essays we hope to build our own watchtower, one that guides future students of William's writings, and encourages readers to appreciate the world William illuminates for us.

The papers in this volume display William's extraordinary eclecticism, and also paint a picture of a complex and insightful individual whose mind was constantly at work, and who was – as we all are – perpetually in a process of self-realisation. William had an independent mind, and injected his works with his own personality and his own intellectual dilemmas. By reading and studying his words we can come to know him, and to appreciate him as a historian and as a man. The process of understanding history was a relentless and life-long pursuit for William. The collected essays reflect the ongoing activity and *energeia* both of William himself and of scholars who endeavour to understand him. The choice of the present participle 'discovering' to honour these shared endeavours is a variant of which William, we hope, would be proud.

→ 2 ←

Gesta Pontificum Anglorum: History or Hagiography?

Anne E. Bailey

THE MODERN DISTINCTION between the genres of history and hagiography is not easily applied to written narratives in the medieval West.[1] Chroniclers frequently inserted hagiographical material and supernatural elements into their historical accounts, and saints' Lives and miracle stories often contained historical matter. Medieval writers happily mixed and matched what we would consider factual history and semi-fictional hagiography to the extent that some modern commentators have included saints' Lives under the rubric of 'history'.[2]

While problematising the slippery boundaries of genre draws attention to the fluid nature of medieval historiography, it does not fully account for the fact that medieval historians consciously wrote in different narrative styles. These 'genres' were signalled by informative titles labelling their work so that the reader would, at a glance, understand that the *chronica*, *historia* or *gesta*, for example, would be different in form, content and purpose from the *vita* or *miracula*. Since medieval writers evidently had little compunction about including hagiographical elements in texts principally conceived as works of history, exploring the use of hagiographical themes in these narratives offers insight into how the past was conceptualised in the Middle Ages. Such an investigation also tells us much about the aims and function of medieval historical writing.

The purpose of this essay is to examine the relationship between history and hagiography in William of Malmesbury's *Gesta Pontificum Anglorum*. William was one of a handful of twelfth-century English writers who turned his hand to both history (in the form of the *chronica* or *gesta*) and hagiography (in the form of the *vita*), although he is best known today as an historian, as he was in the

---

[1] For a discussion of the shifting perspectives on these categories, see F. Lifshitz, 'Beyond positivism and genre: "hagiographical" texts as historical narrative', *Viator* 25 (1994), 95–113.
[2] For example, T. Sizorich, 'Religious history', in *The Oxford History of Historical Writing*, vol. 2, ed. S. Foot and C. F. Robinson (Oxford, 2012), pp. 607, 612–13; S. Foot, 'Annals and chronicles in Western Europe', ibid., p. 350.

Middle Ages.[3] William began the *Gesta Pontificum*, the second of his two great English chronicles, in the 1120s soon after completing the *Gesta Regum Anglorum*.[4] Although he envisaged the *Gesta Regum* and *Gesta Pontificum* as works of history, both volumes included details borrowed and adapted from saints' Lives, and William freely peppered his biographical vignettes of royal and episcopal celebrities with hagiographical motifs and miraculous anecdotes.

The convergence of history and hagiography is a feature of all William's work.[5] However, this aspect of William's writing is particularly evident in the *Gesta Pontificum*, which charts the ecclesiastical history of England from the time of Augustine's mission to William's day in five books organised around different bishoprics.[6] William was a self-conscious and self-reflective writer, and he leaves his readers in no doubt as to the purpose of his project. The *Gesta Pontificum*, he tells us, has a two-fold objective: his 'ordered plan' ('dispositum meum ordine') is first to record the histories of England's bishops, and then to commemorate England's saints 'resting in their parishes' ('in eorum parrochiis requiescentes').[7] The complication here is that many of William's episcopal subjects were also venerated as saints. As a result, the *Gesta Pontificum* is less a neat division of William's subject matter into bishops and saints and more a complex interweaving of history and hagiography.

For the most part, William presents himself as a conscientious historian: he sets out his evidence, dismisses unsubstantiated rumour and voices scepticism about some of the more sensational miracles which he feels obliged to record.[8] At other times his secondary purpose, 'to praise the saints of my country' ('sanctos patriae meae laudare'),[9] becomes more pronounced and we see William the hagiographer at work. His favourite characters often receive extensive hagiographical treatment, most notably in Book Five in which he pays homage to his monastery's patron saint, Aldhelm.

It would seem that, for William, hagiography *was* history. Nonetheless, there are clear stylistic differences between 'history' (passages which follow the chronicle tradition) and 'hagiography' (passages more akin to a saint's Life) in the *Gesta Pontificum*. History and hagiography are therefore useful analytical categories, allowing us to examine how William constructed the past for contemporary consumption.

What follows assesses the two sides of William's writing persona in the *Gesta Pontificum*. In asking how and why William employed hagiographical elements in

---

[3] Thomson, *William of Malmesbury*, pp. 6–8; M. Winterbottom and R. M. Thomson in *Saints' Lives*, p. xxv. Other historian-hagiographers include Eadmer of Canterbury and Symeon of Durham.

[4] For the dating of these two works and their relationship, see *GP* II, pp. xix–xxv.

[5] For example, William was 'noticeably historical' in his saints' Lives: *Saints' Lives*, pp. xiii, xxxiii–xxiv, xxxviii.

[6] For more on the structure of the *Gesta Pontificum*, see *GP* II, pp. xxv–xxviii.

[7] 74. 20.

[8] For the 'art' of history writing in the Middle Ages, see M. Kempshall, *Rhetoric and the Writing of History* (Manchester, 2011).

[9] *GP* bk 4 prol. 1.

Gesta Pontificum Anglorum: History or Hagiography?

what was ostensibly a work of history, the paper argues that hagiographical motifs had various narrative applications for William, such as lionising his favourite religious heroes. Focusing on William's penchant for recording miracle tales, the chapter also suggests that miracles served as a vehicle for the transmission of historical knowledge in the Middle Ages.

William's sources and influences

In questioning why the *Gesta Pontificum* has such a strong hagiographical flavour, it is pertinent to begin by considering William's written sources. Although William obtained much of his information from secular and archival documents such as charters and letters, the bulk of his longer narrative detail is drawn from hagiography.[10] From the outset, William relies on saints' Lives to flesh out the biographies of his episcopal subjects. By 1. 3, for example, he has referred to the hagiography of Goscelin of Saint-Bertin and Eddius Stephanus alongside the *Historia Ecclesiastica Gentis Anglorum* of Bede.

One reason for William's heavy reliance on saints' Lives may be practical, such as a lack of other available sources when relating stories from the remote past (for example, 1. 1–2). His fondness for hagiographical stories may also be instrumental, as when he cites Osbern of Canterbury's *Vita S. Dunstani* 'in order to show readers how venerable ('uenerabilis') Ælfgar was'.[11] In this and similar cases, hagiography functioned as a kind of spiritual character reference for William's historical protagonists, serving to endorse his own opinion that certain individuals were worthy of prestige. Whatever his purpose in turning to hagiographical evidence, it is important to note that William, and presumably his readers, considered a saint's Life a legitimate and valuable source for history.

Whereas William refers to respected hagiographers for stories of individual saints, the greatest influence on the *Gesta*'s hagiographical tone and overall content was Bede, whose *Historia Ecclesiastica* set a precedent for much history-writing in medieval England.[12] Bede, like William, produced saints' Lives as well as histories, and both writers liberally incorporated hagiographical vignettes of holy men and women into their accounts of England's past. William also employed Bede's five-book structure for the *Gesta Pontificum* and drew directly on the *Historia Ecclesiastica* for many of his stories.

Although the *Gesta Pontificum* owes much to Bede, William does not mine the *Historia Ecclesiastica* for material in the same way as he does for his other sources. He rarely simply produces 'cover versions' of Bede's stories, but instead tends either

---

[10] Thomson estimates that William used at least fifty *vitae*: GP II, p. xxxvii. For a discussion of William's sources, see ibid., pp. xxxvi–xli.

[11] GP 74. 9.

[12] See, for example, A. Gransden, 'Bede's reputation as an historian in medieval England', in her *Legends, Traditions and History in Medieval England* (London, 1992), pp. 8–17.

to 'improve' the Bedan version or to refer his readers to the *Historia Ecclesiastica* when he considers his predecessor's information sufficient (for example, 179. 1). It seems likely that the two texts were supposed to be read as companion pieces, to be consulted alongside one another. This suggests that an ecclesiastical readership was intended.

William 'improved' stories found in the *Historia Ecclesiastica* principally by expanding them using information taken from sources not available to Bede. The best-known example is Bede's very brief account of St Aldhelm which, as we shall see, William develops into something resembling a full Life and posthumous miracle collection. Other Anglo-Saxon saints who gained a fuller treatment under William's penmanship include Wilfrid, 'because Bede's history leaves much out' ('quia... multa ex historia Bedae uacant'; 99. 7). Indeed, William records so much extra biographical information about Wilfrid's turbulent ecclesiastical career that he refers to it as a 'digression' ('digressio'; 110. 1).

William was keen to record the political machinations surrounding Wilfrid's disputed career and, perhaps as a consequence, the section on Wilfrid reads more like secular biography than hagiography. However, William also adds hagiographical material to many of Bede's other stories, and in some instances these hagiographical enhancements add a strong sense of historical veracity. An example can be found in Book Two concerning the missionary saint Earconwald. Whereas Bede simply says that Earconwald's litter was a source of posthumous miracles and provides no further information, William – possibly drawing on Goscelin – takes his readers further back in time and provides the missing historical context.[13] Thus we learn that, when too sick to walk, Earconwald was carried around his parishes in a litter. William then adds the story of how, during one of these parochial tours, a river in spate miraculously folded back, allowing Earconwald in his litter to pass across safely to the opposite bank (73. 10–11).

In this example, William not only connects the miracle-working litter with the historical Earconwald in a memorable way, but in showing that the relic had miraculous properties in the saint's lifetime he also offers an explanation – perhaps even a justification – for the relic's later veneration. The detail about Earconwald's mode of transport and the illustrative 'parting of the waters' miracle therefore work together both to validate and to historicise Bede's claim that the litter 'continues to cure people troubled by fever and other complaints'.[14] Moreover, the colourful anecdote with its nod towards a familiar Old Testament precedent (Exodus 14: 21–2) must have stimulated interest in the past because, once told, the story was surely hard to forget.[15] The idea that vibrant story-telling forges connections to the past is a theme to which I will return.

---

[13] Bede, *HE* iv. 6. William may have conflated two stories from Goscelin's *Vita S. Erkenwaldi*: *GP* II, p. 90.

[14] Bede, *HE* iv. 6.

[15] Another example of a biblically inspired miracle defining a missionary saint is the story of Birinus walking on water in *GP* 75. 3–4.

Gesta Pontificum Anglorum: History or Hagiography?

The lives and miracles of the bishops?

The *Gesta Pontificum*, then, contains many fact-filled biographies of historical characters alongside hagiographical episodes praising the merits of English saints. Whereas some historical figures, such as Wilfrid, seem almost entirely to inhabit the secular sphere, others are singled out for stronger hagiographical treatment. An outstanding example is Dunstan, whose entry in Book One reads like a miniature saint's Life (19), and foreshadows the *Vita Dunstani* which William would subsequently compose.

In an account taken almost entirely from Osbern's *Vita*, this earlier biography of Dunstan associates the Canterbury archbishop with a comprehensive range of conventional saintly attributes and activities.[16] These begin before his birth when Dunstan's future sanctity is foretold by a prophetic sign given to his mother – a common motif in hagiography – and continue with stories which present him as a child prodigy (19. 2). As an adult, Dunstan further demonstrates his holiness by combating the Devil, warding off sexual temptation, experiencing visions of the Virgin Mary and using miraculous powers to rescue people from harm (19. 3–10). The saintly attribute of prophecy – which Bede also makes much of throughout his *Historia Ecclesiastica* – is particularly prominent in William's account of Dunstan, as it would be in his later *Vita*.[17] Like other historians of the period, William gives prophecy a political emphasis: Dunstan foretells the death of King Eadwig and the birth of King Edgar, and he warns Æthelred of coming troubles (19. 6, 19. 8–9).[18]

Dunstan was a well-known saint who was canonised in 1029, and became the subject of a clutch of hagiographies.[19] However, William's aim to record the saints 'resting in their parishes' seems to include saints not officially recognised as such. One unofficial 'saint' was Wulfstan II of Worcester, who was not formerly canonised until 1203, but was regarded as a saint by many in William's time. William would go on to write a full *vita* of Wulfstan, but for the *Gesta Pontificum* his source was an Old English Life by the Worcester monk Coleman. In the *Gesta Pontificum* William creates a career biography which frames the bishop's life history around familiar hagiographical elements, and includes tropes particularly favoured by Bede such as saintly powers of foresight and the ability to miraculously extinguish fires (142, 145–8, 149. 1).[20]

Interestingly, William adopts different styles when writing about Wulfstan, depending on whether he is pursuing a biographical or hagiographical story line. For example, William refers to Wulfstan as a bishop when the narrative follows

---

[16] For William's sources, see Thomson in *GP* II, p. 32.
[17] *Saints' Lives*, p. xxix.
[18] For prophecy in history writing, see C. Given-Wilson, *Chronicles: The Writing of History in Medieval England* (London, 2004), pp. 38–48.
[19] *Saints' Lives*, pp. xvii–xxiii.
[20] For Coleman's Life and William's interest in Worcester, see A. Gransden, 'Cultural transition at Worcester in the Anglo-Norman period', in her *Legends, Traditions and History*, pp. 114–16, 120, and Thomson in *Saints' Lives*, pp. xv–xvii, xxvii–xxix.

his ecclesiastical career, but switches to calling him a 'saint' ('sanctus') in episodes detailing his miracles (142–9). The section on Wulfstan finishes with a note of regret that Wulfstan has not been awarded the religious honour due to him. In a less sceptical age, William says, Wulfstan would have 'been raised on high and proclaimed a saint' ('elatus in altum sanctus predicaretur'; 149. 3).

William's distress that Wulfstan was not given due recognition by the ecclesiastical establishment suggests that his tendency towards favouritism, together with his determination to shine a light on deserving but less well publicised 'saints', must have played a large part in William's choice of whom to honour with a hagiographical anecdote. These choices may have been controversial, as was certainly the case with his support for the 'martyred' Earl Waltheof. Waltheof was regarded as a traitor by the Normans for his part in an uprising against King William in 1075, but venerated as an innocent victim by the monks of Crowland, whose prior called him 'sanctus' (182. 4–6). Writing in the wake of the culturally disruptive Norman Conquest and as part of a movement to reclaim the Anglo-Saxon past, William clearly had strong personal, even partisan, views on whom one should consider a saint.[21]

Because William often saw sanctity where others did not, standard saintly attributes – such as prophecy, visions and asceticism – assisted his claim that a particular historical figure was worthy of veneration. However, the most prominent hagiographical trope used by William to mark out his spiritual heroes was the ability to work miracles. Indeed, miracles are a ubiquitous feature of the *Gesta Pontificum*, as they are in Bede's *Historia*.[22] Whether derived from written hagiography or related orally to William during his travels around the country, tales of miraculous occurrences were an integral part of his 'historical vision'.[23]

It is a measure of their importance in William's eyes that miracles enter the narrative early, at the beginning of Book One. After crediting the first two Canterbury bishops, Augustine and Laurence, with miracles, William provides two reasons why miracle stories are important in historical writing. First, he explains that miracle accounts are useful channels of historical knowledge, particularly when they provided information about subjects which historians like Bede only treated 'cursorily' ('breuiter') (1. 2). Secondly, we learn that miracles are a sign of God's favour, and therefore authoritative evidence of sanctity. 'How highly his merits are valued in the eyes of God is shown by remarkable miracles' ('eius merita quanti apud Deum pensentur signa preconantur illustria'), he remarks with reference to Augustine (1. 2). This is a hagiographical commonplace which validates William's high opinion of an individual's worth and, presumably, supports

---

[21] For this theme see, for example, R. W. Southern, 'The sense of the past', in *History and Historians: Selected Papers of R. W. Southern*, ed. R. J. Bartlett (Oxford, 2004), pp. 66–83, esp. 69–77 and, for William, pp. 75–7.

[22] For Bede's miracles, see J. T. Rosenthal, 'Bede's use of miracles in "The Ecclesiastical History"', *Traditio* 31 (1995), 328–35.

[23] For William's 'historical vision', see Rodney Thomson's chapter in this volume, pp. 165–73.

his occasional tenuous assertion that less popular historical individuals merited veneration.[24]

Even while writing in the hagiographical tradition, William is still the discerning historian and this is evident in his often objective approach to miracles. Although he evidently enjoyed recording a few legendary tales of Anglo-Saxon saints – such as the stories of Edmund's decapitated talking head (74. 20–9) and Wærburh's resurrected goose (172. 6–9) – the majority of miracles in the *Gesta Pontificum* are not jaw-dropping wonders. Instead, they tend to be pedestrian healing miracles, or incidents which modern readers might attribute to good fortune, such as the calming of stormy seas, the preservation of buildings from fire and the arrival of timely rainstorms (examples include 224. 4–6; 66. 1; 149. 1–2; 2. 1; 134. 6).

Moreover, William is not averse to voicing scepticism towards hagiographical evidence. Just as he occasionally questions the claims made by certain churches that they possessed famous relics (91. 6; 180. 3; 186. 6), so he sometimes takes an equally distrustful attitude towards more unlikely miracles. Thus, when relating the story of the discovery of the monstrous fish with the key to Ecgwine's shackles in its liver, William comments, 'If we are to believe the old story' ('credendumne putatur quod tradit antiquitas'; 160. 3). He is equally hesitant about the report that a camel was cured by Aldhelm during a journey across the Alps, implying that another animal was more probable (222. 2). While evidently considering it important to record popular stories about the saints, William also expresses the historian's concern to separate fact from fable.

These are examples of William in historical rather than hagiographical mode, wishing to win the trust of his readers. Nonetheless, and with particular reference to the camel miracle, it is important to note that William is not questioning the veracity of these miracles. The camel story is likely to have had an oral provenance, and William acknowledges that miracle tales might become distorted or misunderstood in their telling and retelling, especially if they had travelled by word of mouth across many generations.[25] Miracle tales – no matter how improbable – were important components in William's retelling of history, as the final section of this chapter will argue. First, though, no discussion of the *Gesta Pontificum*'s leaning towards hagiography would be complete without a closer look at the book featuring the camel miracle. This is Book Five which, to all intents and purposes, contains a detailed *vita* of William's favourite saint: Aldhelm.

Book Five: the life and miracles of St Aldhelm?

Book Five of the *Gesta Pontificum* – described by Thomson as 'a monograph in its own right' – differs from the preceding books in that it focuses almost entirely

---

[24] For example, *GP* 182. 6.
[25] Thomson surmises that this story, without any apparent written source, represents 'local tradition': *GP* II, p. 275.

on one religious house, Malmesbury, and on one saint, Aldhelm.[26] In so doing, it manages to incorporate a house-history of Malmesbury Abbey, a biography of a monk-bishop and a hagiography of a saint. It is therefore in Book Five that we can best appreciate the overlap of history and hagiography, not least because William is at his most self-analytical as a writer here.

At the beginning of Book Five, William establishes himself as an objective historian, emphasising the importance of recording verifiable facts: the 'truth of history' ('ueritati historicae') in preference to rumour ('opinio'; 188. 2). He tells us that 'evidence' ('testimonium'), particularly in the form of written texts, is important for inspiring confidence in his readers (189. 4). With respect to St Aldhelm – the principal protagonist in Book Five – these sources include Aldhelm's own letters and a number of Malmesbury Abbey charters, but a great deal of William's information derives from a Life by Faricius of Abingdon (d. 1117). As a monk of Malmesbury, able to read Old English, William evidently felt entitled to think of himself as a better authority on the abbey and its patron saint, and he criticises Faricius for lacking exact knowledge about Aldhelm (prol. 4–5). Like a modern historian, then, William identifies a gap in the market, subtly critiques the failings of his predecessor and brings into play fresh evidence sourced, in this instance, from Malmesbury's own archives.[27]

As William explains in the prologue, Book Five is divided into four sections (187). The first section details Aldhelm's early life as a scholar (188–96), and the second describes Aldhelm's career as an abbot and records Malmesbury's early endowments (196–211). The third and fourth parts recount Aldhelm's lifetime miracles (212–31) and Malmesbury's more recent history, including the saint's posthumous miracles (232–78). The Prologue advises readers that the book should not be considered so much a Life of a saint as a 'witness' ('testimonium') to Aldhelm's life and 'a source of information' ('cognitionis instrumentum'; 187. 1). William's scheme, however, acquires an increasingly hagiographical feel as the book unfolds.

As William embarks on his biography of Aldhelm, it immediately becomes clear that he does not intend to give his hero the same conventional hagiographical treatment he has accorded some of his earlier subjects, such as Dunstan. In the first section describing Aldhelm's early life, the nascent saint is something of a prodigy, but not a spiritual one. Aldhelm's main characteristic – which William never tires of emphasising – is his dazzling erudition. Aldhelm is portrayed as an outstanding scholar rather than as an outstanding holy man. Moreover, William subverts the hagiographical genre by giving familiar tropes a secular twist. Aldhelm converts heathen as we might expect of a missionary saint, but William attributes his success more to his canny rhetorical skills than to his spiritual ones (190).

---

[26] Ibid., p. xliv.
[27] Indeed, Beryl Smalley called William 'a modern historian's historian': B. Smalley, *Historians in the Middle Ages* (London, 1974), p. 90.

Gesta Pontificum Anglorum: History or Hagiography?

William develops these themes in the next section of the book describing Aldhelm's life as an abbot. Here, Aldhelm's sanctity is primarily manifest in his intellectual gifts: he attracts devotees because of his knowledge of letters ('litterarum scientia'), wins victory over his opponents with rhetoric, and soothes his pupils with his teaching (200). William speaks of Aldhelm's 'charm' ('lepos') rather than his piety, and implies that his personal and scholarly qualities attract benefactors and ultimately lie behind Malmesbury's wealthy endowments (200).

The third section of the book opens with William admitting his discomfort in acknowledging that what follows is based on oral sources rather than on written testimony (212. 1). This remark appears to signal a shift in emphasis away from history and towards hagiography, and Aldhelm suddenly appears in a more saintly guise. Focusing on his monastic career, the section portrays Aldhelm as an exemplary monk, exhibiting praiseworthy Benedictine habits which include praying, fasting, stability and poverty (213. 1). William mentions a couple of Aldhelm's flesh-taming mortifications such as reciting the psalms while standing shoulder-deep in icy water (213. 2) and testing his chastity by spending the night with a woman (213. 3–4). Intriguingly, William has Aldhelm warning pupils against reading the works of classical philosophers, contrary to the advice Aldhelm gave to other pupils in an earlier section (214; 193. 4). However, with another repeated trope – the conversion of heathen – William returns to the theme of Aldhelm's rhetorical skills and shows him converting the 'schismatic' Celtic bishops by persuasion (215). Although clearly following a generic hagiographical model in this section, William also has Aldhelm retain what is perhaps his most distinguishing secular characteristic: his aptitude for language.

The rest of the section pushes further into hagiographical mode as William weaves the remainder of Aldhelm's life around his lifetime miracles. The two episodes to which he gives the fullest treatment, a trip to Dover and a journey to Rome, are presented chiefly through action-packed miraculous anecdotes. In the Dover story Aldhelm, strolling along the seashore, haggles unsuccessfully with sailors over the price of a scriptural book. The book finally comes into Aldhelm's possession, but only after he has saved the sailors from shipwreck by sailing after them in a storm and calming the seas by making the sign of the cross (224).

The Roman episode is more important politically because, in recording the granting of papal privileges to Malmesbury Abbey, it contains the legal and moral justification for the monastery's long-term security and prosperity, as well as providing the monks with a kind of foundation myth featuring their founding saint. The magnitude of the episode's importance is underlined by the fact that no fewer than four miracles are associated with it. In fact, the miracles frame the events: there are the 'setting out' miracle marking the place whence Aldhelm embarked on his voyage (217), two miracles performed in Rome (218, 219), and the 'camel-and-altar' miracle highlighting the journey home, as will be discussed in more detail below.

In contrast to Aldhelm's lifetime miracles, the saint's death is a surprisingly unremarkable affair, and William passes over it quickly. Nonetheless, it is an important watershed, as it marks the end of William's third book division and the beginning of Malmesbury's more recent history. This final section of Book Five interweaves history – 'keeping the order of kings and quoting their charters' ('per successionem ergo regum et cartarum appositionem'; 232. 2) – with Aldhelm's posthumous miracles, and includes entertaining interludes such as the anecdote of John the Scot's dinner witticism at the court of Charles the Bald (240) and the legendary story – part romance, part saint's Life, part miracle story – of the slave girl Ælfhild (259). Some historical events are given a hagiographical gloss, such as the coming of the Vikings to Malmesbury, dramatically illustrated by the miracle of the Dane dashed down for trying to loot Aldhelm's shrine (256). The eclectic nature of this section not only demonstrates the wide variety of topics which William thought worth recording, but also suggests that William did not see, as we might, a distinct separation between the historiographical and hagiographical components of his writing.

Towards the end of this final section, miracle stories become more prominent and the historical narrative slips into second place. From the account of Aldhelm's translation – accompanied in the text with a conventional healing miracle (267. 3–4) – William recounts an almost unbroken succession of miracle stories, including four which he himself claims to have witnessed. William's narrative now takes the shape of something much more akin to a miracle collection than a history, reflecting Aldhelm's transition from a live historical character to a dead saint. Because the hagiographical elements gradually overtake the historical material, Aldhelm appears increasingly to inhabit a saintly mantle. Whether or not this change in thematic direction is intentional, by the end of the book Aldhelm the secular scholar and bishop has become a miracle-working saint.

Hagiography and the miraculous in history writing

The *Gesta Pontificum*, then, can be characterised as a series of diocesan histories combined with hagiographical information about a range of English saints.[28] To modern scholars, aware of different narrative genres, the *Gesta Pontificum* is therefore something of a hybrid work incorporating a mixture of history and hagiography. This blend of genres is nowhere better illustrated than in Book Five, where William pursues his overall historical plan of following the chronological succession of bishops, but also includes what is effectively a hagiography of Aldhelm in the form of a Life (*vita*), translation account (*translatio*) and collection of posthumous miracles (*miracula*). William casts Aldhelm as both a historical figure and a saint.

One ubiquitous component of hagiography – the miracle tale – features prominently in the *Gesta Pontificum*, and this element of William's writing allows

---

[28] For example, Thomson in *GP* II, p. xxix.

us to examine how miracles operated within written, and perhaps even within oral, history. In many respects, miracles played much the same role in William's historical writing as they did in conventional hagiography, in that their primary function was to provide proof of sanctity for holy individuals. Miracles, as signs of God's favour, therefore aided William in championing the cause of forgotten or unrecognised English saints. More specifically, miracles divinely sanctioned the remembrance of long-dead saints, and it was important for William to record – and sometimes revive or stimulate – memories of saints in danger of extinction through neglect.

Gathering knowledge about saints was often deemed especially important if there was little or no written evidence. Although in Book Five William is apologetic for his lack of written testimony (536), he nonetheless attributes great importance to 'what is universally believed and has come down all the way from antiquity: things supported by the general agreement of local people, handed down to posterity in an unbroken succession ... so that the saint's miraculous deeds should not perish and go to waste (212. 2)'. This remark is telling, not only in the value that William attaches to oral tradition therein, but also because it indicates the prominence he gives to miracles in that oral tradition. If saints are to be remembered for anything, William seems to suggest, they will be remembered for their 'miraculous deeds'. It is often the case that the further back in time William reached for his evidence the more reliant he was on written and oral hagiography in the form of local legends and miracle tales. The longevity of these stories suggests that hagiography often survived the test of time better than conventional, 'secular' history.

William's accounts of saints who seem to be memorable principally, or exclusively, because of the miracles associated with them, illustrate this point. We might ask, for example, whether the virgin Wærburh would have made much of an impression without her signature miracle of the resurrected goose, or whether Earconwald's litter would have lost its credibility as a wonder-working relic had it not featured in the story of the miraculously parted river. There are two important points here. First, in containing dramatic and unusual detail, both of these stories are highly memorable. Second, William provides few other facts about either of these saints; indeed, the goose story is the only information he supplies about Wærburh's life.

Selecting the most colourful anecdote about a saint and using it as a kind of memory tag may have been a canny narrative tactic on William's part, but it could also reflect the fact that, owing to their memorable content, miracle stories were generally more enduring than stories of everyday historical events. The durability of miracle stories is especially likely to be true for orally transmitted stories; indeed, William tells us that the story of Wærburh's goose was kept alive by the *fama* (tradition) of the locals (172. 6). Modern anthropologists and historians have shown how vivid mental images – 'memory pictures' – function as carriers of knowledge, and it is possible that many of William's visually appealing miracle stories not only operated as mnemonic devices for otherwise forgettable saints, but that they already did so before he committed them to parchment.[29] Miracles, in other words, aided William's objective in keeping alive the memory of saints through their highly memorable deeds.

The mnemonic role of miracles in history-telling is particularly strongly suggested in Book Five of the *Gesta Pontificum*, in an episode with no known written source.[30] This is the story of Aldhelm's trip to Rome to petition Pope Sergius for privileges for Malmesbury Abbey (217–22). A journey to Rome was no mean feat in the eighth century and, as previously mentioned, the outcome of Aldhelm's trip was politically momentous because the privileges acquired from the pope – which William reproduces in full – helped to secure the abbey's future. Given its historical significance, it is striking that the expedition to Rome is presented through a series of self-contained miracle stories rather than as a 'secular' historical narrative, and that the little historical detail supplied appears only as thin descriptive infill.

An important point of interest here is that the somewhat dislocated structure of the Rome episode is reminiscent of *divisio*, a mnemonic technique whereby a medieval reader divided sections of text into shorter segments to aid memorisation.[31] Since each separate segment of William's text revolves around a memorable miracle tale, we might surmise either that William inherited this format from his oral source, or that the structure of the written text reflects his own mental assemblage of a well-known local tale. Although the relative absence of more mundane material supports the argument for an oral provenance, it should be noted that some factual details are included because they are necessary to bind each miracle story together. For example, we learn from the miracle of the miraculously floating chasuble – which was borne aloft by a ray of sunlight after a servant had failed to catch it – that Aldhelm sung mass at the Lateran: a detail potentially lost had it not been attached to a miracle story (218). This kind of mnemonic framing, then, carries with it less memorable – but historically important – factual information.

The strangest of William's Roman miracles, and therefore the most memorable, is the story of the camel and altar (222). This is the final miracle in the Rome sequence, and it depicts Aldhelm returning to England with many foreign goods including a camel and white marble altar. William tells us that, while crossing the Alps, the camel suffered a seizure and collapsed onto the altar which broke in two. Aldhelm, however, quickly came to the rescue. He restored the camel to health and miraculously repaired the broken altar although, reports William, the crack remained visible 'so that the miracle should never be forgotten' ('ut mirabilis signi memoria non obsolesceret'; 222. 3).

This miracle prompts the memory of a significant moment in history in two interrelated ways. First, the mental image which the Alpine accident conjures up is so bizarre – apparently even to William, who questioned the identification

[29] J. Fenton and C. Wickham, *Social Memory* (Oxford, 1992), pp. 11–13; M. Carruthers, *The Book of Memory: A Study of Memory in Medieval Culture* (Cambridge, 1990), pp. 17, 142–4.
[30] See n. 25 above.
[31] Carruthers, *Book of Memory*, pp. 7, 85.

of the altar-smashing beast – that readers were unlikely to forget it, and unlikely to forget its association with this important historical event. Second, there was a visible, tangible reminder of the miracle in the evidence of the cracked altar: William explains that the flaw in the stone 'is still visible to the careful observer' ('curioso tamen perspicua oculo'; 222. 3). In this memory chain, the sight of the cracked altar acts as an *aide-mémoire* of the Alpine drama which in turn triggers the memory of an event with political significance for the Malmesbury community.

There was, moreover, a second physical reminder of Aldhelm's presence in Rome in the shape of the vestment featured in the floating chasuble story. The chasuble was preserved at Malmesbury Abbey where, says William, 'it feeds the eyes of the passing generations' ('pascat oculos succiduarum generationum'; 218. 5). In bridging the gap between past and present, the altar and chasuble not only served as material witnesses to miracles, but also impressed upon viewers the significance of a locally remembered past.

Miracles, then, had the power to transport the imagination back in time into 'history'. The *Gesta Pontificum*, however, also suggests that miracles may have provided a link with the past in a different way. In Book Two, William laments the loss of written historical sources pertaining to English saints. In many places, he says, records of the past have been destroyed, leaving only 'the knowledge of the names of holy men and of any miracles they still perform' ('sanctorum nomina et si quae modo pretendunt miracula tantum sciri'; 95. 2). Here again is an indication of the durability of miracles over other forms of historical knowledge. More than this, the remark suggests that William saw present-day miracles as a lifeline connecting men and women to their local saints and, by extension, to their past. Furthermore, whereas stories of 'old' miracles – such as the camel-and-altar miracle – returned people to the remote past through collective memories, 'new' miracles effectively brought the past into the present by reanimating historical figures and reactivating their powers. If, as William supposes, these more obscure cults had no written sources, the accounts of miracles must have been circulated by word of mouth, which underlines the power of miracle tales to reawaken or to sustain people's interest in past events and characters.[32]

But were these remembered tales of the past really 'history'? We might argue that, when in 'hagiography mode', William is more interested in what we would call 'heritage' than in 'history'.[33] Like modern heritage professionals, he employs time-spanning techniques – in William's case miracles – 'to make the past alive in the present' and create a comforting sense of historical continuity.[34] In this respect

---

[32] For the oral transmission of 'new' miracles, see R. Koopmans, *Wonderful to Relate: Miracle Stories and Miracle Collecting in High Medieval England* (Philadelphia PA, 2011), esp. 9–46.

[33] For heritage vis-à-vis history see, for example, F. J. Schouten, 'Heritage as historical reality', in *Heritage, Tourism and Society*, ed. D. T. Herbert (London, 1995), pp. 21–31; Hyung yu Park, *Heritage Tourism* (Abingdon, 2014). For the potential of 'heritage' approaches to medieval history, see A. E. Bailey, 'Anthropology, the medievalist … and Richard III', *RMS* 41 (2015), 27–51.

[34] Southern, 'Sense of the past', p. 72.

we might note that William is as much interested in preserving the traditions of local communities as he is in memorialising the history of the wider English nation. In the *Gesta Pontificum*, his bishops are national or regional figures, but many of his saints, like Aldhelm, Wærburh and Waltheof, are local heroes who connect local people to localised remembered pasts through miracles.

In discovering William, then, we discover that history can be both 'hagiographical' and 'historical', and that miracles in a historical context often had a purpose beyond that of furnishing a narrative with a conventional hagiographical trope. For William, hagiography was one way of accessing chronologically remote events, and miracle stories played a crucial role in his mission to recover and illuminate the Christian heritage of Anglo-Saxon England.

3

William of Malmesbury and Civic Virtue

Daniel Gerrard

For William of Malmesbury, the writing of history was a serious moral enterprise. In the most important study of William's work to have been published in recent years, Sigbjørn Sønnesyn has shown that William's historical writing must be seen in the context of wider schemes of monastic education, in particular moral education. Many contemporary authors acknowledged the need to write for the purposes of moral improvement, but William's approach was planned with unique skill: he sought to show that English history moved according to a centuries-long teleological development ordained by God, in which the English advanced towards greater political and moral union as a nation, as well as spiritual union with the Divinity. In short, William wrote national history both about and to encourage the development of virtue.[1] Within the nation, however, was an array of smaller distinct communities – the village, the town, the county etc. It is the contention of this paper that William considered these smaller communities to be essentially moral in character too. In consequence, the ways in which he wrote about them were related to his wider arguments about the virtues and vices of the English. In William's view, virtue and vice (and therefore Englishness) were not evenly distributed throughout the land. Some men were more English than others.

Urban communities in William's writings are one obvious candidate for investigation. Indeed, the link between moral development and political cohesion is illustrated most sharply by William's remark in his *Commentary on Lamentations* drawing particular attention to the need for good government in cities:

> What solitude is more wretched than the medley of vices that throngs about the soul when virtues are overthrown? A city is not embellished by the din and ignorance of the commons, but by a court where a few good men take counsel. It does not profit a city to have many inhabitants: they must be good. And the soul is rightly likened to a city, for God has fortified her with natural passions

---

[1] Sønnesyn, *Ethics*, especially pp. 70–95.

and virtues and, into the bargain has redeemed her at the price of His blood and clothed her in the likeness of his countenance.[2]

William wrote a great deal about towns and cities. His *Gesta Pontificum Anglorum* in particular, which arranges the history of the English Church geographically, provides us with a series of short but vivid pen-portraits of English settlements in the early twelfth century. Similar examples are scattered throughout his *Miracles of the Virgin*, he makes some important observations in the *Gesta Regum*, and his *Commentary on Lamentations* is framed around a meditation on the ruin of the city of Jerusalem by the Babylonians. Taken as a body, William's writings are the most useful sources available to us that illustrate how towns and cities were understood in early twelfth-century England.

At its simplest, his discussion of the connection between England's urban and moral development and national character was imperial apology, supporting Anglo-Norman hegemony within the British Isles against the claims of the less urbanised Irish, Welsh and Scots:

> What would Ireland be worth without the goods that come in by sea from England? The soil lacks all advantages, and so poor, or rather unskilful are its cultivators that it can produce only a ragged mob of rustic Irishmen outside the towns; the English and French, with their more civilised way of life, live in the towns, and carry on trade and commerce.[3]

Here William linked economic sophistication with urban development, in order to argue for some nations' superior moral quality, as others have done in subsequent centuries. William projected that sense of superiority into the remote past, claiming in the *Gesta Pontificum* that the 'Scotti', who had overrun Northumbria in the seventh century, did not replace Archbishop Paulinus after his expulsion from York because they 'were more used to lurking obscurely in bogs than to living in high cities'.[4] Unlike more straightforward imperial apologists, such as Gerald of Wales, however, William did not simply adopt a linear scheme of historical development that put the industrious and urbane English ahead of their bog-lurking neighbours. He was, after all, well aware that many English towns had truly ancient and pre-English origins, the physical remains of which

---

[2] *Comm. Lam.*, p. 9: 'Quae enim miserabilior solitudo quam uirtutibus deturbatis uitiorum confusa frequentia? Non est ornamentum ciuitati uulgaris strepitus et imperitia, sed paucorum bonorum curia. Non confert animae multos habitatores habere, sed bonos. Que recte ciuitati comparatur, quia muniuit eam Deus naturalibus affectibus et uirtutibus, et, ne hoc parum esset, sanguinis ui commertio redemit, et uultus sui simulacro uestiuit.' The translation is Winterbottom's in *Lam.*, p. 42.

[3] GR 409. 1: 'Quanti enim ualerat Hibernia si non annauigarent merces ex Anglia? Ita pro penuria, immo pro inscientia cultorum ieiunum omnium bonorum solum agrestem et squalidam multitudinem Hibernensium extra urbes producit; Angli uero et Franci cultiori genere uitae urbes nundinarum commertio inhabitant'; J. Gillingham, *The English in the Twelfth Century: Imperialism, National Identity and Political Values* (Woodbridge, 2000), p. 11.

[4] GP 72. 6: 'magis in paludibus inglorii delitescere quam in excelsis urbibus consuerant habitare'.

were often still visible in his own day.[5] He therefore chose to emphasise that the conquest of Romano-British Britannia by the English had stripped its original inhabitants of their urban status and demoted them to the status of rustics. His description of the campaigns of the early West Saxon king Ceawlin tells how Ceawlin 'savagely pursued [the Britons], expelled them from their cities, and drove them into the land of rocks and forests [i.e. Wales], where they yet remain today'.[6] In short, the passing of Britannia's cities into the hands of the English represented their assumption of political, economic and moral supremacy within the British Isles.[7]

While chastising Britain's other peoples for their moral and economic failures, William addressed the increasingly urbanised England of his own day with rather more subtlety. Like many medieval intellectuals, he borrowed from Antiquity a concept of national identity with three main points of solidarity: a common point of origin, a common language and common customs, or what Sønnesyn has called 'biological, cultural and moral unity'.[8] Some of these criteria self-evidently applied to England's urban communities. There were certainly substantial differences in dialects among English towns in William's day, as he himself repeatedly acknowledged, and English cities were beginning to acquire their own written customs in his period, while their populations had their own cultural distinctiveness which he stressed regularly. Towns therefore had the potential to cut across the key bonds of national solidarity at two points. Nevertheless, it is important to recall Sønnesyn's thesis: William wrote history oriented around the appreciation and imitation of virtue. It is striking, therefore, that William's approach in the *Gesta Regum* was to emphasise the distinctive loyalty and martial valour of the men of London – a city which he tells us both 'belongs to the East Saxons'[9] and is the 'capital' ('caput regni') of the Mercians.[10] His account of moral and military decline in the late Anglo-Saxon period makes grim reading and his view of the Danish campaigns presents a pitiful view of the English forces, characterised by weakness, treachery and cowardice.[11] William saw the Londoners, however, as an important exception, who retained through the Viking age their *virtus* in both senses: 'London was besieged, but defended *probe* (bravely, or perhaps, honourably) by the citizens. As a result the besiegers were hard hit, and in despair

---

[5] His remarks about the surviving Roman structures at Carlisle are well known: *GP* 99. 3–4.
[6] *GR* 17. 1: 'exitum effugerant, infesta persecutes animositate urbibus exuit et in confragosa saltuosaque loca hodieque detrusit'. Compare Æthelstan's ethnic cleansing of the city of Exeter (136. 6). Compare Gildas, pp. 23–4, 28.
[7] Cf. the remarks of Emily A. Winkler, in this volume, pp. 189–201.
[8] Sønnesyn, *Ethics*, p. 111.
[9] *GR* 98. 1.
[10] *GR* 121. 10.
[11] *GR* 165. 3: 'Tantus timor Anglos incesserat ut nichil de resistendo cogitarent; si qui sane antiquae gloriae memores obuiare et signa colligare temptassent, hostium multitudine et sotiorum defectione destituebantur'.

of capturing the city departed.'[12] His account tells briefly not only of the fall of Oxford, Winchester and Bath to Swein, but also of how the Londoners stood apart in character and effectiveness:

> the Londoners, who had their lawful king safely inside their walls, shut their gates. The Danes, attacking furiously, raised their spirits high with the hope of glory; the townsmen charged to their deaths in the cause of freedom, thinking that they to whom the king had himself entrusted would never be forgiven if they were to desert him. Thus, after fierce fighting, the just cause won the day, for the citizens put all they had into the attempt, each man showing his mettle before the eyes of his prince and thinking that to die in his cause was a noble death.[13]

Even after Swein's forces had received the submission of Bath, the Londoners would not have surrendered to the Danes, had not the king himself shamefully fled the city.[14] The men of London played a similar role in the war between Cnut and Edmund Ironside, fighting 'heroically' ('magnanimiter') and driving off the invader's army.[15] The men of London, in other words, are deliberately portrayed as exceptions to the rule of late Anglo-Saxon moral and military decline. They are described repeatedly as a distinct moral community with clearly defined virtues, becoming a superior sort of Englishman, loyal when others were treacherous, and mettlesome when others were weak.

To make the men of London the particular embodiment of English virtue in difficult times, however, occasionally required William to take a creative approach to his sources. He avoided mention of the Londoners' defiance of William I after the Battle of Hastings, instead depicting them as joyously accepting the improving rule of the Conqueror.[16] The fact that the Londoners had supported the ascent to the throne of Harold Harefoot was, perhaps, too well known to be so easily dismissed, but William coped by claiming that they were temporarily corrupted by cultural contact with the Danes. This is important, because it is the only occasion on which William's writing compromises the Englishness of the men of the capital.[17] In contrast, he both emphasised and delegitimised defiance of royal power by

---

[12] Ibid.: 'Lundonia obsessa, sed a ciuibus probe defensa. Quocirca obsessores afflicti et desperantes posse capi ciuitatem discesserunt.'

[13] 'Lundonienses, regem legitimum intra menia tutantes, portas occluserunt. Dani contra ferotius assistentes spe gloriae uirtutem alebant; oppidani in mortem pro libertate ruebant, nullam sibi ueniam futuram arbitrantes si regem desererent, quibus ipse uitam suam commiserat. Ita cum utrimque acriter certaretur, iustior causa uictoriam habuit, ciuibus magna ope conantibus, dum unusquisque sudores suos principi ostentaret et pro eo pulchrum putaret emori.' Note also William's invocation of Virgil, comparing the Londoners to the warriors of antiquity: GR 177. 2–3.

[14] William of Jumièges inverted this sequence of events, writing that it was the Londoners who abandoned the king, not vice versa: *The Gesta Normannorum Ducum of William of Jumièges, Orderic Vitalis, and Robert of Torigni*, ed. and trans. E. van Houts (2 vols, OMT 1992–5), II, p. 18.

[15] GR 180. 5.

[16] GR 247. 1–2. William of Poitiers wrote instead of a small battle fought outside the city: *Gesta Guillelmi*, ed. and trans. R. H. C. Davis and M. Chibnall (OMT 1998), p. 146.

[17] GR 188. 1.

other English towns. William showed no sympathy for the citizens of Caerleon for their resistance to the pagan king Æthelfrith,[18] nor for their 'rebellious spirit' ('contumatia') in revolting against Edward the Elder.[19] Orderic Vitalis regarded the uprising at Exeter in 1068 as a noble act and a spirited defence of ancient liberties. William, however, had little patience with rebels at Exeter and York:

> The city of Exeter, which was in revolt, he [William the Conqueror] easily subdued, aided as he was by the help of Heaven, when part of the walls collapsed of its own accord and gave him admittance; indeed he himself had assaulted it with particular ferocity, protesting that such irreverent men must surely be deprived of divine support, after one of them, standing on the wall, had bared his breech and made the welkin re-echo with the noise of his nether parts to show his contempt for Normans. York, the only remaining refuge for rebels, he almost wiped out, so many of the citizens perished by famine or sword; for that was where Malcolm, king of Scots with his forces, where Edgar and Morcar and Waltheof with English and Danish troops often made a snug nest for tyranny and often cut to pieces William's generals.[20]

William's attitude to York was generally rather different from his glowing view of London. In his view, the men of Northumbria's failure to accept the divinely ordained West Saxon hegemony had allowed for the brutal Viking conquests of the ninth century, and that moral failure had been reflected in their military collapse and the destruction of their metropolis.[21] He related how Æthelstan had demolished the fortifications there 'to leave disloyalty ("perfidia") no place for refuge'.[22] When he came to the question of the Conqueror's treatment of the northern revolt, William again emphasised the mixed garrison of the town of York (which contained English, Scottish and Danish troops),[23] and made the point that the devastation unleashed by the Harrying of the North resulted in the total destruction of the region's cities. Whereas the London of the *Gesta Regum* is an exception to the rule of English corruption, the weakness and disloyalty of other cities is certainly not.

Since William's *Gesta Pontificum* is far less concerned with military and political history, there are fewer opportunities there for townsmen to demonstrate agency, and therefore, virtue or vice. Even so, there are hints that William remained

---

[18] GR 47. 3.
[19] GR 133. 1.
[20] GR 248: 'Vrbem Exoniam rebellantem leuiter subegit, diuino, scilicet iutus auxilio, quod pars muralis ultro decidens ingressum illi patefecerit; nam et ipse audatius eam assilerat, protestans homines irreuerentes Dei destituendos suffragio, quia unus eorum supra murum stans nudatio inguine auras sonitu inferioris partis turbauerat, pro contemptu uidelicet Normannorum. Eboracum, unicum rebellionum suffugium, ciuibus pene deleuit fame et ferro necatis. Ibi enim rex Scottorum Malcolmus cum suis, ibi Edgarus et Marcherius et Waldefus cum Anglis et Danis nidum tirannidis sepe fouebant, sepe duces illius trucidabant.'
[21] GR 120. 2.
[22] GR 134. 4.
[23] GR 249.

concerned with the connection between place and virtue. The most important of William's reflections on towns in the *Gesta Pontificum* is the first, his description of Canterbury:

> The first episcopal see after the English became Christian was, as it still is, at Canterbury. This English city is neither particularly large nor excessively small. It takes good care of its inhabitants both by its geographical position, for the nearby countryside is extremely fertile, and by its unbroken girdle of walls, though it has often had to face the perils of war. It is rich in the ashes of many saints, and can boast of their protection. It has a river to give it water, and woods nearby; and as the sea is only twelve miles away, it is not short of fish. The people in the city and outside it are more than other Englishmen still proudly aware of their long-established nobility, and this makes them the readier to pay honour to others and welcome them as guests, but also the fiercer in driving off those who might do them injury.[24]

Some of William's most important remarks here concern the city's physical and spiritual defences, its 'unbroken girdle of walls' ('integro murorum ambitu'), and its 'ashes of many saints' ('multorum sanctorum cineribus copiosa'). It has often been observed that the walls of a medieval city could be a major focus of urban pride, expenditure and even urban status itself.[25] What did it mean, therefore, for William to write that Canterbury's walls were 'unbroken' ('integer')? Perhaps William was neither making a straightforward architectural observation nor merely asserting Canterbury's claim to be regarded as a city. The word 'integer' is significant: it not only implies that the walls ran continuously around the city, but also connotes ideas like 'untouched', 'unbroken', 'inviolate' and 'incorrupt'. Cicero, an author whom William held in the highest regard, sometimes used it to mean 'morally spotless', and it appears often in the context of Marian devotion.[26] There is a resonance, therefore, between this description of Canterbury's architecture, and his later comment about the 'long-established nobility' of the inhabitants. Canterbury as William invoked it was an ancient city, inviolate and therefore incorrupt, and so was one that retained its antique identity and the dignity and virtues of its citizens. Canterbury was furthermore a city 'rich in the ashes of many saints'. Some significant work over the last few years has highlighted the

---

[24] GP prol. 1–2: 'Prima sedes episcoporum post Christianitatem Anglorum Cantuariae habita est et habetur. Ea urbs est Angliae nec adeo magna nec exiliter parua; qua et positione terrae, quippe soli affinis maxima ubertate, et integro murorum ambitu, licet multotiens Martias fortunas experta, ciues suos fouet, multorum sanctorum cineribus copiosa, patrociniis gloriosa; nec fluminis irriguo nec nemorum oportunitate indiga, preterea maris ad duodecim milia uicinitate piscium fecunda. Gens urbana et rustica, plusquam ceteri Angli conscientiam adhuc antiquae nobilitatis spirans, et ad honorificentiam et hospitium cuiuslibet pronior, ad propulsandas iniurias acrior.'
[25] O. Creighton and R. Higham, *Medieval Town Walls: An Archaeology and Social History of Urban Defence* (Stroud, 2005); J. Wigglesworth, *Science and Technology in Medieval European Life* (Greenwood, 2006), p. 100; O. Creighton, 'Urban defences', in *The Oxford Encyclopedia of Medieval Warfare and Military Technology*, ed. C. Rogers (3 vols, Oxford, 2010), I, pp. 385–90.
[26] A wide range of examples is collected in Lewis and Short. See also *DML*, II, 1419–20.

development from the mid-twelfth century of urban saints' cults, stressing that the creation of narratives which emphasised the sacred history and geography of towns was closely related to their economic and social emergence.[27] There was a strong connection between the sacred history of a town and its dignity, and William was not alone in stressing the importance of physical defences and holy patronage in his encomium of a noble city.[28]

When he came to develop his encomium of Canterbury, however, William was confronted with the historian's core problem: his sources did not tell the story he wanted to read. After all, in the early part of the twelfth century, a generation before the martyrdom of St Thomas, Canterbury was not particularly 'rich in the ashes of many saints'; indeed, for a major metropolitan see it was rather underprovided. The relics of only two major Canterbury saints were at Christ Church: those of the tenth-century reformer, Dunstan, and of one of his successors, Ælfheah, who was murdered by marauding Vikings in 1012. Even if we count the relics of St Augustine at his eponymous monastery, it appears that William was exaggerating somewhat for Canterbury's benefit. A rather shadowy figure with a weak claim to the martyr's palm, Ælfheah was known to William principally through Osbern's long account of Ælfheah's Passion. Osbern had given a central place in his text to an elaborate and detailed description of the destruction of Canterbury in 1012.[29] Worse for William's purposes, Osbern's version specifically describes how the city walls were first abandoned by their inept defenders and then battered with siege machines. In his *Commentary on Lamentations*, William made very clear what he thought of cities that had suffered conquest: when 'the nobles were killed and the temple burned down ... honour gave way to disgrace, veneration to scorn.'[30] The fall of a walled city to invaders meant that divine protection had been with-

---

[27] S. R. Jones, 'Cities and their saints in England, c. 1150–1300', in *Cities, Texts and Social Networks, 400–1500: Experiences of Medieval Urban Space*, ed. C. Goodson, A. Lester and C. Symes (Farnham, 2010), pp. 193–214. Although beginning with mid-twelfth-century material, this approach can certainly be projected even further back. It has been shown, for instance, that the enigmatic Old English poem *Durham* elides the identity of the city of Durham with that of Saint Cuthbert himself: see C. Kendall, 'Let us now praise a famous city: wordplay in the OE "Durham" and the cult of St Cuthbert', *Journal of English and Germanic Philology* 87 (1988), 507–21.

[28] It is worth noting that William used very similar language to describe Canterbury in his *Miracles of the Virgin*, which he wrote several years later. *MBVM*, p. 33: 'Ea ciuitas et multis sanctorum cineribus gloriosa et integro murorum ambitu, quamuis non semel marcias fortunas experta, uiget et pollet'. There are many examples in that later text of William praising cities for their physical defences, and several of him praising them for their relics. It appears that in all his writings, William only praised three cities for having both: Canterbury, Rome and Constantinople. For Rome, *MBVM*, p. 88, for Constantinople, *GR* 355–6. For the use of *romanitas* to establish the status and authority of Canterbury in the early Anglo-Saxon period, see N. Brooks, 'Canterbury, Rome, and the construction of English identity', in *Early Medieval Rome and the Christian West: Essays in Honour of Donald A. Bullough*, ed. J. Smith (Leiden, 2000), pp. 221–46.

[29] Osbern, *Vita S. Alphegi Archiepiscopi Cantuariensis*, in *Anglia Sacra*, ed. H. Wharton (2 vols, London, 1691), II, pp. 123–42.

[30] *Comm. Lam.*, I. 1819–21; *Lam.*, p. 108: 'Sed illis interfectis et isto incenso ... successitque honori dedecus, reuerentiae contemptus'.

drawn from inhabitants who no longer deserved it. Had William acknowledged Ælfheah's death in the terms described by Osbern, he would have been recording Canterbury's failure as a military and as a moral community.

William's task, therefore, was far from straightforward. Although the martyrdom of St Ælfheah helped his case for Canterbury's wealth of relics, the story was simply not compatible with an encomium that stressed the inviolate walls of the city and the moral purity of the inhabitants. He had to choose between them, and it is striking that he chose to sacrifice Ælfheah. His description of one of Canterbury's principal saints is conspicuously vague in the *Gesta Pontificum*: it comprises just a few short lines in which he took care not to mention the sack of the city before referring the reader to Osbern's text and moving swiftly onwards.[31] Ironically, he wrote a fuller description of Ælfheah in the *Gesta Regum*, for there the dignity of Canterbury was less significant, and reference to its sacking could do no harm to his wider arguments.[32]

In a passage unique to the *Gesta Pontificum*, William also took care to assert the ancient dignity, virtue and ferocity of the men of Canterbury. Despite the attention that he paid to individual towns, nowhere else in that text did he single out the men of a particular settlement for their virtues. Even the Londoners, so often praised in the *Gesta Regum* for their loyalty and valour, are mentioned in the *Gesta Pontificum* only with reference to their extensive wealth and trade. In short, the men of Canterbury, as depicted in the *Gesta Pontificum*, occupy a position somewhat analogous to that of the Londoners in the *Gesta Regum*. Each group, in its respective work, represents the English *par excellence*.

If there is merit in this analogy, it should be possible to identify a contrasting site or sites of moral and physical collapse. Perhaps unsurprisingly, York again offers the most plausible comparison:

> Next after Canterbury in importance is York, a large metropolitan city, showing signs of the taste of the Romans. Built on both sides of the River Ouse, it can receive into its very heart ships arriving from Germany and Ireland. It was the first city to be exposed to the furious assaults of the northern peoples; and for the whole time of the English domination it sustained, and lamented, the barbaric invasions of the Danes. Shaken by many a devastation, it was finally laid low by a disaster under King William. Enraged with the people of York because they had taken in and served the needs of the Danes on their arrival, he first starved and then burned the city. He had the entire region, town and country alike, pillaged, and the crops and fruit ruined by fire or flood. Plunder, arson and bloodshed thus hamstrung a province that had once been so fertile. For sixty and more miles round, cultivation ceased, and the soil is quite bare to this day .... Of course, the whole language of the Northumbrians, particularly in York, is so inharmonious and uncouth that *we southerners* can make nothing of

---

[31] GP 20. 3–4. William made no effort to obscure the sack of Canterbury when the primacy was not a significant part of his purpose in writing. See GR 165. 5.
[32] GR 165. 5–6.

it. This is the result of the barbarians being so near, and the kings, once English, now Norman, so far away.[33]

This passage inverts the sentiment of William's description of Canterbury. Though conceding that York had a long history and advantageous location, William blamed the Harrying of the North on the defection of the townsfolk to the Danes and emphasised the city's physical dilapidation. He made no reference to her saints. Where the men of Canterbury are characterised by refinement and virtue exceeding that of all other Englishmen, the men of York are almost barbarians, barely English at all. The pointed contrast can hardly be accidental, and certainly fits into William's view of the relationship between England's two archbishoprics. Canterbury, he seems to suggest, is a city worthy of the primacy, as opposed to that miserable pile of barbarian-infested ruins in the north. He did allow York the accolade of 'caput regni' of the Northumbrians, reproducing the text of Alcuin of York, but he took care to rearrange Alcuin's language to ensure that it could not be used to make an argument for the dignity of the church of York,[34] and the phrase appears only in the context of a miraculous rain of blood on the city which had prefigured its destruction.

If we try to assemble a picture of William's views on cities and their relationship with moral character and national identities in the British Isles, it becomes clear that he did not seek to downplay the moral or physical differences between towns in the service of a unified national identity. Rather, William, who self-identified as a 'southerner',[35] saw a superior version of English virtues in the townsmen of the south-east, specifically among the men of the ecclesiastical and political metropolises. His choice of which city held those virtues depended on whether he was writing secular or ecclesiastical history. In the north and west of England there were other cities with a long history, but these were cities of a lesser sort: they had been repeatedly overrun by barbarians, were given to pointless rebellion or had proven themselves barely English. Even further from the virtuous cities of the south-east were the Irish, Welsh and Scots, who either had no urban

---

[33] *GP* 99. 1–4: 'Secundae post Cantuariam dignitatis est Eboracum, urbs ampla et metropolis, elegantiae Romanae preferens inditum. A duabus partibus Husae fluminis edificata includit medio sinu sui naues a Germania et Hibernia uenientes. Furori aquilonianum gentium prima semper obnoxia, barbaricos Danorum motus toto tempore quo dominate sunt Angli excepit et ingemuit. Quapropter multis ruinis quassata ultima peste sub Willelmo rege concidit. Qui urbanis iratus quod Danis aduentius receptui et consultui fuissent, prius inedia mox flamma ciuitatem confecit. Regionis etiam totius uicos mox flamma ciuitatem confecit. Regionis etiam totius uicos et agros corrumpi, fructus et fruges igne uel aqua lebefactari iubet. Ita prouintie quondam fertilis nerui preda incendio sanguine succisi. Humus per sexaginta et eo amplius miliaria omnifariam, inculta, nudum omnium solum ad hoc usque tempus.... Sane toto lingua Nordanhimbrorum, et maxime in Eboraco, ita inconditum stride ut nichil nos australes intelligere possimus. Quod propter uiciniam barbararum gentium et propter remotionem regum quondam Anglorum modo Normannorum contigit.'

[34] Ibid. 5–6; Thomson, *William of Malmesbury*, p. 163.

[35] See above, n. 33.

heritage or had been driven from it several centuries before. William's history was fundamentally moral, and so too was his geography.

Though he certainly made use of literary conventions in his writing about towns and cities, William of Malmesbury's depictions of cities were as careful and as calculated as his arguments about the progress of the nation. For William, towns were moral communities which had a place within his wider arguments about national progress and character and which are best understood by historians in the context of William's sources and the entire corpus of his works. He handled his material deliberately and firmly, even making creative adjustments to fit his wider purposes.

The wider implications of William's mental moral geography for twelfth-century conceptions of national identity could be substantial. It is often taken as axiomatic that one of the defining characteristics of the modern state is that its capacity for government extends uniformly over its territory, and it has been argued that it is the standardisation of print that has made the formation of modern nationalism possible.[36] Medievalists investigating the apparent resurgence of English national feeling in twelfth-century historical writing, meanwhile, have tended to focus on the development of narratives which contrasted their national character with those of England's neighbours to the west, north and south.[37] This may, however, run the risk of neglecting the distinctions made by contemporaries between the smaller communities (including urban communities) that made up the English nation. Using William's depictions of cities to inform our reading of his national narratives might lead us to conclude that he had a very distinctive view of the nation. That view required neither the printed word nor unity of administration, because the idea of the nation itself, being built on the possession of virtues, was relative rather than monolithic. For William, some towns, and perhaps even some men, were more English than others.

---

[36] B. Anderson, *Imagined Communities: Reflections on the Origin and Spread of Nationalism* (rev. edn, London and New York, 2006), pp. 19, 44.

[37] Esp. Gillingham, *The English in the Twelfth Century*. Also G. Loud, 'The *Gens Normannorum* – myth or reality?', *ANS* 4 (1981), 104–16; H. Thomas, *The English and the Normans: Ethnic Hostility, Assimilation and Identity 1066–1220* (Oxford, 2003); L. Ashe, *Fiction and History in England, 1066–1200* (Cambridge, 2007).

4

The Ironies of History:
William of Malmesbury's Views of William II and Henry I

John Gillingham

'IF OUR CHRISTIAN FAITH admitted such a thing', wrote William of Malmesbury, 'it might be said that just as the soul of Euphorbus is supposed to have passed into Pythagoras of Samos, so also did the soul of Julius Caesar pass into King William'.[1] This, the concluding sentence of chapter 320 of the *Gesta Regum*, combining a reference to Julius Caesar with an allusion to Ovid's *Metamorphoses*, is a spectacular demonstration of Rod Thomson's comment on William of Malmesbury's pen portrait of Rufus: 'It is a sign of William's particular engagement with his subject that more classical reminiscences are deployed by him in characterising Rufus in the *Gesta Regum* than any other [person].'[2] In other ways too William took a great deal of trouble over his characterisation of Rufus.[3] For Heinz Richter, a German student of twelfth-century English historical writing deeply impressed by William's skill in understanding and delineating personality, the portrait of Rufus was his masterpiece.[4] William would surely have been pleased that his characterisation of the king has been identified as 'the most complete and balanced' of those composed by the next generation of chroniclers and, in consequence, as the one 'upon which subsequent historians have primarily relied'.[5] In this essay, however, I shall begin by arguing that nearly all subsequent historians – though not Richter – have overemphasised the darker colours in that portrait, in one case even suggesting

---

[1] GR 320. 4.
[2] R. M. Thomson, 'Satire, irony and humour in William of Malmesbury', in *Rhetoric and Renewal*, pp. 115–27, 121–2.
[3] As we know from the 'noticeable clustering of changes' to the text of the relevant chapters of Book 4 observed by Winterbottom, *GR* II, p. xxv. See also ibid., p. 276.
[4] 'Ein Meisterstück seines Könnens': H. Richter, *Englische Geschichtschreiber des 12. Jahrhunderts* (Berlin, 1938), pp. 54–125, 89–90.
[5] T. Callahan, Jr, 'The making of a monster: the historical image of William Rufus', *JMH* 7 (1981), 175–85, at p. 178. Cf. J. O. Ward, 'William of Malmesbury: chronicler, antiquarian or historian?' in *The Creation of Medieval Northern Europe. Essays in Honour of Sverre Bagge*, ed. L. Melve and S. Sønnesyn (Oslo, 2012), pp. 271–313, at 307 n. 105.

that 'when William talked of Rufus's resemblance to a Roman emperor, Nero might have been a better comparison'.[6]

Without question, William's opinion of the king was far more balanced than Eadmer of Canterbury's. He saw some redeeming features where Eadmer, single-mindedly making his case that Anselm was in no way to blame for the difficulties faced by churches in England, was determined to see none.[7] Although William admired and was influenced by Eadmer's vivid prose, his own values were much more open to the secular world. He not only added much that was in Rufus's favour, but at several key points, he silently disassociated himself from his predecessor's version of events.[8] It has been suggested that the historian was 'captivated by the king's dry wit. William the ironist could not resist being attracted by such a rich sense of irony in another'.[9] But it was no doubt possible for William to enjoy the king's wit while still thinking of him as a 'bad king'. He certainly found much to criticise. He disapproved of the fashions and sexual *mores* of the courtiers, of Rufus's imposing financial burdens on churches, of his lack of piety, of his scorn for many churchmen, particularly monks, and may well have been shocked by his propensity to joke about them and about portents.[10] These criticisms take up the greater part of ten chapters (312–19, 331, 333).

But did he take an essentially negative view of Rufus?[11] After all, in seven other chapters (305–9, 311, 320) his tone is positive, and Rufus was by many criteria a highly successful king. Even Eadmer acknowledged that at the time of his death 'the whole world was smiling upon him', and it seemed to William that 'no kingdom was beyond the reach of his ambition'.[12] In general William admired successful kings, irrespective of their personal virtue.[13]

---

[6] This despite acknowledging that William 'was not fully convinced of the wickedness of Rufus and has much more to say on the magnanimity and generosity of the king': D. Crouch, *The Normans. The History of a Dynasty* (London, 2002), pp. 140, 150.

[7] For a brief assessment of Eadmer's character-assassination of the king, see J. Gillingham, *William II the Red King* (London, 2015), pp. 33–50.

[8] For example, where Eadmer claimed that Rufus had driven Anselm into exile in 1097, William wrote simply that Anselm went 'of his own accord': GR 315. In his brief sketch of Bishop Ralph of Chichester (1091–1123), he noted that 'by his departure Anselm weakened his hopes and those of other good men': GP 96. 5. And see below, pp. 45–7.

[9] Thomson, 'Satire', pp. 121–2.

[10] GR 312, 317–18, 331. Some of the charges were elaborated in the β text of GP 49. 1–6, 55. 3–6. For Caesar's disregard of omens, see Suetonius 59, 77, 81.

[11] For Jean Blacker, William's portrait of Rufus 'may be among the kindest from the period, yet ... it is essentially negative, underscoring the king's anticlerical and immoral behaviour': J. Blacker, *The Faces of Time. Portrayal of the Past in Old French and Latin Historical Narrative of the Anglo-Norman Regnum* (Austin, 1994), p. 61; 'essentially negative' and 'only Æthelred II receives more criticism': Sønnesyn, *Ethics*, pp. 213- 27, esp. 214, 227.

[12] Eadmer, *Historia Nouorum*, p. 116; GR 333. 7.

[13] A. Plassmann, 'Bedingungen und Strukturen von Machtausübung bei Wilhelm von Malmesbury und Heinrich von Huntingdon', in *Macht und Spiegel der Macht. Herrschaft in Europa im 12. und 13. Jahrhundert vor dem Hintergrund der Chronistik*, ed. N. Kersken and G. Vercamer (Wiesbaden, 2013), pp. 145–71, at 160–1, 164–5.

William of Malmesbury's Views of William II and Henry I

As Joan Gluckauf Haahr observed, 'William commended (although with varying degrees of enthusiasm) those kings who ruled strongly'. But she immediately drew a line: 'with the exception of William Rufus whose personal corruption made him, as most subsequent authorities agree, probably the worst king England ever had'.[14] As these words reveal, she read William's *Gesta Regum* through a lens provided by A. L. Poole, who regarded Rufus as 'from the moral standpoint ... probably the worst king that has occupied the throne of England'.[15] Ruth Morse too was in no doubt: 'The paired lives of William Rufus and Henry are strikingly Suetonian .... The lives of the two brothers are meant to contrast. In William of Malmesbury's judgement the elder was a bad man and a bad king.'[16] It may be that she was influenced by V. H. Galbraith's opinion that, for medieval as well as Victorian historians, it was impossible that a bad man could also be a good king. Galbraith mentioned Rufus twice, in both instances pairing him with King John as the villains of medieval and Victorian historians, although we might think that the records of the two kings are as different as they could possibly be. One extended his dominions, acquiring Normandy, Maine and Cumberland; the other lost Normandy, Maine and Anjou.[17]

Nonetheless most recent commentators on William's views of kings and kingship have treated Rufus as his 'bad king' *par excellence*. Even Paul Hayward, who has emphasised 'studied ambiguity' as one of William's most characteristic qualities, has nonetheless seen him as directing his 'readers' derision to those rulers who stole and squandered other people's resources' and has identified Rufus as the 'grossest example of such depravity'.[18] In this vein Björn Weiler noted that 'Rufus was praised as much for his courage and generosity as he was condemned for his greed and unwillingness to rein in his court and household', but while he dealt with William's praise in a couple of sentences, he devoted page after page to his criticisms of the king.[19] Weiler and Sønnesyn have rightly emphasised the

---

[14] J. G. Haahr, 'The concept of kingship in William of Malmesbury's *Gesta Regum* and *Historia Novella*', *Med. St.* 38 (1976), 355, 361.

[15] A. L. Poole, *Domesday Book to Magna Carta* (Oxford, 1955), pp. 98–9.

[16] R. Morse, *Truth and Convention in the Middle Ages* (Cambridge, 1991), p. 162. Also Sønnesyn, *Ethics*, p. 227. This was not, however, how Marie Schütt read the Suetonian section on *mores* in William's narrative of Rufus's reign. She concluded that it was organised so as to leave 'the reader with a comparatively favourable impression': M. Schütt, 'The literary form of William of Malmesbury's *Gesta Regum*', *EHR* 46 (1931), 255–60, at p. 257.

[17] V. H. Galbraith 'Good kings and bad kings in English history', *History* 30 (1945), 119–32, reprinted in his *Kings and Chroniclers* (London, 1982), pp. 125, 127. More recently Rufus has been paired with Æthelred the Unready. Rufus was 'singled out for particular criticism', with only Æthelred II receiving more: Sønnesyn, *Ethics*, p. 214. Cf. Thomson, 'William obviously found Rufus's reign nearly as distasteful and difficult to deal with as that of Æthelred II': *GR* II, p. 267.

[18] For him William's 'flagrantly reductionist' portrait of Rufus's regime 'may well capture its essence': P. Hayward, 'The importance of being ambiguous: innuendo and legerdemain in William of Malmesbury's *Gesta regum* and *Gesta pontificum Anglorum*', *ANS* 33 (2010/11), 75–102, at pp. 75, 92–3.

[19] B. Weiler, 'William of Malmesbury on kingship', *History* 90 (2005), 3–22, at pp. 7–8, 10–18, 20.

element of moral instruction in William's histories as a reminder of the values and approaches he shared with other ecclesiastical historians. That element is unquestionably there, though it is worth noting that in William's most explicit statement in the *Gesta Regum* of history's value as a guide to conduct, his letter to Robert of Gloucester (*GR*, Ep. III), there is no mention of either God or Christian providence, nor is there in the book's prologue to which William directed the earl's attention. William was of course in many ways a typical monk.[20] But it was in the ways that he was different that he was a great historian.[21] Monks, even monks who belonged to the same order, remained individuals. It is, for example, hard to imagine two historians more different than two English Benedictines from the late twelfth century: Gervase of Canterbury and Richard of Devizes. It may be that William of Malmesbury was less bored by the monotony of life in the cloister than the later monk of Malmesbury who claimed that it was this that made him turn to the writing of history.[22] In any case, not all monks shared Eadmer's view of Rufus. The monks of Battle Abbey certainly did not; nor did the monks of Durham.[23] Orderic followed Eadmer's lead in condemning the sexual morals at court, but came close to seeing Rufus as a model duke of Normandy and leader in the traditional Norman struggle against the king of France: 'If Julius Caesar had tried to wrong the king in any way while he had such men about him, he would have dared to test their strength and courage even against Caesar and the legions of Rome.'[24]

If William had thought that Rufus was not a great ruler, why did he play with the idea that Caesar's soul inhabited him? He saw Caesar as a man of great achievements. The *Gesta Regum* begins with Caesar's conquest of Britain.[25] Only two other kings in William's long gallery of rulers were explicitly compared with Caesar: Rufus's father and Rufus's younger brother Henry. His father because William compared his strategy against the English with Caesar's own account of his strategy against the Germans; Henry because he broke a promise made to his

---

[20] So far as I am aware, no-one has ever suggested, *pace* Weiler, 'William of Malmesbury', p. 6, that William was 'untainted by theological concerns', nor *pace* Sverre Bagge, 'Ethics, politics and providence in William of Malmesbury's *Historia novella*', *Viator* 41 (2010), 113-32, at p. 114, that he paid merely 'lip service to the religious and superstitious ideals of his age'.

[21] Thomson, *William of Malmesbury*, passim; J. Gillingham, 'A historian of the twelfth-century renaissance and the transformation of English society, 1066-ca.1200', in *European Transformations*, ed. T. F. X. Noble and J. Van Engen (Notre Dame, 2012), pp. 45-74.

[22] *Eulogium Historiarum*, ed. F. S. Haydon (RS 1858), i. 2. Although I can imagine both that William was sometimes bored and sometimes felt guilty about it.

[23] In Battle Abbey tradition Rufus was the *magnificus princeps* who 'loved, cherished and defended the Church': *The Chronicle of Battle Abbey*, ed. and trans. E. Searle (OMT 1980), pp. 97-9. Symeon of Durham, *LDE*, p. 243. See E. Mason, 'William Rufus and the Benedictine Order', *ANS* 21 (1998-9), 113-44.

[24] Orderic Vitalis, v. 214, 238, 300.

[25] Even when being criticised, Caesar was recognised as a dominant figure – as in Hildebert's great poem, *Par tibi, Roma* (quoted in full by William in *GR* 351. 2-4), where to achieve power over Rome he 'for his private ends / All loyalties, all kindred set at naught'.

brother Robert.²⁶ In Rufus's case William was reminded of Caesar by the story of how the king released his prisoner, Count Helias of Maine, despite the count's proud insistence that he would take up the fight again as soon as he was free. William's version emphasises Rufus's furious admiration for Helias's bold words:

> 'Sod off then, you clown! Get out! You've my permission to do your worst. And, by the face of Lucca, if you beat me, I shall ask nothing from you in return for letting you go now.' He was as good as his word, and at once let him go free.

Since Rufus had no interest in literature, according to William, he could not have been inspired to do this by reading the words with which, in Lucan's *Civil War*, Julius Caesar had released Domitius. 'Rather it was his innate fire of mind and conscious valour that drove him.'²⁷

These appear to be expressions of admiration for the king. This was certainly the view of Heinz Richter, who chose the word 'Bewundernd' to describe them.²⁸ But Richter's fine analysis, published in Berlin in 1938, has remained without influence. Instead, the view has taken hold that William intended the opposite effect. Haahr, for instance, claimed: 'Given his consistently evident disdain for William Rufus, it is hard to believe he was not being ironic'.²⁹ As always with William, ironic interpretation of his words is tempting.³⁰ The most comically blatant instance of his irony is the famous comment on Henry I's sex life: 'all his life long he was completely free from fleshly lusts'.³¹ Orderic, living much further from the court than William did, took a simpler view of Henry I: 'Possessing an abundance of wealth and luxuries, he gave way too easily to the sin of lust; from boyhood until old age he was sinfully enslaved by this vice, and had many sons and daughters by his mistresses'.³² William had no need to conceal his views of Rufus's vices under a veil of irony. As Stubbs pointed out, matters such as the king's extortions and

---

[26] GR 254. 1, 389. 9.
[27] GR 320. 3-4: '"Tu", inquit, "nebulo, tu quid faceres? Discede, abi, fuge! Concedo tibi ut fatias quicquid poteris, et per uultum de Luca nihil, si me uiceris, pro hac uenia tecum paciscar". Nec inferius factum uerbo fuit, sed continuo dimisit euadere. Quis talia de illiterato homine crederet? Et fortassis erit aliquis qui, Lucanum legens, falso opinetur Willelmum haec exempla de Iulio Cesare mutuatum esse. Sed non erat ei tantum studii uel otii ut litteras umquam audiret; immo calor mentis ingenitus et conscia uirtus eum talia exprimere cogebant. Et profecto, si Christianitas nostra pateretur, sicut olim anima Euforbii transisse dicta est in Pitagoram Samium, ita posset dici quod anima Iulii Cesaris transierit in regem Willelmum.' The allusion is to Lucan, *Bellum Civile* 2. 512-15.
[28] Richter, *Englische Geschichtschreiber*, p. 90.
[29] J. G. Haahr, 'William of Malmesbury's Roman models: Suetonius and Lucan', in *The Classics in the Middle Ages*, ed. A. Bernardo and S. Levin (Binghamton, 1990), p. 172 (though 'citing no literature later than 1962!': GR II, p. xlv n. 81). 'With tongue firmly in his cheek': Sønnesyn, *Ethics*, p. 225; 'keinesfalls schmeichelhaft gemeint': Plassmann, 'Bedingungen und Strukturen', p. 161.
[30] 'his view of the world was an ironic one': Thomson, 'Satire', p. 116.
[31] GR 412. 2. On this see A. Cooper, 'The feet of those that bark shall be cut off: timorous historians and the personality of Henry I', ANS 23 (2001), 47-67, at p. 64.
[32] Orderic Vitalis, vi. 98-9.

'his personal peculiarities' could scarcely come into the [Anglo-Saxon] Chronicle but would, twenty years after, 'be amusing enough in conversation'.[33]

How then are we meant to be amused by the mention of Caesar's soul? Since William had explicitly drawn attention to Lucan, did he mean us to understand that Rufus was as demonic as Lucan's Caesar? – that monster who, to quote the Chicago classicist W. R. Johnson, belonged not in a Latin historical epic but in a Vincent Price movie.[34] But even had William hinted at this in his multi-layered ambiguity, it is hard to believe that the main message was not a positive one. The king's release of Count Helias had become legendary. The story, with its dramatic dialogue between the two men, would be told in one form or another by Orderic, Gaimar and Wace, and always admiringly. This was the action that Anselm's biographer, John of Salisbury, characterised as Rufus's great deed.[35] William acknowledged that Rufus had been much admired by knights who flocked to his service from all over Europe this side of the Alps, and he, like Orderic, clearly knew the kind of stories they told about the king. The knights' view was reflected in Gaimar's words: 'Never was there a king held in such affection or in such honour by his men'.[36] But effective leadership in war mattered to monks like William and Orderic as well as to knights. Indeed, William praised his patron, Robert of Gloucester, as a military commander – 'he nobly fulfilled the duty of a knight and leader' – and on the occasion of his invasion of England in 1139 explicitly compared him with Julius Caesar.[37]

When interpreting William's reference to Lucan it is important to note that it ends a chapter that begins: 'On the other hand, the king provided some examples of real greatness of spirit ("quaedam de rege preclarae magnanimitatis exempla")'.[38] William's use of the classics, here as elsewhere, 'amounts to much more than rhetorical/stylistic *Schmuckmittel*'.[39] He measured kings not only by ecclesiastical criteria, but also by the 'classical' notions of *liberalitas* and *magnanimitas*.[40] William measured Rufus in terms of his *liberalitas* and found him

---

[33] *GR* (Stubbs), II, p. cxvii.

[34] W. R. Johnson, *Momentary Monsters* (Ithaca NY, 1987), p. 103. If William of Malmesbury's Rufus was inspired by Lucan's Caesar, and so too Marlowe's Tamburlaine (see W. Blissett, 'Lucan's Caesar and the Elizabethan villain', *Studies in Philology* 53 (1956), 553–75), then Frank Barlow's choice of lines from *Tamburlaine* as the epigraph to his great *William Rufus* makes good sense.

[35] Orderic Vitalis, v. 228–32; Geffrei Gaimar, *Estoire des Engleis/History of the English*, ed. and trans. I. Short (Oxford, 2009), pp. 320–3; Wace, *The Roman de Rou*, trans. G. S. Burgess (St Helier, 2002), pp. 310–11; John of Salisbury, *Policraticus*, ed. C. C. J. Webb (2 vols, Oxford, 1909), 6. 18.

[36] *GR* 314. 1–2, 333. 7–8. Gaimar, *Estoire*, lines 5923–4. And see 'Kingship, chivalry and love. Political and cultural values in the earliest history written in French: Geoffrey Gaimar's *Estoire des Engleis*', in J. Gillingham, *The English in the Twelfth Century* (Woodbridge, 1997), pp. 233–58.

[37] *HN* 2. 31.

[38] *GR* 320. 1.

[39] R. M. Thomson, 'William of Malmesbury and the Latin Classics revisited', in *Aspects*, pp. 391–2.

[40] Richter, *Englische Geschichtschreiber*, p. 91. While it is true that 'just because William wrote like an early imperial Roman historian', it 'does not mean that he also thought like one' (B. Weiler,

wanting; this is evident in his restatement of the Ciceronian distinction between liberality and prodigality, and in his argument that the king's prodigality led to financial oppression.[41]

But what about his *magnanimitas*? The word, which he applied to Rufus three times, although not easy to translate, certainly meant something positive. The first time William used it in the *Gesta Regum* was with reference to Charlemagne.[42] He used it in the prefatory letter to Robert of Gloucester when he was at his most obsequious, referring to the *magnanimitas* of Robert's grandfather (the Conqueror).[43] In the same passage he went on to praise the wisdom of Robert's father, Henry, and the generosity ('munificentia') of his uncle.[44] Like Jean Blacker, I take the uncle here to be not Robert Curthose, as has sometimes been suggested, but Rufus; after all, when the prefatory letter was written, Uncle Robert was either living in prison or had recently died there.[45] *Magnanimitas* certainly included the connotation of an element of courage. Hence, when Geoffrey Martel turned tail before Duke William's advance, William wrote that he failed to display his *solita magnanimitas*.[46] But the word connotes something more: that quality which enables its possessor to face trouble with firmness, to be above taking petty revenge and to disdain meanness. William used it, for example, of Edgar on the occasion when he freed a slave girl with whom he had had sex while believing she was someone else.[47] Of course, *magnanimitas* could also be used ironically, as possibly it was in the case of Edgar and the slave girl. Two clearer examples of irony can be seen when William applied the word to Henry I. In one case he

'William of Malmesbury, King Henry I and the *Gesta regum Anglorum*', ANS 31 (2008/9), 157–76, at p. 158 n. 6), equally it does not follow that because he was a Benedictine he could do no other than express standard Benedictine thoughts.

[41] GR 313–14. Putting aside the question of whether he would have condemned Rufus if he had spent as much on donations to monasteries as he did on donatives to knights, it is worth noticing that he said similar things about his first patron, Queen Matilda: 'her liberality attracted people from around the world, so she was profligate and in consequence oppressed her tenants, damaging them and taking their substance, indifferent to the wrongs done to her people while winning the name of a generous giver': 418; Plassmann, 'Bedingungen und Strukturen', p. 153. In 313–14 William was more concerned about royal extravagance and the luxurious lifestyle of courtiers than about the oppression of the poor.

[42] Referring to a letter as 'a tribute to the greatness of mind and courage of Charles ["magnanimitatis et fortitudinis Karoli"] who spent his whole life fighting pagans': GR 90.

[43] When it came to narrating the Conqueror's life, although he did not use precisely that word, he several times chose closely related ones: 'magnitudo animi' (234. 1), 'magnanimus dux' (244); 'magnanimo parenti' (275. 1).

[44] GR Ep. III. 2: 'Nullum enim magis decet bonarum artium fautorem esse quam te, cui adhesit magnanimitas aui, munificentia patrui, prudentia patris'. The likely date of this letter is discussed in GR II, p. 6.

[45] Blacker, *Faces of Time*, p. 4; pace GR II, p. 10, and Sønnesyn, *Ethics*, p. 101. There is an illuminating parallel in the reference to Matilda in the *HN:* 'in whom alone lay the legitimate succession since her grandfather, uncle and father had been kings' ('Nunc superesse filiam, cui soli legitima debeatur successio, ab auo, auunculo et patre regibus'): HN c. 2 (p. 6).

[46] GR 231. 4.

[47] GR. 159. 1.

referred to the *regiae magnanimitatis motum* which the king felt about his Welsh enemies and which persisted until allayed by hostages, money and livestock.[48] In the second case, in describing the way in which Henry's hatreds and friendships were carried to extremes, he called his treatment of his friends and supporters 'regalis magnanimitas': he exalted them 'until all were jealous of them'.[49]

Had William been equally ironic on the three occasions he ascribed *magnanimitas* to Rufus? The first time he did so was in chapter 308, introducing the story of how out of admiration for an enemy's prowess Rufus took into his service a knight who had unhorsed him. William explicitly compared Rufus's conduct here with Alexander the Great's admiration for the courage of an opponent: 'Bravo, most generous king ('amplissime rex')! You fall not far short of the glory of great Alexander long ago, who ... spared a Persian soldier's life out of admiration for his courage'.[50] Here we have another classical reminiscence, again in the context of Rufus's generous treatment of opponents, and once again, though silently this time, quoting Lucan on Caesar.[51] True, this was an episode from fairly early in Rufus's reign (1091), and in chapter 312 William famously described him as a man 'of high principle (*magnanimitas*)' who after promising beginnings went sadly downhill.[52] But the story of the count of Maine in chapter 320 shows that William's Rufus continued to display magnanimity even at the end of his reign. Moreover, as Marie Schütt noted, William highlighted this same quality in the king's character, although without using the word, in summarising his dealings with Malcolm III's son Edgar. William chose to forget the wrongs done by the father and put Edgar back on the throne: an outstanding instance of generosity worthy of so great a man ('egregia plane et quae tantum uirum decebat pietate, ut paternarum iniuriarum immemor filium suplicem restitueret regno').[53] The cumulative effect of these instances is to make plain that William thought Rufus capable of genuine magnanimity.

---

[48] GR 401. 3: 'donec Walenses, datis obsidibus nobiliorum suorum filiis cum aliquanta pecunia et multo peculo regiae magnanimitatis motum sedarent'. The translations 'commotion of the royal spirit' (Sharpe) and 'king's generous resentment' (Mynors) reveal that this was an unusual kind of magnanimity.

[49] GR 411. 1: 'Odii et amicitiae in quamlibet tenax, in altero nimio irarum estui, in altero regiae magnanimitati satisfiens, hostes uidelicet ad miseriam deprimens, amicos et clientes ad inuidiam efferens'.

[50] GR 309. 2. Thomson identified an epitome of Julius Valerius, *Res Gestae Alexandri Macedonis* as the probable source: GR II, p. 274. Rufus's generosity here has been credited to his father: M. Winterbottom, 'The *Gesta regum* of William of Malmesbury', *JML* 5 (1995), 169.

[51] After Rufus's immediate flash of anger he was calmed down by the knight's explanation, and he spoke 'uultu serenus', a quotation from Lucan's *Bellum Ciuile* (4. 363) describing Caesar's generous treatment of a defeated enemy.

[52] He had 'refrained from all wrongdoing while Lanfranc was alive, when it was hoped he would be a paragon among princes', but by the end of his reign his virtues had degenerated into vices, and where he had been high-minded ('magnanimus') he was now proud: GR 312. 1.

[53] Schütt, 'Literary form', 256. Moreover William later approvingly described Henry's policy towards the Scottish kings as 'conciliatory, following the precedent set by his brother': GR 311. 2, 400. 1.

Nonetheless for William, as for most early narrators of Rufus's reign – though emphatically not for those who wrote in the language of the secular world, like Gaimar and Wace – the king's sudden death proved that, despite all his worldly successes, he had on balance been a bad man. Monks such as William, Eadmer and Orderic, as well as other churchmen like Henry of Huntingdon, were bound to think of Rufus's end, coming at the height of his power, as a death sentence passed on him by God. William duly reported that no less a monk than Abbot Hugh of Cluny had pronounced that this was indeed so.[54] William did not doubt it.[55] But it saddened him too, for in some ways he saw Rufus as an able ruler and an attractive figure. He thought of Rufus as a man to be pitied: he had died without doing penance and his soul could not be saved.[56] Yet had he lived longer, he might have mended his ways. William wrote: 'Naturally gifted with a spirit prolific of great ideas, he would have been a prince without peer in our own time had he not been overshadowed by his father and had not fate (*fata*) overtaken him at an early age, thus preventing the faults occasioned by unlimited power and youthful spirits from being corrected by maturity.'[57]

It may well be that on the subject of Rufus, William's ambiguity was not only studied but also genuinely felt. As Michael Winterbottom noted, 'bravery, magnanimity, panache are qualities that attract the bookish monk of Malmesbury'.[58] William's view of Rufus was not only complex but conflicted too. On one occasion he expressed himself in confusingly convoluted Latin, and the modern conviction that he saw him as a 'bad king' has led to some manipulation of the text and its meaning:

> Vides quantus e liberalitate, quam putabat, fomes malorum eruperit. In quibus corrigendis quia ipse non tam exhibuit diligentiam quam pretendit negligentiam, magnam et uix abolendam incurrit infamiam; immerito credo, quia nunquam se tali supponeret probro se tanto meminisset prelatum imperio. Haec igitur ideo

---

[54] GR 332. 1.
[55] Thus in the β text of *GP* he wrote of a king who scorned God's judgement who 'paid for the wantonness of his acts and words by being pierced though the vitals by an arrow': *GP* 55. 4–5.
[56] GR 333. 8. As Weiler noted, 'few would have described the decline and fall of a ruler like Rufus with quite so much empathy': 'William of Malmesbury and King Henry I', p. 176.
[57] GR 305. 1. It is noteworthy that in *GR* William, except when reporting Abbot Hugh's prophetic statement, used classical rather than ecclesiastical language when referring to the king's death: 'Immensely ambitious, he would have been immensely successful had the Fates allowed him to complete his allotted span or break through the violence of Fortune' ('cum et illi naturaliter inesset ingentia parturiens animus, ad culmen supremae dignitatis euasit: incomparabilis proculdubio nostro tempore princeps, si non eum magnitudo patris obrueret, nec eius iuuentutem Fata precepissent, ne per aetatem maturiorem aboleret errores licentia potestatis et impetu iuuenili contractos'): GR 333. 7. As Bagge pointed out, William saw God's Providence being directly engaged when things went well, but when they turned out ill God stood back and let fortune take its course: Bagge, 'Ethics, politics and providence', pp. 125–30. William FitzOsbern was another prince renowned for *pene prodiga liberalitas* who was struck down by *fortuna*: GR 256. 1–2. More generally on William's use of Fortune, see Rodney Thomson's paper in this volume, pp. 166–8.
[58] Winterbottom, 'The *Gesta regum*', p. 169.

> inelaborato et celeri sermone conuoluo, quia de tanto rege mala dicere erubesco, in deiciendis et extenuandis malis laborans.[59]

This has been translated in the OMT edition:

> You see what a hotbed of evils burgeoned from what he supposed to be generosity. He himself used no diligence to correct them, but rather made a display of negligence, so bringing on himself great and indelible discredit; which in my opinion he thoroughly deserved, for a man would never expose himself to such disgrace who had once bethought him of the great kingdom he was called to rule. So I veil the topic in these few bald and hasty words and I am devoting my efforts to refuting or palliating the evil spoken of him.

A footnote saying 'William surely meant to write *non immerito* or *merito*' explains the unusual translation of *immerito*.[60] But if William believed that Rufus 'thoroughly deserved' his reputation, would he have devoted his efforts to refuting or palliating it? In any case, this passage in chapter 316 comes within that section of his text – chapters 314–17 – that has been identified as containing a 'clustering of changes' that were intended to import a 'less critical view of William II'.[61] Given that in the *Gesta Regum* we have a highly polished text surviving in no less than four manuscript traditions, it passes belief that he would have allowed a word that exactly reversed his intended meaning to remain in all four.[62] I suggest an alternative translation of the crucial sentence:

> By not only failing to show due diligence in correcting [such evil practices], but by making it appear that he did not even care, Rufus earned himself an extremely bad reputation, one that could hardly ever be expunged; this was, in my view, undeserved, for someone who was conscious of the great responsibility he bore as a ruler would never lay himself open to a charge of such infamous conduct.[63]

Whatever we may think of the *merito/immerito* question, it is generally accepted that William's view of Rufus was at least fairly consistently held throughout his surviving works, including the β text of the *Gesta Pontificum*.[64] The same is not true of his view of William I and Henry I. While he certainly admired both as strong and successful rulers, the survival of what Michael Winterbottom has

---

[59] GR 316.
[60] GR I, p. 360 n. a. Cf. Sønnesyn, *Ethics*, p. 224. That William's Latin required emendation had not occurred to John Sharpe whose own translation was described as 'a work of distinction' that paid 'attention to the minutest touch in William's Latin': GR I, p. xxii.
[61] GR II, pp. xxv–xxvi.
[62] All the more since precisely this chapter includes one of his small revisions, in this case substituting 'fomes malorum' (hotbed of evils) in place of 'gurges uitiorum' (whirlpool of vices).
[63] Here, as generally, my translations owe much to Ian Short's mastery of languages.
[64] Thomson in GR II, p. 276. In the β text of *GP* the criticism is more sharply phrased than in *GR* and the other versions of the *GP*, but it is in essence the same. See also, for example, Hayward's discussion of the collapse of Winchester tower, pointing out that the criticisms of Rufus, though slightly softened in the later version, are still there: Hayward, 'The importance', p. 79.

called 'the offensive material that is the glory of β' allows us to see his criticisms of them – criticisms that were so powerfully worded that he subsequently suppressed them.[65] The β text includes, for example, a long passage on William the Conqueror's ecclesiastical policy that is not only very different in tone from what he wrote elsewhere, but amounts to a direct refutation of Eadmer's representation of a harmonious partnership between the king and Lanfranc.[66] It also contains a lapidary description of the ecclesiastical policy of the king who allowed Roger of Salisbury to seize Malmesbury Abbey: 'he snatched everything from everybody ('omnia omnibus eriperet')'.[67]

As for Henry's personal morality, in the β text William wrote that after Anselm's death he

> plunged into a mire of disgrace ('se uolutabro dedecoris immergeret'), and allowed others to fall into it with him. Now that a spirit, in itself fierce and uncontrolled ('feroci per se et lasciuo spiritui') is being further encouraged by bishops who should have stood in the way, no hope remains, nothing is left. Let each look to himself to hope; let him live who can! But where is my distress leading me?[68]

It is easy to understand why William had second thoughts about those words, in tone the most emotionally engaged of any passage in his two great histories. Henry, described in passing by Eadmer as 'the king whom many feared more than they feared God', was on the throne.[69] As William himself wrote, 'all men had love of him on their lips and fear of him in their hearts'.[70] If William did indeed think, as Hayward has suggested, that his readers sometimes needed 'alerting to the rules according to which he has constructed his text', then the phrase 'all men had love of him on their lips' looks very like a clue on how best to read Book Five of the *Gesta Regum* and in particular its prologue.[71] As Alan Cooper noted, irony 'is difficult to detect when we are unable to know the reality against which the irony works'.[72] But the β text suggests conclusively that this prologue is an

---

[65] *GP* II, p. xiv.
[66] *GP* 42. 6
[67] *GP* 96. 7. 'Dismay and fear at Roger of Salisbury's seizure of Malmesbury infect William's work, shaping the way he wrote about England's lords and bishops': Hayward, 'The importance', pp. 93–6, 101. If he had cause to fear Roger of Salisbury, how much more Roger's master?
[68] *GP* 63. 1. Presumably Roger of Salisbury was prominent among those complaisant bishops. Cf. Weiler's view that what made kings like Henry I admirable was that they sought out advisers who would admonish and censure, listened to them and made amends: Weiler, 'William of Malmesbury and Henry I', pp. 162–6.
[69] 'Qui plus Deo a multis timebatur': *HN*, p. 213. In arguing that the 'unexpurgated version' of the *GP* shows that William had no fear of Henry, Weiler takes no account of the strong evidence that at some date after the initial composition he lost his nerve: Weiler, 'William of Malmesbury and Henry I', pp. 167–8.
[70] *GR* 411. 4. Contrast 'Henry I was … loved by his subjects': Weiler, 'William of Malmesbury and Henry I', p. 162.
[71] Hayward, 'The importance', pp. 97–100.
[72] Cooper, 'The feet of those that bark', p. 61.

exercise in sustained irony, in the praise it lavishes on the king, in the references to himself 'remote from the mysteries of the court', and in the mock modesty: 'my personal insignificance' ('personae meae exilitas').[73] Not only here but elsewhere (see above, pp. 41, 44), William was at his ironic best when he portrayed Henry 'as a very good king'.[74]

Famously, another discreet historian, Henry of Huntingdon, felt free after 1135 to write what he really thought about King Henry's lifelong debauchery and oppression of the poor. William's continued close association with the king's son, Robert of Gloucester, meant that this was an opportunity he decided he could not afford to take. He could write openly of Rufus's 'great severity' in his punishment of men involved in rebellion, but he kept silent about King Henry's blinding of his kinsman, Count William of Mortain, in Henry of Huntingdon's eyes a fearful act of cruelty.[75]

In this essay I have argued that, with a few honourable exceptions, historians have consistently misunderstood William of Malmesbury's portraits of William II and Henry I. They have consistently underestimated the extent of his appreciation of William II's qualities as a ruler, including his magnanimity. Far too often they have taken his praise of Henry I at face value. Undoubtedly Henry had the better formal education, and he avoided Rufus's shocking levity in religious matters, but in other ways, for instance in what some churchmen regarded as their oppressive lordship of the Church, the brother kings were more alike in William's eyes than he decided it was politic to make public in the *Gesta Regum*.[76] That some readers have taken William's comments on Rufus's magnanimity as ironic while at the same time seeing Book Five as a reflection of William's genuine admiration for a model king, is one of history's nicer ironies.

---

[73] 'tongue in cheek', Edmund King in *HN*, p. xxiii. Cf., with reference to another prologue, Thomson, 'William ... and the Latin Classics', pp. 391–2. The β text supports Cooper's instinct that William's portrait of Henry I in *GR* was meant to be a subversive one. Similarly Thomson in *GR* II, p. 355: 'overall complimentary but with much subtle undercutting which suggests something of the ambivalence of William's attitude to him. One notices that he did not see fit to dedicate *GR* to his king, despite the claims he made for Henry's good education.'

[74] Contrast 'I fully concur with Weiler's verdict that William's portrayal of Henry is not that of an overly obsequious flatterer, but of a moralist praising what he saw as good kingship': Sønnesyn, *Ethics*, p. 244

[75] *GR* 319, 398. 5–6; Henry of Huntingdon, *Historia Anglorum* x. 1 (pp. 698–701).

[76] Nor indeed, and for the same reason, could he afford to take a different line in *HN*. But the references in Book V prol. to *fama* spreading and *uictura memoria* keeping alive knowledge of those of Henry's actions that he had chosen not to write about may hint at what he hoped would happen.

→ 5 ←

William of Malmesbury and the Jews

Kati Ihnat

JEWS HELD A SPECIAL FASCINATION for William of Malmesbury, judging from their presence in his collection of Marian miracles (*MBVM*). Of the fifty-one tales he included in his collection, six feature Jews as major characters; a seventh mentions them in passing.[1] They are the group of non-Christians that appear most often in the *Miracula*, far more so than Muslims.[2] They also feature with much greater frequency in William's work than in those from which he drew, namely the collections attributed to Dominic of Evesham and Anselm of Bury St Edmunds.[3]

What distinguishes William's collection is not only the prominence of Jews in his stories, but also the ways in which they are depicted. Compared to his known sources, William generally exaggerated claims of Jewish antagonism, depicting Jews as especially staunch enemies of Mary and her followers: Jews blaspheme against Christ and the saints, desecrate icons and images, terrorise Christians and cheat their way to financial and political gain. William was a pioneer in making the Jews the villains of the Marian miracles, a role they came increasingly to inhabit in later collections.[4] Such negative sentiments about Jews pervade his other works

---

[1] These are Theophilus, the Jewish Boy, Theodore and Abraham, Toledo, Toulouse and the Virgin's Image Insulted, as well as Ildefonsus of Toledo (*MBVM* 1, 3–5, 32–3, 51).

[2] There is only one story about Muslims in the collection (50), although they also feature in the story of Guy of Lescar (12).

[3] These contain two (Theophilus and the Jewish Boy; 1, 33) and one (Jewish Boy; 33) respectively. On these collections, see the seminal article by R. W. Southern, 'The English origins of the "Miracles of the Virgin"', *Medieval and Renaissance Studies* 4 (1958), 176–216. Philip Shaw thought William's was earlier than Dominic's, though this seems unlikely: P. Shaw, 'The dating of William of Malmesbury's *Miracles of the Virgin*', *Leeds Studies in English* 37 (2006), 391–405. See also K. Ihnat, *Mother of Mercy, Bane of the Jews: Devotion to the Virgin Mary in Anglo-Norman England* (Princeton, 2016).

[4] Their prevalence in later collections was remarked on by R. W. Frank, 'Miracles of the Virgin, medieval anti-Semitism and the Prioress's Tale', in *The Wisdom of Poetry: Essays in Early English Literature in Honor of Morton W. Bloomfield*, ed. L. D. Benson, and S. Wenzel (Kalamazoo, 1982). On anti-Jewish themes in isolated Marian miracles, see O. Limor, 'Mary and the Jews: three witness stories', *Alpayim* 28 (2005), 129–51; eadem, 'Mary and the Jews: story, controversy, and testimony', *Historein* 6 (2006), 55–71; D. L. Desprès, 'Immaculate flesh and the social body: Mary and the

as well. His liturgical commentary, the *Abbreviatio Amalarii* and his exegetical *Commentary on Lamentations*, both feature an emphatically anti-Jewish gloss.[5] It is hardly surprising, therefore, that more than one scholar has remarked on his 'rabid anti-Semitism'.[6]

To help us understand the underlying reasons why William should paint such an antagonistic picture of Jews in his corpus, this study will explore his portrayal of Jews specifically in the Marian miracles.[7] William was a consummate historian who filled his stories with historical detail.[8] His tendency to use his works of history to criticise the political and ecclesiastical orders raises the possibility that he framed his Marian stories to comment on the world around him.[9] The exaggerated images of magic-practising, money-lending and corrupt Jews could therefore be read as statements about William's views on contemporary scientific learning, economics and social policy, and some of his remarks in the stories certainly point in this direction. Reducing the legends to social commentary is nevertheless risky, for they had an important place in devotional culture, both featuring in and helping to justify the performance of Marian devotion.[10] Seen from this perspective, Jews appear to play an allegorical role, standing in for non-Christian values and ideals that included rejection of Mary and the devotional acts her followers were encouraged to perform in the miracles. But we are still left with the rich historical detail William introduced into his stories that fixed them to a particular context and which seems to render their message less universal. In order to resolve this dilemma, this study will consider key examples of the stories, first uncovering the historical dimension of William's portrayal of Jews, and then exploring the lessons they provide about Marian devotion. Thinking of

Jews', *Jewish History* 12 (1998), 47–69; A. Bale, *The Jew in the Medieval Book: English Antisemitism, 1350–1500* (Cambridge, 2007), pp. 55–104.

[5] For Jews in the *Abbreviatio*, see R. W. Pfaff, 'The *Abbreviatio Amalarii* of William of Malmesbury', *Recherches de théologie ancienne et médiévale* 47 (1980), 100–1. For the *Commentary*, see *Comm. Lam.*, p. xii.

[6] P. Carter, 'The historical content of William of Malmesbury's Miracles of the Virgin Mary', in *The Writing of History in the Middle Ages: Essays Presented to Richard William Southern*, ed. J. M. Wallace-Hadrill and R. H. C. Davis (Oxford, 1981), pp. 127–65, at 153. Articulated in slightly different form with the same meaning in *Comm. Lam.*, p. xii; R. M. Thomson, 'Satire, irony and humour in William of Malmesbury', in *Rhetoric and Renewal*, p. 123; idem, 'William of Malmesbury as historian and man of letters', *JEH* 29 (1978), 387–413, at p. 413; revised version as ch. 1 of idem, *William of Malmesbury*.

[7] On twelfth-century changes in Christian attitudes towards Jews, see (among others) A. S. Abulafia, *Christians and Jews in the Twelfth-Century Renaissance* (London, 1995).

[8] '[William] never allows us to forget that he is an historian, doing what no-one had done before to establish these miracles in time and place': Carter, 'Historical content', p. 165. On William as historian, see also A. Gransden, *Historical Writing in England: c. 550–c. 1307* (London, 1974), pp. 166–81; Thomson, 'William of Malmesbury as historian and man of letters' (see n. 00 above).

[9] This was noted especially by Thomson, 'Satire'.

[10] This was not taken into account by an otherwise thorough exploration of miracle collections in eleventh- and twelfth-century England by R. Koopmans, *Wonderful to Relate: Miracle Stories and Miracle Collecting in High Medieval England* (Philadelphia, 2011).

the miracles as a further expression of William's reflection on Christian ethics, as suggested recently by Sigbjørn Sønnesyn, provides a helpful framework in which to understand these texts, which functioned both as records of actual events and as devotional tools.[11] To take these two dimensions into consideration is to suggest that William featured concrete examples of Jews embodying evil in order to present Mary as the only remedy for sin, both in his immediate historical context and on a universal scale.

One of the most famous of the Marian miracles to feature Jews in William's collection is the legend of 'Theophilus', the proto-Faustian tale of the *vidôme* who made a pact with the Devil in order to regain his ecclesiastical position through the aid of a Jewish necromancer.[12] The story goes back to a sixth-century account by Eutychianus of Adana, which was translated into Latin by Paul the Deacon in the ninth century, and it became 'one of the most important texts inspiring devotion to Mary in late Anglo-Saxon England'.[13] One of the legendaries in which it is found, produced at Worcester Cathedral in the late eleventh century, may have provided a source for William and two of his contemporaries, Honorius Augustodunensis and Dominic of Evesham, who included it in a sermon and miracle collection respectively.[14] William nevertheless changed key elements of the tale. He emphasised the necromancer's devious character, describing him as 'a Hebrew' ("Hebraeus"). A widespread rumour had it that he, being skilled in the black arts, and with command over spells, could contrive anything he liked', and that he was 'an old hand at hunting down innocent souls', who boasted of having captured Theophilus 'in the toils of our arts'.[15] The Jew's talent for hunting

---

[11] Sønnesyn, *Ethics*.

[12] A. Poncelet, 'Index Miraculorum B. V. Mariae quae saec. VI–XV Latine conscripta sunt', *Analecta Bollandiana* 21 (1902), 242–360 at p. 74. *MBVM* 1.

[13] For its early history see: G. W. Dasent, *Theophilus in Icelandic, Low German and Other Tongues* (London, 1845); K. Plenzat, *Die Theophiluslegende in den Dichtungen des Mittelalters* (Berlin, 1926). For a rudimentary stemma see P. Texier, 'Orient, Occident: les avatars du pacte diabolique du clerc Théophile', in *Anthropologiques juridiques. Mélanges Pierre Braun*, ed. J. Hoareau-Dodinau and P. Texier (Limoges, 1998), pp. 777–98, at 782. The version by Paul the Deacon appears as *De Theophilo penitente* in *Acta Sanctorum* for 4 Feb., pp. 483–7, and discussion, pp. 480–3. A study of the Middle English version of the story explained in the context of thirteenth-century legal history is found in A. W. Boyarin, *Miracles of the Virgin in Medieval England: Law and Jewishness in Marian Legends* (Cambridge, 2010).

[14] The legendaries are MSS BL Harl. 3020, ff. 113r–132r, Cotton Nero E. I, ff. 157r–160r, and Harl. 4719, ff. 122v–125r, all listed in H. L. D. Ward, *Catalogue of Romances in the Department of Manuscripts of the British Museum* (3 vols, London, 1883–1910), II, pp. 595–7, 597, 598. The Worcester legendary (Cotton Nero E. I) is discussed in P. Jackson and M. Lapidge, 'The contents of the Cotton-Corpus Legendary', in *Holy Men and Holy Women: Old English Prose Saints' Lives and Their Contexts*, ed. P. Szarmach (Albany, 1996), pp. 131–46. For Honorius's use of it, V. I. J. Flint, 'The commentaries of Honorius Augustodunensis on the Song of Songs', *RB* 84 (1974), 196–211, at p. 202. Dominic included two other stories from the same Legendary, as discussed in J. C. Jennings, 'The writings of Prior Dominic of Evesham', *EHR* 77 (1962), 298–304. For William's sources, see Shaw, 'Dating', pp. 392–3.

[15] *MBVM* 1. 3, 5. For shifting depictions of the magician character over the course of the Middle Ages, see G. Dahan, 'Salatin, du *Miracle de Théophile* de Rutebeuf', *Le Moyen Age* 83 (1977), 445–68,

Christians in the Devil's service nevertheless sees him 'shortly afterwards detected in his illicit ways. He was convicted and beheaded, learning to his discomfiture how severe the laws of the state are.'[16] The fate that befalls the Jew in William's story is notably different from the accounts found in the earlier versions, which reported that the necromancer was only tried by the law.[17]

William's concern with the punishment of the Jewish necromancer could reflect wider anxieties around the interest shown by his contemporaries in magic and science more generally. It was in William's home-ground of south-western England that new advances in scientific learning were being made in the first half of the twelfth century with the help of Jewish translators. Charles Burnett has discussed the active school at Hereford where Christian scholars learned the liberal arts from individuals like Peter Alfonsi, a convert from Judaism and possibly also the physician of Henry I.[18] Alfonsi appears to have helped English scholars translate astronomical works from Arabic, at least one of which survives in an early twelfth-century manuscript from Worcester Cathedral.[19] Alfonsi counted necromancy among the liberal arts, although he differentiated between the manipulation of natural elements and the summoning of demons as two distinct forms of the discipline.[20] Such a distinction may not have been obvious to someone like William, however, who may have seen the new learning in astrology as a direct precursor to the black arts. Another of his Marian miracle stories, 'Love by Black Arts', suggests as much. It features a cleric who is given licence by his bishop to pursue his interest in science.[21] This leads the scholar to take up necromancy in order to seduce women, although he stops short of abjuring Christ and Mary when he successfully summons the Devil. The story is not so far removed from the 'Black Legend' of Gerbert of Aurillac, which William recorded in its first complete version in his *Gesta Regum*.[22] Gerbert became the tenth-century Pope Sylvester

and M. Lazar, 'Servant of two masters: the pre-Faustian theme of despair and revolt', *Modern Language Notes* 87 (1972), 31–50.

[16] *MBVM* 1. 7.

[17] In the version translated by Paul the Deacon, Theophilus's prayer of repentance to the Virgin is interrupted by a lament: 'Why did I have to meet that most nefarious Jew, who is worthy of being burned?' Then, in an aside, it is explained that not long before, the Jew had been found guilty 'by the law and a judge': 'Quae mihi fuit necessitas cognoscendi nefandissimum et comburendum illum Hebraeum? Erat enim ante paululum Hebraeus ille a lege et iudice condemnatus': *Acta Sanctorum*, 4 Feb., 484E.

[18] On these circles, see especially C. Burnett, 'The works of Petrus Alfonsi: questions of authenticity', *Medium Aevum* 66 (1997), 42–79; idem, *The Introduction of Arabic Learning into England. The Panizzi Lectures* (London, 1997), pp. 38–40.

[19] *Introduction of Arabic Learning*, p. 39.

[20] For the inclusion of necromancy among the seven liberal arts, see Peter Alfonsi, *Disciplina clericalis*, ed. E. Hermes (London, 1977), pp. 9–10, 114–15. For the distinction between necromancy as manipulation of natural elements and manipulation of demons, see Peter Alfonsi, *Dialogue against the Jews*, trans. I. M. Resnick (Washington, 2006), p. 150.

[21] *MBVM* 28.

[22] *GR* 167. 1–5. See M. C. E. Vargas, 'Image and Reality of the Magician Figure in Twelfth Century England', Ph.D. thesis (University of Reading, 2011), particularly ch. 2.

II allegedly thanks to a pact with the Devil, made possible by magical knowledge he gained from a Muslim teacher in Al-Andalus. William seems to have thought that non-Christians were an especially good source of illicit learning, as is evident in another passage of the *Gesta Regum* about an old monk at Malmesbury who went searching for the treasures of the Emperor Octavian with the help of a Jew practised in the arts of necromancy.[23] William's evident concern with the risks inherent in accumulating scientific knowledge could explain why he thought the Jewish necromancer in the Theophilus legend deserved the worst possible punishment. The story thus comes across as a cautionary tale, a warning to his fellow monks about the dangers of the new scientific learning being undertaken in England.

Further echoes of William's concerns about the place of Jews in Christian society come through in his version of the story of 'Theodore and Abraham'.[24] A lengthy tale of debt and deceit, it features a Christian businessman fallen on hard times who seeks a loan to rebuild his business. Abandoned by his Christian friends, the man turns to Abraham, a Jewish money-lender, and receives funds in exchange for his pledge of an icon of the Virgin Mary. After his fortunes in business improved, Theodore is prevented from repaying the loan when a storm breaks, so he places the amount in a chest which he sets on the sea with a prayer to Mary. Abraham's lie that he did not subsequently receive the repayment – which he miraculously did – is then exposed by the icon when it comes to life.

Based on the seventh-century legend of the Antiphonetes icon, an image of Christ that served as surety for a loan, as well as similar tales of an image of St Nicholas, William's version of Theodore and Abraham is the first to feature an icon of Mary.[25] William was not only clear as to the identity of the image, but he also produced fairly extreme caricatures of the protagonists. He described Theodore as

---

[23] GR 170.

[24] Poncelet 41 and 55, and *MBVM* 32.

[25] Another version of the story found in many Marian miracle collections from the twelfth century onwards first describes the image as one of Christ, only at the end referring to a carved *Sedes Sapientiae*, depicting Mary enthroned with the infant Christ. This version is edited in T. Crane, *Liber de Miraculis Sanctae Dei Genitricis Mariae (Published at Vienna, in 1731 by Bernard Pez)* (Ithaca NY, 1925), p. 42. For the Greek and Latin history of the story, see B. N. Nelson and J. Starr, 'The divine surety and the Jewish moneylender', *Annuaire de l'Institut de Philologie et d'Histoire Orientales et Slaves* 7 (1939–44), 289–338. The Nicholas legend is found in Honorius Augustodunensis, *Speculum Ecclesiae*, PL 172. 807–1107, at 1035–6, as well as in a late eleventh-century manuscript from Battle Abbey (BL Cotton Tiberius B. V, ff. 55r–56r, 73rv), discussed by A. Harris, 'The performative terms of Jewish iconoclasm and conversion in two Saint Nicholas windows at Chartres Cathedral', in *Beyond the Yellow Badge: Anti-Judaism and Antisemitism in Medieval and Early Modern Visual Culture*, ed. M. B. Merback (Leiden, 2008), pp. 119–41, at 128–9. On the significance of the Marian statues in these stories, see J.-M. Sansterre, 'Vivantes ou comme vivantes: l'animation miraculeuse d'images de la Vierge entre moyen âge et époque moderne', in *Les images miraculaires au premier âge moderne, entre dévotion locale et culte universel*, ed. R. Dekoninck and S. Mostaccio, Special issue of *Revue de l'histoire des religions* 2 (2015), 9–13, and K. A. Smith, 'Bodies of unsurpassed beauty: "living" images of the Virgin in the High Middle Ages', *Viator* 37 (2006), 167–87.

a layman of praiseworthy modesty, though he made his living by a means that especially seduces men into sullying the truth. He was in fact a trader: you can see almost no-one in this line who is afraid to expose his sworn word to perjury if he can turn a penny or two. What is more, when open cheating does not serve, they take advantage of the unwary by craft. Theodorus was not like that at all. He knew nothing whatever about cunning, for he chose to know nothing; and he regarded lying as morally wrong. He did not try to beat down a price or wipe out a buyer's profit. If he gave, he did so gladly and liberally, from a full hand.[26]

By contrast, Abraham is depicted as conniving and deceitful. He may at first weep with sympathy at Theodore's distress, but this quickly turns to impatience coupled with greed as he scours the seas for the return of his debtor.[27] When he sees the chest, he quickly hides it under his bed unbeknown even to his wife, and he unhesitatingly perjures himself in front of the statue, thinking 'the affair to be silly, and [that] he would get away unpunished, even if he sullied our sacred lady by perjury'.[28] Compared to the far more neutral depictions of both characters in earlier versions of the story, William makes a considerable effort to portray Theodore in a good light, at the same time demonising Abraham.[29]

In a lengthy epilogue to the tale, William provides us with considerable insight into his exaggeration of Theodore and Abraham. Concluding that 'from that day on, the unmanageable zeal of the Jews, which before had moved among us in that city, was cooled', William goes on to describe how Mary wrought revenge on the devious, the impious and the perfidious, exposed the rich and arrogant and defended her poor devotees.[30] The tirade ends with a general complaint that 'religion is thought of in terms of treasure, since riches alone are thought to be valuable... in this age, money alone is thought to lighten men's worries, and, with the likeness of tranquillity, ease their minds.'[31] This passage suggests that William had deeper reasons for insisting so forcefully on Theodore's good qualities *despite* his involvement in trade. Abraham, on the other hand, is ascribed the role of the avaricious Jewish money-lender, a stereotype that would become increasingly prevalent in medieval Western culture.

The emergence of this stereotype has generally been linked to the nascent commercial revolution at the turn of the twelfth century, in which Jews increasingly played an important role in the financial sector as money-changers and money-lenders.[32] Scholars have underlined the fact that, in England, Jews held

---

[26] *MBVM* 32. 2.

[27] *MBVM* 32. 11.

[28] *MBVM* 32. 12.

[29] This was remarked by Nelson and Starr, 'The divine surety', p. 328. The other twelfth-century version (ed. Crane, pp. 41–4) vilifies the Christian more so and less so the Jew.

[30] *MBVM* 32. 14.

[31] *MBVM* 32. 14–15.

[32] L. K. Little, 'The function of the Jews in the Commercial Revolution', in *Poverta e ricchezza nella spiritualità dei secoli XII e XIII*, Centro di studi sulla spiritualità medievale (Todi, 1969), pp. 271–87; S. Lipton, *Images of Intolerance: The Representation of Jews and Judaism in the Bible*

these professions to a greater degree than elsewhere in Europe.[33] William of Malmesbury is the first to attest to the Jews' earliest immigration to England, attributing it to William the Conqueror, who may have encouraged Norman Jews to cross the Channel in order to help develop the financial sector as they had done in Normandy.[34] We find evidence for Jews lending money to fund monumental building campaigns, in both the secular and ecclesiastical spheres, as early as the 1130s; the monks of Westminster appear to have become especially indebted to Jewish moneylenders.[35]

It is tempting to hear the complaints of such debtors in William's remark in the story of 'Theodore and Abraham' that 'creditors are so ill-disposed to poor friends that [Abraham] did not imagine that Theodore was unable to put to sea.'[36] Elsewhere, in his *Gesta Pontificum*, William complained bitterly about the mismanagement of Malmesbury at the hands of several post-Conquest abbots, for example Warin of Lire (abbot 1070–87/91), whom William blamed for greed and 'emptying the monks' pockets', and the otherwise praiseworthy Godfrey (abbot 1087/91–1100/5), who allegedly sold off the abbey's most precious items.[37] The story of Theodore and Abraham could thus have provided William with another opportunity to comment on the rampant greed and financial mismanagement he observed around him.[38] William seems to have thought Jews especially susceptible to the lure of material gain; in the *Commentary on Lamentations* he remarked that Jews by definition were 'longing only for the riches of the present life' rather than eternal salvation.[39] He may therefore have embellished the character of Abraham along these lines in order to warn Christians of the dangers of chasing the volatile and corrupting promise of riches, and to criticise those who were doing so.

If the Jews' economic activities posed a threat to the social order as William saw it, he was not especially optimistic about the secular authorities' willingness to curb them, as several of his Marian miracle stories indicate. The story of 'Toledo', which

---

Moralisée (Berkeley, 1999), pp. 31–53.

[33] See R. Stacey, 'Jewish lending and the medieval English economy', in *A Commercialising Economy: England 1086 to c. 1300*, ed. R. H. Britnell and B. M. S. Campbell (Manchester, 1995), pp. 78–101; A. S. Abulafia, *Christian-Jewish Relations 1000–1300: Jews in the Service of Medieval Christendom* (Harlow, 2011), pp. 88–93; H. Pollins, *Economic History of the Jews in England* (Rutherford, 1982); R. R. Mundill, *The King's Jews: Money, Massacre and Exodus in Medieval England* (London, 2010).

[34] Stacey, 'Jewish lending', p. 82. For the historical account, see GR 319. 1.

[35] *Magnum Rotulum Scaccarii vel Magnum Rotulum Pipae de Anno Tricesimo Primo Regni Henrici Primi* (London, 1833), p. 146. On this, see E. Mason, *Westminster Abbey and its People* (Woodbridge, 1996), p. 34. See also the accounts of Osbert of Clare, prior of Westminster in the 1130s, who sought loans from his friends to pay off his debts to Jewish lenders: Osbert of Clare, *Letters*, ed. E. W. Williamson (Oxford, 1929), Epp. 24 and 28 (pp. 100, 107).

[36] *MBVM* 32. 9.

[37] GP 265, 271.

[38] Very similar complaints to the one in the epilogue come in *Comm. Lam.*, II, lines 285–96; GP 49. 5β. 1–8, 73. 22β.2, and GR 84. 7.

[39] *Comm. Lam.*, I, lines 2597–9.

appeared for the first time in the twelfth-century miracle collections, relates how, on the feast of the Assumption, a heavenly voice calls down to the congregation gathered in Toledo Cathedral that the Jews are torturing 'her son'.[40] In seeking out the culprits, the Christians discover the Jews subjecting a waxen image of Christ to the abuses of the Passion, for which the Jews are all put to death. Peter Carter remarked that the narrative could have been inspired by accounts of a massacre of the Jews of Toledo following the death of Alfonso VI of Castille, in 1109.[41] William, however, set his version in the completely different context – of Visigothic Iberia:

> Spain was at one time overburdened by the number of Jews there; and unambiguous rumour insists that it is no less polluted by them nowadays too. For instance, it has more than once been reported that at Narbonne they have a supreme pope, to whom Jews run from all over the world, piling gifts upon him, or deciding by his arbitration any dispute arising among them that requires someone to resolve it. Such a great number of them had swamped Toledo in the time of Reccared [559–601], king of the Goths and ruler of Spain, that they attempted to claim equal rank with Christians in all respects, and used bribery to try to bring about the annulment of regulations passed against them by councils at Toledo. They tested the mettle of the pious king, but the unbelievers could find nothing in his breast that encouraged their arts: their cash was of no interest to the king. Hence the compliment to him in a letter he received from the blessed Gregory, that he did not sell justice for gold: rather he rated justice above gold. You can find the letter in the ninth book of the *Registrum*.[42]

William was clearly familiar with the extensive legislation regulating Jewish activity found in the collections of Visigothic law, the quantity and severity of which have attracted much attention.[43] The situation in Visigothic Spain seems to have contrasted strongly with William's impressions of his own period, in which he alleges that the Jews have so much freedom that they have come to have their own 'pope'. This reference points to the legends that had circulated since *c.* 1000 about a prominent Jewish dynasty, the Kalonymides, based in Narbonne.[44] Raising

---

[40] *MBVM* 4. Found in MSS BnF lat. 2873, f. 27v, lat. 3809A, f. 74v, lat. 14463, ff. 34r–35r, lat. 18168, ff. 93v–94v, Chicago UL 147, f. 9rv (pr. from this copy by E. F. Dexter, *Miracula Sanctae Virginis Mariae* (Madison, 1927), pp. 39–40), Copenhagen, Kongelike Bibl. Thott. 26, 8 ff. 68r–69r, Thott. 128, 2 ff. 17v–18v, BL Add. 25112, ff. 77v–78r, Arundel 346 f. 67r, BL Cotton Cleopatra C. X, ff. 127v–128v, Oxford, Balliol Coll. 240 f. 154rv, Bodl. Libr. Laud. misc. 410, ff. 88v–89r.

[41] Carter, 'Historical content', p. 145.

[42] *MBVM* 4. 1–2. It is worth noting that the Assumption feast was not celebrated in the Visigothic period: Carter, 'Historical content', p. 146.

[43] There is considerable literature on this legislation, but for the most recent study, see *Jews in Early Christian Law: Byzantium and the Latin West, 6th–11th Centuries*, ed. J. Tolan *et al.* (Turnhout, 2014), and the survey article by R. Stocking, 'Early medieval Christian identity and anti-Judaism: the case of the Visigothic kingdom', *Religion Compass* 2 (2008), 642–58.

[44] Noted by Carter, 'Historical content', pp. 147–8. On the Kalonymides, see A. Graboïs, 'La dynastie des "rois Juifs" de Narbonne (IXe–XIIIe siècles)', in *Narbonne: archéologie et histoire* (Narbonne, 1973), pp. 49–54, especially 50, J. Schatzmiller, 'Politics and the myth of origins', in

the spectre of an international Jewish conspiracy, William's remarks explain the events recounted in 'Toledo' as justification for the harsh measures taken by the Visigothic kings against the Jews, and warn of the dangers of leaving Jews to their own devices.

William's admiration for Visigothic policy towards the Jews is palpable, and differs markedly from his attitude towards the protagonist of another story about the Jews of Toulouse. The story of 'Toulouse' was not included in the earlier Marian miracle collections, probably because it does not feature Mary at all.[45] In it William describes how on Good Friday one year, a Christian man hit and killed a Jew for mocking Christ and the saints. The Jews went to the Count of Toulouse to demand justice for the victim, but after some deliberation, the count instead instituted an annual tradition: a Jew would be publically slapped in the church square, the right to deliver the slap having been auctioned off to the highest bidder.[46] Carter has again noted the historical basis for this story. An account of one particular instance in which the Jew being slapped was killed is related in the Chronicle of Ademar of Chabannes.[47] Another reference to the tradition is found in the very charters of Toulouse cathedral, which record a payment by Bishop Amelius (1106–39) 'pro colapho Judaeorum' (for the slap of the Jews).[48] William clearly thought that the *colaphus* tradition was ongoing, which perhaps explains his delight at the events; it must have seemed to him as though the social order was put right by having the Jews pay for their blasphemy.[49] His version further reveals that he held Count William of Toulouse in low esteem for being tempted by offers of bribes from the Jews to punish the Christian murderer, which, had William accepted, would have rendered the count a 'half-Jew' ('semiiudaeum').[50]

The depiction of Count William, while it diverges from that of the kings of Visigothic Iberia, nevertheless chimes closely with William of Malmesbury's portrayal of William II ('Rufus') of England in the *Gesta Regum*, and it may be

---

Les Juifs au regard de l'histoire. Mélanges en l'honneur de Bernhard Blumenkranz, ed. G. Dahan (Paris, 1985), pp. 49–61, at 52–8, and G. Dahan, 'Un miracle de Notre Dame: La Juive Narbonne convertie', in *Medieval Studies in Honour of Avrom Saltman*, ed. B.-S. Albert, Y. Friedman and S. Schwarzfuchs (Jerusalem, 1995), pp. 97–120, at 100–1. Later accounts include Peter the Venerable, *Adversus Iudeorum Inveteratam Duritiem*, ed. Y. Friedman, CCCM 58, p. 70, and Benjamin of Tudela, *Itinerary*, trans. E. N. Adler (London, 1907), p. 4.

[45] The story is unrecognisable in later versions (e.g. *Cantigas de Santa Maria*, no. 286; for more information on this Cantiga, see http://csm.mml.ox.ac.uk/index.php?p=poemdata_view&rec=286), illustrating just how bizarre it must have seemed even to its contemporary readers.

[46] The count is identified as William III of Toulouse (950–1037), who is erroneously referred to as the father of Raymond of St Gilles when he was in fact Raymond's grandfather. Cf. Carter, 'Historical content', p. 150.

[47] Ademar of Chabannes, *Chronicon*, 2. 52: 1–14, ed. P. Bourgain, CCCM 129, pp. 132–6. Carter noted this in 'Historical content', p. 151.

[48] *Cartulaire de l'Abbaye de Saint-Sernin de Toulouse*, ed. C. Douais (Paris, 1887), pp. 200–1.

[49] For an analysis of the humour in the story, see K. Ihnat, 'Getting the punchline: deciphering anti-Jewish humour in Anglo-Norman England', *JMH* 38 (2012), 408–23.

[50] *MBVM* 5. 5.

that William was purposefully drawing parallels between them.[51] His damning portrait of the king concludes with a revealing passage:

> Let me give an example of his [William Rufus's] arrogance, or rather ignorance, towards God. Some London Jews, whom his father [William the Conqueror] had transferred there from Rouen, came to him on some feast-day or other bearing gifts. Prompted by their flatteries, he dared encourage them – no less – to debate against the Christians, saying that 'By the holy Face of Lucca', if they prevailed he would become a Jew himself. The contest was therefore held, to the great alarm of the bishops and clergy, who were filled with fear in their pious anxiety for the Christian faith. And from this dispute, at any rate, the Jews got nothing but confusion, although they have often boasted that they were beaten by party passion and not argument.[52]

We have no other evidence that the London debate took place, but Eadmer of Canterbury, a friend of William's, described a situation in which Rufus was apparently paid by the families of Norman converts to impel these converts to return to Judaism; this is no doubt explained by the forced baptism of Jews in northern France c. 1095, in the wake of the call to the First Crusade.[53] We cannot verify the accusations against Rufus, but English kings did have direct jurisdiction over the Jewish community, according to the so-called Laws of Edward the Confessor (c. 1140).[54] This political arrangement could explain why twelfth-century historians

---

[51] That Rufus was especially singled out for criticism is noted by Thomson, 'Satire', pp. 121–3. For further discussion of William's views on Rufus, see John Gillingham's essay in this volume, pp. 37–48.

[52] GR 317. This passage is taken as the first indication of a Jewish community in England, suggesting Jewish immigration to the island only began after the Conquest. On this early community, see A. M. Hyamson, *A History of the Jews in England* (London, 1928), pp. 14–17; C. Roth, *The Jews of Medieval Oxford* (Oxford, 1951), p. 2; R. B. Dobson, *The Jews of Medieval York and the Massacre of March 1190* (York, 1974), p. 4; E. Rutledge, 'The medieval Jews of Norwich and their legacy', in *Art, Faith and Place in East Anglia*, ed. T. A. Heslop, E. Mellings, and M. Thøfner (Woodbridge, 2012), pp. 117–29; J. Hillaby, 'The London Jewry: William to John', *Jewish Historical Studies* 33 (1995), 1–44; idem, 'Jewish colonisation in the twelfth century', in *Jews in Medieval Britain: Historical, Literary and Archaeological Perspectives*, ed. P. Skinner (Woodbridge, 2003), pp. 15–40.

[53] The same event is referred to in William's later recension of *GR*. The forced baptism of Jews is described in Guibert of Nogent, *Monodiae*: trans. as *A Monk's Confession: The Memoirs of Guibert de Nogent* by P. Archambault (University Park, Penn., 1996), pp. 111–12. For the idea that the Jews of England emigrated from Normandy to escape these very persecutions, see N. Golb, 'Les Juifs de Normandie à l'époque d'Anselme', in *Les mutations socio-culturelles au tournant des XIe–XIIe siècles*, ed. R. Foreville (Paris, 1984), pp. 149–60. Some may have come forcibly baptised, as perhaps suggested by several letters of Anselm about a convert from Judaism: Anselm of Canterbury, *Letters*, trans. W. Fröhlich (Kalamazoo, 1990), Epp. 380 and 381 (pp. 135–6).

[54] These Laws, although compiled c. 1140, state that William I dealt with the status of Jews just four years after the Conquest at a council convened of barons, nobles, churchmen making the following pronouncement: 'Let it be known that all Jews, wherever they may be in the kingdom, must be by law under the patronage and protection of the king; none of them may remove any of their wealth without the permission of the king, because Jews and all they own are the king's property. If anyone should detain/take hold of either their person or their money, the king may demand his property, should he be able to and wish it.': F. Liebermann, *Die Gesetze der Angelsachsen* I (Halle,

expressed anxiety with regards to the close relationship between the king and the Jews.[55] How a king utilised his prerogative with the Jews was viewed as a marker of his integrity and righteousness, and Rufus's apparent laxity with respect to the Jews under his control must have seemed particularly indicative of his weakness as a Christian ruler.[56] Read in this light, the stories of 'Toledo' and 'Toulouse' appear as veiled social commentary, in which a monarch's policy towards to the Jews signifies his leadership qualities.[57] The threat of Jewish violence described in 'Toledo' functioned as a stark reminder of what was at stake should secular leaders fail to keep their Jews in check: 'Toulouse' set a template for appropriate action.

The fact that we can link particular themes in William's miracle stories to contemporary social phenomena makes it tempting to assume that he purposely set out to provide an indirect but acerbic criticism of his society. This challenges Carter's conclusion that the image of Jews in William's miracles 'was not based on experience' but rather derived from literary works.[58] William's adjustments to his sources on the other hand suggest that he was seeking to address social ills that he attributed to the presence of Jews in post-Conquest England, including Jewish involvement in illicit learning, in the growing financial professions and in the corruption of secular leadership. We would nevertheless be wise to heed Sara Lipton's warning that visual depictions of Jews in the Middle Ages were 'not a straightforward reflection of contemporary attitudes towards Jews.'[59] She argues that such images say more about their creators' vision of Christian values and ideal behaviour than about the perceived status of Jews themselves, something that applies equally to narrative works such as William's Marian miracles. It is worth remembering that the prologue to his miracle collection is a lengthy exposition both of Mary's embodiment of Christian virtue in its purest form and of the need to venerate her as a result. His use of Cicero's ethical scheme in this section attributes to Mary the four cardinal virtues – prudence, justice, temperance and courage – and the miracles were meant to act as proof that she put these virtues

---

1903), pp. 627, 650. On relations between Jews and the monarchy, see Abulafia, *Christian-Jewish Relations*.

[55] This type of concern is assumed to have caused the York massacres of 1190, on which see *Christians and Jews in Angevin England: The York Massacre of 1190, Narratives and Contexts*, ed. D. R. Jones and S. Watson (York, 2013).

[56] That William of Malmesbury appreciated Rufus's wit has been suggested by Thomson, 'Satire', p. 121. But in this case, it seems fair to say that threatening conversion to Judaism would have been a step too far.

[57] This argument was used to explain royal policy on the Jews in thirteenth-century France by W. C. Jordan, 'Jews, regalian rights and the constitution in medieval France', *Association for Jewish Studies Review* 23 (1998), 1–16; idem, *The French Monarchy and the Jews: From Philip Augustus to the Last Capetians* (Philadelphia, 1989).

[58] Carter, 'Historical content', p. 152. Elsewhere Carter remarked that 'he never allows us to forget that he is an historian, doing what no-one had done before to establish these miracles in time and place'. Ibid., p. 165.

[59] S. Lipton, *Dark Mirror: The Medieval Origins of Anti-Jewish Iconography* (New York, 2014), p. 94.

into action: 'reasoned arguments can teach that she is able to take pity on the wretched; examples of miracles teach that she actually desires to do so'.[60] It is therefore imperative to go beyond the historical dimension and consider the Jews of William's stories within this wider devotional and ethical framework.

William not only provided a model for right Christian living through the figure of Mary, but also presented the audience of his *Miracula* with examples of Christians honouring Mary with appropriate acts of devotion. In so doing, he participated in a lively cult of Mary developed in Anglo-Norman England that had literary, theological and artistic dimensions, although perhaps its most important expression was liturgical. Like many of the miracle stories compiled in this period, William's feature a host of different liturgical means of commemorating Mary. These included daily and weekly offices and masses, prayers, and the celebration of unusual feast days, such as that of Mary's conception.[61] All of these practices were increasingly being adopted in English Benedictine monasteries around the turn of the eleventh and twelfth centuries, at the same time as the appearance of the first Marian miracle collections.[62] As I have argued elsewhere, this is no coincidence; miracle stories undoubtedly supported the adoption of devotional practices by showing that Mary rewarded these acts with miracles.[63] Not only that, miracle stories themselves became integrated in the liturgy as readings for matins, meal times and *collatio* and were excerpted to provide *exempla* in sermons.[64]

---

[60] *MBVM* prol. 40.

[61] The most important work to date on this is N. Morgan, 'Texts and images of Marian devotion in English twelfth-century monasticism, and their influence on the secular Church', in *Monasteries and Society in Medieval Britain: Proceedings of the 1994 Harlaxton Symposium*, ed. B. Thompson (Stamford, 1999), pp. 117–36, explored in greater detail in Ihnat, *Mother of Mercy*. Other isolated studies of various aspects of this cult are found in A. Gransden, 'The cult of St Mary at Beodericisworth and then in Bury St Edmunds Abbey to c. 1150', *JEH* 55 (2004), 627–53; T. A. Heslop, 'The English origins of the Coronation of the Virgin', *Burlington Magazine* 147 (2005), 790–7; idem, 'The Virgin Mary's regalia and twelfth-century English seals', in *The Vanishing Past: Studies of Medieval Art, Liturgy and Metrology Presented to Christopher Hohler*, ed. A. Borg and A. Martindale (Oxford, 1981), pp. 53–62.

[62] For a comparison of liturgical practices in the miracles and as practised in Benedictine institutions in England, see K. Ihnat, 'Marian miracles and Marian liturgies in the Benedictine culture of post-Conquest England', in *Contextualising Medieval Miracles*, ed. M. Mesley and L. Wilson (Oxford, 2014), pp. 63–98.

[63] Ibid. The same was the case for other saints in Anglo-Norman England, although their cults tended to be associated with particular institutions, contrary to Mary's, which was universal. On other collections, see Koopmans, *Wonderful to Relate*, and S. Yarrow, *Saints and their Communities: Miracle Stories in Twelfth-century England* (Oxford, 2006).

[64] See T. Webber, 'Monastic space and the use of books in the Anglo-Norman period', *ANS* 26 (2013), 221–40, pp. 235–6 on books for reading at the post-meal *collatio*, and pp. 236–9 on the refectory readings, but also see eadem, 'Reading in the refectory: monastic practice in England, c. 1000-c. 1300', *London University Annual John Coffin Memorial Palaeography Lecture* (2010). See also D. J. Reilly, 'Lectern Bibles and liturgical reform in the central Middle Ages', in *The Practice of the Bible in the Middle Ages*, ed. S. Boynton and D. J. Reilly (New York, 2011), pp. 105–25. Miracle stories appear in the sermons of Honorius Augustodunensis, who was based at Worcester in William's time, on which see V. I. J. Flint, 'The chronology of the works of Honorius Augustodunensis',

William would have been especially interested in proper devotional attention being shown to Mary because Malmesbury Abbey had been dedicated to Mary, as William tells us, since its foundation by Aldhelm (d. 709).[65] Additionally, as precentor, William was responsible for the liturgy at Malmesbury.[66] Margot Fassler and Susan Boynton have demonstrated that the liturgy was a crucial element in the construction of communal identity at religious institutions, alongside history-writing and hagiography, and that precentors were often also historians.[67] William would therefore have had a special interest in cultivating the cult of Mary at Malmesbury, and his collection of miracles may have been designed to put the abbey's Marian heritage in writing as well as to participate in her liturgical commemoration there.

It is important to remember, however, that William's miracles do not treat Mary as a local patron saint. The stories depict her actions everywhere in the world, to all kinds of people. This makes his *Miracula* one of the first 'universal' collections, which differ from the ones associated with particular Marian shrines. The local collections, which appeared more or less at the same time as the universal ones, were produced predominantly at northern French institutions that housed Marian relics or images. They were intended to promote pilgrimage to these sites, since the stories concern miracles performed only by those objects.[68] The English collections clearly had a different aim. They convey the didactic message that it is essential to show devotion to Mary anywhere and everywhere, and they illustrate how this devotion is meant to be performed.

Seen in this context, the stories that feature Jews are not so much warnings about social dangers as incitements to turn to Mary in praise and prayer.[69] The 'Theophilus' legend emphasises the idea that prayer to Mary is far more powerful than consorting with the Devil: although Satan might bestow earthly goods, Mary

---

RB 82 (1972), 215–42; eadem, *Honorius Augustodunensis of Regensburg* (Aldershot, 1995), and K. Ihnat, '"Our Sister is little and has no breasts": Mary and the Jews in the sermons of Honorius Augustodunensis', in *The Jewish-Christian Encounter in Medieval Preaching*, ed. J. Adams and J. Hanska (New York, 2015), pp. 119–38.

[65] GP 216. 1.

[66] Thomson, *William of Malmesbury*, p. 3.

[67] M. Fassler, *The Virgin of Chartres: Making History through Liturgy and the Arts* (New Haven, 2009); eadem, 'The office of the cantor in early western monastic rules and customaries: a preliminary investigation', *Early Music History* 5 (1985), 29–51; S. Boynton, *Shaping a Monastic Identity: Liturgy and History at the Imperial Abbey of Farfa, 1000–1125* (Ithaca NY, 2006).

[68] These include Coutances, Soissons, Saint-Pierre-sur-Dives, Rocamadour and Chartres, on which see B. Ward, *Miracles and the Medieval Mind* (Philadelphia, 1982), pp. 142–55; G. Signori, *Maria zwischen Kathedrale, Kloster und Welt. Hagiographische und historiographische Annährungen an eine hochmittelalterliche Wunderpredigt* (Ostfildern, 1995), and idem, 'La bienheureuse polysémie, miracles et pèlerinages à la Vierge: pouvoir thaumaturgique et modèles pastoraux (Xe–XIIe siècles)', in *Marie: Le culte de la Vierge dans la société médiévale*, ed. D. Iogna-Prat, É. Palazzo and D. Russo (Paris, 1996), pp. 599–604. See also M. Bull, *The Miracles of our Lady of Rocamadour: Analysis and Translation* (Woodbridge, 1999).

[69] This is the general argument for the Jews in Marian miracle collections as articulated in Ihnat, *Mother of Mercy*.

has the capacity to forgive even the greatest sin and therefore to grant eternal salvation. The tale of 'Theodore and Abraham' presents charity and trust in Mary as the antidotes to the sins of avarice and pride, as William stated explicitly in his epilogue to the story. 'Toledo' highlights devotion to Mary in her guise as suffering mother at the foot of the Cross,[70] and although 'Toulouse' does not give Mary an explicitly intercessory role, the story sees Christ's resurrection as the ultimate joke played on the Jews.[71] Other stories in William's works, such as the famous tales of the 'Jewish boy' and the 'Virgin's Image Insulted', illustrate the power of the Eucharist and of religious images, as well as the veneration owed to both.[72] In all cases, the behaviour of Jews provides counter-examples to Marian devotion: they worship the Devil when they should honour Mary; they adore money, when they should love Mary; they desecrate images when they should venerate them; they mock the Passion, instead of seeing in it the only means to salvation. The stories also reaffirm this message of devotion by showing that Mary conquers all, since the Jews invariably end up either converting or being punished for their recalcitrance; in fact, William remarks at one point on 'how much Mary's efforts go towards the conversion of her own people.'[73]

Their place in the performance and promotion of devotion to Mary suggests that Jews in miracle stories came to play the role of foil to Christians performing the proper forms of veneration. On this basis, we might conclude that miracle stories privileged a universal moral message over a historical, political one. Ultimately, however, it does not seem essential to distinguish sharply between William's criticism of the ills afflicting his society and the more enduring lesson he wished to provide about Christian virtue. Sigbjørn Sønnesyn and Rodney Thomson have both proposed that the political was ethical for William: writing history necessarily involved engaging with morality.[74] Miracles too could be part of this

[70] This was an important theme emerging in Christian culture around this period, and was fostered especially by monks connected to William, including Anselm, Eadmer of Canterbury and Honorius Augustodunensis, on which see R. Fulton, *From Judgment to Passion: Devotion to Christ and the Virgin Mary, 800–1200* (New York, 2002). On the devotional context of the wax image, which I argue was meant to be understood as a kind of votive, see K. Mesler and K. Ihnat, 'From Christian devotion to Jewish sorcery: the curious history of wax figurines in the Middle Ages', in *Authority and Knowledge in the Long Thirteenth Century*, ed. R. Mazo Karras, E. Baumgarten and K. Mesler (Philadelphia, 2016).

[71] On this see Ihnat, 'Getting the punchline'.

[72] In the 'Jewish Boy' (Poncelet 95), the eponymous protagonist returns home after having inadvertently taken communion with his Christian friends only to be thrown in the oven by his enraged father; he emerges unscathed thanks to Mary's protection. William's version is *MBVM* 33. On this story, see E. Wolter, *Der Judenknabe: 5 Griechische, 14 Lateinische und 8 Französische Texte* (Halle, 1879), and M. Rubin, *Gentile Tales: The Narrative Assault on Late Medieval Jews* (Philadelphia, 2004), pp. 7–29. The story of the Virgin's image insulted (Poncelet 20) sees a Jew take an image of the Virgin Mary and throw it in his latrine. In William's version, as the Jew empties his bowels over it, his organs flow out too, in what seems to be an echo of the fate suffered by the heretic Arius: *MBVM* 51. 1.

[73] *MBVM* 96.

[74] Thomson, 'Satire'; Sønnesyn, *Ethics*.

pursuit. As a form of historical writing – recording events thought to have actually happened – miracles also spoke to deeper truths about right Christian living and devotional practice, and in this sense were timeless.[75] Using miracle stories to comment on pressing social issues and on universal problems were not incompatible aims, and William may have thought that giving concrete, relatable examples only strengthened his case for exalting Mary. The figure of the Jew could have functioned in this scheme as an effective rhetorical device to underline proper and improper approaches to Mary and Christian values both in theory and in the here and now. But it is interesting to note that this very attempt to ground the miracles in a specific historical context seems to have failed. William's miracles were not as popular as other versions of the same tales, which may indicate that the level of historical specificity made them less appealing once they left his immediate milieu.[76] William's miracles can therefore be considered unique in combining political commentary and legendary material to communicate a universal message about his ideal Christian society, one in which Mary triumphed and the Jews were put to shame.

---

[75] The tension between the historical vs. the miraculous or supernatural in twelfth-century historical writing is explored by M. Otter, *Inventiones: Fiction and Referentiality in Twelfth-Century Historical Writing* (Chapel Hill, 1996).

[76] On the influence (and limits thereof) of William's collection, see *MBVM*, pp. lvi–lvii.

⇾ 6 ⇽

Advising the King: Kingship, Bishops and Saints in the Works of William of Malmesbury

Ryan Kemp

THROUGHOUT THE MEDIEVAL WEST, saints and bishops offered crucial advice and fierce admonition to the rulers of political communities. The type of the forceful and reprimanding cleric, however, has so far mostly been studied with reference to the early Middle Ages, at least when compared with his successors in twelfth-century England.[1] Indeed, even William of Malmesbury's views on kingship have begun to be explored only fairly recently.[2] Our understanding has been reshaped by the scholarship of Sverre Bagge, John Gillingham, Paul Hayward, Björn Weiler and, especially, that of Sigbjørn Sønnesyn.[3] As a direct consequence of their efforts, far greater attention is now paid to the moral, ethical and theological dimensions of William's texts. When defining the virtuous exercise of royal power, William emphasised the connection between outward action and inner disposition, and expressed Augustinian and early medieval assumptions about power in the language of classical antiquity. To maintain a virtuous character, however, kings needed the Church. Both Weiler and Sønnesyn have drawn attention to the fact that all the outstanding kings in the *Gesta Regum* had powerful clerical advisors.[4] This paper builds upon their remarks by exploring further interactions between kings, bishops and saints in William's writings. In particular,

---

[1] As noted by B. Weiler, 'Bishops and kings in England, c. 1066 – c. 1215', in *Religion und Politik im Mittelalter: Deutschland und England im Vergleich*, ed. L. Körntgen and D. Wassenhoven (Berlin, 2013), pp. 157–204, at 161–2.

[2] With the earlier exception of the constitutional and legalistic approach adopted in J. Haahr, 'The concept of kingship in William of Malmesbury's *Gesta Regum* and *Historia Novella*', *Med. St.* 38 (1976), 351–71. Cf. Sønnesyn, *Ethics*, pp. 180–1, 247–58.

[3] P. A. Hayward, 'The importance of being ambiguous: innuendo and legerdemain in William of Malmesbury's *Gesta Regum* and *Gesta Pontificum Anglorum*', *ANS* 33 (2011), 75–102; Sønnesyn, *Ethics*; J. Gillingham, 'Civilizing the English? The English histories of William of Malmesbury and David Hume', *Historical Research* 74 (2001), 17–43; S. Bagge, 'Ethics, politics, and providence in William of Malmesbury's *Historia Novella*', *Viator* 41 (2010), 113–32; B. Weiler, 'William of Malmesbury on kingship', *History* 90 (2005), 3–22.

[4] Sønnesyn, *Ethics*, esp. 253–63; Weiler, 'William of Malmesbury on kingship', p. 18.

it extends the discussion to texts other than the *Gesta Regum*, principally to its monumental twin, the *Gesta Pontificum*, which has always received less scholarly attention. Although the succession of kings and the development of a nation were common historical frameworks through which contemporaries reflected upon the progress of a moral community, they were not the only approaches to the past available to twelfth-century writers. How did William depict kings known to him from texts with rather different structures and intended audiences? How far did he draw upon an insular, as much as a classical and patristic, inheritance? With these questions in mind, this chapter argues that the notion of clerical oversight was of fundamental importance to William's historical and political vision. He regarded it as essential to the well-being of the realm. His normative expectations of secular and ecclesiastical power were the product of a political culture rooted in early medieval traditions and practices. The following will proceed in three steps. I begin with William's depictions of one of his exemplars of clerical oversight: St Dunstan. The historian explored the relationship between the archbishop and the various rulers he served in considerable depth. These detailed descriptions establish a basis for comparison with prelates closer to William's own time, whose interactions with kings were more ambivalent. Secondly, by examining a range of examples from across William's oeuvre, we can judge how William thought kings and clerics interacted in the vast majority of historical circumstances. In doing so, it is important to look beyond those interactions that have garnered the greatest modern critical attention. After all, such encounters do not necessarily reflect the breadth of William's interests or those of his audience. Interpreting this greater range of examples allows us to see how William judged a variety of historical scenarios against his own expectations of royal and clerical behaviour. These judgements, in turn, enable us to highlight some of the underlying tenets of his political, moral and historical outlook, and to offer suggestions for their possible origins.

Of all clerical advisors, William paid most attention to Dunstan. William was not alone in believing that the saint's co-operation with King Edgar had brought about a golden age: Eadmer began his *Historia Nouorum* with a description of their partnership,[5] whilst Goscelin of Saint-Bertin, in his *Life of St Wihtburh the Virgin*, described how, in the memory of the English, no other reign had seen such a remarkable group of saints.[6] For William, too, Dunstan was an extraordinary figure and the exemplar of the admonishing bishop. William's depictions vary between texts, however, and require comparison in order to illustrate his selective use of the source material at his disposal. In the *Gesta Regum*, Dunstan first appears when rebuking King Edgar for abducting and raping a nun. The saint reprimands Edgar, forcing him to do penance for seven years. According to William, it is to

---

[5] Eadmer, *Historia Nouorum*, p. 3; trans. Bosanquet, p. 3.
[6] Goscelin of Saint-Bertin, *The Hagiography of the Female Saints of Ely*, ed. R. C. Love (OMT 2004), pp. 67–9.

Edgar's credit that he submitted, notwithstanding his royal status, and even refused to wear a crown during this period of atonement.[7] In William's rendition, there remains, however, a sense that Dunstan was not wholly effective in his chastisement. William goes on to describe Edgar taking several other mistresses.[8] An indignant Dunstan used all his powers against the king, but William does not record anything further about the prelate's success or failure. Their relationship is sketched in greater detail in the *Gesta Pontificum*. Indeed, in the *Gesta Regum* William points his readers towards the *Gesta Pontificum* as a work in which he would 'beat out something for the instruction of our countrymen'.[9] There, William is far more explicit in relating Edgar's utter reliance on Dunstan's advice. God inspired the king to look to the saint in all matters. The king did everything the prelate asked. Dunstan applied the spur when Edgar delayed in any matter and, without respect for the king's person, shaped the monarch's character into a model for his subjects.[10] These remonstrations, in turn, improved the morality of the entire kingdom. Both the nobility and the lower orders followed their king, doing nothing to contravene the law, precisely because they knew their master was himself subject to Dunstan's teachings. Military discipline improved, criminals were executed, while the holiness and learning of king and archbishop reinvigorated monastic life. Their partnership thus brought about a peaceful, lawful, religious and even –according to William– an agricultural and meteorological golden age.[11] William makes clear that these benefits stemmed from St Dunstan's teachings, spread from him to the king, and from the king to the people. There is thus a clear shift of focus between the *Gesta Regum* and the *Gesta Pontificum*, away from the actions of the king and towards those of St Dunstan. Good fortune flowed from the saint's virtues, sanctity and advice.

William's *Vita Dunstani* conveys a similar image: the effectiveness of Dunstan's teachings ensured that a receptive Edgar treated offenders severely, favoured the pious, and was approachable to monks.[12] No one stole or plundered during his reign without risking his or her life. Edgar was constantly founding monasteries or doing 'something great and politically important'.[13] William does not, however, mention Edgar's penance and its cause. After the king's death, in a chapter without parallel in his known written sources, William recorded an oral tradition current amongst the English which claimed that they had never had so great a king, one to

---

[7] GR 159. 2–160. 1.
[8] GR 159. 1.
[9] GR 149. 3: 'et ad scientiam nostrorum procudere'.
[10] GP 18. 2.
[11] GP 18. 3–5. Ideas of pollution, divine retribution, and climatological change, as a consequence of royal sin, spread initially from an Irish context to the Anglo-Saxon and Frankish kingdoms and became the dominant themes of Carolingian political discourse. See R. Meens, 'Politics, Mirrors of Princes and the Bible: sins, kings and the well-being of the realm', *EME* 7 (1998), 345–57.
[12] VD 2. 14. 1.
[13] VD 2. 14. 1: 'non magnum aliquod et patriae necessarium fecerit'.

be remembered in every age.[14] Both Edgar and Dunstan receive praise throughout William's oeuvre, but in the *Gesta Pontificum* and the *Vita* Dunstan's role is more fundamental. In these texts, Edgar simply does whatever he is told, whereas in the *Gesta Regum* the efficacy of Dunstan's oversight is not necessarily total. The difference reflects the distinct aims and intended audience of each text. Where the *Gesta Regum* was at least partly aimed at a courtly lay readership,[15] Rodney Thomson has argued that the *Gesta Pontificum* was intended as a monument to the achievements of the English Church and English monasticism. Hence no single individual was an appropriate dedicatee.[16] Though William does not articulate his purpose explicitly, either in the *Gesta Pontificum* or in his *vitae*, it is clear that he wished to celebrate England's saints and rescue their histories for posterity. The saints' Lives he produced were commissioned by the religious communities at Worcester and Glastonbury who in turn provided him with both hospitality and source material.[17] In the light of this context, it is hardly surprising that William's depiction of Dunstan varied. William tailored his depiction of the saint, and made a selective use of his sources, with his audiences and their expectations in mind. Whereas in the *Gesta Regum* King Edgar is placed at the centre of the narrative, when celebrating the saint either in his own right or as part of a wider narrative of the English Church William instead emphasised how justice stemmed, in the first instance, from the archbishop, not the king. The importance of clerical oversight was a constant in William's texts, but he felt able to vary his focus on the partners in this relationship, depending on the nature of the text, and its presumed recipients and readers. In the *Gesta Regum*, kings had brought Christian rule to England with the aid of bishops as spiritual and moral advisors. Secular rulers were here the primary agents of political and historical change.[18] In his other historical and hagiographical works, by contrast, William is far keener to praise the exploits of clerics, even while paying due attention to kings. Saints and bishops were more closely connected both to his own religious community and to those who commissioned his *vitae*. He thus had good reason for placing them at the centre of his narrative. Indeed, Dunstan's other interactions with kings in the *Vita Dunstani* allocate primacy to the archbishop in maintaining and restoring royal justice. He thus lectured King Edmund, his nobility and the lower orders, 'at a time when justice had long been under threat, to bring the tottering land back to its former state'.[19] Similarly, it was Dunstan, who, during the reign of the sickly King Eadred, ensured that justice prevailed throughout the realm, who took care

---

[14] *VD* 2. 18. 1; cf. *GR* 160. 3, where the wording used to praise Edgar is similar.
[15] In terms of the dedicatees and the inclusion of more geographically wide-ranging, entertaining, and lengthy digressions than offered in the *Gesta Pontificum*. *GP* II, pp. xxx–xxxii.
[16] *GP*, p. xxii.
[17] *Saints' Lives*, pp. xiv–xv.
[18] Sønnesyn, *Ethics*, pp. 205–6.
[19] *VD* 1. 14. 2: 'et iam dudum laborante iustitia labefactatum regno consuleret in statum priscum erigeret'.

that those were corrected who had gone astray, and who allowed no-one to sin, thereby ensuring that everyone adhered to the judgements of God and the law.[20] Moreover, Dunstan did not take credit for this, but attributed it to the king's good will and piety, thus gaining advantage for the king by his own labours, and his fear of God.[21] Dunstan's fierce admonitions of both Eadwig and Æthelred are also well known.[22] Throughout these texts, whether by predicting the deaths of kings or the destruction of their realms, censuring tyrants, dragging them out of bed, combating the dangers of sinful women, ruling in a king's stead, saving his life, or lecturing his nobility on the importance of justice, Dunstan was William's most effective example of clerical oversight. The kingdom's well-being was owed, ultimately, to both his virtue and his influence at court.

Closer to William's own time, the archbishops of Canterbury left much to be desired when compared to Dunstan. In the *Gesta Regum*, William the Conqueror makes himself subservient to Lanfranc's wisdom and accepts all his recommendations.[23] Lanfranc also plays a pivotal role in the succession of William Rufus by acting 'as the most powerful influence in affairs'. He not only 'reared him and made him knight', but also forced Rufus to promise to act in accordance with what was right and fair.[24] Rufus might have become a paragon of virtue, according to William, had the king not instead been overwhelmed by vice on the death of his mentor.[25] In the *Gesta Pontificum*, William describes Lanfranc's interactions in greater depth. William the Conqueror recognised Lanfranc's wisdom from 'the dignity of his countenance and the wit of his retorts'.[26] Although the revised version of the text shows the king treating the archbishop with delight and respect, the more critical original (version β) paints a less rosy picture, with far less agency ascribed to the king. This version of William's text contained a number of highly critical comments on earlier kings and prelates which were later erased, adapted, or substantially rewritten. William likewise softened the earlier and harsher judgements in later versions of the *Gesta Regum*. It is impossible to know what prompted these changes: a reaction from his readers, a change in political circumstances or in William's own judgement, outlook and enthusiasm towards the writing of history may provide possible causes.[27] In this unedited version, we are, however, fortunate in having William's judgement of episcopal behaviour set in the context of a more critical and forthright depiction of the political elite in

---

[20] *VD* 2. 22.
[21] *VD* 2. 22. 3.
[22] On Eadwig see *GR* 147; *VD* 2. 27, on his death ibid. 1. 31, and 2. 3–4. 1 on his attacks on the Church and the rebellion against him. On Æthelred see *GR* 164; *VD* 2. 21–2. On the lack of royal justice see *VD* 2. 25 and for the effect of Dunstan's prophecy on the coming of the Danes, 2. 34. 1–2.
[23] *GR* 269. 2.
[24] *GR* 305. 3: 'Accessit etiam fauori eius maximum rerum momentum, archiepiscopus Lanfrancus, eo quod eum nutrierat et militem fecerat'.
[25] *GR* 312. 1–2.
[26] *GP* 24. 4: 'ex dignitate frontispitii et facetia responsi interiora coniectans'.
[27] *GR* II, p. 276; *GP* II, pp. xiv–xxv.

general. Where this earlier version is more critical of the king, Lanfranc's virtue emerges more clearly as an astute and calculated struggle against the king's vice. A single glance from Lanfranc is said, by William, to quell the Conqueror. The archbishop 'managed the king with a holy skill, not sternly upbraiding what he did wrong, but spicing serious language with jokes'.[28] This, William claimed, was the best means by which Lanfranc could influence the king. A more aggressive line, William implies, would have been fruitless against the king's natural stubbornness.[29] Overall, William is highly critical of the king's arrogance which, he concludes, had overwhelmed Lanfranc so that he was unable to withstand his ruler's vices.[30] Unlike his predecessors, Lanfranc had to be more tactical and astute in his handling of the king. He studied the king's character, for example, before making 'quiet interventions and timely suggestions'.[31] Only in this way, William concluded, could Lanfranc 'preserve what the saints had begun in Edgar's reign'.[32] In composing this account, William did not merely follow in the wake of his sources. He reflected on, and compared, the examples at his disposal. Although William recognised that Lanfranc's achievements paled in comparison to those of Dunstan, he nonetheless argues that the archbishop deserved a favourable judgement for having had to act alone and in the face of fierce opposition, in his sole promotion of royal justice and virtue.[33]

Similar themes emerge from William's depiction of St Anselm. William argues that Anselm's lack of influence over Rufus was at least partly due to an absence of support from his episcopal colleagues.[34] As in the case of Lanfranc and Rufus, Anselm's support for Henry I was crucial in securing the king's succession. Indeed, in William's writing, clerics repeatedly extract promises of good conduct during such moments of royal weakness. In the *Gesta Pontificum*, during Henry's struggle with his brother Robert, William recounts how the king leant on Anselm, letting him in on all his secrets and promising to pass good laws, when in fear for his life and throne.[35] Anselm returned the favour by both intimidating suspected magnates and by lecturing them, at every opportunity, on the importance of faith and the dangers of treachery.[36] William describes how, when Robert landed in England, Anselm roused the common people in support of their king by offering himself as a guarantor of the king's future good conduct. William claims that the power of Anselm's appeal was such that many subsequently rushed to take up

---

[28] GP 42. 6β 1.
[29] GP 42. 6β 1.
[30] GP 42. 6β 1.
[31] GP 42. 6β. 8.
[32] GP 44. 6: 'Magnum id et laudandum, ut quod sedula sanctorum benignitas tempore regis Edgari inchoauerit, iste labefactari non permiserit'.
[33] GP 44. 6.
[34] GR 315.
[35] GP 55. 11β.
[36] GP 55. 11β.

their swords.[37] Version β underscores the importance of Anselm's oversight, and does so again in the context of a more forthright condemnation of the king. As with Lanfranc and Rufus, William complains bitterly that, had Anselm only lived longer, Henry would never have plunged into his later disgraces, urged on by other less virtuous bishops who should instead have reprimanded him. William's despair at this turn of events is palpable: having related the failure of the episcopate, he launches into a bitter lamentation.[38] In the later version, a somewhat more measured William claims that there was good in Henry's heart, but it required 'kindling words' and 'wholesome exhortations' to stir it to life.[39] William thus suggests that oversight over the Norman kings, provided by Lanfranc and Anselm, had benefited the kingdom, but that their interventions were often less dramatic than those of Dunstan. Their actions rarely translated into harmonious co-operation or fierce opposition, instead often occupying a grey area of compromise.[40] Their methods had to be more indirect and their successes were often fleeting, frequently gained only during moments of royal weakness and crisis. In the case of the Conqueror, William's depiction of the king contrasts with that of Eadmer, who paints a picture of harmonious co-operation. William praised Eadmer as a historian, drew upon his texts extensively for his depiction of Lanfranc and Anselm,[41] and it is reasonable to infer that they were acquainted.[42] William's depiction of the relationship between the Conqueror and his archbishops thus represents a deliberate departure from one of his most important sources. Eadmer claimed that Lanfranc had the king's ear, was his principal advisor and made him a more faithful servant of God as part of a wider renewal of religious life.[43] Eadmer also asserted that both Lanfranc and Anselm were held in high esteem and were able to keep the king's 'usual harshness' in check.[44] Though Eadmer and William agreed on the control the king exercised over both temporal and spiritual affairs, they differed in how far his archbishops were able to influence that control. Both expected an archbishop to act, in William's words, as 'a spokesman for all, a standard bearer in the van, a shield to protect the public weal'.[45] The sketch that

---

[37] GP 5.
[38] GP 63.
[39] GP 63. 1: 'Hic est contemplari quanta materia boni in regis pectore fuerit, si quis tam ingenuae fidei scintillas fomento uerborum animaret et in maiores uires bonis ammonitionibus excitaret'.
[40] William's verdict has proved influential. H. E. J. Cowdrey described the collaboration between Lanfranc and the Conqueror as 'though cordial and fruitful ... not without its complexities ... Lanfranc had sometimes to differ in silence and occasionally to come to terms with invincible resistance. Lanfranc's skill and achievement lay in his ability to acknowledge the balance involved and in his knowing when to differ to the king as supreme'. See GP II, p. 46; H. E. J. Cowdrey, *Lanfranc* (Oxford, 2003), pp. 186–8, 228–9.
[41] GR II, pp. 68–269, 279; GP II, pp. 45–50, 56, 59, 61.
[42] GR II, p. 15; GP II, p. xl; Thomson, *William of Malmesbury*, pp. 46–7, 72–5, on William's contacts with Canterbury.
[43] Eadmer, *Historia Nouorum*, p. 12; trans. Bosanquet, pp. 12–13.
[44] Eadmer, *Historia Nouorum*, p. 24; trans. Bosanquet, p. 23.
[45] GP 47. 4: 'qui esset os omnium, uexillifer preuius, umbo publicus'.

William draws of his near-contemporary prelates, however, contrasts with both his own depiction of a tenth-century golden age, and Eadmer's of the Conqueror. William doubtless had to take into account his audience's knowledge of the more recent events, and sources that might have told a story different from Eadmer's. He thus had to contend with a rather different horizon of expectations, compared to his treatment of tenth-century England. While he knew Eadmer's account, and clearly respected his skill as a historian, William drew his own conclusions about the effectiveness of episcopal oversight in modern times.

William naturally gave considerable attention to dealings between kings and the archbishops of Canterbury, and so have modern scholars using his works. In addition to these often colourful encounters, however, William recorded many other interactions between kings and their clerical advisors. The following examples are far from exhaustive, but the expectations of royal and episcopal behaviour that they reveal are all the more striking for being ubiquitous throughout William's oeuvre. Numerous partnerships between monarchs and ecclesiastical advisors, as described by William, highlighted the importance of clerical oversight. William describes in detail Æthelstan's dealings with Archbishop Oda of Canterbury and stresses that Aldhelm, first abbot of Malmesbury, had been an especially effective and important advisor of kings.[46] In William's view, the power of English episcopal saints arose from the military support they provided, their advice, the education they offered, the concessions they gained for their communities, and the odd curse or lightning strike.[47] The *Gesta Pontificum* reports how Archbishop Ealdred of York only agreed to crown William the Conqueror after the king swore to rule with moderation. Episcopal approval of the king was conditional on the king's conduct. When the king reneged on his promise, Ealdred unleashed a terrifying curse. The frightened ruler had to be calmed by his advisors and Ealdred died before they could be reconciled.[48] In William's interpretation of English history, clerical exhortations, or their absence, had a decisive impact on royal character. The seventh-century King Ecgfrith of Northumbria was defeated in battle, so William recorded, a year to the day after his new wife had forced the venerable St Wilfred from court.[49] Likewise, King Cnut only became a great ruler once he was aided by 'men of high quality and wisdom',[50] including Archbishop Æthelnoth, who put the fear of God into the king when he misbehaved. Edward the Confessor was taught, specifically, 'the sacred principles of kingship' by Archbishop Eadsige.[51]

---

[46] GP 246. 1–2. Cf. Æthelstan calling on Aldhelm to save him during an assassination attempt: GR 131. 6–7. As close advisor of King Ine cf. GR 35. 4. William recorded how Ine, on Aldhelm's advice, founded Glastonbury Abbey.

[47] For Wulfstan's cursing of the rebels see GP 144. On other military involvements, see Bishop Wærstan being ambushed whilst bringing reinforcements to Æthelstan: GP 80. 4. The same incident was described in GR 131. 6.

[48] GP 19–20.

[49] GP 100. 33–6.

[50] GR 184. 1: 'summi et sapientissimi uiri'.

[51] GR 197. 2: 'et ab Edsio archiepiscopo sacra regnandi precepta edoctus'.

The so-called 'gifts of kingly character', possessed by King Ine of Wessex, had been 'encouraged by the lively admonitions' of Aldhelm.[52] Another king of Wessex, Ecgberht, had placed his son Athulf into the care of Bishop Swithhun of Winchester, who, William claims, taught him how to rule.[53] Bishop Ealhstan of Sherborne also helped the same youth 'to learn the art of kingship' and inspired him to resist the Danish invasions.[54] Clerical advisors, throughout William's interpretation of English history, had taught good kings, who were willing to listen, how to rule and provided them with crucial support. Those rulers who failed to listen to their exhortations, or who had broken guarantees of good behaviour, were left to face the consequences, both in this life and the next.

However, England's saints and bishops played a fundamental role in the development of the kingdom, well beyond their criticism and tutoring of kings and their sons. The story of Alfred's vision of St Cuthbert, included in both of William's major works, emphasises that England had been paying the penalty of her sins during the Viking invasions, but was now offered mercy 'thanks to the merits of her home-bred saints'. Alfred would become a proper king again if, and only if, he won the favour of God's messengers.[55] The survival not only of Alfred, but of his dynasty and the kingdom itself, were predicated on God's mercy as announced by His prophets, a mercy dependent on the devotion of Alfred's successors. This very offer of mercy, though, would never have occurred had it not been for the merits of England's saints.[56] Their virtue gave Alfred and the kingdom the chance of redemption. As St Peter informed Edward the Confessor in a vision experienced by a Glastonbury monk, the kingdom was God's to do with as He wished.[57] He had chosen to give this political community a second chance because of the many saints it had produced. They, not the community's secular rulers, had secured this offer of mercy. These saints were not only at the centre of William's narrative of England's historical and political development; the narrative itself would have been cut short without their virtue.

Only bad and immoral bishops failed to heed prophecies such as those of the Glastonbury monk. Archbishop Stigand, for example, treated the dying words of Edward the Confessor with derision, unaware, to William's regret, of the disaster to come.[58] Ruin also faced those rulers who failed to respect and honour the memory of holy men and women. All kings, according to William, feared St Frideswide,[59] while Cnut's impiety towards the corpse of the saintly daughter of King Edgar caused her to leap at him from her tomb. The shock made the king fall backwards, in

---

[52] GP 209. 2: 'Has animi regalis dotes animabat stimulis monitionum pater Aldelmus'.
[53] GP 75. 14.
[54] GP 79. 3: 'sedulis ammonitionibus ad scientiam regni stimulabat, contra Danos'.
[55] GP 130. 2: 'modo tandem indigenarum sanctorum meritis super eam misericordie suae oculo respicit'.
[56] Cf. the same event in GR 121. 3.
[57] GP 83. 5.
[58] GR 226–7.
[59] GP 178. 3.

the process suffering a fortuitous knock to the head that persuaded him to improve his behaviour.[60] Cnut should have known better. After all, William recorded, the king had earlier built St Edmund's ditch out of fear. He had 'learned what was right' after his own father, Swein Forkbeard, had been killed by the saint for violating his territory.[61] William Rufus characteristically declined to show any such respect or veneration for the memory of saintly individuals. Indeed, William has the king openly proclaim that no saint could possibly help him, sarcastically remarking that 'of course those long dead are concerned to interfere in our affairs'.[62] Rufus thus neatly expresses the antithesis of William's own consistent view that saintly and clerical oversight was a fundamental necessity for good rulership.

How widely did William's contemporaries share his values and views? It is worth recalling that his works were part of a wider culture of moral instruction, one popular with an intellectually, culturally and politically significant lay and clerical elite.[63] William showed real concern to preserve the memory of particularly virtuous reprimanding clerics. They were, after all, the most effective challengers to abuses of royal power. The opening of William's *Vita Wulfstani*, for instance, describes how recent examples of virtuous conduct were more likely to be influential than those found in Holy Scripture, as the former were closer and more relevant to a contemporary audience.[64] With access to at least fifty saints' Lives, the lengthy accounts of Eadmer and Bede, and documents, letters, and observations collected during his own extensive travels, William was able to deploy an extraordinary range of examples of royal and clerical interaction.[65] William expressed his expectations and assumptions through the depictions of a diverse set of individuals, events and contexts: their cumulative effect is considerable. Few readers could have failed to appreciate the relevance and importance of these examples of royal and ecclesiastical behaviour to the well-being and preservation of their own religious communities and the realm as a whole. Despite the varying emphases in his works, the overall image of royal and ecclesiastical power that William wished to present is clear. Although the interactions between prelates and rulers may appear formulaic, their repetition was essential because of the nature of his readership. William's audiences were unlikely to read his texts from start to finish in one sitting, but instead drew upon them as repositories of good deeds

---

[60] *GP* 87. 7–9.
[61] *GP* 74. 28: 'Fossatum Cnuto rex fieri percepit, patris sui Suani miserabili fine ad bonum edoctus'.
[62] *GP* 55. 3β. 3: 'Scilicet ea cura iam olim mortuos sollicitat, ut nostris intersint negotiis!'
[63] Otto of Freising and Alexander of Telese, among others, made comparable statements on the importance of history as moral instruction in texts also directed at a powerful lay audience. See B. Weiler, 'Thinking about power before Magna Carta: the role of history', in *Des chartes aux constitutions: autour de l'idée constitutionnelle en Europe (XIIe–XVIIe siècles)*, ed. F. Foronda and J. P. Genet (Publications de la Sorbonne/École Française de Rome: forthcoming); Weiler, 'Bishops and kings'.
[64] See *VW* 1. prol. 11–15. 1–2.
[65] Listed in detail *GP* II, pp. xxxvii–xl.

Advising the King

to emulate and bad ones to shun.⁶⁶ The *Gesta Pontificum*, for example, had an overwhelmingly local audience in the first instance, but was copied at many other priories and abbeys besides Malmesbury itself.⁶⁷ The text influenced dozens of writers, including John of Worcester, Symeon of Durham, William of Newburgh, Geoffrey of Monmouth, Wace, Ralph of Diss, the author of the *Liber Eliensis*, Gervase of Canterbury, and possibly Henry of Huntingdon and Orderic Vitalis.⁶⁸ William's *vitae* were also used by the communities that commissioned them.⁶⁹ Although the *Gesta Regum*, of course, had a much wider reach and popularity (including on the continental mainland), these ecclesiastical audiences should not be seen as insulated from wider political and lay culture. As Nicholas Vincent has observed, the itineraries of the Angevin kings resembled a near-perpetual pilgrimage, in a ceaseless round of visits to religious centres, where rulers prayed, made offerings, displayed humility, and asked for saintly intercession.⁷⁰ William's texts thus contributed towards written traditions, sustained by communities who were in frequent contact with kings. The examples he recorded continued to be copied and utilised and had a resonance not necessarily dependent on their place within the text as a whole. The continued influence and popularity of William's writings, and their commission in the first instance, reflected an appreciation not only for his intellectual and historical abilities but also for the views he espoused.

What were the sources for William's particular focus on the importance of clerical oversight for the well being of the realm? Many of the fundamental biblical parallels, particularly with the Books of Samuel and Kings, are immediately recognisable. The prophets anointed and admonished the kings of Israel, linking the monarchs directly to the ultimate source of their God-given authority. Crucially, these prophets warned kings who went astray that, if they continued to promote sin and idolatry, then God's favour would be withdrawn. God transferred Saul's kingdom to David because the former had ignored such warnings. David, in turn, was admonished by Nathan for his own transgressions and adulterous behaviour.⁷¹ Both Nathan and Zadok later secured the succession of Solomon, but after the king's adultery with strange women and his refusal to be corrected God left only one tribe to David's successors.⁷² The role of the prophets, as described in the

---

⁶⁶ The episodic nature of William's narrative, and other examples of monastic *gestae*, lent itself to a context in which monks listened to, and reflected upon, short examples of moral correctness on the pattern of the Gospels. See R. D. Ray, 'Medieval historiography through the twelfth century: problems and progress of research', *Viator* 5 (1974), 33–60 at p. 41; T. Riches, 'The function of the *Gesta Episcoporum* as archive', *Jaarboek voor Middeleeuwse Geschiedenis* 10 (2007), 7–46.

⁶⁷ *GP* II, pp. xlv–l.

⁶⁸ The twenty-one copies which survive indicate a 'steady, if unremarkable. popularity': *GP* II, pp. xlvi–l.

⁶⁹ And hardly anywhere else: see *Saints' Lives*, pp. xxv–xxvii.

⁷⁰ N. Vincent, 'The pilgrimages of the Angevin kings of England, 1154–1272', in *Pilgrimage. The English Experience from Becket to Bunyan*, ed. C. Morris and P. Roberts (Cambridge, 2002), pp. 12–45.

⁷¹ 1 Kings (1 Sam.): 15; 2 Kings (2 Sam.): 12.

⁷² 3 Kings (1 Kings): 1; 3 Kings (1 Kings): 11.

remainder of the Books of Kings, was to ensure that kings were made aware both of when they had broken God's commandments, and of the consequences their transgressions would bring to their own people.

England's saints and bishops fulfilled the same function in William's texts. The kings who followed episcopal advice succeeded, whereas those who did not faced divine retribution that invariably wrought disaster upon their people. Cuthbert's promise to Alfred thus established a similar kind of pact to that established by God, through the biblical prophets, with the kings of Israel. William had access to insular traditions that emphasised this very theme. The sixth-century monk Gildas, whom William admired, asked what hope there was for the British when the Israelites had been punished for failing to listen to their watchmen. Those who should have been overseeing their flock were instead haughty, envious and drunk.[73] Fortunately, there were far more successful partnerships in the *Historia Ecclesiastica* of William's great model, Bede. William regarded himself as following in Bede's footsteps and mined his text extensively.[74] Bede wrote of his own model partnerships between royal and clerical authority, hailing the co-operation between St Aidan and St Oswald.[75] Bede's account provided the foundation for William's own narrative of the development of the English as a civilised Christian people.[76] Bede, however, wrote a history of conversion. He championed humble, modest kings who gained great earthly power through their preaching and acceptance of the faith and sought to banish from his audience's memory the apostate kings who had allowed idolatry to flourish.[77] William's narrative was not the same as Bede's, and he did not focus on the virtues of humility and modesty to the same degree. Nonetheless, from both these insular traditions, and from his reading of the Bible, William had access to models of royal-episcopal behaviour which helped to frame his own interpretation.

What other, perhaps more indirect, sources might have influenced William? There are striking resemblances between William's depictions and the ideas found in the seventh-century treatise on social and political morality, the Pseudo-Cyprian *Twelve Abuses of the World*. The abuses included the unjust king who, because he did not correct others, faced war, disruption, the death of loved ones, and even diminishing agricultural returns as lightning strikes and beasts ripped apart his

---

[73] Gildas, pp. 24–5.
[74] *GP* II, p. xxxv.
[75] Bede, *HE* iii. 5–6 on Bishop Aidan and Oswald.
[76] *GP* II, p. xix.
[77] On the importance of humility and modesty, see Bede, *HE* iii. 6 on Bishop Aidan and King Oswine. Apostate kings deserved to be forgotten: Bede, *HE* ii. 5 on King Eadbald, and at iv. 2: 'so all those who compute the dates of kings have decided to abolish the memory of those perfidious kings'.

fields.[78] The subsequent, connected abuse was the neglectful bishop.[79] These watchmen were meant to warn the wicked of God's judgement in order to give the sinners a chance to repent. If the sinful died without having been forewarned, then the bishop was ultimately responsible. Hence, the treatise claimed that bishops must act like watchtowers, correcting by word and by deed. There is no evidence that William knew the text directly, but treatises like the *Twelve Abuses of the World* lay behind the re-emergence of the mirrors for princes genre under the Carolingians.[80] Both William and the clerics of his text fit comfortably within a peculiarly, but not exclusively, Carolingian vocabulary of admonition, correction and atonement.

There were also, of course, innumerable sources behind specific sections of William's texts. His presentation of Dunstan drew upon an extensive Canterbury tradition, which also urged its readers to model themselves on Dunstan's character and emphasised his asceticism, authority and proximity to royal power.[81] This was never a matter of slavish copying, however. Nicola Robertson has shown how twelfth-century authors, including William, placed Dunstan at the centre of the Benedictine reform movement in a way that contemporary accounts did not.[82] William's depictions of the interaction between royal and clerical authority bear a further striking resemblance to the *Institutes of Polity* of Wulfstan, bishop of London, Worcester, and archbishop of York (d. 1023). This work put forward a vision of a justly ordered realm strongly influenced by both Carolingian and English reformers. It called not for humility or withdrawal from the world, but for an alliance among those who worked, fought and prayed.[83] Both king and

[78] Pseudo-Cyprian, *De XII Abusivis Saeculi*, ed. *Texte und Untersuchungen zur Geschichte der altchristlichen Literatur* 34 (1909), 1–61. On passages quoted here see *Vincent of Beauvais: The Moral Instruction of a Prince with Pseudo-Cyprian: The Twelve Abuses of the World*, trans. P. Throop (Charlotte, 2011), pp. 115–33, at 127–9; J. Grigg, 'The just king and De duodecim abusiuis saeculi', *Parergon* 27 (2010), 27–51.

[79] *The Twelve Abuses of the World*, trans. Throop, pp. 129–30.

[80] R. Meens, 'Politics, Mirrors of Princes and the Bible: sins, kings and the well-being of the realm', *EME* 7 (1998), 345–57; G. Koziol, 'Leadership: why we have mirrors for princes but none for presidents', in *Why the Middle Ages Matter: Medieval Light on Modern Injustice*, ed. C. Chazelle and S. Doubleday (London, 2012), pp. 183–98. William was familiar with important texts and figures in this tradition including its classical forbears. He knew at first hand Einhard's *Vita Karoli*, Seneca's *De Clementia*, and various texts of Gregory the Great. He was also familiar with figures such as Hincmar of Reims and Alcuin through texts other than the Mirrors for Princes they produced. On the possibility that William had himself visited Aachen, and on his familiarity with a corpus of Carolingian chronicles at Metz, see *GP* II, pp. 214–15; M. Tischler, *Einharts Vita Karoli: Studien zur Entstehung, Überlieferung und Rezeption* (2 vols, Hannover, 2001), II, pp. 1392–1402.

[81] The author known as B urged his readers to model themselves on Dunstan's character: *The Early Lives of St Dunstan*, ed. and trans. M. Winterbottom and M. Lapidge (OMT 2012), p. 9. See D. Rollason, 'The concept of sanctity in the early Lives of St Dunstan', in *St Dunstan: His Life, Times, and Cult*, ed. N. Ramsey (Woodbridge, 1992), pp. 261–72.

[82] N. Robertson, 'Dunstan and monastic reform: tenth-century fact or twelfth-century fiction?', *ANS* 28 (2006), 153–67, at pp. 166–7.

[83] *The Political Writings of Archbishop Wulfstan of York*, trans. A. Rabin (Manchester, 2014), p. 102.

people would thrive if the ruler embraced justice and zealously aided those who enforced it. He should apply his learning, purify his people, heed divine teachings and reject all injustice.[84] The king's counsellors should be the messengers of such teachings. If a king did not listen to their proclamations of justice, he ignored and challenged God himself. If the bishops failed to curb injustice, they too rejected God and their own flock. Wulfstan's expectations of clerics and kings, like William's, were bound together.

The works of tenth-century Benedictine reformers, epitomised by the *Regularis Concordia*, similarly urged the integration of monasteries, Church and society, with the king as the focus of loyalty, unity and authority. Such Christian political theory bound together monarchy, episcopacy and monasticism. One modern account has described how the works of this movement legitimated new norms by making reference to an earlier golden age, by searching for inspiration amongst long-dead figures of the past, disregarding the pre-Reform Church as degenerate.[85] This description bears obvious resemblances to William's own techniques. In other words, he was indebted to an ideology that urged a closer relationship between powerful reprimanding prelates and the king, one which originated in Carolingian texts and rhetoric.

William's works were part of a long tradition that promulgated an outlook which combined particular expectations for secular and ecclesiastical power. Episcopal oversight was essential, whether in local, royal or national contexts. William sought to preserve the memory of particularly virtuous reprimanding clerics, whom he regarded as among the most effective safeguards against abuses of power. These clerics preached the fundamental importance of clerical oversight for the welfare of the realm: a kingdom ultimately owned by God and only granted mercy because of the holy men, women and saints who helped to provide such oversight. There were patterns of deep continuity behind his expectations, which resemble the political discourse of the Carolingians, transmitted and enhanced by the tenth-century Benedictine reform movement. Scholars such as Timothy Reuter and Geoffrey Koziol have noted that the influence of the early medieval period upon twelfth-century political conduct and depiction has too frequently been ignored.[86] Although William travelled extensively, it is important to remember that his texts were primarily produced in a thoroughly Benedictine intellectual environment, immersed in classical, patristic and early medieval literature and thought. He was not the only writer to react with embittered disappointment

---

[84] Ibid., pp. 103–9.
[85] C. Cubitt, 'The tenth-century Benedictine reform in England', *EME* 6 (1997), 77–94, at pp. 89–90.
[86] G. Koziol, 'England, France, and the problem of sacrality in twelfth-century ritual', in *Cultures of Power: Lordship, Status, and Process in Twelfth-Century Europe*, ed. T. N. Bisson (Philadelphia, 1995), pp. 124–48, at 124–6; T. Reuter, 'Velle sibi fieri in forma hac. Symbolic acts in the Becket Dispute', in *Medieval Polities and Modern Mentalities*, ed. J. L. Nelson (Cambridge, 2006), pp. 167–92.

when contemporaries failed to live up to expectations and standards derived from the past. To judge by the frequency with which past exemplars and models of behaviour were evoked during political crises, such as the Becket dispute, the written traditions to which William contributed remained popular.[87] The celebrations surrounding the eight-hundredth anniversary of Magna Carta, for example, have provided a timely reminder that bishops and clerics played the decisive role in the production, proclamation, and preservation of that most famous expression of oversight over royal power.[88] The same frustration felt by William, that more recent archbishops only gained fleeting concessions from kings during moments of weakness and crisis, had perhaps now manifested itself in a rather different form. However indirectly, William's texts contributed towards a political culture and collective memory built from past exemplars. Fortunately for modern historians, the jest of William Rufus had been incorrect: the long dead could, and did, interfere in the affairs of the living.

---

[87] For a discussion of how these traditions influenced political actions, see Weiler, 'Bishops and kings', pp. 193–203; S. MacLean, 'Recycling the Franks in twelfth-century England: Regino of Prüm, the monks of Durham, and the Alexandrine Schism', *Speculum* 87 (2012), 649–81.

[88] N. Vincent and D. Carpenter, 'Feature of the Month: June 2015 – Who did (and did not) write Magna Carta', *The Magna Carta Project* (accessed 29th December 2015 http://magnacartaresearch.org/read/feature_of_the_month/Jun_2015_3); S. Ambler, *Bishops in the Political Community of England, 1213–1272* (Oxford, 2017).

7

Roman Identity
in William of Malmesbury's Historical Writings

William Kynan-Wilson

WILLIAM OF MALMESBURY was fascinated by Rome and *romanitas*. He wrote about the city, the Romans and their history at length, and in a variety of contexts and styles, including: a papal biography (1119), a digest of ancient Roman history (1129), a description of the city's topography (*Gesta Regum* 352), and a now-lost account of his abbot's journey to Rome (the *Itinerarium Iohannis abbatis*, c. 1140).[1] William also exhibits a deep interest in Roman style. This is most apparent at the opening of the *Gesta Regum* (bk 1 prol. 4) where he describes English history as broken, barbarous and in need of seasoning with Roman salt ('Romano sale condire').[2] This allusive statement can be read on several levels: it suggests judicious authorship, variety and good taste, preservation and entertainment, as well as the influence of ancient Roman literature, particularly satire.[3] Above all, it immediately alerts the reader to two recurring and related facets of William's historical writing: first, the author's comparisons between Norman England and ancient Rome; and second, William's intention to inform his own writing style with a Roman quality.

In part, William lends his writings a Roman polish through his extraordinary handling of classical texts. It has been estimated that he knew over one hundred classical works.[4] A constituent element of William's classicism is the manner in

---

I wish to acknowledge the support of the Danish Council for Independent Research, and Aalborg University, and to thank Lyndsay Coo, John David Wilson, and the editors of this volume for commenting on this paper.

[1] GR (Stubbs), I, pp. xxxviii–xl (*Itinerarium Iohannis*); Thomson, *William of Malmesbury*, pp. 119–36 (papal biography), and pp. 7 and 63–6 (ancient digest).
[2] References and translations are taken from the OMT editions of William's work.
[3] Thomson, 'Satire, irony and humour in William of Malmesbury', in *Rhetoric and Renewal*, p. 116; M. Winterbottom, 'The language of William of Malmesbury', ibid., p. 132.
[4] N. Wright, 'William of Malmesbury and Latin poetry: further evidence for a Benedictine's reading', *RB* 101 (1991), 122–53 and '*Industriae Testimonium*: William of Malmesbury and Latin poetry revisited', *RB* 103 (1993), 482–531; Thomson, *William of Malmesbury*, pp. 7 and 48–61, and idem, 'William of Malmesbury and the Latin Classics revisited', in *Aspects*, pp. 383–93. On

which he attributes Roman qualities to important characters in his histories. This chapter examines how and why William crafts and appropriates Roman identity; it focuses on his descriptions of British figures *in* Rome and how, through dexterous displays of classical learning, eloquence and rhetoric, these characters *perform* in a Roman manner.

Two extended scenes merit particular attention: first, William's retelling of the martyrdom of St Kenelm; and second, a debate between cardinals and the sons of Norman aristocrats. A close reading of these passages demonstrates the specular quality that Rome assumes in William's writing: when recounting the Roman identity of others, William writes with an acute awareness of his own *romanitas*.[5] The Roman flavouring was meant to elevate both William's status as a writer and the prestige of English history.

William's conception of romanitas

Despite his interest in things Roman, William neither visited the city nor ventured to the Italian peninsula in person. His knowledge of Rome was mediated almost exclusively via textual sources. Even when writing about the Romano-British remains that he saw at Carlisle (*Gesta Pontificum* 99. 3–5) his description is adorned with specialised classical terminology and his interpretation informed by ancient Roman history.[6]

Nowhere does William indulge in overt or prolonged discussion of Roman identity or Romanness; he does not even use the word *romanitas*. Nonetheless, William twice connects national identity with literary style. In the *Gesta Regum* (31. 1–2), he describes the Roman manner as 'careful' and 'considered' ('circumspecte'), and in the *Gesta Pontificum* (196. 6) he defines the Romans as writing 'with brilliance' ('splendide'). These passages are challenging to interpret considering the disjuncture between these two definitions.[7] However, it is evident that he identifies a distinctive Roman style, and it will be seen that it holds largely positive associations for him. Throughout the *Gesta Regum* and *Gesta Pontificum*, William refers positively to the Roman traits of specific *individuals*. For example, William praises Bishop Ithamar of Rochester for the 'positively Roman accomplishment of his learning' (*Gesta Pontificum* 72. 5) and he extols the 'Roman elegance' of Osbern's writing (*Gesta Regum* 149. 3) and Aldhelm's Latin (*Gesta Pontificum* 195).

William's structural borrowings from classical texts see J. G. Haahr, 'William of Malmesbury's Roman models: Suetonius and Lucan', in *The Classics in the Middle Ages*, ed. A. S. Bernard and S. Levin (New York, 1990), pp. 165–73.

[5] This paper strengthens and expands upon Michael Winterbottom's suggestion: 'Though he [William] does not exactly make this claim, he perhaps regarded himself as, if not a proto-Roman, at least an honorary one.' Winterbottom, 'The *Gesta regum* of William of Malmesbury', *JML* 5 (1995), 167.

[6] W. Kynan-Wilson, '*Mira Romanorum artifitia*: William of Malmesbury and the Romano-British remains at Carlisle', *Essays in Medieval Studies* 28 (2012), 35–49.

[7] Winterbottom, 'The *Gesta regum*', p. 167.

By contrast, William defines the contemporary Romans *collectively* in pejorative terms. He makes an important distinction between Rome's glorious past and her present decline, and he frequently compares the two: in his eyes the contemporary Romans are corrupt, avaricious and ignorant. William even decries them for their rhetorical ploys (*Gesta Pontificum* 70. 1), despite admiring the same qualities in Anglo-Norman figures. In short, the modern-day Romans are shown to be unworthy of their illustrious heritage. These criticisms are unexceptional within contemporary medieval literature, but William's originality lies in his mode of amplification.[8] He reinforces English eloquence in Rome by simultaneously highlighting Roman degradation. A vivid example of this contrast is when William calls Rome former 'mistress of the world' ('domina orbis terrararum'), that is now a 'meagre town' ('oppidum exiguum', *Gesta Regum* 351. 1). In the same breath, he terms the city a 'holy storehouse' ('caeleste promptuarium', ibid. 353. 1) that now houses a mad and avaricious populace. In this passage, William not only proclaims his Romanness, he also displays it by referring to a line in Virgil's *Aeneid* (1. 282), the original context of which proclaims the eternity of the Roman Empire. With intentional irony, William redeploys this passage whilst commenting on the fall of Rome – by implication, Norman England assumes Rome's mantel. The correct performance of *romanitas* is an integral element of Roman identity, as is most evident in William's descriptions of British figures in Rome.

Roman Manners in Rome

The city of Rome is a recurring backdrop in William's historical writings. He records dozens of figures travelling from the British Isles to Rome, particularly kings, saints and bishops. William eulogises several characters for exhibiting their learning and eloquence in Rome, including Lanfranc (*Gesta Pontificum* 42. 3), Anselm (ibid. 52), Herbert Losinga (ibid. 74. 18), Wilfrid (ibid. 100 and 106), and Aldhelm (ibid. 219. 4).[9] For example, William records that Wilfrid learnt Roman customs ('Romanas consuetudines') in the Roman manner ('pro Romano more', *Gesta Pontificum* 100. 6–7) in the papal city. As an aged litigant, Wilfrid returns to Rome and answers his accusers with such eloquence that the Romans applaud him (ibid. 106. 1–2). Equally, on Anselm's arrival in Rome, Pope Urban II hails him as being supreme in the liberal arts throughout the Latin world (ibid. 52. 1). Anselm's brilliance becomes apparent during a council when the pope cries out for the archbishop's aid, declaring: 'Now, master, there is need of your knowledge

---

[8] For an overview of medieval attacks on Rome see J. Yunck, 'Economic conservatism, papal finance, and the medieval satires on Rome', in *Change in Medieval Society: Europe North of the Alps 1050–1500*, ed. S. Thrupp (New York, 1964), pp. 72–85; R. M. Thomson, 'The origins of Latin satire in twelfth-century Europe', *Mittellateinisches Jahrbuch* 13 (1978), 73–83.

[9] Anselm and Lanfranc were both Italian by birth, but William adopts them as honorary Normans.

and of the services of your eloquence' (ibid. 53. 2). William is keen to emphasise that Rome needs England and the English.

The figures that William imbues with Roman qualities are favoured characters in his narrative. Indeed, he is disappointed that the evidence for Bede's presence in Rome is uncertain (*Gesta Regum* 57). He believes that Bede travelled to the papal city, but he cannot prove it. Nonetheless, the mere prospect of this journey allows William to connect his intellectual idol to notions of ideal Roman oratory. In a familiar refrain, he states that Bede's learning was unsurpassed in the Latin world and that Rome was in great need of him. William then quotes Seneca the Elder's definition of a good orator ('An orator is a good man with skill in speech', *Controversiae* 1. pr. 9) before styling Bede as 'our orator of the Church' (*Gesta Regum* 59).

Wit, splendour, classical learning, erudition and eloquence, underpinned by supreme Latinity, were all crucial elements in emulating a Roman style, which in turn reflected ancient Roman character. The symbolism of conducting oneself in a Roman manner in Rome finds its fullest expression in a story about St Kenelm that William recorded twice (*Gesta Regum* 211 and *Gesta Pontificum* 156. 3–6). By examining William's reworking of an earlier *vita* in telling this story it is apparent how he crafts his own Roman identity and stresses Anglo-Norman appropriation of Rome.

St Kenelm and Roman eloquence

Kenelm was a ninth-century Mercian prince who probably died in battle, and was buried at the Benedictine abbey of Winchcombe in Gloucestershire.[10] His cult appears to date from the revival of the abbey by Oswald bishop of Worcester in 969.[11] Two Latin texts detail Kenelm's martyrdom, but William knew and used only the later version known as the *Vita et miracula* (*c.* 1066–75), which was probably produced by a monk of the abbey or possibly by the Flemish hagiographer Goscelin.[12] In this version, Kenelm is a child of seven years entrusted to his sister, who, in a bid for the throne, has the young prince murdered in a wood. This despicable crime remains unknown in England, and the whereabouts of Kenelm's body a mystery, until a miraculous event occurs in Rome (§10–11):

> For as Pope Leo the Younger[13] was celebrating the rites of mass in the presence of a multitude of people, behold a dove whiter than snow appeared from above

[10] D. H. Farmer, *The Oxford Dictionary of Saints* (5th edn, Oxford, 2004), pp. 279–80.
[11] W. Levison, *England and the Continent in the Eighth Century* (Oxford, 1946), pp. 252–8; R. Love, *Three Anglo-Latin Saints' Lives* (OMT, 1996), p. cxi.
[12] The first, a set of Lections, is known as the *vita brevior* (third quarter of the eleventh century). Love, *Anglo-Latin Saints' Lives*, pp. xc–xci, xciii–iv and xcvii–ci; P. A. Hayward, 'The idea of innocent martyrdom in late tenth- and eleventh-century English hagiology', in *Martyrs and Martyrologies*, ed. D. Wood (Studies in Church History 30: Oxford, 1993), pp. 81–92.
[13] This specific pope is difficult to identify. Love, *Anglo-Latin Saints' Lives*, p. 64 n. 4.

in the sight of everyone, and it carried in its gentle beak a snow-white parchment inscribed with golden letters in English, which it put down on the altar of St Peter, and then disappeared high into the sky.

The holy and apostolic father looks with trembling at the strange crisp sheet written all over with unfamiliar words and letters, and implores the throng of diverse nations flocking together to St Peter, to indicate whether anyone among them might understand anything of the text of this letter. There were, among the assembly of so many lands, a good number of Englishmen, even Mercians, either staying at the English school in Rome set up by former kings of the English people, or just recently arrived from England. By them the holy letter is read out, and its interpretation is as follows . . . .[14]

The passage continues by detailing the discovery of Kenelm's body. The sister and her accomplices are duly punished and various miracles are performed.

William's two versions of the story are nearly identical to one another, save for minor alterations in the word order; I quote from the *Gesta Regum*:

> Siquidem membrana super altare sancti Petri superne columba ferente delapsa necis et sepulchralis loci per ordinem index. Quae quia elementis Anglicis erat conscripta, a Romanis et aliarum gentium hominibus qui aderant frustra legi temptata. Sed salubriter et in tempore astitit Anglus, et linguae inuolucrum Latialiter Quiritibus euoluens effecit ut Apostolici epistola regibus Anglis compatriotam martirem indicaret.
>
> A parchment carried by a dove fluttered down upon the altar of St Peter's with precise details of [Kenelm's] death and burial-place which, being written in English characters, the Romans and men of other nationalities who were there tried in vain to read. By good luck an Englishman appeared in the nick of time, who untied the knot of language, speaking good Latin to those men of Rome, and ensured that a letter from the pope should make known to the English kings this martyr of their own nation.[15]

William's story concludes in similar fashion to that of its model, with the discovery and veneration of Kenelm's body and the punishment of his treacherous sister. Scholars have seldom compared the original text with William's reworking, which has been described as a 'freely written' version of the *Vita et miracula*.[16] William retains the overall sense of the earlier account, but he alters certain details in order to emphasise three crucial elements that I will now explore: (i) the Roman setting, (ii) the nameless translator and (iii) the translator's Roman manner. The overall effect of these revisions is to present the English as the rightful appropriators of Rome. More precisely, it will be proposed that in this story William assumes a Ciceronian identity.

---

[14] Ibid, pp. 64–7.
[15] GR 211. 1–2.
[16] Love, *Anglo-Latin Saints' Lives*, p. cxxxvii.

First, a significant portion of William's narrative focuses on the scene in Rome: almost a quarter of the *Gesta Regum* (22%) and *Gesta Pontificum* (23%) versions are devoted to the moment at St Peter's basilica, whereas the same episode in the *Vita Kenelmi* is a brief section in an extensive narrative. The Roman context of the story is important to William: Roman style acquires greater weight and purpose when demonstrated in Rome before the Romans. Second, William underlines the critical moment of translation. In the model text, the translation is a collective endeavour by 'a good many Englishmen', but instead William describes a single unidentified Englishman who 'untied the knot of language' (*Gesta Regum* 211. 2 and *Gesta Pontificum* 156. 5). The image of untying language is especially ornate and rhetorical.[17] Third, William uses unusual classical terminology to demonstrate the anonymous Englishman's exemplary Latin, which in turn reflects his own Latinity. He writes: the Englishman 'untied the knot of language, speaking good Latin ["latialiter"] to those men of Rome ["Quirites"]'. At this point the author's language requires close reading.

In both the *Gesta Regum* and *Gesta Pontificum*, William uses an uncommon yet telling word to describe the anonymous Englishman's Latin. He employs 'latialiter', a late Latin term meaning 'in Latin', or more specifically, as derived from 'latiatim': 'in the Roman manner, or according to the Roman custom'.[18] 'Latialiter' is rarely found in medieval British Latin texts: Ælfric Bata (*fl. c.* 1010), Osbern Pinnock of Gloucester (*fl.* 1150–75), who is known for his exotic language, and Ralph of Diss (d. *c.* 1199/1200) are the only other authors known to have used this term.[19] However, it appears to have been a favourite of William's. He also uses it in his *Historia Nouella* when describing a council held at Winchester in 1139. In this passage, Henry of Blois, bishop of Winchester, was officially declared papal legate in a letter from Pope Innocent II. Following this announcement, Henry made a speech: 'in Latin (in a Roman manner) to educated men' ('latialiter ad litteratos habitus').[20] The context is crucial to our understanding of William's language: the newly appointed papal legate is depicted as instantaneously speaking in the Roman tongue. The author describes the audience as men of culture, thereby suggesting that Henry's Roman eloquence was recognised by those present. William shapes his language to fit the context of the scene: voice is matched with meaning. In his retelling of Kenelm's life, William uses 'latialiter' in a similar way. The Englishman does not simply speak in Latin; he speaks in a Roman manner *in* Rome and *to* the citizens of Rome.

The precision of William's language is more apparent in the *Gesta Regum* version of Kenelm's life.[21] William initially describes the Romans as 'Romani', but

---

[17] For William's thoughts on translation see *GP* 80. 1 and 240. 5.
[18] *DML*, p. 1565.
[19] Ibid.; A. G. Rigg, *A History of Anglo-Latin Literature 1066–1422* (Cambridge, 1992), p. 62.
[20] *HN* 25 (my translation).
[21] 'Quirites' is only used in the former text – a rare difference between the *GR* and *GP* texts. Nonetheless, the sense of 'good Latin' ('latialiter') is retained in both versions.

at exactly the moment when the Englishman speaks to the crowd in Rome the terminology shifts in a subtle yet significant manner. William labels the Romans 'Quirites', a classical term used by an orator when addressing an assembly of people. Once more, William chooses the right terminology for the right moment.[22] Furthermore, Cicero favoured this word, which is rarely found in Anglo-Norman Latin literature.[23] The ancient Roman orator ranks alongside Virgil as one of William's prime antique models.[24] It has been estimated that William knew at least nineteen and perhaps as many as twenty-eight works by Cicero, and he produced a substantial compendium of Ciceroniana (CUL Dd. 13. 2).[25] William rarely quotes Cicero's work, but he consistently cites Cicero as *the* paradigm of eloquence. William extols him as the 'king of Roman eloquence' ('rex facundiae Romanae', *Gesta Regum* 132. 1) and as a figure 'whose brilliance makes him the idol of the Latin world' ('cuius adorat sales tota Latinitas', *Gesta Regum* bk 5 pr. 1).[26] The use of 'Quirites' in this scene should therefore be added to the known list of Ciceronian allusions in William's writing, but more importantly it illuminates William's layered descriptions of Anglo-Norman eloquence in Rome that essentially reveal his own Roman style.

William's modifications to the *Vita Kenelmi* emphasise the latinity of a single, nameless Englishman in Rome. William's sophisticated classical lexicon fits the context in two respects: first, he knows that his language is an appropriate way in which to address a crowd in Rome; and second, that Cicero – his model of rhetorical eloquence – favoured this term. In sum, the anonymous Englishman with a Ciceronian style is presented as a superior figure to the Romans.

Michael Winterbottom rightly posits the anonymous Englishman as a general model for William, who was similarly marshalling English history into a Latin idiom.[27] The story of Kenelm doubles as a metaphor for English history and culture, which William sought to preserve from oblivion (*Gesta Regum* bk 2 pr. 2). It is a tale of revelation, self-realisation and the resurrection of memory. The English had flocked to Rome to venerate the city's great saints, and yet unbeknown to them a holy saint lay hidden in their homeland. But Winterbottom's analogy may be pressed even further. William surely saw the nameless Englishman who spoke

---

[22] On the relationship between rhetorical ornamentation and context see M. Kempshall, *Rhetoric and the Writing of History, 400–1500* (Manchester and New York, 2011), p. 303.

[23] Livy also used this term frequently, but William does not appear to have known any Livy. Thomson, *William of Malmesbury*, p. 207; GR II, p. 459; GP II, p. 390. On the use of 'Quirites' see S. P. Oakley, *A Commentary on Livy*, I (Oxford, 1997), p. 697 and DML, p. 2636.

[24] Thomson, *William of Malmesbury*, pp. 48 and 141; idem, 'William of Malmesbury and the Latin Classics revisited', p. 386.

[25] Thomson, *William of Malmesbury*, pp. 51, 55–6 and 207.

[26] In the preface to his *Polyhistor* (lines 12–14), William criticises some of Cicero's writings, but this is in the context of being unsuitable for Guthlac's instruction. Elsewhere, William partly justified his use of pagan authors owing to their eloquence. Thomson, *William of Malmesbury*, pp. 29, 31 and 52; *Polyhist.*, p. 37; J. O. Ward, 'What the Middle Ages missed of Cicero, and why', in *Brill's Companion to the Reception of Cicero*, ed. W. H. F. Altman (Leiden, 2015), pp. 319–20.

[27] Winterbottom, 'The Language of William of Malmesbury', p. 132.

exemplary Latin as an idealised and demi-oblique personification of himself. When praising the character's oratory, William writes with an acute awareness of his own Ciceronian style. This is an extended example of William's reflective *romanitas*.

Debating with cardinals

Thus far, these scenes of high eloquence have all been intentionally located in Rome. William includes a few instances of Roman style beyond the city walls, but always in relation to Roman culture. For instance, Henry of Blois's Roman elocution and William's description of the archaeological remains at Carlisle both include classical Latin that fits the context. The most explicit comparison of Roman and Anglo-Norman culture is found towards the end of the *Gesta Regum* (406) when William reports a peace conference in Normandy between the kings of England and France. The same meeting is recorded by a number of contemporary historians, including Eadmer, Orderic Vitalis and Hugh the Chanter.[28] However, in contrast to these other accounts, William marginalises the politics of the event and instead recasts this meeting as a dialectical debate between young Norman nobles and the cardinals of Rome:

> and when it proved impossible by force of reasoning to withstand their volleys of argument, the cardinals were not ashamed to confess that these western territories had a far more flourishing literary culture than they had ever heard of or imagined in their own country. So the outcome of this meeting was a declaration by the pope [Calixtus II] that for the justice of his case, his eminent wisdom, and copious eloquence, the English king [Henry I] had no superior.

In this scene, William clearly sets out the Anglo-Norman inheritance of Rome that has been implicit throughout, and he also demonstrates it. The setting of a classically inspired dialectical debate presents an appropriate stage upon which the Norman aristocracy can perform in a Roman manner. Moreover, William replicates the debating skills of the Normans through his own rhetoric by referencing an appropriate passage from Cicero (*De Inuentione* 2. 48) on rhetorical amplification and argumentation in the preceding line (406. 1). Once more, Roman identity is appropriated by Norman figures through learning and eloquence and in contrast to the decline of the Romans (here represented by the cardinals).

From homage to parody: the appropriation of Roman identity

The literary appropriation of Roman character has a long history, but its medieval episode has received little attention.[29] William of Malmesbury's material is an

---

[28] GR II, p. 368.
[29] On this tradition and the lack of medieval examples, see C. Edwards, *Writing Rome: Textual Approaches to the City* (Cambridge, 1996), pp. 16–18 and 112–14. Greater attention has been given

early and especially sophisticated example of acquiring and projecting Roman identity. Indeed, literary expressions of *romanitas* are particularly pronounced in twelfth-century Anglo-Norman writings on Rome.

In his *Historia Pontificalis* (*c.* 1164–70), John of Salisbury includes a scene analogous to William's Ciceronian Englishman at St Peter's. In this passage, John describes a 'certain grammarian' ('quidam grammaticus') versed in Horatian satire who doubles as a persona of the author. The unnamed grammarian mocks Henry of Blois for purchasing antique statues in Rome using lines from Horace's *Satires* (2. 3. 16–17 and 64).[30] John likens Henry to the failed antiques dealer Damasippus, but the author's own Horatian self-identity has been overlooked. Henry of Blois is undoubtedly teased for his suspect antiquarian tastes, but the real punch line is aimed at the Romans. The two Anglo-Norman figures ridicule the citizens of Rome as undeserving of their antique heritage: the grammarian quips that by removing these idols the bishop was saving the Romans from their inveterate idolatry. John demonstrates his *romanitas* through a set of sophisticated allusions to an iconic Roman writer (Horace) delivered in the most Roman of genres (satire), and, symbolically, in Rome itself.[31]

An alternative example of appropriating classical Roman identity is found in Master Gregory's enigmatic and curious late twelfth-century description of Rome, entitled the *Narracio de Mirabilibus Urbis Romae*.[32] I read this text as a parodistic account of an English cleric who intentionally misreads Rome to humorous effect.[33] An early and effective illustration of the text's subversive nature is found in the opening chapter where Gregory surveys the city's panorama. When gazing down upon Rome, Gregory likens himself to Julius Caesar returning victoriously from Gaul and he self-importantly quotes lines from Lucan's *De Bello Ciuili* (3. 91–3, 1. 511–14 and 1. 199–200) to this effect.[34] Throughout the text, Gregory's classical learning is knowingly pompous and artfully misplaced, and on repeated occasions he ironically mocks the Romans for their ignorance. With great skill

---

to Anglo-Saxon evocations of *romanitas* than examples in the twelfth century, for example see N. Howe, *Writing the Map of Anglo-Saxon England: Essays in Cultural Geography* (New Haven and London, 2008), pp. 101–24.

[30] *Historia Pontificalis*, ed. and trans. M. Chibnall (2nd edn, OMT 1986), pp. 79–80. For a full discussion see W. Kynan-Wilson, 'Damasippus' craze: re-reading John of Salisbury's account of Henry of Blois in Rome', in *Henry of Blois: Patron, Prelate, Prince*, ed. W. Kynan-Wilson and J. M. Munns (forthcoming).

[31] See Quintilian (*Institutes* 10. 1. 93–5) on satire as a Roman genre.

[32] The text can be securely yet broadly dated to between 1118 and 1327, but I favour a late twelfth-century date owing to the tone of the text and its similarities with the *Mirabilia Urbis Romae* (dated *c.* 1143). See W. Kynan-Wilson, 'Rome and *Romanitas* in Anglo-Norman Text and Image, circa 1100–1250' (University of Cambridge, doctoral thesis 2013), pp. 91–162; Cf. *The Marvels of the City of Rome*, trans. J. Osborne (Toronto, 1987), pp. 10–15.

[33] To date, previous scholars have read Gregory's work as a serious albeit unusual description of Rome. For a detailed reading of this text as a parody see Kynan-Wilson, 'Rome and *Romanitas*', pp. 91–162.

[34] *The Marvels of the City of Rome*, pp. 18–19.

and knowledge of Rome, the author parodies Anglo-Norman visitors to the city who uttered classical quotations at every corner and assumed an antique persona.

In each instance, classical texts, specialised terms and rhetorical skill are used as indices of Roman identity: William as a Ciceronian orator, John of Salisbury with his Horatian mask, Henry of Blois as the foolish Damasippus and Master Gregory in the comic guise of Caesar. Indeed, there is a shift in the type of *romanitas* on display and the contexts in which it is found in these three Anglo-Norman texts: the concept of Roman identity transmutes from learned and nuanced homage in William's historical writings into an exaggerated and entertaining mode in Master Gregory's parody. The *Narracio* demonstrates just how established this rhetorical mode of displaying *romanitas* in Rome had become.

Conclusion: Rome as mirror

This paper has examined a series of passages in which William consistently describes eloquent and classically learned British figures in heightened contrast to the Romans: Anselm, Aldhelm, Lanfranc, Herbert Losinga, Wilfrid, the anonymous figure at the Vatican and the sons of Norman counts all fit this mould. Implicit in each example is William's own rhetorical skill and learning: his *romanitas* underpins that of others. Crucially, these scenes not only assert Romanness – they also display it. William does not want these claims to Rome to read as idle boasts. In this sense, the act of seasoning is as important as the Roman salt itself.

William's purpose in invoking *romanitas* in this manner appears to be twofold. First, this material offers an insight into William's self-identity as a writer. He wants to situate himself within a grander tradition of historical writing and literature that extends beyond local and national examples to the great writers of antiquity. Indeed, William identifies four figures as supreme examples of learning and eloquence within the Latin world: Cicero (*Gesta Regum* bk 5 pr. 1), Bede (ibid. 59. 1), Lanfranc (ibid. 267. 2 and *Gesta Pontificum* 24. 3) and Anselm (ibid. 52. 1 and 65. 5). To this list should be added Virgil, who William admired and referenced on many occasions. William does not openly induct himself into this pantheon, but the implication is clear and unavoidable. Far from feeling alienated and inferior in relation to Rome, William sought to be the equal of the ancients.[35]

Second, in addition to elevating his own status as a writer, William sought to elevate the standing of Anglo-Norman culture and its history. At important junctures in his *Gesta Regum* (bk 1 pr. 4 and 2 pr. 2), William laments the broken and forgotten nature of English history. William's mission is to show that writing English history is a worthwhile endeavour. He wants to counter what he views as the parochial, incomplete and inelegant state of English history. Through the

---

[35] 'William saw himself in a direct line of descent from the ancient writers he quotes and recalls, and as the equal of the historians among them.' Thomson, 'William of Malmesbury and the Latin Classics revisited', p. 391. Cf. idem, *William of Malmesbury*, p. 32.

projection and appropriation of Roman character William is able to elevate Norman history onto an international stage, to situate it within a grander tradition of European historiography and to imbue it with literary merit.[36]

In this way, Rome assumes a specular quality in William's writing: it is a mirror with which he implicitly compares and defines Norman England, as well as his own identity as a writer. In so doing, he aims to cast himself and his nation as the cultural appropriators of Rome. He was not alone in doing so. The emulation and appropriation of Rome is one of the grandest traditions of the medieval period, and William's Rome-seasoned histories are amongst the earliest and most sophisticated literary instances of this rich cultural phenomenon.

---

[36] On William and European historiographical tradition see Winterbottom, 'The language of William of Malmesbury', p. 132.

→ 8 ←

William of Malmesbury and the Chronological Controversy

Anne Lawrence-Mathers

WILLIAM OF MALMESBURY'S POSITION as cantor at Malmesbury received little attention in his brief autobiographical comments, and was consequently accorded little significance by later historians. However, the connection between the office of cantor and that of chronicler in the cases of several well-known English writers of the twelfth century has received increasing attention in recent years. As David Rollason has pointed out, Symeon of Durham's role of cantor or precentor (the terminology was variable) meant that he had overall responsibility for the monastic library, the scriptorium, and the complex arrangements associated with the recording and commemoration of the significant dead.[1] A similar point applies to Eadmer of Canterbury, who moved from hagiography to historical writing after his own period of service as cantor. The position of the cantor in relation to historical writing in the monasteries of Anglo-Norman England may never have been as powerful as it was in continental Europe, as argued by Miriam Fassler. Nevertheless, she traces a shift in the role during the eleventh century – namely, that the cantor took over the role of *armarius* or librarian and had fewer responsibilities for the technical aspects of musical performance – which also affected English houses.[2] William of Malmesbury's understanding of this role is currently being explored by Paul Hayward.[3]

However, whereas scholarly attention has focused on the role of the cantor/ *armarius* as custodian of books, liturgical observance and remembrance, this article will address a related, but distinct, aspect of the cantor's duties, namely, his need for expertise in computus, and the light this sheds on William's views on correct historical dating.

---

[1] D. Rollason, 'Symeon of Durham's *Historia de Regibus Anglorum et Dacorum* as a product of twelfth-century historical workshops', in *The Long Twelfth-Century View*, pp. 95–112.

[2] M. E. Fassler, 'The office of the cantor in early western monastic rules and customaries: a preliminary investigation', *Early Music History* 16/5 (1985), 29–51, at pp. 47–51.

[3] P. A. Hayward, 'William of Malmesbury as a cantor-historian', in *Medieval Cantors and their Craft: Music, Liturgy and the Shaping of History, 800–1500*, ed. K. Bugyis, A. Kraebel and M. Fassler (Woodbridge, 2017).

As cantor, William would have known that the timing of the monastic day was a highly technical matter closely tied to the timing and the cyclically varying details of the *Opus Dei*, based on the movements of the heavenly bodies. The ringing of the bells to signal the various canonical hours was a serious matter, which required the cantor's expert advice, since these hours were meant to be calculated on the basis that there should always be twelve hours between sunset and dawn and another twelve between dawn and sunset. The result was that the actual length of day and night hours varied constantly with the seasons, and that it was only at the equinoxes that all twenty-four hours were of the same length as one another. The hours of varying length were referred to as 'artificial' hours, and those of unvarying length as 'natural' or 'equinoctial' hours. That both types of hour were known in Anglo-Norman monasteries is clear, since relevant calendars have notes of the number of 'equinoctial' hours of darkness and of light in each twenty-four-hour period of each month, although regulations for the *Opus Dei*, and the parts of the monastic day organised around it, still apparently used 'artificial' hours. Equally, because the dating of Easter determined much of the ecclesiastical calendar, including the timing of the moveable feasts and Lent, a cantor had to understand the complex rules that governed the correct selection of the paschal full moon and of Easter Sunday.

Textbooks on computus, such as Bede's, set out rules and tables for such calculations over cycles of 532 years. The cantor, in order to do his job properly, needed a grasp of the mechanics of time, the calendar and the calculation of dates. William of Malmesbury's appreciation of the ramifications of time-calculation is apparent in his remarks on both ecclesiastical institutions and learned individuals. His comments on the removal of the New Minster, Winchester, to Hyde offer a small example, and one which William found interesting enough to repeat.[4] In the *Gesta Regum*, William tells of King Alfred's death, burial in Winchester Cathedral, and reburial in the grand church of the New Minster. These events took place two centuries before the removal of the New Minster to Hyde, and yet William inserts a comment on the latter at this point in his narrative. William's explanation is that the Old and New Minsters were so close to each other that the sound of services in one disturbed the other, suggesting that they took place at very similar times but did not exactly correlate. William hints that other factors were also involved in the decision to move the New Minster. Nevertheless, an occasion on which small differences in the timing of services played such a major role in the history of a powerful monastic community was of clear significance to the cantor-historian. In an age of clock time it is not obvious that calculations of timing for a service could differ between two institutions in the same city following the same Rule. However, in the period when time-keeping was dependent upon local observation of astronomical phenomena, small variations could very easily arise, and the cantor's sphere of activity would be most affected.

---

[4] *GR* 124; *GP* 78. 1–2.

William of Malmesbury and the Chronological Controversy

The importance which William of Malmesbury accorded to the calculation of time as a matter of both intellectual complexity and political significance is demonstrated by his description of the career and abilities of Bishop Robert of Hereford. The most relevant passage is in the entry for Hereford in the *Gesta Pontificum* (164. 1). Robert is described as very learned in all the liberal arts, but 'especially skilled with the abacus, the lunar computus and the courses of the stars across the heavens'. William's own familiarity with the most advanced writers in the field of computus and chronology is evident in his reference to Marianus Scotus, a leading expert on both who died in Mainz at the end of the eleventh century. It was Bishop Robert who brought to England Marianus's Chronicle, which contained many chronological calculations and arguments. William was sufficiently interested to note that Marianus had made an extensive study of the works of chronographers, and had as a result argued against the 'errors' made in the fundamental work of the sixth-century computist, Dionysius Exiguus. As William suggests, this was a brave and lonely eminence, since Dionysius's work had become the basis of both the Church calendar and the official dating of the Christian era. Nevertheless, William states that Marianus proved that Dionysius had contravened the 'evangelical truth', and that as a result, no fewer than twenty-two years had been lost from the correct reckoning of the Christian era. These years had been painstakingly recovered by Marianus and placed into the cycles of time calculated by computists and chronographers.

However, although William was convinced of the erudition and value of Marianus's work as a chronographer, he was considerably less positive about Marianus as a chronicler. He dismisses the chronicle that follows the chronology in Marianus's work as 'large and highly diffuse' ('magnam et diffusissimam'), and reports with satisfaction that Bishop Robert had not only brought the entire work to England but also done the world a service by extracting and communicating its key points. Robert compiled these into a short overview ('defloratio'), which William describes as more valuable than its prolix source. Strikingly, William not only admires the chronographical skills of Marianus and Robert, and understands the computistical and astronomical work which underpinned them, but also accepts that Marianus was correct in asserting that Dionysius's calculation of the Christian era was out by twenty-two years.

The phrase 'evangelical truth' ('evangelicam veritatem'), used by Marianus to support his calculations, and repeated by William, echoes Bede's use of the phrase 'Hebrew truth' in his fundamental *De Temporum Ratione*. Bede used this term to stress that his own calculations of the world era and the ages of the world were based securely upon the correct text of the Old Testament, as opposed to the faulty translation of the Septuagint. An example is provided by the first entry in Bede's World Chronicle, which constitutes Book V c. 66 of the *De Temporum Ratione*: 'The first Age of this world, then, is from Adam to Noah, containing 1,656 years according to the Hebrew Truth, and 2,242 according to the Septuagint'.[5] Bede was Marianus's precursor in another, even more fundamental way, since he noted (rather cryptically) that there was a problem with the computistical data given by Dionysius for the year of Christ's crucifixion. Bede says, in his chapter on 'The Years of the Lord's Incarnation' (c. 47), that the computist who wishes to find the year of the Lord's Passion should be able to do so if he tries hard enough, since the way to do it is known. Bede had explained that a complete, computistical Great Cycle comprises 532 years, after which all the astronomical and computistical details found in any given year will repeat. Bede's next step was to point out that year 1 of Dionysius's Great Cycle rather confusingly corresponded in its astronomical details to year 532 of the Incarnation, as Dionysius himself noted. This meant that the details for year 1 of the Christian era would be those of year 2 of the Cycle. Bede notes that Christ was thirty-three years old at the time of the Crucifixion, according to the Gospels. As he then states, anyone wishing to find the year equating to that of the Crucifixion should add 33+1 (=34) to 532.[6] It should be year 35 of Dionysius's Great Cycle, which would be the sixteenth year of the second nineteen-year, luni-solar cycle of the twenty-eight which make up a Great Cycle, and should therefore exhibit the details shown in that section of Dionysius's tables. The uncertainty was potentially worsened by the fact that the actual month and day of Christ's birth are not given in the Gospels, meaning that the relationship between a year in the Roman calendar (which would begin on 1 January) and a fully accurate 'year of the Incarnation' depended on the Church's fixing of the date of Christmas. In his own chronological writings Bede used Christmas Day as the start of each year 'of grace', and was followed widely in this, although the date of the Annunciation (25 March) was a popular rival.[7]

The way Bede proceeds in c. 47 shows that there remained a much worse problem: 'And so, with the Cycles of Dionysius open before you, if you find in the 566th year that *luna* 14 falls on Friday, and is the 8th kalends of April, then give thanks to God .... But if you fail to find such a year in the place you expected, blame the carelessness of the chronographers or, even better, your own slowness.' Bede's silence regarding the Cycle year puts the blame for any uncertainty onto the chronographers, whose alignment of Cycle years and Incarnation years might be faulty, or more simply onto the computist attempting to resolve all this data. Bede avoids spelling out that the relevant years in Dionysius's Cycle do not, in fact, have the correct details for the date of the Easter full moon as specified above. Just how high the stakes were in making the calculation is revealed in Bede's next sentence. He declares that it would be effectively heretical not to believe that the Crucifixion took place on a Friday, on the fifteenth day of the lunar month, on a date in the Roman calendar fixed by the doctors of the Church.[8] Bede, who

---

[5] Bede, *The Reckoning of Time*, trans. F. Wallis (Liverpool, 1999), p. 157.
[6] Ibid., pp. 127–9.
[7] C. R. Cheney, *Handbook of Dates* (corrected edn, London, 1970), pp. 1–5.
[8] Bede, *The Reckoning of Time*, pp. 128–9.

found himself facing accusations of heresy over his calculation of the world ages, and of the final one in particular, goes no further than this, but the requisite years in Dionysius's Cycle do not in fact display the necessary computistical data (as set out above). These were established by the Old Testament calculations for the Passover, the Gospels' testimony as to the days of the week on which the Crucifixion and Resurrection took place, and patristic views on the calendar dates of these days. It was therefore unfortunate that neither the year corresponding to 566 in Dionysius' Cycle nor the years on either side of it provided the days of the week, of the lunar month and of the solar year, specified by the Bible and the Church fathers.

This problem had, of course, not escaped the notice of computists between Bede and Marianus. Indeed, Abbo of Fleury proposed a solution at the beginning of the eleventh century: the necessary data could be found in the year usually regarded as year 12 of the Christian era.[9] However, such observations remained the preserve of specialists, and the 'scandal' was both potentially serious and without an obvious solution. In the absence of an agreed solution to this problem, the dominant practice was to maintain the status quo. Marianus's innovation was to point out, in full and technical detail, the nature and seriousness of the problem, and then not only to propose a solution but also to work it through. Like Abbo, he observed that all the requisite data could be found if one went back twenty-two years in the Cycle. He further accepted that doing so necessitated a recalculation of world history up to that point, as well as a redating of subsequent years, to make Cycle years, years AD and historical events correlate. Moreover, he carried out that work in his Chronicle, presenting his evidence throughout the narrative.[10] It was this thoroughness that made his chronological work so convincing to both Robert of Hereford and William of Malmesbury, even though they estimated his skill as an historical writer differently.

The *Gesta Regum* provides further evidence of the seriousness with which William treated Marianus's chronological work. In chapter 292 William repeats information about Marianus. He then criticises contemporary scholars, claiming that they either ignore new discoveries or condemn them as mere novelties, even when such discoveries are in accordance with truth. Both the context and the echo of Marianus's usage of the phrase 'evangelical truth' make it clear that this is the discovery most in question, and suggest strongly that William is convinced by Marianus's arguments.[11] However, his political awareness and appreciation of the effects of power are demonstrated by his conclusion to this passage. He observes, sadly, that knowledge cannot succeed on its own merits, but must have

---

[9] P. Verbist, *Duelling with the Past: Medieval Authors and the Problem of the Christian Era, c. 990–1135* (Turnhout, 2010); and P. Nothaft, *Dating the Passion: The Life of Jesus and the Emergence of Scientific Chronology* (Leiden, 2012).

[10] See P. Nothaft, 'An eleventh-century chronologer at work; Marianus Scottus and the quest for the missing twenty-two years', *Speculum* 88 (2013), 457–82.

[11] GR 292. For Marianus's work see Nothaft (as n. 9 above).

Discovering William of Malmesbury

the support of powerful patrons if it is to be accepted. Although pure knowledge might suggest that all dates should be adjusted forwards by twenty-two years (for instance, 1125 should become 1147) as Robert of Hereford strongly argued in his treatise on Marianus's work, William did not believe that a theoretical argument alone would bring about this change. William then tells a story about another learned computist and astronomer, his contemporary Walcher, prior of Malvern. Apparently confirming the lack of general interest in this advanced subject, the anecdote concerns not Walcher's ability to use an astrolabe and to draw up lunar tables, skills attested elsewhere, but rather his status as witness to the story of a miracle that took place at Fulda.[12] It is worth noting that Walcher himself carefully emphasised that his new tables were to be used for medical and other non-spiritual purposes, suggesting that he had no intention of criticising the lunar tables, which were part of established computistical practice. Taken together, these pieces of evidence from the *Gesta Regum* show that William, as a chronographer, fully understood Marianus's work and was convinced by it, even though, when writing as an historian, he bowed to established practice.[13]

No chronicle survives from twelfth-century Hereford, but any scholar trained under Robert of Hereford would have been well versed in Marianus Scotus's new dating system. Their solution to the problem of having two dating systems would presumably have been the same as that of John of Worcester, whose own bishop and patron, Wulfstan (bishop 1062–95) was a close friend of Robert of Hereford. John used both dating systems in his own chronicle, giving priority to that of Marianus.[14] William of Malmesbury, whose works were more directly addressed to secular patrons than was the Worcester chronicle, was more circumspect: despite his comments on the strengths of Marianus's work, he used only the established dates. However, the twelfth-century compendium of computus texts and materials from Malmesbury, now Oxford, Bodl. Libr., MS Auct. F. 3. 14, provides evidence that he too studied and perhaps even taught Marianus's system at Malmesbury. The volume not only contains William's handwriting but also his preliminary inscription on its flyleaf (now f. ii^v). This short poem testifies to the importance which William attributed to the highly technical contents of the volume: 'Ecclesiae codex multarum materiarum/Sicut ager plenus variarum delitiarum / Willelmi nomine faciet post funera clarum' ('This, the Church's book of many materials, is like a field full of various delights, and will bring renown to William's name after his death'). This is no small claim for a set of technical treatises, and it is one that William composed and wrote out himself.

---

[12] GR 293.
[13] For Walcher, see C. H. Haskins, *Studies in the History of Medieval Science* (Cambridge MA, 1924), pp. 113–20; for comment on the lunar tables see R. Mercier, 'Astronomical tables in the twelfth century', in *Adelard of Bath; an English Scientist and Arabist of the Early Twelfth Century*, ed. C. Burnett (London, 1987), pp. 87–118, at 113–14.
[14] For brief comment on this see *The Chronicle of John of Worcester: Vol. II: The Annals from 450–1066*, ed. and trans. R. R. Darlington, J. Bray and P. McGurk (OMT 1995), pp. xviii–xix.

The first step in seeking an explanation for William's high estimation of this volume is to review the contents and the physical evidence of the manuscript itself.[15] A contents list, probably by William, includes: Isidore's *De Natura Rerum* and Bede's work of the same name, Bede's *De Temporibus, De Equinoctio*, and *De Temporibus II* (now known as *De Temporum Ratione*), the computistical treatise of Helperic, two letters on the calculation of Easter (used by Dionysius but here copied separately), two 'letters' by Dionysius himself, an anonymous *Ciclus Magnus Paschae, Liber Rotberti Hereforde Episcopi de Annis Domini*, Hyginus's *De Spera Celesti*, and a collection of anonymous texts on the astrolabe here called *Regulae de Astrolabio*. This list is interesting both for its information and for the unusual presentation of standard texts. Only small selections from Dionysius's fundamental work are included. The fact that the letters of Dionysius are immediately followed by the tables for the Great Cycle suggests that the tables will also be his – but they are actually those of Marianus, as will be shown later. The ambiguity appears to be deliberate, since Marianus is not named, and Robert of Hereford's treatise in support of Marianus's arguments is described here simply as dealing with 'annis Domini'. There appears to be a deliberate progression in the texts' arrangement, from material things, to time and the dating of the fundamental events of the Christian era, and finally to the heavenly sphere and the tool with which it may be observed and analysed.

There is further evidence of planning for the volume in a preface of sixteen lines, entered onto f. 1r before the work of Isidore, but not identifiable as part of the preface for any of the texts in the volume. It addresses the reader using the first person plural and sets out key points relating to the origin and significance of the art of 'number or computus' ('haec ars quae numerus uel compotus dicitur'). One of its important assertions is that the art of computus is a branch of philosophy which began with the Chaldeans, Hebrews and Egyptians and was adopted by the Greeks and Romans. The author also asserts that computus involves the study of the various signs and names given to numbers. Only once these points have been grasped, the author seems to suggest, can the study of time and its divisions be properly undertaken. This is emphasised by the final sentence of the preface: 'Deinde etiam oportune interrogandum est quot sunt diuisiones temporis' ('Thereafter fittingly the number of the divisions of time should also be investigated'). Although the preface does not appear to be in William's own hand, his personal interest in the volume, and the preface's similarity to others in William's works suggest that he may have composed it. For instance, William uses the introduction to his *Miracles of the Virgin* (admittedly much longer) to set out the evidence provided by earlier writers, before moving on to point out the need for a text which will address a new type of reader and user.[16]

---

[15] For description and analysis see Thomson, *William of Malmesbury*, pp. 83–5.
[16] *MBVM*, pp. 13–15.

William's authorship of this preface must remain uncertain, but his interest in providing both background information and notes on textual selection is established.[17] The historical approach taken in the preface, demonstrating the antiquity of the study of numbers and computus, leads into the apparently historical organisation of the first texts in the collection. First of all comes a letter by Isidore of Seville, here used as an additional element of the preface. As would be expected of a volume edited by William of Malmesbury, the selection of works by Bede is both full and clearly articulated, with no confusion between his two works on time and its calculation, as was often the case. Examples are too numerous to list, but Cambridge, St John's College A. 22, is representative. In this high-quality manuscript from Reading Abbey, datable to *c.* 1132, Bede's shorter and longer works are elided in both its contents list and the headings in the text itself. After this very standard opening to the collection, a surprise is encountered on f. 120(B)r, where the anonymous tables for the Great Cycle begin. These cover 532 years in the usual fashion, by providing twenty-eight tables of nineteen years each. The obvious expectation is that they will be the tables of Dionysius Exiguus, as updated by Bede, but this is not the case. Instead, notes added at the top of the first set express a degree of scepticism about Dionysius's work. The 'current' cycle is identified as that 'in which we are' and its first year is given as 1064 'according to Dionysius'. Still more remarkable, the repeated use of the phrase 'according to Dionysius' suggests doubt about the accuracy of the identification of the Great Cycle in which Christ was born. The point is that the year of Christ's birth would be year 2 of a Great Cycle calculated by Dionysius, as Bede had shown. Thus, if Marianus's recalculation were accepted and the Incarnation moved back by twenty-two years, Christ would have been born late in the preceding Great Cycle – a rather major difference.

Equally significant is a note in red, placed in the left hand margin and starting beside year 2: 'Incarnatio iuxta dionisium in anno xxiii incar[nationis] secundum historiam evangelii' ('The Incarnation according to Dionysius in the twenty-third year of the Incarnation according to the Gospel narrative'). This calculation implies the application of Marianus's earlier date for the Incarnation; the scepticism expressed about Dionysius's dates, and the support for Marianus's arguments, are both very clear. The source of these notes is suggested by those found in the equivalent positions in the Great Cycle Tables in the partly autograph copy of John of Worcester's chronicle which is now Oxford, Corpus Christi College 157.[18]

The first runs: 'Incarnatio iuxta dionysium in anno viii tiberii cesaris; hoc est in anno xxiii incarnationis secundum historiam evangelii' ('The Incarnation according to Dionysius in the eighth year of Tiberius Caesar; this is in year 23 of the Incarnation according to the Gospel narrative'). The Worcester tables, like

---

[17] See Thomson, *William of Malmesbury*, pp. 32–3.
[18] The manuscript is described in R. M. Thomson, *A Descriptive Catalogue of the Medieval Manuscripts of Corpus Christi College, Oxford* (Cambridge, 2011), pp. 82–3.

those in the Malmesbury manuscript, enlist Bede as an expert who disagreed with Dionysius, even though they demonstrate that Bede's calculation was different. An entry in the same hand as that against year 2, though here in black, identifies year 10 as that of the 'Incarnatio iuxta Bedam'.[19] Against year 13, in red and in the left margin, is a note stating: 'Resurrectio Christi vi kal. aprilis luna xvii teste evangelio' ('Resurrection of Christ on 6 kal. April [27 March] and day 17 of the lunar month, according to the Gospel'). A careful comparison of the Great Cycles of time was being undertaken at Worcester, as is shown by an instruction in red, in the same hand, at the bottom of p. 56: 'Gesta prioris cicli ad sinistram require; secundi vero ad dextram; gamma notat tertium sic: Γ' (Look for the events of the first Cycle on the left; those of the second Cycle on the right; and gamma marks those of the third Cycle thus: Γ). This system has been carefully applied in Corpus 157, with events of both the second and third Cycles entered into the right-hand margin, and gammas identifying those of the third Cycle.

Even the more guarded Malmesbury version of the tables makes its allegiance to Marianus clear in its annotation against year 13 of the Cycle. Like that to year 2, it is in red; and its wording is identical to that in Corpus 157. Further evidence is provided by the note to the twenty-seventh of the twenty-eight nineteen-year tables, found on f. 132r of Auct. F. 3. 14. Here an entry states that this should be the true year of the Incarnation 'according to the Gospel', just where Marianus's work would place it. Moreover, the same enquiry into possible patterns of events across the three Great Cycles was apparently pursued at Malmesbury, and is represented in the tables in the same way. Events which took place in the first Cycle are noted in the left margin, those which happened in the second Cycle in the right, and those in the third and 'current' cycle are on the right but identified by an upper-case gamma. An example is provided by year 3 where, on the right, is entered: 'Γ Regis willelmi adventus in anglia' (Third Cycle: Arrival of King William in England).

Neither William nor John was simply copying the work of the other, since Corpus 157 omits the entry for William the Conqueror, noting instead: 'Γ Obit Eadwardus rex anglorum / Normanni venerunt in angliam. A quibus haroldus rex anglorum occisus est' (Third Cycle: Death of Edward, king of the English. The Normans came to England. They killed Harold, king of the English). BL, Cotton Nero C. V is a copy of Marianus's Chronicle which provides further evidence of William's allegiance to Marianus's recalculation of time and history. This copy derives from Marianus's autograph (now BAV, Pal. lat. 830). It is believed to have been brought to England by or for Robert of Hereford himself, and was certainly at Hereford Cathedral by c. 1150.[20] Its Great Cycle tables represent the ultimate

---

[19] This calculation by Bede is based upon the fact that the year accepted as AD 42 offered a Crucifixion date of 23 March; if this were accepted as the year of the Passion then the year of the Nativity would be AD 8/9, which would be year 9/10 of the Cycle. I am very grateful to Philipp Nothaft for his generous discussion of this and other points.

[20] M. Gullick, 'The English-owned manuscripts of the *Collectio Lanfranci* (s. xi/xii)', in *The*

origin of those in both the Malmesbury and the Worcester manuscripts. The tables begin on f. 17^v of this section of the manuscript, and they and their headings are the same as those found in Corpus Christi 157. The note against year 2, entered into the left margin, is the same as that in the Worcester manuscript, as are the notes against year 10. Similarly, the explanation at the bottom of the page, concerning the representation of the chosen events of the three Cycles, is the same, including the use of Γ. In this version, however, fewer events of the third Cycle have been entered. This close correspondence between the copies of the tables in the three manuscripts does not enable identification of the immediate source of the Malmesbury copy, but it does confirm William's belief in Marianus's calculation of the correct Christian era.

This interest in patterns and cycles of time is clearly inherent in computus, but is especially strong in the work of Marianus and Robert, as is shown by the headings to the chapters of Robert's treatise, listed on f. 133r of Auct. F. 3. 14. Chapter Eight is here described as demonstrating that the Incarnation, and the Redemption carried out by Christ (here called the Second Adam), took place on the same day of the week as the Creation and Fall of the First Adam ('De congruitate incarnationis et redemptionis per secundum adam in eadem feria in qua primus adam creatus et transgressus est'). Chapter Fifteen moves on to the more advanced consideration that the Fall and the Redemption took place on the same day of a solar month.

For Marianus and Robert the establishment of these points of reference was part of the quest to establish the correct dating of the Incarnation and thus of the Christian era. Chapter Seven demonstrates this through its discussion of how the information concerning the weekday, the day of the lunar month, and the date in the solar calendar of Christ's Passion and Resurrection can be used to ascertain the date of the Incarnation and the number of years which have elapsed since it took place. However, for William of Malmesbury and John of Worcester, the wider analysis of cycles of time was clearly also an important part of the research inspired by the new dating of these fundamental events. Such an interest was not new: Bede's *Hymn on the First Six Days and Six Ages of the World* is just one of many works exploring related parallels.[21] Bede found it striking that God created and illuminated the world on the First Day and that this giving of light to its inhabitants initiated the First Age. In a similar way, the Second Day saw the placing of the world in the midst of the waters, just as the Second Age was begun when Noah's Ark was placed in the midst of the earthly waters of the Flood. Bede's own career had demonstrated the perils of such calculations, since it was because of his supposedly erring calculation of the Sixth Age (and thus the end of earthly time), set out in both his works on Time, that he was accused of heresy.[22]

Legacy of M. R. James, ed. L. Dennison (Donington, 2001), pp. 99–117, at 104–5.

[21] See Bede, *On the Nature of Things and On Times*, trans. C. B. Kendall and F. Wallis (Liverpool, 2010), pp. 180–5.

[22] For recent discussion see P. Darby, *Bede and the End of Time* (Farnham, 2012), pp. 36–42.

The early medieval controversy over the world ages was no longer an issue in William's time; but Marianus's fundamental challenge to the established system of dating had the potential to be just as controversial. William's handling of this problem was strategic. He accepted the work of Marianus and Robert in the context of the technical works collected together in Auct. F. 3. 14 but retained the standard system in his chronicles. This prudent procedure shows both the depth of his interest in the issues at stake and his awareness of what would and would not be generally acceptable outside the circle of specialists.

Equally significant evidence of William's acceptance of Marianus's and Robert's arguments is the placement of these subversive tables at the heart of William's collection of computistical texts and immediately before his copy of Robert of Hereford's treatise making the case for Marianus's work. This is one of eleven known copies of all or part of the work, almost all of which originated in England.[23] Copies were held at Durham and Worcester as well as Malmesbury and presumably at Hereford (although no copy with this provenance has been identified). The version in Auct. F. 3. 14 is complete, and includes an account of the Domesday Survey[24] found in only four other copies.[25] The rest omit Domesday, but have a chapter on the Paschal Great Cycle not found in the first group and not taken from Marianus. The Domesday account is found in a shorter form as an addition to the text of Marianus Scotus's Chronicle in BL, Cotton Nero C. V (at f. 158v). It is clear, therefore, that there were two versions of Robert's text, and that Malmesbury's copy is of what might be called the 'English Edition'.[26]

What matters for this enquiry is that William, in compiling a volume of computistical works for his abbey at a fairly early stage in his own career and probably soon after a visit to Worcester, chose to include Marianus's and Robert's work on dating.[27] It is equally significant that he placed Robert's treatise alongside a set of tables for the Great Cycle which also derives from the work of Marianus, and which seems to have been available in England only at Hereford, Worcester and Durham.

Taken together, these points make it almost certain that William, a computist-chronicler like John of Worcester and Symeon of Durham, was so impressed by this material that he chose to incorporate it into his collection of fundamental texts on natural philosophy and computus. His removal of all reference to the name

---

[23] See G. Schmidt, 'Le récit sur le recensement de 1086 et la tradition manuscrite de l'*Excerptio Roberti de Chronica Mariani Scotti*', at https://www.academia.edu/14660689/Le_r%C3%A9cit_sur_le_recensement_de_1086_et_la_tradition_manuscrite_de_l_Excerptio_Roberti_de_Chronica_Mariani_Scotti (and forthcoming) (accessed 17/01/2016).

[24] See W. H. Stevenson, 'A contemporary description of the Domesday Survey', *EHR* 22 (1907), 72–84.

[25] See n. 23.

[26] For brief discussion of Marianus's chronicle and its influence see H.-W. Goetz, 'The concept of time in the history of the eleventh and twelfth centuries', in *Medieval Concepts of the Past*, ed. G. Althoff, J. Fried and P. Geary (Cambridge, 2002), pp. 139–66, at 145–6.

[27] Thomson, *William of Malmesbury*, pp. 5 and 83–5.

of Marianus, and his careful presentation of Robert's text, are both explained by his awareness of the lack of support for such a bold redating of the Christian era. The very fact of this awareness makes William's decision to give his support to the technical accuracy of Marianus's chronology all the more important. William's belief in Marianus's arguments is demonstrated by his decision to have both the tables (with their controversial assertions) and the supporting treatise copied into 'his' volume, and by the value attributed to the contents of the volume in his verse inscription. The evidence of this manuscript suggests that William was convinced of the troubling 'fact' that the Christian era, and thus the current date, was wrong by twenty-two years.

The textual contents of the volume are given additional emphasis and status by the presence of unusual illuminations. Of these, the most complex is sketched out on f. 19v. This image is placed between Isidore's *De Natura Rerum* and Bede's work of the same name, and appears to be an elaboration of the standard 'T-O' style of world map, which frequently accompanied Isidore's work. In Auct. F. 3. 14, however, four medallions dominate the diagram, containing a sketched bust of Christ, two anonymous profile busts, and the head and hands of an *orans* figure. Although the image is unfinished, it evokes simple *mappae mundi* and appears to echo images of the Crucifixion. It thus encapsulates the volume's repeating theme of the cycles of time and salvation history and, by its very presence, provides further proof of the unusual importance given to this collection of technical works.

Another, less complete, diagram is found on f. 4r, at the end of Isidore's discussion of the month. This diagram is comparable in layout to those found in other copies of Isidore's work, but is not identical in detail to any in the manuscripts examined for this study. The unfinished nature of these images is puzzling, since the one on f. 19v at least is the work of a skilled draughtsman and the iconography is ambitious. The simplest explanation is that the limner was available for only a limited period, and so unable to finish the work; indeed, the volume seems to have been produced under some pressure of time. Some of its vellum is rather rough, and the number of contributing scribes is high, both of which suggest that the book needed to be produced quickly.[28] This may suggest a special enthusiasm on William's part, and perhaps a desire to involve other members of his house in the project.

A further piece of evidence that William was enthusiastic about this volume and its contents is provided by the notes of important events in Cycle 3, inserted into the margins of the tables of the Great Cycle from f. 120(B)r to f. 132v: they continue throughout most of William's own life, but go no further than this. The last such entry is noted against the last year of the fourth nineteen-year table. In the standard calculation of the Christian era, this would equate to *c.* 1140. The level of William's care for this section of the volume is shown by the thoroughness of the corrections to Robert of Hereford's text. These included changing the names

---

[28] See n. 15.

of the authorities cited (e.g. from Daniel to Ezechiel, in Chapter Ten) and may be in William's own hand.

Overall, the evidence of Auct. F. 3. 14 makes it clear that William regarded what might be called 'the chronological controversy' as both a matter for specialists, and something of great significance for those who understood it. On a more practical level, he also accepted that the radical suggestions put forward by Marianus and Robert were not likely to be popular in the wider world. Thus his own historical writings still used the established dating system, although he cared enough to record for posterity his sorrow about the fact that scientific accuracy was subordinate to political power.

9

William of Malmesbury and Durham: The Circulation of Historical Knowledge in Early Twelfth-Century England

Stanislav Mereminskiy

TODAY, WILLIAM OF MALMESBURY is considered not only the most erudite and well-read historian of the Anglo-Norman age, but also one of the best travelled. Rodney Thomson, in his invaluable commentary on the *Gesta Pontificum Anglorum*, gives a list of some thirty-six places in England, Wales and Normandy definitely or presumably visited by the Malmesbury historian.[1] There can be no doubt that much of the information in some of William's works, including the *Gesta Pontificum*, *Gesta Regum*, *De Antiquitate Glastonie Ecclesie* and *Vita Wulfstani*, derives from first-hand experience. Antonia Gransden considered William's work the prime example of 'realistic observations' and thought it 'likely that most (perhaps all) of William's descriptions were based on personal observation, not hearsay'.[2] Similarly, S. B. Wright claimed that 'personal travel experience is omnipresent' in the *Gesta Pontificum* and stressed 'William's emphasis on eyewitness experience'.[3] However, it is only for a handful of these places that William presents us with evidence that he visited them in person. In fact, in the *Gesta Pontificum* only once does William state that he personally saw the site he describes:[4] the church at Sherborne, thought to have been built by Aldhelm.[5] Of course, this limited direct testimony does not mean that we should take a hypercritical point of view and turn William into a sort of armchair scholar. For

---

[1] *GP* II, pp. xli–xliii.
[2] A. Gransden, 'Realistic observation in twelfth-century England', *Speculum* 47 (1972), 34.
[3] S. B. Wright, 'The soil's holy bodies: the art of chorography in William of Malmesbury's *Gesta Pontificum Anglorum*', *Studies in Philology* 111 (2014), 664–5.
[4] William also personally attests some miracles performed by saints: Swithhun of Winchester (*GP* 75. 43) and Ivo of Ramsey (181. 9–10), but he does not say where he met the beneficiaries of those miracles. He also describes some miracles at the tomb of St Aldhelm at Malmesbury, which he saw in person (273–8).
[5] Ibid. 225. 1: 'habuitque sedem Scireburniae, ubi et aecclesiam, quam ego quoque uidi, mirifice construxit'.

many places, such as Canterbury, Glastonbury and Worcester, the sheer volume and nature of his information make it almost certain that William had been there in person. But in other cases, close scrutiny of his text demonstrates William's heavy dependence on written sources.

The greater weight of written material can be traced, for example, in his account of regions of northern England. William Kynan-Wilson recently demonstrated that the descriptions of churches in Ripon and Hexham in the fourth book of the *Gesta Pontificum* (100. 22–3 and 117. 1) are almost entirely based on a single literary source, the *Vita Sancti Wilfridi* by Stephen of Ripon.[6] The famous description of Roman remains in Carlisle – including an inscription of 'Marii uictoriae' (99. 3–4) on the front of a triclinium, although it has no parallels in known written sources – also exhibits, according to Kynan-Wilson, a large number of bookish *topoi* and clichés, for example, from the famous poem on Rome by Hildebert of Lavardin (c. 1055–1133). William used those descriptions to stress his idea of the present dilapidated state of northern England set against its former glory.[7] In addition, he was probably eager to show off his classical erudition, for instance by using an exotic word like *triclinium* or interpreting the inscription 'Marii uictoriae' so as to identify the Cumbrians with the old Germanic tribe of the Cimbri, defeated by the Roman general Marius in 101 BC.[8] In fact, during a survey at Carlisle Castle in 1987, archaeologists found a portion of a third-century Roman altar with fragments of a dedicatory inscription to various Roman gods by a military tribune, Marcus Aurelius Syrio. When it was discovered, the stone was being used as the lintel of the door into the solar of De Ireby's Tower. According to the archaeologists, it had probably been in that place since the end of the thirteenth century. Because the stone shows signs of exposure to weather, it must have been somewhere outdoors before that time, that is, it could have been visible to an early twelfth-century observer.[9] The altar shows signs of burning, which Kynan-Wilson associates with William's idea that an attempt had been made to burn the *triclinium*.[10] It is noteworthy that William recorded only a part of the inscription. Kynan-Wilson's idea that it was intentional selection for narrative purposes appears reasonable but there is an alternative possibility: that William received the information about the inscription at second hand, maybe even by hearsay. We will return to such a possibility later.

---

[6] W. Kynan-Wilson, '*Mira Romanorum artifitia*: William of Malmesbury and the Romano-British remains at Carlisle', *Essays in Medieval Studies* 28 (2012), 37.

[7] Cf. also William's comments on the same in *GR* 54. 1–2: 'Plaga, olim et suaue halantibus monasteriorum floribus dulcis et urbium a Romanis edificatarum frequentia renidens, nunc uel antiquo Danorum uel recenti Normannorum populatu lugubris, nichil quod animos multum allitiat pretendit'.

[8] Ibid. 37–44.

[9] R. S. O. Tomlin and R. G. Annis, 'A Roman altar from Carlisle Castle', *Transactions of the Cumberland and Westmoreland Antiquarian and Archaeological Society* 89 (1989), 77 (with photograph of the stone).

[10] Kynan-Wilson, '*Mira Romanorum artifitia*', p. 38.

Another chorographic piece in the third book of the *Gesta Pontificum*, a brief but elegant description of Durham, has strong parallels with a written source as well. The passage is worth quoting *in extenso*:

> Durham is a hill, gradually and with a gentle slope swelling up from the level plain. Though, thanks to its lofty site and precipitous cliffs, it bars the approach of any enemy, moderns have sited a castle on the top. Below, at the castle foot, flows a river rich in fish, like many or indeed almost all of those in Northumbria. For salmon are superabundant in the west and north of England, so much so that the local peasants feed their pigs on discarded fish.[11]

It is striking that the main part of this description has a close parallel in the first six lines of the famous Old English poem *De situ Dunelmi et de sanctorum reliquiis quae ibidem continentur carmen compositum* (or simply *Durham*):

> Is ðeos burch breome   geond Breotenrice,
> steppa gestaðolad,   stanas ymbutan
> wundrum gewæxen.   Weor ymbeornad,
> ea yðum stronge,   and ðer inne wunað
> feola fisca kyn   on floda gemonge.[12]
>
> The city is famous throughout the kingdom of Britain,
> built on high, the rocks around it
> wondrously grown up. The Wear runs round it,
> a stream strong in waves, and within it dwell
> many kinds of fish in the thronging of the waters.[13]

In both descriptions we have basically the same elements: a lofty rocky hill, a strong castle built on that cliff, and a river under the hill that is rich with fish. The only independent detail in the *Gesta Pontificum*, an anecdote about Northumbrian peasants feeding their pigs with salmon, looks like a perfect example of hearsay used to embellish an image of a region abundant with natural resources, but rather uncivilised. The poem *Durham* now survives in a unique manuscript (CUL Ff. 1. 27, p. 202), probably made in Durham c. 1188.[14] Previously, there existed a second copy in another twelfth-century manuscript (in the Cotton collection)

---

[11] GP 130. 8: 'Dunelmum est collis, ab una uallis planitie paulatim et molli cliuo turgescens in cumulum. Et licet situ edito et prerupto rupium omnem aditum excludat hostium, tamen ibi moderni collibus imposuerunt castellum. Ad radices pedis castelli defluit amnis piscosus, ut pleraque et omnia pene Northaimbrie flumina. Ita enim istius in patribus occidentalibus et aquilonalibus Angliae superfluit ut rustici proiectis piscibus sues pascant.' Trans. M. Winterbottom.
[12] T. O'Donnell, 'The Old English *Durham*, the *Historia de sancto Cuthberto*, and the unreformed in late Anglo-Saxon literature', *Journal of English and Germanic Philology* 113 (2014), 132.
[13] Translation by T. O'Donnell (ibid., 133).
[14] On the probable dating and original composition of that manuscript see C. Norton, 'History, wisdom and illumination', in *Symeon of Durham: Historian of Durham and the North*, ed. D. Rollason (Stamford, 1998), pp. 61–105.

of probable Durham origin,[15] but the leaf with the poem perished in the fire of 1731. Fortunately, before the fire, Rev. G. Nicholson, archdeacon of Carlisle, transcribed the text of *Durham* from that manuscript, and it was published in 1705 by George Hickes.[16] There are also some early modern transcripts, but Daniel O'Donnell has demonstrated that they all derive from the Cambridge manuscript and therefore they are of no independent value.[17] The poem was traditionally dated *c.* 1104–7, as it is mentioned in Symeon of Durham, *LDE*,[18] but recently Thomas O'Donnell has argued for an earlier date, *c.* 1050–83, that is, prior to the monastic reform at Durham.[19]

William was sufficiently skilled in Old English to have translated Coleman's vernacular *Life of St Wulfstan* into Latin. He also made use of other texts in Old English, including the *Anglo-Saxon Chronicle*, and the Old English translation of the Rule of St Benedict. So it is possible that he knew the poem *Durham* despite its limited circulation, and that he used it for his description of Durham. The evidence may not be strong enough to claim this with certainty; but what we can say without doubt is that William's description of Durham, like the ones of Ripon, Hexham and Carlisle, is laced with images that had a literary origin.

It is impossible to prove beyond doubt that William read or had in his possession any text of Durham origin. Of course, *Gesta Pontificum* 129–35 reveal numerous parallels with various Durham historical texts, foremost *LDE* and a collection of the miracles of St Cuthbert. There are virtually no direct quotations, but that is not unusual for William of Malmesbury's works. As Thomson points out, 'William may have spoken with Symeon, or taken notes from him, rather than having the work at his elbow'.[20] In this section, in addition to some material from Bede's *Historia Ecclesiastica* and prose *Life of St Cuthbert*, and a couple of quotations from Alcuin's letters concerning the devastation of Lindisfarne by the Danes in 793, William presents a series of anecdotes: on the wanderings of the saint's relics during the first wave of Viking invasion (129), on St Cuthbert's appearance to King Alfred (130. 1–4), on his prophecy to the future bishop, Edmund (130. 5–7), and on the sudden rain during the saint's translation in 1104 (135). Their source is difficult to establish. With the list of Lindisfarne and Durham bishops in the *Gesta Pontificum* one reaches more solid ground. William's list is virtually the same as that which appears among the preliminary materials to John of Worcester's Chronicle; on the other hand it differs from sources of certain or probable Durham origin: *LDE*, the tract *De Primo Saxonum Aduentu*, and the list added in the early

---

[15] Now BL Cotton Vitellius D. XX + Miscellaneous Burnt Cotton Fragments, Bundle I.

[16] *Linguarum Veterum Septentrionalium Thesaurus Grammatico-Criticus et Archæologicus* (2 vols, Oxford, 1705), I, pp. 178–9.

[17] D. P. O'Donnell, 'Junius's knowledge of the Old English poem *Durham*', *ASE* 30 (2001), 231–45.

[18] Symeon of Durham, *LDE* III. 7 (p. 166): 'illud Anglico sermone compositum carmen ubi cum de statu huius loci, et de sanctorum reliquiis que in eo continentur agitur'.

[19] T. O'Donnell, 'The Old English *Durham*'.

[20] *GP* II, p. 182.

twelfth century at Christ Church Canterbury to the 'Parker manuscript' of the *Anglo-Saxon Chronicle*.[21]

If William had access to a full text of *LDE*, it is puzzling that he decided to omit a great deal of it, including subjects that might have been of obvious interest for him, such as the story of the great Gospel-book, now known as the Lindisfarne Gospels. Thomson also notes that William 'clearly had no idea that the bishopric was at Chester-le-Street, 883–995,'[22] though it is clearly stated in *LDE* and the *Historia de Sancto Cuthberto*. In fact, we cannot claim that William consulted *any* books from the cathedral library of Durham, even though the library obviously had some volumes that could have attracted the attention of a bibliophile like William of Malmesbury, such as the books associated with Bede, whom William fervently admired. Of obvious interest to William would have been the early twelfth-century codex containing Regino of Prüm's Chronicle and the *Annales Mettenses Priores* (now Durham Cathedral Library, MS C. IV. 15), but Joan Story has recently demonstrated that it was most likely imported to Durham from the Continent *c*. 1130, after Symeon of Durham's death or retirement.[23]

It is striking that William has very little to say about Durham Cathedral's new building, although it was impressive and innovative,[24] and his interest in architecture in general and his observations on the introduction of Romanesque architecture into England in particular are well known.[25] In the *Gesta Regum* and *Gesta Pontificum*, but only rather generally, William mentions the construction of a new cathedral and buildings for the monks in Durham, a project initiated by William of Saint-Calais and completed by his successor Ranulf Flambard.[26] In the *Gesta Pontificum* he recounts a miraculous fall of timbers supporting the vault of the presbytery in the new cathedral before the translation of Cuthbert's relics.

---

[21] Both *GP* and John of Worcester *pace* the Durham source omit three names (Heathuredus or Eadredus; Ecgredus; Eanbertus) between Ecgberht and Eardulf. *GP* gives Milredus for Tilredus, but that name is written over erasure in the main manuscript of John of Worcester (Oxford, Corpus Christi College 157, p. 45). The copy from Bury St Edmunds Abbey (now Bodl. Libr., Bodley 297, p. 39), copied from Corpus Christi 157 before some corrections had been made there, has the correct name – Tilredus. William also, against all other witnesses, inverts the episcopates of Æthelric and Æthelwine.

[22] Ibid., p. 185.

[23] J. Story, 'Frankish annals in Anglo-Norman Durham', in *Wilhelm Levison (1876–1947). Ein jüdisches Forscherleben zwischen wissenschaftlicher Anerkennung und politischem Exil*, ed. M. Becher and Y. Hen (Siegburg, 2010), pp. 145–60. On that manuscript see also S. MacLean, 'Recycling the Franks in twelfth-century England: Regino of Prüm, the monks of Durham, and the Alexandrian Schism', *Speculum* 87 (2012), 649–81.

[24] M. Thurlby, 'The roles of the patron and the master mason in the first design of the Romanesque cathedral of Durham', in *Anglo-Norman Durham*, ed. D. Rollason et al. (Woodbridge, 1994), pp. 161–84.

[25] *GP* II, pp. xxxix–xl; R. Allen Brown, 'William of Malmesbury as an architectural historian', in *Mélanges d'archéologie et d'histoire médiévales: en l'honneur du Doyen Michel de Bouard* (Geneva, 1982), pp. 9–16, repr. in his *Castles, Conquests and Charters: Collected Papers* (London, 1989), pp. 227–34.

[26] *GR* 445. 2, *GP* 133. 3–4, 134. 4.

William is the only authority for that story, but it is exactly the stuff he may have heard from Durham monks.[27] Those are interesting details, but William was much more expansive when describing other building projects of Anglo-Norman prelates, for example at Salisbury or Worcester. It may be relevant that, as far as is known, Malmesbury Abbey had no confraternity agreement with Durham, and William's name is absent from the Durham *Liber Vitae*.[28]

However, if we review the evidence from Durham, we do find some suggestions that there was contact between William of Malmesbury and the Durham monks. First of all, quotations from both the *Gesta Regum* and *Gesta Pontificum* are found in the well-known Durham historical compilation, *Historia de Regibus Anglorum et Dacorum* (hereafter *HR*), which survives, in its final form, in a single manuscript (now CCCC 139) and is usually attributed to Symeon of Durham. The quotations from the *Gesta Regum* are a selection of anecdotes about King Edgar and King Edward the Confessor. They occur for the first time in CCCC 139, produced most probably in Durham in the 1160s. They have no analogues in the various texts that represent earlier stages of *HR* than CCCC 139.[29] According to a penetrating study by Derek Baker, those anecdotes seem to be used as space-filling texts at the end of a quire. Other quotations from the *Gesta Regum* occur as space-filling texts in other parts of CCCC 139 as well.[30]

Unlike those anecdotes, a lengthy quotation from the *Gesta Pontificum* (240), describing the career of the Carolingian scholar John the Scot, seems to have been an integral part of *HR* from the beginning.[31] This can be demonstrated, since the story in question occurs not only in *HR* as represented in CCCC 139, but also under the same year (s. a. 884) in its cousin text, the so-called *Historia post Bedam* (hereafter *HPB*). This means that this lengthy quotation from *Gesta Pontificum* was already present in the common prototype of those texts (hereafter proto-*HR*), which was compiled no later than 1130 and quite probably in c. 1121,[32]

---

[27] *GP* 135.

[28] BL Cotton Domitian A. VII, f. 25r. See *Durham Liber Vitae: London, British Library, MS Cotton Domitian A. VII: edition and digital facsimile with introduction, codicological, prosopographical and linguistic commentary, and indexes including the Biographical Register of Durham Cathedral Priory (1083–1539)* by A. J. Piper, ed. D. Rollason and L. Rollason (3 vols, London, 2007), III, p. 127.

[29] On the textual history of *HR* see now D. Rollason, 'Symeon of Durham's *Historia de Regibus Anglorum et Dacorum* as a product of twelfth-century historical workshops', in *The Long Twelfth-Century View*, pp. 95–112.

[30] D. Baker, 'Scissors and paste: Corpus Christi, Cambridge, MS 139 again', in *The Materials, Sources and Methods of Ecclesiastical History*, ed. D. Baker (Oxford, 1975), pp. 109–11.

[31] CCCC 139, ff. 81v–82r, printed in *Symeonis Monachi Opera Omnia*, ed. T. Arnold (2 vols, RS 1882–5), II, pp. 115–17. Cf. *Chronica Magistri Rogeri de Houedene*, ed. W. Stubbs (4 vols, RS 1868–71), I, pp. 46–7.

[32] The best available discussion of relation between *HR* and *HPB* is D. Rollason, 'Symeon of Durham's *Historia de Regibus Anglorum et Dacorum*', pp. 105–7. However, to the three manuscripts of *Historia post Bedam* listed by Rollason (Oxford, St John's College 97; BL Royal 13 A. VI; London, Inner Temple Petyt 511. 2), one must add one more, Oxford, All Souls College 36 (s. xii). It has additional material from books 1, 2 and 4 of Henry of Huntingdon's *Historia Anglorum* and seems to represent a fuller text than all the other copies.

that is either very soon after the publication of the *Gesta Pontificum* (c. 1125) or even before.[33]

It is also remarkable that the story of John the Scot is found in the fifth book of the *Gesta Pontificum*, the book which concerns the life of St Aldhelm and the history of Malmesbury Abbey and survives now only in William's autograph copy (Oxford, Magdalen Coll. lat. 172). There are few reasons to postulate the existence of other copies of the fifth book.[34] Besides William's autograph copy, only a lost archetype of the 'First Recension' of the *Gesta Pontificum* (dubbed β in the OMT edition) may have had an abbreviation of the fifth book. This abbreviation is extant in a copy of β, a twelfth-century manuscript, now BL Cotton Claudius A. V, from the Benedictine priory of Belvoir, Lincolnshire or the Cistercian abbey of Bridlington, Yorkshire,[35] but that abbreviation does not include the story of John the Scot, so it could not be the source for *HR*.[36]

The most likely explanation of how the story of John the Scot found its way into proto-*HR*, is that Symeon or another Durham writer briefly reviewed William's autograph or an even earlier draft, and copied a story he liked. We know that William loved to edit and polish his own works constantly, and as the story of John the Scot in proto-*HR* is virtually identical to its final version in Magdalen Coll. lat. 172, it seems more probable that the Durham author consulted the already finished book rather than a rough draft. If we allow for an earlier dating of proto-*HR* (c. 1121), it may indicate that the fifth book of the *Gesta Pontificum* was written originally separately, before the rest of the work.

Of course, it is theoretically possible that both William of Malmesbury and the compiler of proto-*HR* independently copied the story of John the Scot from a third source. But it is extremely unlikely, as the story has every sign of William's own confection, based on a number of classical and early medieval sources. For

---

[33] Another early user of the 'First Recension' of *GP* was the Worcester-based author of *Cronica de Anglia* (written between 1125 and 1137), probably John of Worcester himself, but, unlike proto-*HR*, his work has no material from the fifth book of *GP*: P. Hayward, 'The *Cronica de Anglia* in London, BL, Cotton MS Vitellius C. VIII, fols. 6v–21v: another product of John of Worcester's history workshop', *Traditio* 70 (2015), 159–236.

[34] In the sixteenth century copies of the fifth book were added to several manuscripts (now CUL Ff. 1. 25, CCCC 43 and Cambridge, Trinity Coll. R. 7. 13) by secretaries of Matthew Parker, archbishop of Canterbury, but they have no independent textual value.

[35] The manuscript has the fifteenth-century Belvoir ex-libris, but the style of initials is similar to Bridlington books: A. Lawrence-Mathers, *Manuscripts in Northumbria in the Eleventh and Twelfth Centuries* (Woodbridge, 2003), pp. 184–5 (possible Bridlington connections). The late twelfth-century library catalogue from Durham Cathedral has an entry 'Gesta pontificum Anglorum' (*Catalogi Veteres Librorum Ecclesiae Cathedralis Dunelmensis*, ed. B. Botfield, (London, 1838), p. 3; the new edition of medieval Durham catalogues, as part of CBMLC, is still unpublished) that might be β itself or its lost descendant, as no surviving manuscripts of *GP* have known Durham connections. The same catalogue also mentions 'Miracula de sancta Maria' (*Catalogi Veteres*, p. 4), which may be William's *Miracula*, though there are other possibilities as well, e.g. Dominic of Evesham's work on the same subject: J. C. Jennings, 'The writings of Prior Dominic of Evesham', *EHR* 77 (1962), 298–304.

[36] *GP* I, pp. xxii–xxiv.

Discovering William of Malmesbury

example, a pun on the similarity of *sottus* and *Scottus* occurs in various sources from the Carolingian age onwards;[37] an anecdote about schoolboys murdering John with their *styli* is clearly based on Seneca and a story of Saint Cassian of Forlí, related by William in his *Miracles of the Blessed Virgin Mary*.[38]

It is not easy to say why the compiler of proto-*HR* selected the story of John the Scot for inclusion in his own work. In the early twelfth century Durham had no copies of the works of John the Scot. Although as far as I know Symeon never mentions John apart from the references in proto-*HR*, he clearly had some interest in the Greek fathers and even wrote a letter to Hildebert of Lavardin on dubious matters in the works of Origen.[39]

Another interesting indication of possible links between Malmesbury and Durham is a fragment of a letter of Pope Sergius (687–701) to Abbot Ceolfrid of Wearmouth-Jarrow, added in the early twelfth century to an eleventh-century copy of Bede's *Historia Ecclesiastica* (now Durham Cathedral Library, B. II. 35). This fragment belongs to a group of additions, dated by Richard Gameson to before c. 1130: the anonymous Life of Bede (*BHL* 1069; ff. 119–23), an extract from Pope Sergius's letter (f. 123v) and Bede's *Historia Abbatum* (ff. 123v–129r).[40] All three texts are connected with Bede, who is mentioned in the papal letter. But Rodney Thomson has demonstrated that it was William of Malmesbury who interpolated Bede's name into the original text of the letter.[41] It is possible that the interpolated version of the letter came to Durham not from Malmesbury, but from a third place, such as Worcester, where John of Worcester copied it along with William of Malmesbury's version of the *Liber Pontificalis*.[42] But the Durham manuscript adds a unique and highly interesting rubric to the letter: 'Ex epistolis sancti aldelmi'.[43] The exact meaning of these words is obscure to me, but the mention of Aldhelm may indicate a connection with Malmesbury.

Ultimately, one cannot be certain that William used any Durham literary texts, although he was obviously familiar with oral stories and traditions concerning St Cuthbert and Durham. It is possible, then, that William never visited Durham,

---

[37] The earliest example, perhaps, is a ninth-century poem by Theodulf of Orleans against an Irishman Cadac-Andreas: K. Sidwell, 'Theodulf of Orleans, Cadac-Andreas and Old Irish phonology: a conundrum', *JML* 2 (1992), 55–62; B. Bischoff, 'Theodulf und der Ire Cadac-Andreas', *Historisches Jahrbuch* 74 (1955), 92–8. Gerald of Wales in *De Principis Instructione* tells a similar story (perhaps based on *GP*, *HR* or *HPB*) about Alcuin and Charlemagne (*Giraldi Cambrensis Opera*, vol. 8, ed. G. F. Warner [RS 1891], p. 42).

[38] *GP* II, p. 292.

[39] R. Sharpe, 'Symeon, Hildebert, and the errors of Origen', in *Symeon of Durham: Historian of Durham and the North*, pp. 282–300.

[40] R. Gameson, *The Manuscripts of Early Norman England c. 1066–1130* (Oxford, 1999), p. 81.

[41] Thomson, *William of Malmesbury*, pp. 166–7.

[42] Ibid.

[43] I was not able to examine the Durham manuscript *de visu*, but the rubric is present in its fourteenth-century copy (BL Burney 310, f. 171v) and is mentioned in its description by T. Rud, *Codicum Manuscriptorum Ecclesiae Cathedralis Dunelmensis Catalogus*, ed. J. Raine (Durham, 1825), p. 142.

but met Symeon or another Durham monk elsewhere, perhaps in Worcester, Canterbury or York.[44]

Here it may be useful to return to William's description of the Roman ruins in Carlisle. For Symeon, as for other Durham monks, Carlisle was an important place in the early decades of the twelfth century. Carlisle was under Durham's jurisdiction from its re-establishment by William Rufus to 1101, when, after Ranulf Flambard's forfeiture, it was transferred to the archdeaconry of Richmond in the diocese of York. That was a heavy loss for the Durham monks, who were eager to regain Carlisle. Symeon himself even wrote (before *c.* 1122) a polemical tract in which he defended Durham's jurisdiction over that city.[45] Carlisle appears to be the subject of a passage which was later mostly erased from the main manuscript of *LDE*, perhaps after the collapse of Durham's hopes.[46] It is quite possible that Symeon, who entered the Durham community in the early 1090s, personally visited Carlisle or at least knew a great deal about it.

So, a story might be hypothesised as follows: William of Malmesbury learns about the Roman remains in Carlisle from Bede's *Life of Cuthbert* and is intrigued because of his obsession with classical antiquity. He thoroughly interviews Symeon on the subject and then uses his own imagination and knowledge of classical writers to compose his famous description of the Roman ruins. William might have visited Durham, Hexham, Ripon or Carlisle in person, but even if he did, his description nevertheless bears striking parallels to literary sources. This fact once again reminds us that William's writings belonged to a highly learned, erudite tradition, that operated, to use Lars Boje Mortensen's apt definition, 'through strong intertextual grounding'.[47] The erudite nature of his writing brings us to the problem of William's audience. In the prologue to Book II of the *Gesta Regum* the Malmesbury historian asked his readers to send him new information, in order that he might at least add it 'in the margin'.[48] Unfortunately, we know very few names of those potential informants. However, the range of William's contacts might be partly reconstructed through careful analysis of the sources he used and the transmission of his works, as in the example of a probable quotation from William's personal manuscript of the *Gesta Pontificum* in a Durham historiographical compilation. The evidence we have demonstrates intensive circulation in the early twelfth century of many historiographical works between various English religious communities: Canterbury, Malmesbury, Worcester, Durham, Bury St

---

[44] The description of York, unlike Durham, in my opinion seems to reflect some first-hand experience, including such vivid detail as the heavy Yorkshire accent. Yorkshire indeed was a region of intense Scandinavian settlement, as well as Cumberland, where there was also a strong Celtic element. However William says nothing about the speech of the people of Carlisle.

[45] R. Sharpe, 'Symeon as pamphleteer', in *Symeon of Durham: Historian of Durham and the North*, pp. 214–29.

[46] Ibid., pp. 217–18.

[47] L. B. Mortensen, 'Comparing and connecting: the rise of historiography in Latin and vernacular (12th–13th cent.)', *Medieval Worlds* 1 (2015), 25–39 at p. 30.

[48] GR bk 2 prol. 3.

Edmunds and others. This dynamic exchange of information and ideas helped to shape the rather uniform vision of the English past that had a significant impact on future historical writing.[49]

---

[49] I wish to warmly thank Rodney Thomson, Anne Lawrence-Mathers, Paul Hayward, William Kynan-Wilson and all the participants of 2015 Oxford Conference 'William of Malmesbury and his Legacy' for discussing my paper and giving valuable comments and advice. The author is responsible for any remaining flaws.

→ 10 ←

William of Malmesbury as Librarian: The Evidence of his Autographs

Samu Niskanen

If I single out this activity [namely, building up a library], I think I have every right to do so, for in this area especially I have been inferior to none of those who went before; indeed (if I can say this without boasting) I have easily surpassed them all. May there be someone to look after the present stock! I have collected much material for reading, approaching the prowess of my excellent predecessor at least in this respect; I have followed up his laudable start as best I could. Let us hope there may be someone to cherish the fruits of our labours![1]

IN HIS CAPACITY AS PRECENTOR OF MALMESBURY ABBEY, William was also its librarian.[2] As expressed in the passage from his *Gesta Pontificum* quoted above, he had, to his knowledge, supplied the abbey with more books than any of his predecessors. This paper studies that accomplishment from two perspectives. Surveying the corpus of William's extant autographs, I shall first attempt to characterise his objectives with regard to the production of books for the library of his house. Scrutinising one of his autographs in a more detailed manner, I shall then observe how he approached and used his sources when copying books with the assistance of his scribes. These two discussions are in essence commentaries on the quoted extract, and together they seek to form a concise account of how William performed his duty to collect books as librarian.

I wish to express gratitude to Dr James Willoughby for the benefit of his advice and help.

[1] *GP* 271. 2: 'Quod studium si predico, uideor id quodam meo proprio iure facere, qui nullis maioribus in hoc presertim loco cesserim, immo, nisi quod dico iactantia sit, cunctos facile supergressus sim. Sit qui modo parta conseruet: ego ad legendum multa congessi, probitatem predicandi uiri in hoc dumtaxat emulatus. Ipsius ergo laudabili cepto pro uirili portione non defui. Vtinam sit qui labores nostros foueat!' The translation is Michael Winterbottom's.

[2] The office of precentor involved responsibility for liturgical music and supervision of the library and book production in the scriptorium: R. W. Sharpe, 'The medieval librarian', in *The Cambridge History of Libraries in Britain and Ireland*, vol. 1, ed. E. Leedham-Green and T. Webber (Cambridge, 2006), pp. 221–2.

His hand has been detected in twelve manuscripts.[3] Of these, he was the sole scribe for two, and he collaborated with other scribes for the remaining ten. The two manuscripts by him alone contain the *Collectio Canonum Quesnelliana*, an early collection of conciliar decrees, and a working copy of his *Gesta Pontificum*.[4] The remaining ten books include three volumes of ancient classics,[5] two of patristic texts (including William's original collection of extracts from the works of Gregory the Great),[6] two containing works by two medieval philosophers (one Carolingian and one contemporary),[7] an anthology of biblical exegesis,[8] a collection of extracts connected to Roman history from Troy to William's day,[9] and a collection of *computistica*.[10]

To what extent are these twelve survivors representative of the whole corpus of books made under William's supervision in his role as librarian? The passage quoted above hints that he produced many more books than the twelve extant, and this is certified by the fact that only three of his nineteen original works survive in autographs.[11] Any answer in absolute terms to the question posed above will, therefore, be a mere guess. The problem must be tackled in relative terms: one can reflect upon it in the contexts of what we know of his literary outlook and the development of monastic libraries during his time. Using that approach, I shall discuss two features, which seem to me the most striking, of the body of William's twelve extant autographs.

First and foremost, this corpus reflects his extraordinary acquaintance with ancient pagan classics, which are the focus of three volumes, as noted above. The Latin classics were one of his central preoccupations: he was perhaps better versed in them than was any other member of his generation in England.[12] Furthermore, the medieval transmission of ancient classics was, in most cases, connected to the needs of the schoolroom.[13] Such a purpose characterised also William's mission

---

[3] For a detailed discussion of each manuscript, see Thomson, *William of Malmesbury*, pp. 80–96.

[4] Oxford, Oriel Coll. 42 and Magdalen Coll. lat. 172 respectively.

[5] CCCC 330, Bodl. Libr., Rawl. G. 139, and Oxford, Lincoln Coll. 100.

[6] CUL Ii. 3. 20 (Gregory the Great) and BL Royal 5 F. iv (Ambrose).

[7] BL Royal App. 85 and Cambridge, Trinity Coll. O. 5. 20 (originally from the same volume, Johannes Scotus Eriugena), and Lambeth 224 (Anselm).

[8] Oxford, Merton Coll. 181.

[9] Bodl. Libr., Arch. Seld. B. 16.

[10] Bodl. Libr., Auct. F. 3. 14.

[11] R. W. Sharpe, *A Handlist of the Latin Writers of Great Britain and Ireland before 1540* (2nd edn, Turnhout, 2001), pp. 784–6. My count excludes *Vita S. Aldhelmi*, forming the last part of *GP*. The survivors are *Gesta Pontificum Anglorum*, *Deflorationes ex Libris Beati Gregorii Papae*, and *Epistola de Iohanne Scoto*. It is, of course, possible that William did not produce autograph books of all his works as he could have dictated or used wax tablets for the first version.

[12] See R. M. Thomson, 'William of Malmesbury and the Latin Classics revisited', in *Aspects*, pp. 383–93.

[13] See J. M. W. Willoughby, 'The transmission and circulation of Classical literature: libraries and *florilegia*', in *The Oxford History of Classical Reception in English Literature 1: The Middle Ages*, ed. R. Copeland (Oxford, 2016), pp. 205–6.

as librarian, as exemplified by MS CCCC 330, a copy of Martianus Capella's *De Nuptiis Philologiae et Mercurii*. The book consists of two originally separate volumes, both earlier than William's lifetime. His contribution was to furnish it with a gloss, which was extracted from that by Remigius of Auxerre and was to serve as an aid in teaching.[14]

Secondly, just two of William's autographs contain patristic theology. One of these is his own compilation of extracts from the writings of Gregory the Great and the other is an anthology of Ambrosian treatises. The diminutive share of patristic works in William's extant autographs contrasts with the body of manuscripts by the scribe of the *Textus Roffensis*, a monk of Rochester Cathedral Priory and William's contemporary. The hand of the Rochester scribe has so far been observed in fifteen manuscripts, of which ten are almost exclusively devoted to patristic treatises.[15] Was William less inclined to transmit patristic theology than this man? Absence of evidence, of course, does not necessarily equate to evidence of absence. Furthermore, in about 1320 Malmesbury Abbey possessed no fewer than sixty-nine titles of the works of Augustine and many more unspecified titles by other Fathers.[16] The bulk of the abbey's late medieval patristic collection is likely to have been produced during the twelfth century, during or after – not before – William's day.[17] The abbey had boasted a major library during the time of Aldhelm (†709), but his collection, which may have comprised more than one hundred books, had been decimated owing to fire and negligence by William's lifetime.[18] Because William credited himself with being the principal collector

---

[14] This purpose is reflected also in *GP* 271. 3 (immediately after the quoted passage) in relation to the time of Abbot Godfrey: 'Monachi, qui uulgares tantum litteras balbutiebant, perfecte informati'.

[15] In addition to his patristic books, a further two include works by patristic and medieval authors. His autographs are: CUL Ff. 4. 32 (Augustine); CCCC 332 (patristic and medieval theology); Cambridge, Trinity Coll. O. 2. 44 (patristic and medieval theology); O. 4. 7 (Jerome and pseudo-Jerome); Eton Coll. 80 (Jerome); BL Royal 5 B. XII (Augustine); 5 C. I (Augustine); 6 A. IV (Ambrose); 6 C. IV (Ambrose); 8 D. XVI (John Cassian); 12 C. I (contemporary monastic authors); 15 A. XXII + Cotton Vespasian D. XII, which come from the same volume (Roman and English histories); Lambeth 76 (patristic authors); Bodl. Libr., Bodley 134 (Augustine); Rochester, Dean and Chapter Library A. 3. 5, now on deposit in Kent Archives, Maidstone, as MS DRc/R1 (*Textus Roffensis*). This list is a combination of N. R. Ker, *English Manuscripts in the Century after the Norman Conquest* (Oxford, 1960), p. 31, and M. B. Parkes, *Their Hands before Our Eyes* (Aldershot, 2008), p. 96, n. 45. For his work as a copyist, see S. Niskanen, 'The treatises of Ralph of Battle', *JML* 26 (2016), pp. 205–6.

[16] *Registrum Anglie de Libris Doctorum et Auctorum Veterum*, ed. R. A. B. Mynors, R. H. Rouse and M. A. Rouse (CBMLC 2: 1991), p. 103.

[17] In *GP*, immediately before the passage quoted at the opening of this essay, William remarked that during the period of Abbot Godfrey (1087×1091–1100×1105) '[l]ibri conscripti nonnulli, uel potius bibliothecae primitiae libatae': *GP* 271. 1.

[18] M. Lapidge, *The Anglo-Saxon Library* (Oxford, 2006), p. 127. It is now a moot point whether or not William had recourse to any of his manuscripts; Thomson, *William of Malmesbury*, p. 114. As one might expect, there is much overlap between patristic works that Aldhelm and William knew at first hand. Yet differences are also notable, of which Augustine is a case in point; cf. Lapidge, *Anglo-Saxon Library*, p. 179, and Thomson, *William of Malmesbury*, pp. 204–5.

of books for his house, it seems reasonable to suggest that his team copied many more patristic treatises than the twelve surviving autographs would indicate. His acquaintance with patristic literature as attested by quotations and allusions in his own works would support that assumption.[19] Even so, the contrast between the corpora of surviving books copied by William and the Rochester scribe is so stark that it almost certainly implies different objectives. The Rochester scribe's mission was more focused on patristic literature than William's. A booklist written by the Rochester scribe in 1122/3, which records more than one hundred volumes, shows that the extant corpus of his autographs did not constitute an anomaly in the library of his church.[20] Patristic authors prevailed at Rochester. Emphasis on the Fathers was part of a wider trend, with several English monastic houses building up substantial patristic collections at the beginning of the twelfth century. The books acquired by Abbot Faricius of Abingdon are a well-known instance.[21] William's autographs and the other books identified as made or kept at Malmesbury in the twelfth century (admittedly, very few in number) do not betray such an emphasis.[22] Its library, under his leadership, seems to have embraced a more varied selection of material.

Two factors may account for the lack of a strong focus on patristic theology at Malmesbury. First, the paucity of such books in the corpus of his extant autographs would be in line with William's project as author. His literary calling was not that of a theologian, but a historian, as he admitted when attempting biblical exegesis at an advanced age.[23] Another factor may have been his view that modern scholarship could surpass earlier learning. In expressing his high esteem for the *Chronicon* of Marianus Scotus (d. 1082), William noted that he regarded Marianus as superior to all earlier authors in the field of chronography.[24] As an afterthought, he added the jeremiad that owing to the prevalent inclination for 'the opinion of the ancients', many of his generation did not accord 'to new discoveries, however plausible, the unimpassioned acceptance they deserve'.[25] Indeed, he plainly placed one contemporary author 'above all his predecessors' in the field of theology: Anselm (†1109), abbot of Bec and archbishop of Canterbury. The compliment was not mere rhetoric, but an assessment which William explicitly justified; whereas

---

[19] Ibid., pp. 202–14.

[20] *English Benedictine Libraries: The Shorter Catalogues*, ed. R. Sharpe, J. P. Carley, R. M. Thomson and A. G. Watson (CBMLC 4: 1996), B77, pp. 469–92.

[21] *English Benedictine Libraries*, B2, pp. 5–6.

[22] The best list of the surviving Malmesbury books is the one available through the electronic resource *MLGB3*, a completely revised and updated edition of N. R. Ker, *Medieval Libraries of Great Britain*. http://mlgb3.bodleian.ox.ac.uk.

[23] 'Olim enim cum historias lusi, uiridioribus annis rerumque laetitiae congruebat rerum iocunditas', *Comm. Lam.*, prol. 7–8.

[24] Cf. Lawrence-Mathers's paper in this volume, pp. 93–105.

[25] GR 292. 2: 'Quare sepe mirari soleo cur nostri temporis doctos hoc respergat infortunium, ut in tanto numero discentium, in tam tristi pallore lucubrantium, uix aliquis plenam scientiae laudem referat: adeo inueteratus usus placet, adeo fere nullus nouis, licet probabiliter inuentis, serenitatem assensus pro merito indulget.'

earlier theologians had enforced belief by their authority, Anselm corroborated belief by reason, 'proving [it] by irresistible arguments'.[26] While William certainly did not dismiss patristic theology as obsolete, we may presume that as librarian he regarded an extensive focus on the Fathers as disadvantageous conservatism.

A concrete manifestation of William's admiration for Anselm is London, Lambeth Palace Libr. 224, the source for my investigation into his methods of copying books and supervising his team.[27] In comparison to his other extant autographs, Lambeth 224 is of merely average quality.[28] It is the content of the book that makes it special: the Lambeth manuscript is our most extensive medieval Anselmian anthology in a single volume.[29] It contains all but one of Anselm's treatises and 214 of his letters, close to half of the surviving correspondence. Table 1 summarises the contents and, as identified by Thomson, the stint of each hand, omitting brief intrusions.[30]

The most notable absentees from the anthology are Anselm's prayers, with the exception of the *Meditatio Redemptionis Humanae*, which was often transmitted together with the treatises. In William's time the prayers were widely available, circulating in various compilations either together with selections of Anselm's treatises or independently. In the surviving Anselmian anthologies his treatises are often (but not always) followed either by his letters or his prayers.[31] The absence of the latter from William's collection and the inclusion of the former were surely his editorial decisions. He preferred the correspondence to the prayers.

---

[26] GP 46. 4–5: 'cogitata omnium antecessorum euicit .... Credulitatem enim nostram, quam illi auctoritate extorquere uolunt, ille ratione roborat, quod credimus ita esse nec aliter esse posse inuincibilibus approbans argumentis.'

[27] I must lodge an objection to an earlier consensus. According to this argument, established by Richard Southern and followed by others, William found Anselm's letters uncollected and in disarray when visiting Canterbury in search of materials for his historical works in 1120 or soon after. Attempting to arrange Anselm's archive, he took some of it back home. The fruits of this project included MS Lambeth 224, and, more importantly, a new impetus on the part of Christ Church's brethren to properly preserve Anselm's writings. R. W. Southern, *Saint Anselm. A Portrait in a Landscape* (Cambridge, 1990), pp. 459–81. This narrative is mistaken. William's role in the transmission of Anselm's literary corpus was not as crucial as Southern maintained. His project amounted to a local affair, which did not impinge upon the codification of his correspondence at Christ Church. This is because William demonstrably relied on earlier collections. See S. Niskanen, *The Letter Collections of Anselm of Canterbury* (Turnhout, 2011), pp. 94–103.

[28] With regard to its codicological and palaeographical properties, the manuscript is fairly conventional for a twelfth-century library book containing contemporary theological treatises: the parchment is rather poor, the size insignificant, the decoration rare, and the script informal book-hand.

[29] CUL Dd. 9. 5 is about as extensive but it consists of two originally separate volumes. Only in 1612 was William's achievement in this respect exceeded; the printed edition of Anselm's works by Jean Picard was the first collection to include more titles by Anselm than William's manuscript. But even that edition was published in four volumes.

[30] Thomson, *William of Malmesbury*, p. 87.

[31] Exceptions to this rule are manuscripts that have only a few letters; Brussels, Bibl. Royale 2004–10; Cambridge, Peterhouse 246; BL Cotton Claudius E. I; Royal 5 E. XIV, 8 D. VIII; Oxford, Merton Coll. 19 (in which the letters and the prayers occur in two originally separate units). BnF lat. 15694; Worcester Cath. F. 41; F. 142; BAV Vat. lat. 10611.

Table 1

Folios	Work	Hand
1r–22v	*Monologion*	Scribe A (till f. 12va l. 26) Scribe B
22v–32v	*Proslogion*	Scribe B
32v–40r	*Epistola de Incarnatione Verbi*	Scribe A
40r–63r	*Cur Deus Homo*	Scribe A (Prologue) Scribe B
63v–74v	*De Conceptu Virginali et de Originali Peccato*	Scribe A
75r–85v	*De Concordia Praescientiae et Praedestinationis*	Scribe A
86r–v	*Ep. 971*	Scribe A and William
87r–89r	*Meditatio de Redemptione Humana*	Scribe A
89r–95r	*De Grammatico*	Scribe A
95r–102v	*De Veritate*	Scribe A
102v–108v	*De Libertate Arbitrii*	Scribe A
109r–120v	*De Casu Diaboli*	Scribe A
120v–174r	*Epistolae* including *Epistola de Incarnatione Verbi (prior recensio)*, *Epistola de Sacrificio Azimi*, *Epistola de Sacramentis Ecclesiae*	Scribe A (3 letters) William (138 letters) Hand VII (45 letters) Hand VIII (28 letters)
174r–185r	*De Processione Spiritus Sancti* Not mentioned in William's list of contents	a new hand of s. XII^1, completed s. XIV

All references to the printed editions of Anselm's works are to *Sancti Anselmi Opera*, ed. F. S. Schmitt (Seckau, Rome, Edinburgh, 1938–61).

The treatises were copied by two trusted scribes: Scribe A and Scribe B, whose hands occur also in some of William's other manuscripts. With the exception of the *Monologion*, their stints embrace whole works or sections. The reason for William's decision not to copy any of the treatises by himself may have been his liberal approach to transmission, discussed below. His tendency to omit words, phrases and sections would have risked Anselm's line of reasoning since even a small omission, if not judiciously deliberated, could have rendered the treatises' intricate argument void. From this viewpoint, assigning to his team such texts that had to be copied verbatim was a natural decision.

This then is a big difference between William's work and that of his team. He did not allow his assistants any of the editorial liberties in which he himself so readily indulged. He required that they produce a faithful copy, suggesting that he did not trust their editorial judgement as much as his own. Their work as copyists was not perfect, but of average quality in comparison with our other early Anselmian manuscripts, an assessment that applies also to the stints of his two most trusted assistants, Scribes A and B.[32] A somewhat amusing instance is the failed emendation by Scribe B of Anselm's renowned ontological argument in 'Sumptum ex libello', an authorial abstract of the *Proslogion*, which followed the work proper. This man distorted one of the most famous philosophical arguments into nonsense.[33]

Anselm's correspondence was copied by William, two otherwise unknown scribes and, for a short sequence, Scribe A. The team drew on multiple sources. Since some of these can be identified with certainty, the manuscript provides us with textual evidence for William's use of exemplars, unmatched by any other of his surviving autographs. For by comparing the text of the Lambeth manuscript with that of its sources, we can identify his editorial touches with confidence. As regards his other autographs, one cannot be certain whether their distinct textual variants were his own alterations or derived from his sources. Conclusions drawn from the textual criticism of Anselm's letters in MS Lambeth 224 are, therefore, more firmly based than those derived from William's other autographs with respect to his methods of transmitting the works of other authors. Table 2 summarises the stints of each copyist in the letter section of the Lambeth manuscript, the sources, and the arrangement of the letters included.[34] *F* is BL Royal 5 F. IX and α stands for a hypothetical collection of Anselm's Norman correspondence, now lost.[35]

William allotted each of his assistants a single principal source to copy. He himself copied letters from two sources, *F* and α. The latter seems to have consisted of single-sheet letters, rather than a single volume.[36] For Anselm's Norman career (ending with his promotion to the archbishopric in 1093), William relied on α where he could, but in doing so rearranged the letters according to their sequence in *F*. Such an editorial approach suggests awareness of the textual status of his two sources. While *F* presented the letters in a better arrangement, α offered a truly excellent text.

---

[32] I have not detected conscious scribal individuality at any level in the text copied by his assistants. This assessment results chiefly from textual evidence systematically harvested from the correspondence. As regards the treatises, I relied primarily on the critical apparatus of their modern edition and secondarily on my own observations.

[33] Lambeth 224, f. 28v. When correcting the passage, he failed to notice one of his several omissions in it.

[34] The few short intrusions from other sources (such as M82, which is *Ep*. 337) are not recorded in the table.

[35] It is possible, although unlikely, that the α source was BL Cotton Nero A. VII. The textual criticism is impeded by the fact that while the Cottonian manuscript offers a nearly perfect text, William's is often idiosyncratic.

[36] Niskanen, *The Letter Collections of Anselm*, pp. 97–100.

Table 2

Letters	Source	Arrangement	Hand
M1–3	α		Scribe A
M4–17	F	F	William
M18–79	α	First F, then α (possibly with alterations)	William until M34, then hand VII
M80–107	Historia Nouorum, iii and iv	Historia Nouorum	Hand VIII
M108–37	F	F	William
M138–214	F	F, hierarchical	William
* M138–49, pope		– original	William
* M150–2, king of England		– reversed	
* M153–62, queen of England		– original	
* M163–4, rulers other than kingdoms		– reversed	
* M165–6, Marchioness Matilda of Tuscany		– original	
* M167–71, archbishops and bishops		– initially original, then reversed	
* M172–96, Canterbury		– original	
* M197–203, prelates of other kingdoms		– reversed	
* M204–10, monks		– initially original, ending reversed	
* M211–14, nuns		– original	

As for Anselm's correspondence as archbishop of Canterbury (covering the period 1093–1109), the team had recourse to two sources, manuscript *F* again and Eadmer's *Historia Nouorum*, which incorporated several letters to and from Anselm. William had an assistant, Hand VIII, copy the letters from the final part of book iii and those from book iv of *Historia Nouorum* (M80–107). It is unclear why the letters in books ii and iii were excluded. After Hand VIII had finished his stint, William started working on his own, copying more than one hundred letters from

F (M108–214). Without a single error, he omitted all letters in F that Hand VIII had copied from Eadmer. He passed over three other letters, but each omission appears to have been intended.[37] It was an achievement that he managed to avoid duplication although relying on multiple sources and supervising several scribes.

The way William rearranged the Canterbury letters reflects his conception of social hierarchies, as well as his overriding interest in domestic affairs as opposed to foreign ones. He first copied thirty letters from F (M108–37) following the order in which they appear in that manuscript. Then, on encountering a letter to the pope (Ep. 272), he decided to rearrange the remaining eighty-odd letters according to the status and rank of Anselm's correspondents. First comes Anselm's papal correspondence, then his correspondence with the English king, then with the English queen, then with rulers of other kingdoms and states; and then with archbishops and bishops, and so on, as indicated in Table 2 above. In that archbishops and bishops did not precede secular sovereigns, the sequence hints at a rather conservative world view. William plainly did not regard the priesthood as a social determiner that would have placed the clergy above all laity.

William's choices in rearranging the material offered by his exemplars give us insight into how he read them. The above-mentioned sections defined by social hierarchy, with some exceptions, reflect F's arrangement, but in a curious way. William's papal section complies with the order in F.[38] The next group, consisting of correspondence between Anselm and King Henry, reverses F's arrangement. Then the letters exchanged with Queen Matilda again follow the order in F. The organisation of material in his manuscript continues in this pattern; in transcribing material from F, William, for mysterious reasons, leafed the volume back and forth.

When copying Anselm's text, he edited at will. One of his favourite editorial devices was omission, demonstrating that he wished to progress efficiently. Sometimes he only provided a few lines of a single letter. More often, his omissions were shorter, consisting of a few words or a sentence or two. In particular he passed over formulaic valedictions and short afterthoughts immediately before (and sometimes after) them.[39] He likewise tended to abbreviate salutations.[40] Except for his inclination to abridge and skip sections at the beginning and end of letters, it is often difficult to characterise the purpose of his omissions. Perhaps he had not devised a clear-cut editorial policy. However, on occasion a morally didactic emphasis seems to have guided him. A case in point is a letter to Bishop Fulk of Beauvais about the heresy of Roscelin of Compiègne. In copying this letter, William completely omitted a section on Roscelin and his teaching. This suggests that he felt that Roscelin was either too unimportant or too much of a

---

[37] Ep. 416 is a lengthy theological treatise. Epp. 467 and 470 are concerned with the excommunication of Thomas II of York by Anselm in 1109.

[38] Epp. 283, 303, where M includes the first words and refers the reader to Liber pontificalis for the full text.

[39] Epp. 1, 3, 6, 13, 17, 29, 31, 61, 121.

[40] Epp. 31, 49.

heretic to be introduced to his readers. What he chose to transmit of the letter was a moralistic exhortation against excessive confidence in reason over faith.[41]

Another way in which William frequently altered Anselm's text was in the rearrangement of short distinct expressions, most often two successive words. Such transpositions could take place anywhere, but the practice occurred much more frequently in the middle or at the end of a phrase or sentence than at its beginning. Comparable alterations have been observed also in other texts copied by William, for instance in Alcuin's letters.[42] Because medial positions are about as frequent as final positions for transposition, it does not seem that William was attempting to refine Anselm's prose by imposing on it his preferred accentual types of the *cursus*.

I propose that frequent transpositions resulted from his method of copying the text in front of him, and not from any deliberate attempt to revise Anselm's diction. My impression is that he read a complete unit from his source – a phrase or a clause, or maybe even a sentence (rather than two, three words) – and then copied that unit from memory. That explanation would also account for the types of changes that follow. William very frequently replaced words with new ones. 'Internum' became 'intimum' (*Ep*. 7); 'quo modo' became 'quoquo modo' (*Ep*. 1); 'praefatus' became 'suprafatus' (*Ep*. 89), 'illis' became 'ad ea' (*Ep*. 8); 'os' became 'cor' (*Ep*. 3), and so on. He changed prefixes to nouns and verbs. For instance, 'diiudicare refugiat' became 'iudicare diffugiat' (*Ep*. 37). He added prepositions, such as those he inserted into serial expressions in which Anselm had only provided the first noun with a preposition (as in *Ep*. 73).

William's haste is apparent when he abbreviated phrases of a few words into their initials and did this imperfectly.[43] For example, in *Ep*. 414, his source, F, read 'caro concupiscit aduersus spiritum, spiritus autem aduersus carnem' in line with other manuscripts and the Bible (Gal. 5: 17).[44] William wrote 'caro concupiscit aduersus s. et s. a. c.'. The word *et* was his addition. Comparable inadvertent touches took place in salutations abbreviated by the same method. As is evident from the agreement of the best manuscripts (including his source), the greeting of *Ep*. 280 ended 'debitam subiectionem et fidele seruitium'. William idiosyncratically wrote 'd. s. et f[ideles] o[rationes]'.[45] These alterations, together with the use of abbreviations, are clearly the result of haste.

Although one encounters such deviations as are observed here in all medieval manuscripts, their frequency in Lambeth 224 is far greater than average. Poorly copied manuscripts may be exceptions, but their textual deviation is explained by scribal error. William's digressions almost always make sense, and they are not to be categorised as mistakes. On the other hand, few of his alterations were the

---

[41] *Ep*. 136.
[42] Thomson, *William of Malmesbury*, pp. 161–3.
[43] He picked up the habit from his source, F, but applied it more frequently.
[44] See also somewhat similar cases in *Epp*. 233: 10 and 249: 28.
[45] See also *Ep*. 289: 2–3.

result of careful deliberation. Rather, they betray a mind swiftly processing the exemplar's text and taking a consciously flexible approach to the act of transmission. The resulting text – neither a fine-tuned rendition of the original nor a bad copy – reflects how William instinctively engaged with what he read.

His flexibility and originality are apparent in his revision of his team's work. Although his assistants entered the occasional correction, this was primarily his responsibility. He sometimes consulted the source from which the text had been copied, but often he did not. The latter is evidenced by the fact that many of his revisions are idiosyncratic, not supported by other manuscripts, with the exception of those deriving from his.[46] This is to say that he took revision mainly as a matter of conjecture, without recourse to the exemplar or another manuscript.[47] Where the tradition was corrupted, the combination of his fine ear and liberal attitude could yield textual conjectures superior to the readings in our other manuscripts.[48]

William's approach to transmission contrasted with Anselm's. In a letter to one of his monks, Anselm emphasised that when commissioning a copy of a work, he preferred 'an intact fraction to a corrupt whole'.[49] William's mission as librarian was to produce a decent stock of books for his brethren, not to make a few perfectly accurate copies. The undertaking was apparently so large that it could not have been tackled without some amount of compromise. William's personal literary preferences, as one might expect, affected the selection of works to be copied. If patristic treatises were a genuine emphasis in the collection produced under his supervision, that emphasis was rather less apparent than in the corpus of books copied by the prolific Rochester scribe discussed above. William's personal interest in the Latin classics and perhaps also in contemporary learned literature was conducive to a selection of texts that was varied, rather than focused, in character. Also important is the fact that William was an author, and a most productive one at that; he would have had less time and energy to invest in restocking the library of his abbey than most of his fellow precentors-cum-librarians acting in comparable institutional settings. This may have been a factor that contributed to his swift method of copying. Yet William's swiftness was not carelessness: as expressed in the quotation that opens this essay, he regarded the stock of books he copied with the aid of his team as a major contribution, of which as librarian he had every reason to be proud.

---

[46] Niskanen, *The Letter Collections of Anselm*, pp. 103–7.
[47] An instance of accurate conjecture is, for example: *Epistolae de Incarnatione Verbi prior recensio*, f. 122rb, line 10: dicit] dicitur, above which William interlined 'uel dicit'.
[48] *Epp.* 73 and 87.
[49] *Ep.* 60.

11

William of Malmesbury: Medical Historian of the Crusades

Joanna Phillips

BOOK 5 CHAPTER 410 of William of Malmesbury's *Gesta Regum Anglorum*, which describes the mostly forgotten crusade of Sigurd, co-king of Norway, in 1106/8–10, contains a curious vignette about the emperor's sojourn in Constantinople:

> In that same city his men began to die like flies, and he himself [Sigurd] thought out a remedy, making the survivors drink wine more sparingly, and not unless mixed with water. Such was his penetrating intelligence: he put a pig's liver into the unmixed wine, and finding it soon dissolve away in the harsh liquor, he first foretold that the same thing would happen in the human body and then obtained visual confirmation by post-mortem examination of one who had died.[1]

Although at first one might pass over this passage as an oddity, the fact that it is only found in William's text encourages closer examination. Sigurd's crusade is mentioned – very briefly – by only two other Latin chroniclers, Albert of Aachen and Fulcher of Chartres, but this episode is absent from their histories.[2] Moreover, it is not described in the vernacular sagas that record Sigurd's crusade in detail; these concentrate instead on Sigurd's good relations with the Byzantine Emperor, Alexius Comnenus.[3] Sigurd's crusade has been mostly forgotten since

---

[1] GR 410. 3: 'Hominibus suis in eadem urbe cateruatim morientibus remedium excogitauit, ut reliqui parcius et aqua mixtum uinum biberent, ingenti ingenii acrimonia ut, porcino iecore mero iniecto moxque pro asperitate liquoris resoluto, idem in hominibus fieri primo presagerit, post etiam quodam defuncto extinterato uisi addisceret'. I am grateful to Rod Thomson for bringing this passage to my attention.

[2] Albert of Aachen, *Historia Ierosolimitana*, ed. and trans. S. Edgington (OMT 2007), pp. 799–809; Fulcher of Chartres, *Historia Hierosolymitana*, ed. H. Hagenmeyer (Heidelberg, 1913), bk 2. 44 (pp. 543–8).

[3] The sagas which describe Sigurd's journey are: *Morkinskinna*, ed. T. M. Andersson and K. E. Gade (Ithaca NY, 2000), pp. 322–5; *Fagrskinna*, ed. A. Finlay (Leiden, 2004), pp. 256–7; *Ágrip af Nóregskonungaşogum*, ed. and trans. M. J. Driscoll (2nd edn, London, 2008), pp. 73–5; Snorri Sturluson, *Magnússona Saga*, in *Heimskringla: History of the Kings of Norway*, trans. L. M. Hollander

its military impact was fairly limited, and indeed William does not dwell on Sigurd's sieges of Tyre and Sidon. How and why, then, did this episode make its way into William's text, and how should we interpret it? If we consider William as an historian of crusading, the twelfth-century medical context in which he wrote, and his other discussions of medical incidents occurring during the crusades, we will see that he was a chronicler with a very keen interest in medical experiences, whose discussion of them could contain subtleties relating to the importance of leadership, place and the crusading endeavour.

William has been somewhat overlooked as an historian of the crusades because of the relatively late date of the composition of the *Gesta Regum* in relation to other narratives of the First Crusade, and William's reliance on other written sources.[4] However, recent trends in the study of medieval chroniclers, including those narrating the crusades, suggest that these reasons for excluding William from crusading scholarship are no longer valid, if indeed they ever were. If we do not search for 'truth' but rather look to the chronicler's representations of events then there is much to be discovered in the subtext of their writing, especially regarding matters of health.[5] Some background to William's interest in crusading is apposite. His account of the First Crusade (1095–9) and details of the early history of Outremer occupy most of book 4 of the *Gesta Regum*.[6] William also briefly comments on the participation of Edgar the Ætheling in the crusade of 1101, and, as mentioned, he describes the crusade of Sigurd of Norway.[7] William's sources of information on the crusades have been detailed by Rodney Thomson. Fulcher of Chartres's *Historia Hierosolimitana*, in two redactions, formed the basis of William's account of the First Crusade. He added material from Bernard the Monk's *Itinerary*, the anonymous *Gesta Francorum*, a version of the canons of the Council of Clermont and a now-lost *Itinerarium Urbis Romae*.[8] Although English participation in the First Crusade was limited, William seems to have been acquainted with crusaders from the retinue of Eustace of Boulogne, perhaps

---

(Austin, 1964), sec. 1–13 (pp. 689–99).

[4] R. M. Thomson, 'William of Malmesbury, historian of crusade', *RMS* 23 (1997), 121–34, at 122, revised version in his *William of Malmesbury*, ch. 10.

[5] In utilising this approach, this paper is influenced by the ways in which the central premises of the so-called 'linguistic turn' have been taken up by historians working on medieval chronicles. Of particular relevance to this paper, see especially M. Bull, 'Narratological readings of crusade texts', in *The Crusader World*, ed. A. Boas (London, 2016), pp. 646–60, which proposes a methodology for studying crusader narrative texts regardless of whether they represent authentic histories or not. On the representation of health and illness in medieval chronicles, I. McCleery, 'Medical "emplotment" and plotting medicine: health and disease in late medieval Portuguese chronicles', *Social History of Medicine* 24 (2011), 125–41. See also S. Menache, 'Chronicles and historiography: the interrelationship of fact and fiction', *JMH* 32 (2006), 333–45.

[6] GR 343–88.

[7] GR 251. 2–3, 410.

[8] Thomson concludes that although William's account was similar to that of Orderic Vitalis in the *Historia Ecclesiastica*, there is nothing to suggest that their work was interdependent: Thomson, 'Historian of crusade', p. 123.

because the counts of Boulogne held a substantial amount of land in England, and he may have heard their memories of events.[9] These oral reports, and those of travellers who followed their compatriots to the Holy Land soon after the capture of Jerusalem in 1099, may explain why William's accounts of the post-crusade careers of Godfrey of Bouillon, his brother Baldwin, Raymond of Toulouse and Robert Curthose seem to be independent of any other surviving written source.[10]

William tells us in the *Gesta Regum* that he had studied medicine ('Physic, which cures the sick body, I went deeper into [than Logic]'), and his interest in health and the human condition is apparent throughout the text: the sick are a recurrent presence in his narrative of the crusaders' march through Italy, across the Balkan peninsula, and into Asia Minor.[11] However, William's accounts of the experience of sickness do not tally exactly with the writing of other crusading chroniclers.

For example, in his description of the siege of Antioch (1097–8), like most other crusading chroniclers he describes food shortages, but unlike Albert of Aachen, Baudri of Dol and Gilo of Paris, makes no reference to an outbreak of plague, nor to the illnesses suffered by the crusading leaders Raymond of Toulouse, Godfrey of Bouillon, Adhémar of Le Puy and Stephen of Blois.[12] At the siege of Jerusalem in 1099, when most authors agree there was a dire shortage of water, William claims that there was no cause for concern, and that the only shortage of water was for the animals.[13]

William's interest in health and wellbeing becomes particularly evident when he juxtaposes matters of health with discussions of geography. Describing the foundation of the city of Constantinople, he tells us that Emperor Constantine wished to build a city 'in a place where fertile soil and temperate climate conspired to make men healthy, for being born in Britain he hated excessive heat'.[14] William's description of Antioch also highlights the salubrity of the city, where 'the Orontes ... with its fast-flowing waters, made even colder by their headlong

[9] William states that some of the men who fell at the battle of as-Sinnabrah (28 June 1113) were known to him personally: *GR* 385. 1, an episode analysed in A. V. Murray, 'A little-known member of the royal family of crusader Jerusalem in William of Malmesbury's *Gesta Regum Anglorum*', *Notes and Queries*, n. s. 43 (1996), 397–9, at 399, and *GR* II, p. 342.

[10] Thomson, 'Historian of crusade', pp. 123–4.

[11] *GR* bk 2. prol. 1: 'physicam, quae medetur ualitudini corporum, aliquanto pressius concepi'. For references to the sick, *GR* 353. 2–3, 357. 6.

[12] Raymond of Aguilers records the illnesses of Godfrey of Bouillon and Raymond of Toulouse: *Historia Francorum*, in *Receuil des historiens de Croisade. Historiens occidentaux*, 5 vols (Paris, 1844–95), III, pp. 231–309, at 243, 259; Raymond of Toulouse's illness is also mentioned by Gilo, *Historia Vie Hierosolimitane*, bk 7, lines 372–3, ed. and trans. C. W. Grocock and E. Siberry (OMT 1997), p. 184. Stephen's illness is acknowledged in Albert of Aachen, bk 4: 13 (pp. 266–8); Baudri of Bourgueil, *Historia Hierosolymitana*, bk 3: 12, in *Receuil des historiens de Croisade. Historiens occidentaux*, IV, p. 71; Peter Tudebode, *Historia de Hierosolymitano Itinere*, c. 61, in *Receuil des historiens de Croisade. Historiens occidentaux* III, p. 203. Adhémar's death is widely attested, although only linked to a widespread epidemic by Albert of Aachen in bk 5: 4 (p. 342).

[13] *GR* 369. 2.

[14] *GR* 355. 2: 'ut illic urbem diuino iussu fundaret ubi et soli ubertas et caeli temperies mortalium saluti conuenerit; quia enim in Britannia natus fuerat, ardores solis exosus erat'.

course, carries with it an admixture of fresh air to ensure the health of the inhabitants'.[15] Medieval medical theory relied on the Hippocratic concept that health was governed by four substances, or humours, within the body: blood, black bile, yellow bile and phlegm. Illness was thought to be the result of imbalance of the humours, which could be kept in balance or restored to equilibrium through the careful management of environmental factors affecting the body.[16] In humoral understandings of the body and health, geography and climate played an important role, and William's understanding of this is especially allied to the ideas presented in Hippocrates's *Airs, Waters, and Places*.[17] This Greek medical treatise details how wind direction, water temperature, quality of sunlight and other environmental factors influence health. Each person, it was thought, had an individual balance of the four humours – his or her 'constitution' – which was largely a product of the environment in which they had grown up; William's reminder to his readers that Constantine was born in Britain subtly alludes to these ideas.

The degree to which *Airs, Waters, and Places* was known in the twelfth century is a subject of some debate, but elements of the theories it contains are clearly detectable in William's work.[18] Although we know that William studied medicine, we know neither where nor with whom, nor of what his medical reading consisted; neither is it possible to trace the medical ideas he references directly to specific medical authorities. His understanding could have developed as he absorbed a wide range of non-medical reading. One of the attractions of humoralism as a medical system was its simplicity; its basic concepts could be easily understood by the non-specialist, and medieval chronicles are suffused with references to humoralism and contemporary medical theory.[19] Like many other twelfth-century authors, William does not dwell on the complexities of humoral imbalance or environmental conditions; rather, the experience of health and an understanding of contemporary medical theory are factors intrinsic to his perception of the world and these are incorporated into his wider discussions of political and military events.

---

[15] GR 359. 1: 'Orontem [...] fluentis rapacibus et ipso impetu frigidioribus salubris aurae temperie saluti medetur ciuicae'.

[16] For more on the system of humoralism, see V. Nutton, 'Humoralism', in *Companion Encyclopedia of the History of Medicine*, ed. W. F. Bynum and R. Porter (2 vols, London, 1993), I, pp. 281–91.

[17] *Airs, Waters and Places*, in *Hippocratic Writings*, ed. G. E. R. Lloyd, trans. J. Chadwick and W. N. Mann (Harmondsworth, 1978), pp. 148–69.

[18] The debate is summarised in S. Cavallo and T. Storey, *Healthy Living in Late Renaissance Italy* (Oxford, 2013), p. 78. While the text itself may not have been known, a commentary by Galen may have been. We ought perhaps to look for an indirect transmission of its central ideas, as suggested by P. Biller, 'Proto-racial thought in medieval science', in *The Origins of Racism in the West*, ed. M. Eliav-Feldon, B. H. Isaac, and J. Ziegler (Cambridge, 2009), pp. 157–80, at 162–3, and R. Bartlett, *Gerald of Wales: A Voice of the Middle Ages* (Stroud, 2006), p. 148.

[19] As Thomson and Winterbottom (*GR* II, p. 305, nn. to c. 347. 8–9) note, the dependence of character on climate (and presumably the corollary that health depended on environment) was an assumed fact in the twelfth century, and an idea that would have been very familiar to William.

Medical Historian of the Crusades

The humoral understanding of health and place propagated the idea that peoples from different climates had different physical characteristics, and this idea is clearly articulated in the *Gesta Regum*. In William's retelling of Pope Urban II's speech calling the First Crusade in November 1095, the pope assured his listeners of their natural advantages over their projected enemies:

> It is in fact well known that every nation born in an Eastern clime is dried up by the great heat of the sun; they may have more good sense, but they have less blood in their veins and that is why they flee from battle at close quarters: they know that they have no blood to spare. A people, on the other hand, whose origin is in the northern frosts and who are far removed from the sun's heat, are less rational but fight most readily, in proud reliance on a generous and exuberant supply of blood. You are a race originating in the more temperate regions of the world, men whose readiness to shed your blood leads to a contempt for death and wounds, though you are not without forethought; for you observe moderation in camp, and in the heat of battle you find room for reason.[20]

William here describes the crusaders as physically different from their enemies from the East and even from their neighbours closer to home; the reference to peoples from the northern frosts presumably implies Scandinavians. The passage is a close paraphrase of Vegetius's *Epitoma Rei Militaris* on the warlike qualities of different peoples, itself drawn from Aristotle's *Politics*.[21] The distinction between the East and the temperate regions is informed by the contemporary view of the world as divided into different climatic zones, whose inhabitants had intrinsically different physical qualities, through which William indicates that the crusaders were predisposed to victory.[22] The borders William draws around the temperate regions seem to be rather fluid. His view of where England fits into this schema is particularly interesting, and is revealed in his infamous comment on the breadth of the appeal of the crusade: 'The time had come for the Welshman to give up hunting in his forests, the Scotsman forsook his familiar fleas, the Dane broke off his long drawn-out potations, the Norwegian left his diet of raw fish.'[23] The

---

[20] GR 347. 8: 'Constat profecto quod omnis natio quae in Eoa plaga nascitur, nimio solis ardore siccata, amplius quidem sapit, sed minus habet sanguinis; ideoque uicinam pugnam fugiunt, quia parum sanguinis se habere norunt. Contra, populus qui oritur in Arctois pruinis, et remotus est a solis ardoribus, inconsultior quidem sed largo et luxurianti superbus sanguine promptissime pugnat. Vos estis gens quae in temperatioribus mundi prouintiis oriunda, qui sitis et prodigi sanguinis ad mortis uulnerumque contemptum et non careatis prudentia; namque et modestiam seruatis in castris, et in dimicatione utimini consiliis.'

[21] Vegetius 1. 2. On William's familiarity with Vegetius, see Thomson, *William of Malmesbury*, pp. 58–9. My thanks to James Titterton for pointing out the debt this passage of the GR owes to Vegetius.

[22] For more on contemporary understandings of geography and ethnography, see I. Metzler, 'Perceptions of hot climate in medieval cosmography and travel literature', *RMS* 23 (1997), 69–105; Biller, 'Proto-racial thought'; and, for a particularly twelfth-century perspective, Bartlett, *Gerald of Wales*, pp. 147–8, 164–71.

[23] GR 348. 2: 'Tunc Walensis uenationem saltuum, tunc Scottus familiaritatem pulicum, tunc Danus continuationem potuum, tunc Noricus cruditatem reliquit piscium'.

English are conspicuously absent from this barbed remark which describes their neighbours to the west, north and east, implying that William may instead wish to suggest that England, like continental Europe, was in the temperate zone. But he described Godfrey of Bouillon and Tancred's decision to stay in Jerusalem after the capture of the city in 1099 as a serious risk to their health, because they were 'heroes who from the cold of uttermost Europe plunged into the intolerable heat of the East .... Besides the fear of barbarian attacks, exposed to constant apprehension from the rigours of an unfamiliar climate ... either the air they breathed would be loaded with pestilence, or they would be killed by the fury of the Saracens.'[24] Although these two leaders of the crusade came from rather different climates (eastern Germany and southern Italy respectively), William classes them both as northerners relative to the Saracens. The importance William places on the relationship between geography and health is a manifestation of his strong sense of English self-identity as a native of north-west Europe.[25] William draws on humoralism and contemporary understandings of geography to conceptualise the crusaders, a disparate group, as intrinsically united by their common origin in the temperate zone. In taking this approach he gives special prominence to the north and west of Europe – especially the English region, into which he draws Godfrey and Tancred – and allies the English with the crusaders from the temperate regions.

The logical extension of the medieval association between climate, place and health was that while some climates were naturally healthier than others (as seen in his description of Antioch), a person would always be healthiest in the climate in which he or she had grown up and to which that person was acclimatised. Thus Godfrey and Tancred's decision to remain in the east really was a risk to their health. William's description of this decision conveys his view of the crusade as an expression of providential will: despite the danger to their health, Godfrey and Tancred, William records, trusted in God's protection.[26] William's panegyric biography of Godfrey, later the first Latin ruler of Jerusalem, expands on this theme, integrating issues of health, politics, kingship and crusading. In the narrative structure of William's biography of the duke, who claimed the 'place of honour' among the crusader leaders, Godfrey's experience of the crusade is framed, punctuated and determined by his health.[27] William describes how Godfrey was present at the

---

[24] GR 372. 1: 'uiri qui ab extremo Europae frigore in importabiles se Orientis calores immerserint ... qui preter metum barbaricorum incursuum semper pro incommoditate ignoti poli suspecti ... non dubitarent subsistere ubi uel pestifero afflarentur aere uel Saraceni occiderentur rabie'.

[25] William's sense of self-identity, most evident from a political and cultural perspective, has been explored by, *inter alia*, J. Gillingham, 'The beginnings of English imperialism', *Journal of Historical Sociology* 5 (1992), 392–409, at pp. 394–5, repr. in his *The English in the Twelfth Century* (Woodbridge, 2000), pp. 1–18, at pp. 5–6, and chapter 1 of K. A. Fenton, *Gender, Nation and Conquest in the Works of William of Malmesbury* (Woodbridge, 2008).

[26] GR 372. 2.

[27] GR 373. William's clear partiality towards Godfrey may be as much a manifestation of the fact that Godfrey assumed a semi-mythical status as the ideal crusader soon after his death, later being counted among the Nine Worthies, as of William's good relations with Empress Matilda and

siege of Rome by the Emperor Henry IV in 1084, but his interest in the siege is narrow.[28] Unconcerned here with military events – except to laud his hero by saying that Godfrey was the first to breach the walls – William instead relates how Godfrey's health was ruined by the siege: he contracted a fever, either from quenching his thirst from a barrel of poisoned wine found in a cellar during the battle for the city, or by the unhealthy mists arising from the Tiber.[29] In identifying the vapours of the river as one of the possible causes for Godfrey's illness, William makes reference to a common medieval theory of disease causation: the deleterious effects of the airs produced by unhealthy rivers or marshes. Air quality was thought to have a strong effect on the body, and certain types of air, particularly those arising from standing water such as marshes, were thought to be especially dangerous.[30]

William has a teleological purpose in giving us such detail about Godfrey's fever, a 'febrim quartanum', which apparently caused him to lose his hair and nails: it directly led to Godfrey's assumption of the cross. According to William, the 'continual but slow fever' ('continuae sed lentae febris') continued to affect Godfrey and the duke despaired of recovery. However, on hearing the news of the planned expedition to Jerusalem, he swore

> that he would go thither, if God in His mercy would grant him health. Having formulated this vow, he regained his strength to such a degree that, with his limbs renewed, upright and broad-chested, as though he had put years of decrepitude from him, he shone with new-created youth.[31]

With his hero now at the peak of health, William reinforced his presentation of Godfrey's physical resilience through a story describing his exemplary leadership: Godfrey came to the rescue of one of his knights who had been attacked by a lion while foraging at the siege of Antioch, dealing the animal a mortal blow with his hunting spear. The lion managed to wound Godfrey, but William leaves us to assume that the duke made an easy recovery.[32] However, in other early twelfth-century versions of the story, Godfrey's encounter with the beast (in these cases, a

---

her half-brother Robert of Gloucester; Godfrey was in imperial vassal. Although William strove to remain impartial, he acknowledged the difficulties of doing so as an historian: GR bk 4 prol. 1.

[28] Godfrey was probably not actually present at this siege: A. V. Murray, *The Crusader Kingdom of Jerusalem: A Dynastic History, 1099–1125* (Oxford, 2000), p. 25. However, Albert of Aachen also assumes his presence: bk 5: 13 (pp. 354–5).

[29] GR 373. 3–4. Exactly why the wine should have been poisoned is not explained.

[30] C. Rawcliffe, *Urban Bodies: Communal Health in Late Medieval English Towns and Cities* (Woodbridge, 2013), pp. 120–2; P. Horden, 'Disease, dragons and saints: the management of epidemics in the Dark Ages', in *Epidemics and Ideas: Essays on the Historical Perception of Pestilence*, ed. T. O. Ranger and P. Slack (Cambridge, 1992), pp. 45–76, at 71.

[31] GR 373. 4–5: 'illuc se iturum uouit, si Deus propitius ei salutem largiretur; quo uoto emisso ita ducis uires refloruisse ut nodosos integer artus et spatioso erectus pectore, quasi squalentibus annis exutus, recenti emicaret iuuenta'.

[32] GR 373. 6.

bear) is recorded rather differently.[33] Gilo of Paris's crusade poem recounts how Godfrey was gravely wounded, but impressed those around him by continuing to command while confined to a litter.[34] Two other chroniclers, while ostensibly lauding Godfrey, imply a more complex story. Albert of Aachen says that Godfrey, coming to the rescue of a helpless pilgrim, was mauled by the bear and managed to injure himself, getting his legs entangled with his own sword and inflicting a deep wound on his thigh. The injury of their leader delayed Godfrey's contingent for some time and so, through his self-inflicted injury, Godfrey is seen to fail in the role of military leader.[35] Guibert of Nogent's version is even more critical: he records that the duke had gone out in search of sport, but upon being bitten by a bear was injured so badly that his contingent was delayed and 15,000 men abandoned him. In this version, Godfrey's injury may not have been self-inflicted, but the consequences for his followers are serious.[36] In William's hands, though, Godfrey's accident became the daring rescue of one of his sworn men, the action of a model leader which in no way compromised his commitment to the crusade.

The respite from his chronic illness, which Godfrey enjoyed during the crusade, ended soon after the Battle of Ascalon in August 1099, the engagement that, after the capture of Jerusalem in July, secured the position of the nascent crusader settlement in the East. Apparently, during the lull in hostilities at the end of 1099, Godfrey 'had an attack of his old fever as a result of this unwonted leisure'.[37] Once again, Providence had a hand in this: William explains that it was God's will to take His servant to Him, and so Godfrey died in July 1100.[38] Throughout his highly selective biography of the duke, William consistently uses Godfrey's health as an instrument of Providence. By describing as an act of God Godfrey's return to health in order to fight gloriously in the crusade and secure the kingdom of Jerusalem, William reflects broader contemporary interpretations of the crusaders as implements of God's will: Godfrey's health, furnished by God, directed him to the crusade and took him to Paradise when the crusade was over.

Let us return then to William's story of Sigurd's crusade, and to the health problems of the Norwegian crusaders in Constantinople. This vignette could be interpreted through a modern, scientific lens as a case of alcohol poisoning as a result of overindulgence in the local beverage.[39] To draw this conclusion,

---

[33] For a detailed examination of this event, see N. Hodgson, 'Lions, tigers, and bears: encounters with wild animals and bestial imagery in the context of crusading to the Latin East', *Viator* 44 (2013), 65–93, at pp. 84–93.
[34] Gilo of Paris, bk 4, lines 390–9 (pp. 94–5).
[35] Albert of Aachen, bk 3. 4–5 (pp. 144–5).
[36] Guibert of Nogent, *Gesta Dei per Francos*, 7. 12, ed R. B. C. Huygens (Turnhout, 1996), pp. 285–7.
[37] GR 373. 7: 'regem otii desuetudine febrim antiquam nactum fuisse'. By this stage, Godfrey was king of Jerusalem, according to William, although whether he actually took that title is disputed.
[38] GR 373. 7–8.
[39] GR II, p. 374.

however, would to be to enter the disputed ground of retrospective diagnosis.[40] Alternatively, we can enter William's conceptual world, and to place this passage in the context of his understanding of humoral and climatic theory, his interpretation of the crusade, and his views of different nations and peoples. It should be noted that in twelfth-century medical opinion, wine was considered to be very healthy, being humorally warm and dry, able to balance the humours and strengthen the body when drunk in moderation: excess of anything was considered unhealthy, and too much wine was thought to over-heat the body.[41] Considering the medieval medical theories of the adaptation of people to their climatic surroundings, which, as discussed, were important to William, it follows that he would have thought that wine produced in a foreign place could be unhealthy for visitors. Perhaps the problem was not simply that the Norwegians drank too much wine, but that the wine was of the wrong origin and did not suit their constitutions. Moreover, contemporary medical advice was to mix wine with water in order to manage its effect on the body. The mixing of water and wine for medical purposes could be complex, depending on the specific ailment, time of year and type of wine, but it was also usual to dilute wine for ordinary drinking.[42] Sigurd's advice to his men – to dilute their wine – was current in ancient Greece, and was considered important for the healthy consumption of wine until the early modern period.

More puzzling is William's report that the body of a dead soldier was examined to discover the cause of his death. The implication from the prominence of the liver in Sigurd's diagnosis is that Sigurd had the man dissected, although William's language is not explicit. It would be extremely unusual if autopsy, the dissection of a body to determine cause of death, were implied, since this practice was virtually unknown in Western Europe before the fourteenth century. A handful of stories of autopsies were recorded in Byzantium in the eleventh and twelfth centuries, although the veracity of the incidents described is questionable, and the first recorded autopsy in Italy was not until 1286.[43] It is, however, possible that the concept or idea of autopsy for medical diagnosis, if not the physical practice, was

---

[40] On retrospective diagnosis, the practice of diagnosing medical conditions in the past, see J. Arrizabalaga, 'Problematizing retrospective diagnosis in the history of disease', *Asclepio* 54 (2002), 51–70; A. Cunningham, 'Identifying disease in the past: cutting the Gordian Knot', *Asclepio* 54 (2002), 13–34; P. D. Mitchell, 'Retrospective diagnosis, and the use of historical texts for investigating disease in the past', *International Journal of Paleopathology* 1 (2011), 81–8.

[41] M. W. Adamson, *Food in Medieval Times* (Westport, 2004), p. 51; Cavallo and Storey, *Healthy Living*, pp. 218–20.

[42] J. Jouanna, *Greek Medicine from Hippocrates to Galen: Selected Papers* (Leiden, 2012), pp. 188–9. See also p. 41 above.

[43] L. J. Bliquez and A. Kazhdan, 'Four testimonia to human dissection in Byzantine times', *Bulletin of the History of Medicine* 58 (1984), 554–7; R. Browning, 'A further testimony to human dissection in the Byzantine world', ibid. 59 (1985), 518–20; but see the important qualifications raised by V. Nutton and C. Nutton, 'The archer of Meudon: a curious absence of continuity in the history of medicine', *Journal of the History of Medicine and Allied Sciences* 58 (2003), 401–27, at pp. 404–5, n. 10. On the date of the first Italian autopsy, K. Park, 'The criminal and the saintly body: autopsy and dissection in Renaissance Italy', *Renaissance Quarterly* 47 (1994), 1–33, at p. 4.

known in twelfth-century Byzantium, and this provides a rationale for the inclusion of the story in William's chronicle, given that the event described apparently took place in Constantinople; he may have been prepared to accept the report of such an unusual procedure, given that it took place in an alien land. William gives no indication of shock or surprise at the concept of an autopsy, which ought to have been unfamiliar to him. Perhaps he would have been inclined to accept it as a manifestation of the alterity he already perceived in the toxicity of the local wine to the crusaders and the implied insalubrity of the location.

How does William's inclusion of this story fit in with his interpretation of the crusade? Not only does it represent his interest in health, place and illness, but it is also an opportunity for him to reinforce his presentation of the ideal crusader leader. The role of Providence is less obvious here than in his biography of Godfrey; the solution to the problem of the wine is attributed solely to Sigurd himself without any divine assistance. However, there is some corroboration between the depictions of the two men: William's description of Sigurd as learned and wise, concerned above all for the condition of his men, parallels William's story of Godfrey and the lion, in which Godfrey responded to the danger of one of his knights. William thus emphasises that a crusading leader should be constantly attentive to the health and wellbeing of his men.

William's evidently sophisticated level of medical understanding tells us much about how health and crusading were interpreted in the twelfth century, and about William himself. The representations of health in the crusading sections of the *Gesta Regum* allow us to appreciate the wealth of contemporary medical insight that these parts of the text convey. The experience of health is integrated into William's political, military and biographical narrative of early twelfth-century crusading, and this integration shows that he was interested in more than the politico-military significance of the events he describes. Perhaps this is actually a manifestation of William's own strong sense of self-identity as a writer on the periphery of Europe, leading him to demonstrate that crusading in the East could be a risky endeavour for north-westerners. William's prevailing message, however, is that those crusaders who suffered from the health risks of crusading could be preserved by Divine Providence, the crusade being, of course, the 'gesta Dei per Francos'.

→ 12 ←

German Emperors as Exemplary Rulers in William of Malmesbury and Otto of Freising

Alheydis Plassmann

ONE OF MEDIEVAL GERMANY'S MOST CELEBRATED HISTORIES, Otto of Freising's *Historia de Duabus Ciuitatibus*, or as he himself called it *De Mutatione Rerum*, penned between 1132 and 1146, is often cited as evidence that the so-called Twelfth-Century Renaissance reached Germany.[1] Otto studied in Paris and wrote excellent Latin, which seems to prove this point. Nevertheless, while most twelfth-century historians looked for their inspiration to works of classical learning, Otto's work is deeply influenced by Augustine's *De Ciuitate Dei* and his model is not classical Roman thought. Although his treatment of Augustine is rather innovative, he still adheres to the Church Father's late antique pessimism. Otto cast his work in the mould of providential history, which – at least in theory – treats the whole world as its subject. As his narrative progresses, Otto tries to bring to light God's actions in the world, while also emphasising that no human can really perceive God's will. In doing so, however, Otto is somewhat ambivalent. Sometimes the rise of the Church in and after the Investiture Controversy leads him to suggest that the final disunion of the *ciuitas permixta* (the mixed state), is drawing near and therefore Judgement Day is not far distant. At other times, he seems to think that the rise of the Church will be followed by decadence and decline, as had been the case with every other empire down to his own times. Otto of Freising's other great work, the *Gesta Friderici* is, at first sight, astonishingly different. Begun in 1156, this work, commissioned by his nephew Barbarossa himself, is characterised by a far more positive view of history and the world. In it Otto describes the beginnings of Frederick Barbarossa's reign as a new dawn for the empire and in this way turns the *Historia*'s view of the imminent end of the world upside down. However, despite these two seemingly incompatible texts, Otto of Freising's view of world history is internally consistent,

---

[1] S. Bagge, 'German historiography and the Twelfth-Century Renaissance', in *Representations of Power in Medieval Germany*, ed. B. Weiler and S. MacLean (Turnhout, 2006), pp. 165–88.

as Hans-Werner Goetz has pointed out.[2] Otto simply chose to analyse the turn of events differently after his nephew gained the throne. As he saw it, a new power cycle was about to begin and it is Frederick who gets the benefit of it.

Like Otto, William of Malmesbury is one of the most well-respected historians of the twelfth century, whose Latin and learning make him an excellent example of the boom of historiography in Anglo-Norman England.[3] For William, the secular and the spiritual were two sides of the same coin, an idea he addressed in the 1120s in his *Gesta Regum* and *Gesta Pontificum*, both of which focused on England. William's intentions have been the subject of much debate, but whereas Otto's purpose was to unveil the vanity of the world, William's aims were didactic, practical and to the point. He wanted to show how rulers and bishops should act for the common good. In contrast to Otto the common good might be achieved even if kings did not behave virtuously, nor was it dependent on an overlying arc of providentially determined history.[4]

So Otto wrote about the world and William wrote about England. Although we might expect from the titles of their works that Otto might deal at least in some chapters with English rulers, since the whole world is his subject, and that none of William's chapters in his English history would touch on Germany, the reverse is true. Otto hardly mentions any English kings, while William provides long chapters on the German emperors and their Frankish predecessors. William is not well informed about German affairs, as is evident if we compare his work with German versions of the same stories. His genealogy of the late Carolingians and their supposed connections to the Ottonian emperors is a mess,[5] and many

---

[2] For Otto of Freising compare especially the work of H.-W. Goetz, *Das Geschichtsbild Ottos von Freising, Ein Beitrag zur historischen Vorstellungswelt und zur Geschichte des 12. Jahrhunderts* (Cologne, 1984); S. Bagge, *Kings, Politics, and the Right Order of the World in German Historiography, c. 950–1150* (Leiden, 2002), pp. 364–88; J. Ehlers, 'Ab errorum tenebris ad veram lucem. Otto von Freising entdeckt den Ursprung seiner Zeit in der christlichen Spätantike', in *Die Suche nach den Ursprüngen. Von der Bedeutung des frühen Mittelalters*, ed. W. Pohl (Vienna, 2004), pp. 307–15; L. Hageneier, 'Die frühen Staufer bei Otto von Freising oder Wie sind die Gesta Friderici entstanden?', in *Grafen, Herzöge, Könige – der Aufstieg der frühen Staufer und das Reich (1079–1152)*, ed. H. Seibert (Ostfildern, 2005), pp. 363–96; I do not claim that this list is exhaustive.

[3] On William there are numerous studies by both his editors. Thomson, *William of Malmesbury*, incorporates many of these studies; also Sønnesyn, *Ethics*; B. Weiler, 'William of Malmesbury on kingship', *History* 90 (2005), 3–22; idem, 'Royal justice and royal virtue in William of Malmesbury's Historia Novella and Walter Map's De Nugis Curialium', in *Virtue and Ethics in the Twelfth Century*, ed. I. Bejczy and R. Newhauser (Leiden, 2005), pp. 317–39; idem, 'William of Malmesbury, King Henry I and the Gesta regum Anglorum', ANS 31 (2009), 157–76; further J. Gillingham, 'The beginnings of English imperialism', in idem, *The English in the Twelfth Century – Imperialism, National Identity and Political Values* (Woodbridge, 2000), pp. 3–18 (first published in *Journal of Historical Sociology* 5 (1992), 392–409).

[4] On William's focus on the outcome of royal policy instead of the morally right behaviour compare A. Plassmann, 'Bedingungen und Strukturen von Machtausübung bei Wilhelm von Malmesbury und Heinrich von Huntingdon', in *Macht und Spiegel der Macht – Herrschaft in Europa im 12. und 13. Jahrhundert vor dem Hintergrund der Chronistik*, ed. N. Kersken and G. Vercamer (Wiesbaden, 2013), pp. 145–71.

[5] GR 112. 1: He confused Louis III the Blind with Louis IV the Child and took Henry I for

of his stories about German emperors are legendary and attributed to the wrong ruler. He is not alone in this regard: Otto also does not get it right in every case. But the factual basis of their tales is not important for their outlook on the function of world history, of the history of kings and kingdoms and of history's connection to God's purpose. It can be reasonably assumed that both selected only accounts of events that fitted their view of history.

Thus, in seeking to discern their ideas about history, it is not important to establish whether the events they describe actually occurred. That William's purpose was to write about English history raises the question of why he even wrote about emperors. Although Otto's reasons for writing about the predecessors of his half-brother Conrad III and his nephew Frederick are obvious, the function of the German emperors in William's text is a different matter. Otto gives a clear-cut explanation for history that in his eyes provides us with at least a glimpse of unfolding divine purpose, whereas William's outlook is more complicated. I hope to shed light on William's view of world, imperial and regnal history by contrasting it with Otto's. By juxtaposing William's tales of emperors with Otto's less subtle use of emperors as moral examples we might arrive at an explanation of why William does not stick to the title of his work. I will now focus on emperors whom both saw as predecessors of the contemporary German kings: Charlemagne, Louis the Pious, Charles III, Henry III and Henry IV.

Charlemagne

It is no surprise that Otto describes Charlemagne in a positive way: as a just and pious ruler who serves the Church. At the very beginning of his reign, he decided to go on a pilgrimage to Rome.[6] Otto sees him as the apostle of the Saxons whom he persuaded to convert to Christianity after many wars.[7] His many conquests predestined him to become emperor, although his coronation is as much a reward for him as it is a punishment for the Byzantine empress Irene, who had the audacity to reign despite being a woman.[8] Charlemagne's reign is a turning point: from this point onward, the Roman Empire is transferred to the West.[9] Thus, Charlemagne's assumption of emperorship is a good example of how historical events were usually believed to have unfolded. Otto explicitly sees

---

a son of Conrad I. As Thomson said in *GR* II, p. 218: 'At this point one notes again that most of William's information about Germany, Italy, and the papacy is in the form of folk-tales, saga, and legend.' On his knowledge of German affairs see now S. Pätzold, 'Germania – Alemannia – Regnum Teutonicum. Die Darstellung des ottonisch-salischen Reichs in den *Gesta regum Anglorum* des Wilhelm von Malmesbury', *Historisches Jahrbuch* 136 (2016), 201–66.

[6] Otto of Freising, *Chronica sive de Duabus Ciuitatibus*, v. 26, ed. A. Hofmeister (MGH srg 45), p. 254. Translations of Otto are my own.
[7] Ibid., v. 27, p. 254.
[8] Ibid., v. 29, p. 255. Otto additionally points out that Charlemagne is suitable to become emperor, v. 30, p. 256. This and the remark about Irene's guilt Otto added to his source Frutolf.
[9] Ibid., v. 32 (p. 257).

Charlemagne's reign as the climax of Frankish rule after its rise under Charles Martel and Pippin, just as Otto the Great's reign represents the climax of Ottonian rule.[10] Apart from the image of Charlemagne as exemplary ruler, whose many achievements and virtues are catalogued, his rule is a model in the narrative for how the sine-wave of history functions.

For William, too, Charlemagne is exemplary: pious, a patron of learning, kind and successful in war.[11] To be informed about him is simply part of a good education: 'I regard ignorance of their [the Carolingians'] descent as a serious gap in knowledge seeing that they are not only our neighbours but the people mainly responsible for the Christian empire'.[12] His rise to the imperial crown is a model of moderation: '[Charlemagne] did not presume to take the title of emperor, though often invited to assume it by Pope Hadrian'.[13] Only the accord of the Roman people and the pope could impose the title on him. This does not cause him to fail in his imperial duties though; 'He later came to defend it [the title] with proper spirit against the emperors of Constantinople'.[14] It is symptomatic of Charlemagne's exemplary role even in 'foreign' affairs that William cites a letter of Alcuin describing Charlemagne's righteous indignation at the intrigues and murder at the Northumbrian court.[15]

William's treatment of the pacts of friendship between Charlemagne and Offa of Mercia is in the same vein, contrasting the Mercian ruler with the morally superior Frank: '[Offa] could not easily find in Charles's character anything sympathetic to his own mode of proceeding'.[16] 'Relying on this relationship, Offa, although the object of many men's hatred, ended his days in peace and comfort.'[17] This is not the only time Charlemagne intervened in England. Offa's daughter, accused by William of being a poisoner, was justly punished with exile from Charlemagne's court.[18] Charlemagne functions as a model of princely perfection whose mighty

---

[10] Ibid., vi. 24, p. 286 seq.

[11] GR 65 and 66: Charlemagne is friendly towards Alcuin and shows interest in his teachings; 367. 3: Charlemagne founded a library in Jerusalem; 68 and 135: his military exploits. According to 135. 4 his military success is due to the possession of the holy lance, which only came to the possession of the German kings under Henry I. For the lance see H.-W. Goetz, 'Heilige Lanze', in *Lexikon des Mittelalters* vol. 4 (Munich, Zürich, 1989), col. 2020 seq.; and *Die Heilige Lanze in Wien. Insignie, Reliquie, 'Schicksalsspeer'*, ed. F. Kirchweger and G. Wolf (Vienna, 2005).

[12] GR 67: 'quia progeniem eorum nescire dampnum duco scientiae, cum et confines nobis sint et ad eos maxime Christianum spectet imperium'.

[13] GR 68. 6: 'et ab imperatoria appellatione, quanuis sepe ab Adriano papa inuitaretur, temperans'.

[14] GR 68. 7: 'postea tamen animositate qua decebat contra imperatores Constantinopolitanos defendens'.

[15] GR 72. 3.

[16] GR 90: 'quanuis non facile quod suis artibus conduceret in Karoli animo inuenerit'.

[17] GR 94: 'cuius familiaritate fretus, licet multorum impeteretur odio, dulci tamen uitam consumpsit otio'.

[18] GR 113. 17 seq. Charlemagne's main motive seems to have been his affronted vanity, because Eadburh would rather have married one of his sons than himself. The story is found already in Asser, *Vita Alfredi*, cc. 13–14, ed. W. H. Stevenson (2nd edn, Oxford, 1959), pp. 12–14 (GR II, p. 87).

rule influences England, although it is made clear that from the Frankish perspective that happened only tangentially.[19]

For William, Charlemagne is a good example of how a ruler can be successful. However, as is often the case in William's work, the ruler's success depends on circumstances. William elaborates on this when speaking of Charlemagne's relationship with the Church. In a speech put into the mouth of Pope Gregory VI William mentions the alleged investiture privilege that Hadrian I gave to Charlemagne for practical reasons:

> over such great distances it was in those days impractical to ask the Holy See to lend its approval to every single elected candidate, while there was a prince at hand, known to do nothing for love of gain, but to install religious persons in his churches in accordance with canon law.[20]

In Charlemagne's time, it was reasonable to give land and rights to churchmen so that the Church could aid in taming the newly baptised peoples subjected to Charlemagne's rule.[21] In the time of Henry V, two centuries later, it was reasonable for rulers to renounce investiture and concede to the Church the liberty it wanted. Only after the settlement between Henry and Pope Calixtus at Worms does William praise Henry V as a ruler who almost reached Charlemagne's grandeur.[22] In William's *Gesta Regum* Charlemagne's rule is not just shown as morally exemplary, but also as successful.

Louis the Pious

Otto dismisses the many problems of the reign of Louis the Pious in just one sentence, claiming that they are hearsay: 'The emperor Louis who, because of his wife's wrongdoings, as is said, was expelled and thereafter reinstated, died in the twenty-sixth year of his reign.'[23] The partition of the Frankish realm after his death is brought about by God:

---

[19] On Charlemagne as a model of kingship in legends cf. F. Wolfzettel, 'Karl der Große', in *Enzyklopädie des Märchens*, vol. 7 (Berlin, New York, 1993), cols 981–1002.

[20] GR 202. 7: 'Preterea per tot terrarum interstitia nequibat requiri sedes apostolica ut unicuique electo assensum commodaret suum, dum esset prope rex qui nichil per auaritiam disponeret, sed iuxta sacra canonum scita religiosas personas aecclesiis introduceret.' This 'privilegium' is a forgery. William's editors are not sure where William got his knowledge of the false investiture-privileges (*GR* II, pp. 194 seq. and 385). David Scotus, a close intimate of the emperor Henry V, might be the source as in other cases regarding developments in Germany: cf. *Die falschen Investiturprivilegien*, ed. C. Märtl (MGH fontes 13), p. 113 n. 361.

[21] GR 420. 2.

[22] GR 438. The comparison of Henry V with Charlemagne probably derives from David Scotus (*GR* II, p. 391), William's source, but it is revealing that William mentions this only after the Concordat of Worms.

[23] Otto of Freising, *Chronica*, v. 34 (p. 259): 'Igitur Lodewicus imperator propter mala opera uxoris suae regno, ut dicitur, pulsus ac postmodum restitutus XX°VI° imperii sui anno diem obit extremum'.

> Since God, in order to make plain for mortals the miseries and the twists of fate, did not want the Frankish realm, to which after innumerable changes, as I told above, the Roman Empire was transferred, to remain on the high point it had reached, he allowed for it to be divided miserably and therefore be desolated and diminished.[24]

The reasons for the well-known quarrels within the Carolingian family are not explained. Despite the fact that Louis's sons from the first marriage repeatedly tried to ensure the disinheritance of their youngest half-brother, Otto does not even mention that Charles the Bald had a different mother from Lothar I and Louis the German. Louis the Pious just happens to be the king in whose reign the time of decline took place, so that Louis's involvement in, if not blame for, the complicated inheritance is passed over. The decline of the empire is not man-made, but an inevitable development.

For William, on the other hand, the struggles of the sons and the father are family problems. He sees Louis the Pious as a 'mild and simple-hearted prince', whose only fault was that he paid more attention to Charles than to his other sons. His son Lothar – and only he – showed unprecedented cruelty towards his father and frequently imprisons him, if we are to believe William's claims.[25] From the *Gesta Pontificum* we learn that Lothar pretended to be indignant at the 'incestuous' marriage of his father to Judith, although the real motive for his protest was envy.[26] Louis's simplicity is mirrored by the English king Edward the Confessor. His reign was, according to William, a success, not because of any particular competence on Edward's side but because God favoured him and his magnates supported him.[27] Louis the Pious was unlucky that his close family and other magnates did not support him; he was obviously not sufficiently pious to warrant divine intervention. As with Charlemagne, Louis fits into the pattern William sets up for successful and unsuccessful kingship: Louis was unsuccessful because he did not manage to bring his magnates and sons to heel.

Charles III

For Otto, Charles III the Fat's reign illustrates the vicissitudes of history, not over several generations but over the course of a single life:

---

[24] Ibid., v. 35 (p. 259): 'Igitur cum regnum Francorum, ad quod post innumeras, quas supra dixi, mutationes regnum Romanorum devenerat, cum et ipsum ad ostendendas mortalium miserias ac instabiles mundi rotatus auctor omnium Deus in illo, ad quem profecerat, statu manere nollet, in se ipsum miserabiliter dividi ac per hoc desolari et imminui permisit'.

[25] GR 110. 1.

[26] GP 6. 7.

[27] GR 196. 2. On William's picture of Edward the confessor compare also Sønnesyn, *Ethics*, pp. 189–93, and Plassmann, 'Bedingungen und Strukturen'. On the Confessor cf. F. Barlow, *Edward the Confessor* (3rd edn, New Haven and London, 1997), and *Edward the Confessor. The Man and the Legend*, ed. R. Mortimer (Woodbridge, 2009).

That king, who at the division of the East Frankish kingdom between brothers got the smallest part, reached the top, when he received both the Western and the Eastern realms as well as the imperial crown, but later came down to such poverty that he even lacked bread.[28]

Otto does not describe Charles as a particularly incompetent or bad ruler, however, emphasising instead the mystery and obscurity of God's methods.[29]

William, too, paints a rather positive picture of the reign of Charles III. He describes a vision experienced by Charles, based upon a written source designed to promote one of the emperor's possible heirs. In this vision, Charles sees all his predecessors – uncles, brothers and his father – receiving punishment in purgatory for the evil committed in their reigns. Charles also sees there the kings' bishops and magnates who had sinned by counselling war instead of peace, by loving murder and robbery, and by being driven by greed.[30] A king does not rule alone, and his advisers, the bishops in particular, have a duty to set their king on the right path. William gives numerous examples of this, both in the *Gesta Regum* and the *Gesta Pontificum*, and he drives home this point by drawing on this rather obscure German source to show that this duty is universal.[31]

Henry III and the Salians

Although, in Otto's eyes, history repeats itself under the Ottonian kings and emperors, the continuous up-and-down undergoes a variation with the Salians. This dynasty started well with Conrad II, who was as an exceptionally virtuous king: 'He was a king who was strong in war, prudent in council, wise in law and everyday negotiations, devoted to the Christian religion, and modest, just as befits a king.'[32] This high praise is quite unusual for Otto, who seldom ponders the characteristics of kings at all; he prefers to phrase his criticism subtly. When Conrad passes judgment on three bishops, Otto does not offer his opinion as to whether this was according to the law or otherwise.[33] However, on the way

---

[28] Otto of Freising, *Chronica*, vi. 9 (p. 270): 'Rex iste, qui in divisione orientalis regni inter fratres minimam portionem acceperat, ad tantum primo fastigium, ut tam orientalia quam occidentalia regna cum Romano susceperit imperio, ad tantam postremo deiectionem venit, ut panis quoque egeret'.

[29] This might be due to his sources. Neither Frutolf-Ekkehard nor Regino, *Annales Hildesheimenses*, or *Annales Mellicenses* go much into detail regarding Charles III and none of them tells of his failings as a ruler. The *Annales Fuldenses*, which do go into detail on Charles's shortcomings, were not used by Otto. On Charles III the Fat cf. S. MacLean, *Kingship and Politics in the Late Ninth Century, Charles the Fat and the End of the Carolingian Empire* (Cambridge, 2003).

[30] GR III. On the sources for this vision cf. Thomson, *William of Malmesbury*, p. 148 seq.

[31] On the bishops' duty to counsel their prince cf. Plassmann, 'Bedingungen und Strukturen', and Ryan Kemp in this volume, pp. 65–79.

[32] Otto of Freising, *Chronica*, vi. 28 (p. 291 seq.) : 'Erat autem idem rex armis strenuus, consilio providus, sapientia tam forensi quam civili preditus, in religione Christiana satis devotus, humilitate, quae regem decebat, adornatus'.

[33] Ibid., vi. 31 (p. 296).

Discovering William of Malmesbury

home Conrad's army is afflicted by an illness, which might be interpreted as divine punishment of the emperor.[34] His son Henry III takes after his father: 'In every virtue he was not only his father's equal but surpassed him.'[35] Nevertheless, already in Henry III's reign a new rising star can be perceived: the papacy. Although not every pope Henry appointed was elected canonically, Popes Leo IX and Alexander II struggled in defence of the Church's freedom, and the upward curve of the now important papacy would carry the popes to unanticipated climaxes of power; 'She, who was small and moderate, became a mountain, as everybody can see'.[36] For Otto, this rise of the Church is the portent of the imminent Judgement Day, as the Roman Empire, identified with the fourth and final Empire of Daniel's prophecy, comes to its end.[37]

William's account of Henry III's reign does not even come close to his usual standard of accuracy.[38] He tells us how Gunnhild, Henry III's first wife, was accused of adultery and managed to clear her name through trial by combat.[39] In this particular case, William might have combined several tales: the legend of Kunigunde, Henry II's wife, who proved her innocence by ordeal,[40] and a rumour about Agnes, Henry III's second wife, accused by some of having had an affair with a bishop after Henry's death and who, like Gunnhild in William's version, became a nun afterwards.[41] Henry III purportedly one night observed his sister carrying her clerical lover on her back through the freshly fallen snow,

[34] Ibid., vi. 31 (p. 297).
[35] Ibid.: 'Hic per omnia patrem in virtutibus non solum equasse, sed et transcendisse perhibetur, regnum moderatissime gubernans'.
[36] Ibid., vi. 36 (p. 305): 'Ipsa vero, quae antea parva fuit et humilis, in quantum montem excreverit, ab omnibus iam videri potest'.
[37] Ibid., vi. 36 (p. 306).
[38] Some English historians borrowed these stories from William of Malmesbury or they might have taken them from a similar or identical source. For this see *GP* II, pp. 182–5.
[39] *GR* 188. 8. On Henry's marriage to Gunnhild who died early cf. J. Laudage, 'Heinrich III. Ein Lebensbild', in *Das salische Kaiser-Evangeliar. Der Kommentar Bd. 1*, ed. J. Rathofer (Münster, 1998), pp. 87–145, at 94. On this story, which seems to have been popular in England, cf. also *GP* II, p. 181 seq. The confusion of Gunnhild and Kunigunde might also be due to the fact that Gunnhild was also called Kunigunde in Germany. This story of the slandered queen has many variants; one suspiciously similar is the ballad of Sir Aldingar, on which cf. P. Christophersen, *The Ballad of Sir Aldingar, Its Origin and Analogues* (Oxford, 1952), p. 20 seq. I thank Linda Dohmen (Bonn) for this information. She will publish a Ph.D. thesis on queens suspected of adultery: L. Dohmen, *Tocius mali causa, Untersuchungen zu den öffentlich erhobenen Vorwürfen der Unzucht gegen die Gemahlinnen der Karolinger* (forthcoming).
[40] On the Kunigunde-legend cf. E. Roth, 'Kunigunde, Hl.', in *Enzyklopädie des Märchens* vol. 8 (Berlin and New York, 1996), cols 608–10; B. Schneidmüller, 'Heinrich II. und Kunigunde. Das heilige Kaiserpaar des Mittelalters', in *Kunigunde – consors regni – Vortragsreihe zum tausendjährigen Jubiläum der Krönung Kunigundes in Paderborn (1002–2002)*, ed. S. Dick (Munich, 2004), pp. 29–46.
[41] Lampert of Hersfeld, *Annales*, ed. O. Holder-Egger (MGH SS 38), pp. 1–304, here and a. 1062, 79 seq. On this cf. M. Black-Veldtrup, *Kaiserin Agnes (1043–1077), Quellenkritische Studien* (Cologne, Weimar, Vienna, 1995), pp. 356–65; C. Zey, 'Vormünder und Berater Heinrichs IV. im Urteil der Zeitgenossen (1056–1075)', in *Heinrich IV*, ed. G. Althoff (Sigmaringen, 2009), pp. 87–126, at 101 seq., no. 58.

so that nobody would realise that he had been with her. The emperor chose not to expose them but gave the cleric a bishopric and his sister a nunnery on the condition that there would be no more 'riding pleasures'.[42] Although William uses the story to exemplify Henry's sense of humour, we find another version of it, attributed to Charlemagne and his daughter, recorded in Germany, a little later than the *Gesta Regum*, in the *Codex Laureshamensis*. Here it is a story of how an emperor should act after advice, exemplified by Charlemagne, generally agreed to have been the best of emperors.[43]

William tells another story about Henry III: another cleric at his court was embarrassed by the emperor when, after having spent a night in his mistress's bed, he was ordered by Henry to celebrate mass. The cleric stubbornly refused and was banished by the emperor but brought back and rewarded with a bishopric, on condition however that he give up his love.[44] Another story, first told by the German chronicler Lambert of Hersfeld, recounts a public conflict between the abbot of Fulda and the bishop of Hildesheim,[45] over the right to sit at the emperor's right hand.[46] In William's account (wrongly involving Henry III rather than IV, and the archbishop of Mainz instead of the bishop of Hildesheim) the public quarrel between the prelates is instigated by the Devil, and Henry spoiled the Devil's triumph by declaring a day of public almsgiving.[47] The last anecdote William relates about Henry III is intended to underline the emperor's vigorous fight against simony. When Henry was a child, a certain cleric delighted him with a new toy, and in childish pleasure, the future emperor promised him a bishopric. He made good that promise when the cleric asked for the bishopric, but a near-death

---

[42] GR 190.

[43] *Codex Laureshamensis*, ed. K. Glöckner (2 vols, Darmstadt, 1929–36), I, c. 19 (p. 298 seq.). On this legend cf. E. Frenzel, 'Eginhard und Emma', in *Enzyklopädie des Märchens* vol. 3 (Berlin, New York, 1981), cols 1020–3. She argues that William of Malmesbury was the source for *Codex Laureshamensis*, but this leaves open the question of why one source names Charlemagne and the other Henry III. The other significant difference in the two versions of the king who catches his female relative with her lover is the fact that Henry III in William's story searches for a clandestine settlement and offers an ecclesiastical office to the two lovers, while Charlemagne in the other version simply allows the couple to marry. Thus the 'sister / daughter caught in the act' is more likely a folk-tale motif. On the story in *Codex Laureshamensis* cf. also G. Althoff, 'Colloquium familiare – colloquium secretum – colloquium publicum. Beratung im politischen Leben des früheren Mittelalters', *Frühmittelalterliche Studien* 24 (1990), 145–67, at p. 148, also in idem, *Spielregeln der Politik im Mittelalter, Kommunikation in Frieden und Fehde* (Darmstadt, 1997), pp. 157–84, at 160 seq.

[44] GR 191. S. Sønnesyn, 'Ad bonae uitae institutum'; *William of Malmesbury and the Ethics of History* (Bergen, 2007), p. 373 seq., stresses that these stories are more than anecdotes, since their point is to demonstrate the emperor's prudence in not making the affairs public.

[45] Lambert of Hersfeld, *Annales*, anno 1063. Cf. G. Althoff, *Heinrich IV* (Darmstadt, 2006), pp. 57–9.

[46] GR 192. On the importance of the seat to the right cf. H.-W. Goetz, 'Der "rechte" Sitz. Die Symbolik von Rang und Herrschaft im Hohen Mittelalter im Spiegel der Sitzordnung', in *Symbole des Alltags – Alltag der Symbole – Festschrift für Harry Kühnel zum 65. Geburtstag*, ed. G. Blaschitz and H. Kühnel (Graz, 1992), pp. 11–47.

[47] GR 192. 3.

experience made Henry repent and repeal the investiture.[48] William might have heard of the severe illness which Henry incurred, apparently in 1045,[49] but the story that he tells only otherwise appears in England and seems to incorporate a very broad definition of simony. William finishes his account of Henry III with yet another surprising anecdote, the legend of a hind that once carried the emperor to safety.[50] William would have more stories to tell, he says, 'which I omit, not wishing to overtax my credit with the reader'.[51] William's purpose in going to such lengths regarding Henry III is not as clear-cut as it is with the Carolingians, but once again he is addressing the ideal relationship between king and princes. The emperor cares for the moral purity of his clergy, but does not show this publicly. He changes them for the better but without undermining their authority. His choice to do so with humour is not a specifically Christian virtue, but a courtly one, which had its origin in the eleventh century.[52] Only the story of Gunnhild, who was not exactly treated in a gentlemanly way at the German court, casts a shadow over the otherwise ideal king whose abhorrence of simony as well as his unblemished conduct overall might serve as an example for Henry I in England, though William does not state this explicitly.

Henry IV

For Otto of Freising Henry IV is, like Charles the Fat, a fine example of how things can go wrong in this bleak world. Otto does not elaborate on Henry's reign, concentrating instead on his last year. 'Against the law of nature' his son Henry V rebelled against his father.[53] The emperor's subsequent downfall is another example of how secular power is nothing in the face of eternity. Just like Charles the Fat, he ended life as a beggar.[54] Every incident that might belie this interpretation is declared void by Otto. Happy events only reinforce his interpretation of history as signalling the imminent end of the world. For example, the fact that in Henry IV's reign Jerusalem has been won for Christendom is balanced by a decline of morals and virtues, which in Otto's eyes is obvious to everybody.[55] The growth of both good and bad conditions is a symptom of the coming apocalypse. Otto

[48] GR 193.
[49] On this Hermann of Reichenau, *Chronicon*, ed. G. Pertz (MGH SS 5), pp. 67–133, a. 1045, 125: Laudage, 'Heinrich III', p. 118.
[50] GR 194. 1. For the hind as a helpful animal cf. L. Blum, 'Hirsch, Hirschkuh', in *Enzyklopädie des Märchens* vol. 6 (Berlin, New York, 1990), cols 1067–72, Stith Thompson, *Motif-Index of Folk-Literature* (rev. edn, vol. 1, A-C: Copenhagen, 1955), B 557.3: deer carries man.
[51] GR 194. 1: 'et quibusdam aliis, quibus ideo supersedeo quia estimationem lectoris supergredi nolo'.
[52] On *hilaritas* as a courtly virtue cf. J. Bumke, *Höfische Kultur, Literatur und Gesellschaft im hohen Mittelalter* (3rd edn, Munich, 1986), p. 427 seq.; C. J. Jaeger, *The Origins of Courtliness* (Philadelphia, 1985), pp. 168–73.
[53] Otto of Freising, *Chronica*, vii. 9 (p. 319 seq.): 'contra legem naturae'.
[54] Ibid., vii. 12 (p. 323).
[55] Ibid., vii. 9 (p. 320 seq.).

German Emperors as Exemplary Rulers

leaves the reader to decide whether Henry's enforced abdication was an outward sign of his damnation or an ordeal to be endured while he was alive so that his soul could be saved.[56] The portents of doom intensify after Henry IV's death when his son Henry V behaves just like his father.[57] Henry IV, Otto's grandfather, fits into the pattern of the Roman Empire's decline like everybody else, whereas Otto withholds judgement on whether Henry IV was damned personally. Two reasons might have caused Otto to reserve judgement on Henry's personal salvation: for outlining the purpose of history Henry IV was personally of no significance, and Otto might have been reluctant to openly declare his own grandfather damned.

William's view of Henry IV's reign is not as jumbled as is that of Henry III, but, unsurprisingly, investiture is a central subject. In mentioning Henry IV's death William memorialises him as a tyrant: 'He inflicted much oppression on the Roman world by his folly and wickedness.'[58] I would argue that by *orbis Romanus* William means the Church. The next time he mentions Henry IV is in the context of Robert Guiscard's life, when William gives a brief account of Henry's war on Pope Gregory VII, which prompted Robert Guiscard to come to the pope's rescue. Henry was 'angry with the pope because he excommunicated him for investing bishops', a rather short explanation for a complex conflict.[59] In William's account of Gregory's life, he goes into detail about Canossa and the election of opposing kings. He seems to have borrowed information from propagandistic sources produced by the opposition to Henry IV in Germany.[60] He claims that the unrelenting pope refused to see the penitent king when he approached barefoot, with scissors and a comb. The pope did not want to give absolution to someone who 'had committed sacrilege and incest with his sister'.[61] Henry's actions against Gregory are thus an act of revenge for the pope's refusal to absolve him. Henry was victorious against his adversaries but succumbed to fate when his own son instigated his downfall.[62]

Thus, Henry is introduced as a rather unsympathetic figure, which might be due to William's sources that were clearly influenced by anti-Henry propaganda virulent in Germany. When William turns his attention to Germany for the last

---

[56] Ibid., vii. 11 (p. 322 seq.).

[57] Ibid., vii. 14 and 15 (pp. 325–31).

[58] GR 225. 5: 'E uestigio quoque Henricus, pius Romanorum imperator, defunctus successorem Henricum filium habuit, qui multas oppressiones orbi Romano fatuitate nequitiaque sua intulit'.

[59] GR 262. 3.

[60] Ibid., 266. On the altogether bleak picture of Henry IV instigated by the opposition cf. Althoff, *Heinrich IV*, pp. 254–73; idem, 'Noch einmal zu den Vorwürfen gegen Heinrich IV. Genese, Themen, Einsatzfelder', in *Heinrich IV*, pp. 255–67, and S. Patzold, 'Die Lust des Herrschers. Zur Bedeutung und Verbreitung eines politischen Vorwurfs zur Zeit Heinrichs IV.', ibid., pp. 219–53.

[61] GR 266: 'Denique fertur quod, inter eum et imperatorem primi tumultus initio, illum nudipedem et forcipes cum scopis portantem nec etiam foribus admiserit, abominatus hominem sacrilegum et sororii incesti reum.' This special accusation is imminent in Bruno of Merseburg, *Saxonicum Bellum*, ed. H.-E. Lohmann (MGH. Deutsches Mittelalter 2), c. 9 (p. 18), cf. on this as well, Althoff, *Heinrich IV*, p. 271 seq.; Patzold, 'Lust des Herrschers', p. 222 seq.

[62] GR 266. 4.

time he seems to give a more unbiased account and produces a remarkable summary of Henry's reign:

> That was the period when the pitiful and almost disastrous tenure of the imperial power by Henry ... was for fifty years a grievous burden to the Germans. Himself neither uneducated nor idle, he became by some freak of fortune a general target, so much so that whoever took up arms against him thought himself to be serving the cause of religion.[63]

This implies that although Henry might have had his faults, he had the misfortune to rule in times of exceptionally adverse circumstances. The closest parallel in the line of English kings is Æthelred the Unready who, like Henry, was according to William 'neither uneducated nor idle', but had to fight against very severe odds.[64] The summary of Henry's reign which parallels the assessment of Æthelred seems to represent William's opinion better than the single tales scattered in different contexts and influenced by German sources. The overall characterisation of Henry William provides is nevertheless much more positive than Æthelred's: he was an able warrior, educated with wide reading, eloquent, gave alms, and most importantly, his enemies came to an unhappy end:[65] William tells the story of an unnamed enemy of the emperor who was consumed by mice.[66] Apart from making the wrong decisions regarding investiture, Henry IV is an example of a king who had the odds stacked against him and therefore fits into William's idea that kingly abilities count for nothing if the time is not right. In this, he is not

---

[63] GR 288: 'Illa fuit tempestas qua Henrici ... miserabile et pene funestum per quinquaginta annos Alemannia ingemuit imperium. Erat is neque ineruditus neque ignauus, sed fato quodam ab omnibus ita impetitus ut rem religionis tractare sibi uideretur quisquis in illum arma produceret.'

[64] Ibid., 165. 11-12. On Æthelred in the *Gesta Regum* cf. Sønnesyn, *Ethics*, pp. 175–80, and Plassmann, 'Bedingungen und Strukturen'.

[65] GR 289. 2.

[66] Ibid., 290. Although he does not provide the name of this man, in German histories the unfortunate bishop goes by the name of Hatto of Mainz and he is said to have lived in the tenth century. The story of Hatto and the mice is in *Chronica minor minoritae Erphordensis*, ed. O. Holder-Egger (MGH srg 42), anno 918 and 969 (pp. 619 and 621); cf. J. Banaszkiewicz, 'Die Mäusethurmsage – The symbolism of annihilation of an evil ruler', *Acta Poloniae Historica* 51 (1985), 5–32; G. Althoff, 'Verformungen durch mündliche Tradition: Geschichten über Erzbischof Hatto von Mainz', in *Iconologia sacra. Mythos, Bildkunst und Dichtung in der Religions- und Sozialgeschichte Alteuropas. Festschrift für Karl Hauck zum 75. Geburtstag*, ed. H. Keller and N. Staubach (Berlin and New York, 1994), pp. 438–50; J. Fried, '"Vor fünfzig oder mehr Jahren". Das Gedächtnis der Zeugen in Prozeßurkunden und in familiären Memorialtexten', in *Pragmatische Dimensionen mittelalterlicher Schriftkultur*, ed. C. Meier and V. Honemann (Munich, 2002), pp. 23–61, at 43–56. The folk-tale motif of a bad man eaten by vermin is found in other sources as well: Thietmar of Merseburg, *Chronicon*, vi. 82, ed. R. Holtzmann (MGH srg, n.s. 9), p. 372; *Gallus Anonymus, Cronicae et gesta ducum sive principum Polonorum*, ed. K. Maleczyński (Monumenta Poloniae Historica, n.s. 2: Krakow, 1952), i. 3 (p. 12); Giraldus Cambrensis, *Itinerarium Kambriae* ii. 2, ed. J. F. Dimmock, *Giraldi Cambrensis Opera* 6 (RS 1868), p. 110 seq. On this motif cf. H.-J. Uther, 'Mäuseturm von Bingen', in *Enzyklopädie des Märchens* vol. 9 (Berlin and New York, 1999), cols 445–50; *Historische Sagen. Von der Antike bis zur Gegenwart*, ed. L. Petzold (Wiesbaden, 2008), pp. 37–40.

that far from Otto's pessimistic outlook on the futility of men's efforts. However, circumstances can change, and they can be changed by men's actions. William's account of Henry V is significant for showing this. Henry managed to reconcile himself with the pope and conclude the investiture controversy, and afterwards William compares him to Charlemagne.[67] With the bishops at his side, Henry V had the opportunity to equal his grand predecessor.

Conclusion

Otto and William both use German emperors (and their Frankish predecessors) as examples of the rules of history, be it the rules of rise and fall, be it the rules of success and failure. But neither use them as exemplary rulers who are to be emulated – barring Charlemagne, perhaps. Otto subordinates the outlines of their reigns rigorously to the overall pattern he sees in history. That is, the constant vicissitudes of history will only come to an end if at some day in the future the Roman Empire fails. And in the *Historia de Duabus Ciuitatibus* this end is in the not so distant future, while in the *Gesta Friderici*, Otto seems to maintain that the cycles of history carry on. The events he describes provide evidence for his analysis of history and he repeats this series of events in an almost tedious fashion. Otto's purpose is highly didactic. If the reader observes and realises the vanity of efforts to rectify the secular world, he can concentrate on Heaven and join the ranks of the good people who balance the growing evil in the world. It is significant that Otto only mentions the situation in England once, and this is to further prove his point. The anarchy in England after Henry I's death is another portent in line with many others.[68]

William uses the German emperors just as he uses the English kings. Their reigns are lessons on the conditions of ruling and on how these all cohere: he focuses on the abilities of the emperor, sometimes his virtues, his handling of princes and bishops, the princes' behaviour, and the role of the Church and how it might fall in line to back a successful ruler. William concentrates on the here and now. His outlook on salvation is more personal and secular than Otto's. The king must have a successful and peaceful reign so that the bishops can do their duty by prompting Christians to a better life. It is unlikely that William would have approached the German emperors much differently if he had had better source material or if he had been better informed. He could have used anecdotes and legends about other rulers and shaped them accordingly. Perhaps he left out some stories that did not fit into his system. For William the end of the world is not an issue, but the conditions for successful rule are at the heart of his work, and they are the same in England as in Germany.

---

[67] *GR* 438, cf. p. 22 above.
[68] Otto of Freising, *Chronica*, vii. 21 (p. 341).

Discovering William of Malmesbury

Both William and Otto are far too sophisticated to give simple explanations for the workings of history, whether world history or regnal history, but both align their narrative to their ideas about history. For Otto, history repeats itself and this can be exemplified by the Roman Empire whose ups and downs determine the fate of the world. To describe historical events in depth, whether by explaining personal involvement or blame or even the question of one's soul's salvation, is not important, and Otto prefers to give general outlines not obscured by too many details. Thus, even if he had chosen to include other regnal histories the same pattern would have been perceivable. William, on the other hand, wants to highlight the complexity of the factors that drive history and for him that means that it is necessary to find the same factors at work in Germany and elsewhere. Only by showing that similar situations lead to similar results in England and Germany do his observations on English history gain any validity. That is why Otto does not have to talk about other kingdoms, only the Roman Empire, and why William has to go into detail about conditions in Germany.

13

Lector amice:
Reading as Friendship in William of Malmesbury

Sigbjørn Sønnesyn

> Anselm, priest of Canterbury, argues;
> William, monk of Malmesbury, writes;
> May you, reader and friend, embrace both in gratitude.[1]

THESE LINES, in William of Malmesbury's own Leonine verse, head the list of contents of his collection of the works of Anselm of Canterbury in London, Lambeth Palace Library 224.[2] For many readers of William of Malmesbury the direct address to the reader, from the writer's own hand, is arresting, even poignant. Are these lines addressed to a specific reader at a given time, or to any reader at any time? Did William take into account the extreme durability of parchment and ink when he wrote these lines? Are we, as his present-day readers, included in the prospective audience he addresses? We will never know, but it is clear from the editorial verse heading his computistical collection in Bodl. Libr. Auct. F. 3. 14, that he saw himself as writing for an audience beyond his own lifetime: 'Let this book of many subjects and belonging to the Church, as a field full of varied delights, make William's name famous after his burial.'[3] So we may assume that he is addressing posterity as well – including ourselves.

Moreover, we are not only addressed as readers, but as friends. In our present linguistic framework, moral language has become emotive: friendship might be

---

[1] Lambeth 224, f. 2r: 'Disputat Anselmus presul Cantorberiensis / Scribit Willelmus monachus Malmesberiensis / Ambos gratifice complectere, lector amice.' I wish to thank the editors of this volume for suggesting a number of significant linguistic and substantial improvements.

[2] For William as a collector of Anselm, see Samu Niskanen's chapter in this volume, pp. 117–27, which significantly revises R. W. Southern, *Saint Anselm: A Portrait in a Landscape* (Cambridge, 1990), pp. 400–2 and 470–3. For William as collector of texts more generally, see the magisterial study in Thomson, *William of Malmesbury*. For William as poet, see M. Winterbottom, 'William of Malmesbury *versificus*', in *Anglo-Latin and its Heritage: Essays in Honour of A. G. Rigg on his 64th Birthday*, ed. S. Echard and G. Wieland (Turnhout, 2001), pp. 109–27.

[3] Bodl. Libr. Auct. F. 3. 14, f. 2v: 'Eclesie codex multarum materiarum / Sicut ager plenus variarum deliciarum / Willelmi nomen faciet post funera clarum.'

153

seen as a passive emotional state; reading, on the contrary, as an active intellectual endeavour.[4] But we should be wary of seeing William's formulation 'reader and friend' as a mere figure of speech, or of postulating that William is bestowing his friendship as a reward for our labour in reading the texts that Anselm composed and that he himself copied. Such instrumental pledges of friendship might be revoked with the same ease with which they are given. Furthermore, some scholars have recently suggested that the monastic language of friendship in the late eleventh and twelfth centuries – particularly that of Anselm of Canterbury himself – was a literary artifice constructing an ideal spiritual friendship through the act of writing itself, but shut off from genuinely interpersonal relationships of the extra-textual world.[5] According to this view, William's address tells us more about the literary devices he seeks to employ than about his desire to form bonds with his reader.

In this paper I would like to explore an alternative to these extremes of literary artifice and conceptual contradiction: the possibility that William saw reading as a process through which genuine friendship between writer and reader could develop. To do this we must study the notions of friendship and reading as they occurred in William's own intellectual context, and the possible points of convergence between them. Did William approach his readers as potential friends in the full sense of the term as found in the classical and patristic literary and intellectual heritage that gave him such joy?[6]

Phrasing the question in this way requires a summary of the classical and patristic notions of friendship with reference to which, as we shall see, William elaborated his own views. These traditions were informed by the famous definition of friendship that Cicero, above all, worked out for the Romans, and Augustine adapted for Christian doctrine.[7] In *De Amicitia*, which William knew well, Cicero defined friendship as 'nothing else than the unanimity, with benevolence

---

[4] On the emotivist turn in moral language, I accept and follow the argument presented in A. MacIntyre, *After Virtue* (2nd edn, London, 1985), pp. 6–35.

[5] See in particular R. J. McDonie, 'Mysterious friends in the prayers and letters of Anselm of Canterbury', in *Friendship in the Middle Ages and Early Modern Age: Explorations of a Fundamental Ethical Discourse*, ed. A. Classen and M. Sandidge (Berlin/New York, 2011), pp. 309–48. For the view that high medieval monastic culture was creating an artificial, purely literary reality, see M. B. Pranger, *The Artificiality of Christianity: Essays on the Poetics of Monasticism* (Stanford CAL, 2003).

[6] For William's joy in classical and patristic thought and literature, see in particular Thomson, *William of Malmesbury*, pp. 40–75. For an overview of the concept of friendship from Antiquity to the high Middle Ages, see in particular J. McEvoy, 'The theory of friendship in the Latin Middle Ages: hermeneutics, contextualization and the transmission and reception of ancient texts and ideas, from c. AD 350 to c. 1500', in *Friendship in Medieval Europe*, ed. J. Haseldine (Stroud, 1999), pp. 3–44; cf. A. Classen, 'Introduction: Friendship – The quest for a human ideal and value from Antiquity to the Early Modern time', in Classen and Sandidge, *Friendship in the Middle Ages and Early Modern Age*, pp. 1–185.

[7] See McEvoy, 'Theory of friendship'. Cf. E. G. Cassidy, '"He who has friends can have no friend": Classical and Christian perspectives on the limits of friendship', in *Friendship in Medieval Europe*, pp. 45–67, and Sønnesyn, *Ethics*, pp. 33–41.

and love, concerning all things human and divine.'[8] It was only within such a framework, united in adherence to a common goal or vision, that true virtue could be developed and perfection reached. This scheme was retained by Augustine and the Latin Fathers; but within the Christian view it was love of God alone that formed the *clef de vôute* on which the whole edifice depended.[9] Friendship was a mutually perfective relationship, within which the reciprocal love between friends was sustained by their mutual love of one ultimate object, and their mutual support in the attainment of it.[10]

As such, spiritual friendship founded on a shared love of God came to be seen as the principle by which the monastic brotherhood in the Latin West could create perfective communities in which monks could attain spiritual fulfilment. Although William, in his *Commentary on Lamentations*, seems to borrow such ideas directly from writers like Augustine and Gregory the Great, his line of argument is in perfect harmony with that other staple monastic text in the early medieval West, John Cassian's *Collationes* or Conferences. In the sixteenth Conference, John Cassian warns against utilitarian or instrumental friendships, and holds aloft the spiritual friendship founded on love of God as the only bond capable of sustaining a truly monastic brotherhood.[11] Cassian starts from the bare fact that bonds of love and friendship may come to be in many ways, and between the good and the bad alike.[12] But, like Cicero and the Roman tradition before him, Cassian finds that only one kind is truly stable and mutually perfective: that is the bond of virtue, of a shared love of the common good.[13] As Cicero claimed for the classical *res publica*, and Augustine for the *ciuitas Dei*, Cassian held that only a perfect union of wills centred on a common conception of the true good could make brothers live together in one house, and thus forge the truly monastic kind of friendship.[14] It is not enough to live in the same place in order to live *in unum*. This should be understood not in terms of place but spiritually. For it is to no avail if people of conflicting habits and aim are united in one dwelling, and it is not an obstacle for those of equal virtue to be separated by any interval of space. For the dwelling together in God by character and practice, not by places, conjoins brothers in a united dwelling.[15]

In Cassian's view, God is both the ultimate source and the terminus of love, and He becomes perceptible to the individual in the movement of the love He feels in Himself: 'For up to that point do we perceive this divine being, that we may

---

[8] Cicero, *De amicitia* 6. 20.
[9] See above all McEvoy, 'Theory of friendship'.
[10] Ibid. For a different view, see C. S. Jaeger, 'Friendship of mutual perfecting in the *Confessions* and the failure of Classical *amicitia*', in Classen and Sandidge, *Friendship in the Middle Ages and Early Modern Age*, pp. 185–200.
[11] See C. Stewart, *Cassian the Monk* (Oxford, 1998).
[12] John Cassian, *Collationes* xvi. 2.
[13] Ibid. xvi. 3.
[14] Ibid.
[15] Ibid.

sense this saying of the apostle to live manifestly in ourselves: "because the charity of God is poured forth in our hearts, by the Holy Ghost who is given to us."[16]

The trajectory of Cassian's argument is similar to that found in his close contemporary St Augustine, and later in Gregory the Great, but in Cassian it is adapted to a specifically monastic setting. William knew both Cassian's and Gregory's writings intimately, and their works were fundamental to monastic intellectual life from the time of their composition until after William's lifetime. His discussions of *amicitia* in the *Commentary on Lamentations* were based on a sophisticated and comprehensive framework of classical and patristic heritage.

William never set down a cohesive account of friendship in the way Aelred of Rievaulx famously did. Yet the reality and value of bonds of charity and love between human beings were clearly central to his life and thought, and we find constant reminders of this throughout his works. The most detailed references to friendship, however, occur in his *Commentary on Lamentations*.[17] Friendship, William explains here, can be a solace in the inescapable sufferings of temporal existence and an aid in overcoming the temporal to escape to the transcendent and eternal: 'Nature has given mortals no greater joy than to be joined by ties of friendship.'[18] But true friendship must be based on eternal and unchangeable foundations. William issues stark warnings against utilitarian friendships based on material benefits and love of earthly and transitory things; in so doing, he demonstrates his adherence to the notion of friendship that had become an integral part of western monasticism.[19] It is this elaborate and cohesive definition of true friendship that confers significance on William's warnings against false friends.

William elaborates on the theme of utilitarian friendship when commenting on Lamentations 1: 2: 'There is none to comfort her among all them that were dear to her'. 'Riches win friends, riches attract many to give comfort amid minor losses. But if riches, inconstant as they are, take flight, you may see that the comforters follow fortune, not friendship.'[20] The fickleness of opportunistic friends in times of adversity is a common theme in classical as well as Christian literature, and William explicitly alluded to this tradition in the *Gesta Regum*.[21] In the *Commentary*, the topic is posited within an overall scheme of ordered love, in line with the paradigm

---

[16] Ibid. xvi. 13.

[17] For the moral theology underlying *Comm. Lam.*, see Sønnesyn, *Ethics*, pp. 42–59.

[18] *Comm. Lam.*, I. 19 (p. 108); *Lam.*, p. 149: 'Nullum maius natura donauit gaudium mortalibus quam ut amicis consotientur affectibus'.

[19] For monastic friendship, see B. P. McGuire, *Friendship and Community: The Monastic Experience c. 350–1250* (Kalamazoo MI, 1988); and also E. Gilson, *The Mystical Theology of St. Bernard* (London, 1940), pp. 10–12; J. P. Haseldine, 'Friendship and rivalry: the role of *amicitia* in twelfth-century monastic relations', *JEH* 44 (1993), 390–414.

[20] *Comm. Lam.* I. 148–50 (p. 13); *Lam.*, p. 46: 'Opes enim conciliant amicos, opes in minimis detrimentis multos adhibent consolatores. Quae si mobilitate sua fugam fecerint, tunc uideas illos fortunam sequi, non amicitiam.'

[21] For the classical and patristic world, cf. e.g. Ovid, *Trist.* 1. 9, Boethius, *Consolatio Philosophiae* III, 5 pr., 13–14, and John Cassian, *Collationes* xvi. 2. For William and the *GR*, see e.g. 47. 4.

of Christian thought that dominated the monastic traditions of the West. 'Love', William says, 'is the fount and eye of all good things: ... just as it produces all the virtues by means of love of God and one's neighbour, so by its discretion it guards against anyone being deceived by heedless compassion.'[22] William here invokes a doctrine of love elaborated most fundamentally by Augustine, in which Scriptural moral teaching was united with classical ethical discourse.[23] The virtues, a basic element of most classical moral paradigms, are presented as flowing out of Christ's injunction to love God above all and one's neighbour as oneself.[24] Ordered love, following Augustine, was the necessary and sufficient precondition of growth in virtue. That is not to say that all the principal ideas characterising this tradition originated with Augustine, but rather that he elaborated and combined them in a profound and influential way. This influence reveals itself through the ways in which Christian scholars could use the disparate moral schools of the classical world.[25] Consequently, in what follows I will refer to this tradition as Augustinian.

In the generation preceding William's, Anselm of Canterbury, highly respected by William, had reiterated Augustine's doctrine of ordered love, emphasising that only God should be loved for His own sake, and everybody and everything else for God's sake.[26] According to this mode of thought, loving creatures and things for personal benefit or pleasure was disordered love. Such disordered love characterised false friends, who loved their friends not for God's sake or for the good of the other, but for the potential benefits to be derived from the other's material resources: 'It is not us they love, but our possessions.'[27] But just as such people are not really our friends, so our possessions are not really our possessions. 'Those things are not ours that can be carried away by a tyrant's violence or fleeting fortune. The only good things possessed by the soul are those that, while God's grace attends, the soul, as long as it remains free, cannot lose, whatever fear or pressure it is subject to.'[28] William follows the Augustinian tradition of combining insights from the ancient world with those of Christian thought and practice. Both the Stoics and the Church Fathers taught a basic *contemptus mundi*, an attitude of

---

[22] *Comm. Lam* III. 49–51 (p. 251); *Lam.*, p. 299: 'Est enim caritas fons et oculus bonorum omnium: fons quia est origo uirtutum, oculus quia custos. Sicut enim omnes uirtutes per dilectionem Dei et proximi producit, ita, ne quis inconsiderata compassione fallatur, per discretionem custodit.'

[23] See above all Augustine's *De Doctrina Christiana*; see also e.g. O. O'Donovan, 'Usus and fruitio in Augustine's *De Doctrina Christiana*', *Journal of Theological Studies* n.s. 33 (1982), 361–97.

[24] A wonderfully concise and emphatic summary of this idea is found in John of Salisbury's *Policraticus* 7. 11, ed. C. C. J. Webb (2 vols, Oxford, 1909), II, 661a-b. Webb's apparatus shows how much John's discussion throughout these crucial chapters of book VII owes to Scripture, Augustine and Boethius.

[25] I have described this process in more detail in Sønnesyn, *Ethics*, pp. 21–41.

[26] See S. O. Sønnesyn, '*Ut sine me amet summam essentiam*: The Eudaemonist Ethics of St Anselm', *Med. St.* 70 (2008), 1–29.

[27] *Comm. Lam.* I. 2 (p. 13); *Lam.*, p. 46: 'adeo non nos sed nostra diligunt'.

[28] Ibid.: 'Non enim sunt nostra quae uel uis tirannica uel fortuna uolatica potest auferre. Sola sunt animi bona quae nullo terrore, nullo impulsu, Dei gratia comitante, liber amittit animus.'

reservation towards the transitory things of this world; but while the Stoics justified this in the good soul as an end in and of itself, the Church Fathers emphasised the inadequacy of every worldly end compared to the supreme good in God.[29] The error that causes men to pursue false goods and thus render themselves unable to form true bonds of friendship stems from failure to perceive this basic fact: 'But the common-or-garden friend is not aware of things of that kind; he is in pursuit only of the perishable, he is subservient only to the transitory.'[30]

The only truly trustworthy basis for friendship, within this broadly Augustinian scheme, is God and humanity's love for Him: 'Let us make God our friend: a friend who knows not how to fall away, knows not how to die; who values not wealth but good sense; who weighs not money but the mind.'[31] Love, then, must be regulated, and only a love of God above all, since He is goodness, and of everything and everybody else for God's sake, can provide the correct ordering of love that constitutes true friendship. It is through sharing a love of the supreme good that human beings can be united by bonds of true friendship; and God is that true supreme good that above all offers an unshakeable bond between friends: 'Happy then the man who loves his friend in God and his enemy for God!'[32]

These reflections on the true nature of friendship do not constitute a cohesive and comprehensive conceptual account, but they help us situate William's thinking within the tradition of the patristic reception of the Roman concept of *amicitia*. The exclamation 'Felix qui amat amicum in Deo et inimicum pro Deo' echoes a passage from Gregory the Great's Homilies on the Gospels, which says that 'true charity is to love your friend in God and to love your enemy for the sake of God – 'Caritas uera enim est et amicum diligere in Deo et inimicum diligere propter Deum.'[33] The passage that includes these words was chosen by William to represent Gregory's teaching on charity in the *Defloratio Gregorii*.[34] Both the content and form of this collection are highly relevant for our present concerns. William's collection differs from most contemporary *deflorationes* of the pope's works in containing extracts from across the entirety of Gregory's oeuvre.[35] In his preface, William dedicates his work to his monastic brethren at Malmesbury, and offers it for the instruction of all, but particularly for those who for some

---

[29] For the differences between Stoic and Patristic moral thought, see M. Colish, 'Cicero, Ambrose, and Stoic ethics: transmission or transformation?', in *The Classics in the Middle Ages*, ed. A. Bernardo and S. Levin (Binghampton, 1990), pp. 95–112, particularly at 99–100. I am grateful to Emily Winkler for pointing out to me the Stoic parallels here.

[30] *Comm. Lam.* I, 157–9 (p. 13); *Lam.*, p. 46: 'Verum illa uulgus amicorum non nouit; tantum caduca uenatur, tantum transitoriis ancillatur'.

[31] Ibid. (pp. 13–14): 'Paremus nobis Deum amicum, qui nesciat labi, qui nesciat mori, qui non estimet censum sed sensum, non ponderet nummum sed mentem'.

[32] Ibid. (p. 14): 'Iccirco felix qui amat amicum in Deo et inimicum pro Deo'.

[33] Gregory I, *Homeliae in Evangelia* i. 9. 6 (CCSL 141, p. 63).

[34] Now only preserved in a single manuscript, CUL Ii. 3. 20. The preface and *capitula* are printed as an appendix to D. H. Farmer, 'William of Malmesbury's Commentary on Lamentations', *Studia Monastica* 4 (1962), 283–311, at pp. 308–11.

[35] Farmer, 'William of Malmesbury's Commentary', p. 308.

reason were not able to consult the full text of Gregory's works.[36] The excerpts are organised under thematic chapter headings in a sequence leading from the fundamental principles of faith, hope and love to the practical and particular application of these principles in Christian life.[37]

In the passage to which William alludes in the *Commentary*, Gregory emphasises biblical teaching about the basic unity of ordered love. Gregory insists that 'there are two precepts of charity, that is, love of God and love of neighbour.'[38] Love of God and love of neighbour, then, are basically one; the latter is grounded in, and a visible manifestation of, the former:

> On earth, the Spirit is given so that one's neighbour may be loved; the Spirit is given from heaven so that God may be loved. In the same way, then, that there is one single charity and two precepts, so there is one Spirit and two gifts – first from God existing on earth, after from heaven, because in the love of neighbour is learned how it is possible to attain to love of God.[39]

The love expressed in friendship is only possible if nourished by the loving unity with God that is the gift of the Holy Spirit. Elsewhere in the *Commentary* William echoes Gregory's insistence that love is the root from which all other virtues grow:

> For love is the fount and eye of all good things: 'fount' because it is the origin of the virtues, 'eye' because it is their guardian; just as it produces all the virtues by means of love of God and one's neighbour, so by its discretion it guards against anyone being deceived by heedless compassion.[40]

Love, then, as defined by the tradition from which William draws his main inspiration, is not a passive emotional state, but the very core of human life as a whole; it is the guiding principle for the activities and practices that make us human. Friendship, in its true sense, is the required arena in which this love can grow and reach perfection.

Although Gregory, Cassian and other patristic writers were ancient authorities by William's time, their thoughts were still constitutive of the English Benedictine

---

[36] CUL MS Ii. 3. 20, f. 2r: 'Ad instructionem communem deflorationes ex libris praecelentissimi pape Gregorii in hoc uolumine compegi, ea potissimum intentione ut si quis nostrum uel ualitudine uel occupatione uel etiam desidia impediente multis legendis non uacat, hic in promptu inueniat quibus et animam pascat et uitam componat'.

[37] For a contemporary appraisal of the *Defloratio*, see Robert of Cricklade, *De Connubio Patriarche Iacob* II, 22 (Bodl. Libr., Laud. misc. 725, f. 129v). Printed in R. W. Hunt, 'English learning in the late twelfth century', *TRHS*, 4th ser. 19 (1936), 19–42, at p. 32, repr. in *Essays in Medieval History*, ed. R. W. Southern (London, 1968), pp. 117–18.

[38] CUL Ii. 3. 20, f. 5r: 'Duo sunt autem precepta caritatis, Dei uidelicet amor et proximi'.

[39] CUL Ii. 3. 20, f. 5v: 'In terra datus spiritus ut diligatur proximus; e caelo datus spiritus ut diligatur Deus. Sicut ergo una est caritas et duo precepta, ita unus est spiritus et duo data. Prius a consistente Domino in terra, postmodum e caelo, quia in proximi amore discitur qualiter perueniri possit ad amorem Dei.'

[40] *Comm. Lam.* III. 49–51 (p. 251); *Lam.*, p. 299: for text, see p. 22 above.

monasticism in which William received his own education. I have argued elsewhere that the general tenor of William's argument aligns him to the spirituality elaborated in Anselm of Canterbury's thinking – and we should recall that the phrase 'lector amice' is found at the top of a collection of Anselm's works – but the ideas William propounds are not limited to the sophisticated spiritual theology of the *lux Angliae*.[41]

In his *On the Eight Points of Monastic Life*, Ralph, abbot of Battle 1107–24, lays out fundamental tenets of monastic existence in a brief and succinct manner suitable for novices, but does not depart from the ideals expounded in greater depth and complexity in William's *Commentary*. Crucially for our present purposes, Ralph emphasised that the *caritas* that unites all Christian into one communion is not restricted to an emotional state, but on the contrary leads on to shared practices that develop and perfect the bonds of friendship uniting those who participate in them. In a monastic context, this was above all the *Opus Dei*, the continuous praise for and supplication to God in liturgical worship. Therefore, the injunction to love God and neighbour is followed by another, to participate assiduously and sincerely in the liturgical cycle of prayer:

> [Monks] should not neglect to render the service they owe to God, because, when they perform the praises and thanksgiving that they will perform before God in another life, they even here, in this life, begin to taste beforehand what they, when they have reached that place, will render continuously and without end.[42]

The notion of foretasting, *praegustare*, is in perfect keeping with the shared tenet of the patristic and mainstream classical schools of philosophy, that the highest good for human beings was not a state or a sensation, but an activity, *energeia*.[43] The bliss that is the property of the communion of saints consists of the full realisation of all human faculties in the eternal act of perfect worship, face to face with God.[44] The foretaste of this action is *ipso facto* the blessedness of the saved. It is through participating in practices aimed at the attainment of a common end that virtues are formed. The shared pursuit of the good through virtue is the true bond of lasting friendship, and in this the fathers of the Church and the founders of monasticism closely followed the Romans.

The ideals we find expressed in a succinct and distilled form in Ralph of Battle,

---

[41] For William's description of Anselm as the light of England, see GR 328. For the correspondences between William's thought and Anselm's, see e.g. Sønnesyn, *Ethics*, pp. 40 and 51–3.

[42] Ralph of Battle, *Octo Puncta a Monachis Obseruandis*: Bodl. Libr., Laud. misc. 363, f. 28v: 'precipitur eis ut seruitutium quod Deo debent non negligant reddere, quia sic agentes laudes et gratias quas in alia uita Deo acturi sunt, hic interim, dum uiuunt, incipiunt praegustare, quas ibi, cum peruenerint, iugiter et sine fine semper habent persoluere.'

[43] See Aristotle, *Nichomachean Ethics*, 1098a16–18. The role played by the basic, Aristotelian approach to ethics in classical and medieval thought is chronicled in T. H. Irwin, *The Development of Ethics* (3 vols, Oxford, 2007–11), vol. I.

[44] For William of Malmesbury's appropriation of this intellectual heritage, see Sønnesyn, *Ethics*, pp. 21–69.

Lector amice: Reading as Friendship

I argue, are the same as those William promulgated in his *Commentary*, the same as those Anselm described in his idiosyncratic combination of rational clarity and spiritual intensity, and the same as those codified in Cassian's monastic writings and in the Rule of St Benedict itself. Bonds of friendship were developed through shared practices centred on liturgical worship, in which all other forms of communal action were consummated. Who would know that better than William, cantor of Malmesbury, who made his *Abbreviation of Amalarius* specifically to enable his fellow monks to practise this *res pernecessaria* in an informed way?[45]

There is an almost universally acknowledged organic unity between moral and intellectual development within the traditions, classical, patristic and monastic, from which William drew his inspiration.[46] The human mind was not seen as a disembodied intellect that happened to be trapped in a body, but as part of a living, embodied organism; the human mode of perceiving Truth was embodied. Human beings attained truth primarily through shared practices; consequently, for the full significance of a text to be appreciated, it had to be translated into practice by the reader, and become embodied in the reader's own way of living. We find in historiographical texts, both classical and medieval, an emphasis on imitation and on embodying the lessons of the past as an irreducible part of seeing them for what they are;[47] we find in moral philosophy an emphasis on practice, training and on apprenticeship;[48] we find in metaphysical speculation a mystical element at the point where texts give way to individual experience.[49] Within the Christian and monastic traditions, *lectio diuina* needed to issue in *operatio*, in the embodiment of the Word of God in the reader's way of life, and liturgical texts needed to be prayed rather than simply read or analysed in order be fully efficacious.[50]

In John 15: 14, in the context of a long address by Christ on the precept to love God above all and one's neighbour as oneself, Christ tells his disciples that 'you are my friends, if you do the things I command you.' Love of God and love of neighbour need to issue in action, in obedience and in embodying the commands communicated to post-apostolic generations through Scripture and tradition. Friendship, whether with God or with man, was not formed within the mind or within the soul, but in the agency and activity of the whole human person. Reading

---

[45] See R. W. Pfaff, 'The "Abbreviatio Amalarii" of William of Malmesbury', *Recherches de théologie ancienne et médiévale* 48 (1981), 128–71.

[46] I have discussed this in greater detail in S. Sønnesyn, '"Qui recta quae docet sequitur, uere philosophus est." The Ethics of John of Salisbury', in *A Companion to John of Salisbury*, ed. C. Grellard and F. Lachaud (Leiden, 2014), pp. 307–38.

[47] See e.g. A. Gransden, 'Prologues in the historiography of twelfth-century England', in *England in the Twelfth Century*, ed. D. Williams (London, 1990), pp. 55–82; and G. Simon, 'Untersuchungen zur Topik der Widmungsbriefe mittelalterliche Geschichtsschreiber bis zum Ende des 12. Jahrhunderts', *Archiv für Diplomatik, Schriftgeschichte, Siegel- und Wappenkunde* 4 (1958), 52–119, and 5–6 (1959–60), 73–153.

[48] See Sønnesyn, 'Ethics of John of Salisbury'.

[49] See in particular B. McGinn, *The Growth of Mysticism* (London, 1993).

[50] See D. Robertson, *Lectio Divina: The Medieval Experience of Reading* (Collegeville, 2011), particularly pp. 90–3.

was not enough; action had to follow.⁵¹ This is the context within which we need to view William of Malmesbury's notion of reading.

With this conceptual scheme as our guide, it is not hard to find William adhering to this mode of thought. William intended his historical works to be read and imitated in practice to facilitate the reader's moral and intellectual development. This is just as true of his spiritual works and collections of classical and patristic literature.⁵² In the introduction to his *Defloratio Gregorii*, for instance, he makes it quite clear to his readers that he has omitted discussions of complex, abstract questions in order to focus on what is directly useful to and easily accessible for his monastic brethren:

> You will note that I have not picked out anything from the solutions to profound questions, but that I have only inserted that which is useful for the emendation of living, for the edification of the soul, for the hope of salvation.

Discussion of *quaestiones* can be left to the idle, William says, while monks ought rather to focus on the moral significance of Gregory's text: 'Let others, therefore, excerpt *quaestiones*; let us turn to the pursuit of what we have professed.'⁵³

William's privileging of embodiment of ideals rather than ideals held in the abstract is emphasised in the first *capitulum* of the *Defloratio Gregorii*, which deals with the virtue of faith. Here, William has chosen to focus on Gregory's exposition of faith as issuing in practice, citing the Gospel of John and the letter of James. In the same way that love of God that does not issue in love of neighbour is not really love at all, faith, as belief in the existence of God, is not meritorious if it does not result in a life of loving and trusting Him: 'For we are only truly faithful when we fulfil in actions what we have promised with words.'⁵⁴

This argument, based on the same biblical passages as those used by Gregory, occurs frequently in William's *Commentary on Lamentations*. In the same vein, in the preface to his *Abbreviation of Amalarius* William states that his main aim in compiling the text is to provide the monks with what they need to carry out their primary duty, right worship expressed through liturgical prayer,⁵⁵ and

---

⁵¹ See Stewart, *Cassian*; Robertson, *Lectio Divina*, J. Leclercq, *The Love of Learning and the Desire for God*, trans. C. Misrahi (Fordham, 1961), and B. Stock, *Augustine the Reader: Meditation, Self-Knowledge, and the Ethics of Interpretation* (Cambridge MA, 1996).

⁵² See Sønnesyn, *Ethics*, passim.

⁵³ CUL Ii. 3. 20, f. 2r: 'Illud porro animaduertere potestis me nichil de solutione profundarum quaestionum deflorasse, sed ea tantum posuisse quae sunt ad emendationem uitae, ad edificationem animae, ad spem uenie. De questionibus otiosorum est disputatio, sed secundum Socratis dictum, quod super nos, nichil ad nos. Quod si quis forte abiecerit in capitulis de resurrectionem et tormentis Gehennae et uidendo Deo quaestiones uentilari, commodius et consultius faciet si ad moralitatem ea retorqueat, in quibus quasi e speculo intuebitur quid maxime debeat sperare, quid timere. Quaestiones ergo excerpserint alii; nos ad quod professi sumus studium deriuemus.'

⁵⁴ Ibid., f. 2v: 'Tunc enim ueraciter fideles sumus, si quid uerbis promittimus, operibus implemus'.

⁵⁵ See the preface to his *Abbreuiatio Amalarii*, ed. Pfaff, pp. 128–9.

in the preface to the *Polyhistor* he states that the excerpts are intended for the instruction of the good life, 'ad bonae uitae institutum'.[56] William explicitly invokes this primary function of reading in his account of his efforts as librarian of Malmesbury Abbey:

> I have collected much material for reading, approaching the prowess of my excellent predecessor at least in this respect; I have followed up his laudable start as best I could. Let us hope there may be someone to cherish the fruits of our labours! The monks, who had been mere stutterers in common or garden learning, were now given a proper education. The service of God was liberally endowed and put into effect as a matter of urgency, with the result that no monastery in all England excelled Malmesbury, and many yielded precedence to it.[57]

The main purpose of reading, on William's account, is to inform monastic practice, culminating in liturgical observance. William's portrait of his hero Bede propounds the same ideal: 'His faith was sound, his style unpretentious but agreeable; in all his biblical commentaries he sought out material from which his reader might absorb the love of God and his neighbour, rather than the means of displaying a pretty wit or sharpening a rusty pen'.[58]

William's phrase 'lector amice' should remind us of the symbiotic unity of friendship and reading in William's intellectual world as well as in his works. In order to be effective, the relationship between reader and author had to be modelled on the relationship of friends. Friendship was not a passive emotional state, and reading was not an abstract intellectual pursuit: both found their consummation and perfection embodied in the lives of human beings united in striving for a shared end. William sought to make his readers his friends in this way; by his own admission, he wanted his readers to use the texts he produced not as storehouses of information or as starting points for abstract speculation, but as a basis for a way of life directed towards loving God and neighbour. If William's readers used his works in this way, they would, by the true definition of friendship, become his friends in the most intimate and meaningful way.

---

[56] See *Polyhistor*, p. 37.
[57] GP 27. 2; cf. Niskanen above, p. 117, where the citation and Latin text are given.
[58] GR 59. 1: 'Nam et fidei sanae et incuriosae sed dulcis fuit eloquentiae, in omnibus explanationibus diuinarum scripturarum magis illa rimatus quibus lector Dei dilectionem et proximi combiberet quam illa quibus uel sales libaret uel linguae rubiginem limaret.'

→ 14 ←

William of Malmesbury's Historical Vision

Rodney M. Thomson

On 31 December 1974 Richard Southern wrote to Roger Mynors, after receiving a typescript copy of Mynors's translation of William of Malmesbury's *Gesta Regum Anglorum*:

> I've read ... the whole ... with immense interest, excitement sometimes, growing respect mostly – and with a daunting sense of how much needs to be done to annotate [William] in a way that will do justice to the complexity of his historical vision, the variety of his sources and the way in which he uses them, the nature of his personal interjections, the intensity of his antiquarian imagination, not to speak of the poor old facts. I feel quite shaken by the experience.[1]

What Southern meant by 'historical vision' one can only conjecture, but I imagine that he meant history seen as having a pattern and perhaps a purpose, and its recording as reflecting and emphasising those features, possibly with a view to the moral improvement of the reader. William certainly thought all these things, but it is not easy to be confident about describing his thoughts precisely or in detail: he is not often overt about them, and his rare expressions of them are scattered about his works; he could be ambivalent, even contradictory, and he changed his mind over time. Southern was right to use the word 'complexity'. I shall nonetheless attempt to describe William's 'vision' under three heads which seem to me to bring into focus what was most important for him: God, Empire, and the kingdom or nation of England. Hopefully, I will not be thought to be merely 'yoking disparate ideas by violence together'.[2]

---

[1] Southern and Mynors were to have collaborated on a new edition and translation of *GR* for the OMT series. In the event, a disagreement between them over the development of William's text as reflected in the surviving manuscripts prevented this from happening. The nature of the disagreement is explained by Michael Winterbottom in *GR* I, p. vi; II, pp. xviii–xx.

[2] I paraphrase Samuel Johnson's famous characterisation of the metaphysical poets in his *Lives of the Poets* (Preface to the *Life of Abraham Cowley*).

God

As one would expect, William wrote providential history of a kind. It is in the main conventionally orthodox, with one exception: it is noticeably not apocalyptic. God intervenes in and regulates the course of history, but there is no mention of the Last Days or Last Judgement in William's historical writings, or of the Seven Ages (all of these do feature in his *Commentary on Lamentations*),[3] no sense of history moving towards a denouement or even that the dark days of William's time – which he thought darker as he grew older – might herald the Last Judgement. Instead, history is seen as an apparently or potentially unending series of rises and falls in the fortunes of individuals and communities: rises and falls which might be manifested politically or militarily, but which were essentially moral, the falls preponderating.[4] This is epitomised in his echo of Seneca the Elder at *Gesta Regum* 337. 5, after praising the early Cistercians: 'Such is human weakness, whose unfailing principle it is that nothing won by great toil can long endure'.[5]

For William, God intervened in human history in two ways: in the first instance, He did so directly and miraculously. William happily mixed hagiography in with history, and indeed seems hardly to have made a distinction between them.[6] On the one hand, the narratives of the *Gesta Regum* and *Gesta Pontificum* include numerous miracle stories; on the other, his hagiographical works are unusually 'historical' in their concern with such things as precise dating and details of context.[7] These features, incidentally, partly explain why these particular works of his were not popular: they could not easily be reduced to lections for liturgical use. But in one way these miracles did *not* signify God's direct action, in that they were nearly all mediated: they were the work of saints. Most of William's saints were leaders in the Church hierarchy, but their miracles occurred mainly at a local level, involving individuals, who might, however, be important.[8] William rarely cited miracles as causative agents in large-scale historical events involving whole communities.

Secondly, William shows God as intervening indirectly and in a non-miraculous way, generally in the role of a judge visiting punishment upon whole communities: the various invasions of England, from the Saxons to the Normans, are prominent examples. In particular, William saw the Norman Conquest in this

---

[3] *Lam.*, pp. 58, 72, 229, 274, etc.

[4] T. Summerfield, '"Ut quod intendo ..."; William van Malmesbury's *Gesta Regum Anglorum*', in *Koningen in kronieken*, ed. R. E. V. Stuip and C. Vellekoop (Hilversum, 1998), pp. 59–76, esp. 69–70. See the paper by Alheydis Plassmann in this volume, pp. 139–52.

[5] 'Et profecto fiet pro humana debilitate, cuius perpetua lex est ut nichil maximis laboribus partum diu possit consistere.' See also *GR* II, n. ad loc.

[6] See the paper by Anne Bailey in this volume, pp. 13–26.

[7] *Saints' Lives*, pp. xxix–xxx, xxxiv–viii.

[8] See, for instance, William's treatment of Aldhelm in *GP* 261–2, 266–70, and 272–7. Most of his miracles occurred at or not far from Malmesbury itself. Quite different are the miracles of the Virgin Mary related in *MBVM*. In that work the Virgin's role as 'mediatrix' between the first two persons of the Trinity and mankind is made explicit: *MBVM* 1. 8, 9. 2, 17. 6, bk 2 prol. 2–3 etc.

William of Malmesbury's Historical Vision

light, with increasing intensity as he grew older. God used the Normans, however unworthy they might be, as His instrument to punish the wayward English.[9] The identification of this kind of intervention was a matter of interpretation by the historian: the narrative of events itself, as William tells it, unfolds according to 'normal' human motivation and 'normal' chains of cause and effect.

But William was ambivalent in a number of ways. First of all, he was too observant a historian to conclude that morality always determined historical outcomes, and so his historiography left a role for pure chance. 'Fortuna', sometimes personified as a kind of goddess, is invoked in his major works nearly as often as God's will: a dozen times in the *Gesta Pontificum*, thirty-four times in the *Gesta Regum*. He makes some remarkable overt comments about this: 'Our life is a dice-board, on which Fortune with her unexpected throws makes game of mortal men'.[10] And in the same work (the *Gesta Regum*), describing William Rufus's undeserved good luck, he indulged in what might be thought very unmonastic levity: 'He so completely benefited from the play of chance that God might have been thought to be vying with Fortune to do him service'.[11] Both God and the Fates are invoked, apparently indiscriminately, at *Gesta Pontificum* 246. 4–5, where William relates the youthful death of King Æthelstan:[12]

> nothing he did was comparable to what he might have done, for his great deeds were cut short by the Fates' impatience. He was taken from this world at Gloucester; it was a death that came too early, and one that ill-befitted such a noble spirit; but God thought otherwise.... The sun had lit up Scorpio with its twelfth dawn / When he struck down the king with his tail.

As Michael Winterbottom demonstrates elsewhere in this volume, William in several places in his historical works equates the sting of the scorpion's tail with Fortune's cruelty.[13] In this particular passage he extends the metaphor to the zodiacal *Scorpio*, which he equates with Fortuna/the Fates. How their activity relates to God's in decreeing Æthelstan's premature death is not made clear, nor is it easily to be discerned.

Did he refine or resolve this apparent contradiction into a consistent theology? Perhaps; at one point in the *Commentary on Lamentations*, written later than his

---

[9] R. M. Thomson, 'William of Malmesbury's anti-Norman diatribe', in *The Long Twelfth-Century View*, pp. 113–21, at 114–15.

[10] GR 17. 2: 'Inter haec tamen, quia fatalis alea incertis iactibus in huius uitae tabula mortales eludit.' One is reminded of the *Verworfenheit* ('Thrown-ness') of some existentialist thinkers of the twentieth century.

[11] GP 50. 1: 'ita in omnibus usus est placido allusu fortunae ut uideretur cum eo Deus benefitiis certare.'

[12] 'nichil ad comparationem fatiendorum fuit quod fecit, quia ingentes actus festinata dies fatis abrupit. Immatura ergo morte, et quae animositatem illam, si Deus uoluisset, non deceret, mundo in Gloecestra exemptus.... Sol illustrarat bisseno Scorpion ortu, / cum regem cauda surruit ille sua.'

[13] See below, pp. 204–5.

major historical works, he observes 'Wherefore, if it is proper to say so, not knowing how to deal with us, you [that is, God] left us to be the prey of Fortune.'[14] In other words, God puts pressure on humankind as far as is consistent with free will, but in the face of determined obstinacy withdraws and gives chance free reign. In his *Historia Nouella*, as Sverre Bagge has noted, William wrestled with this problem in a particularly interesting way.[15] In the prologue to book 1, written at a time when it seemed that Earl Robert of Gloucester and Empress Matilda would be victorious, he states his intention to transmit to posterity 'those things that, by a wonderful disposition of God, have happened in England in recent times.... For what is more to the advantage of virtue or more conducive to justice than recognising the divine pleasure in the good and the punishment of those who have gone astray?'[16] However, after the capture of Robert and Matilda by Stephen's men in the second half of 1141, William was forced to write a narrative in which the just had *not* triumphed, and this he explained not in terms of God's providence but of the fickleness of Fortune. In a new prologue to book 3 he wrote that he wished to 'unravel the trackless maze of events that befell England, with the aim that posterity should not be ignorant of these matters through our lack of care, it being worth while to learn the changefulness of Fortune and the mutability of the human lot, by God's permission or bidding.'[17]

Secondly, although William clearly did not object to miracles per se, he sometimes toned down or rejected a miraculous explanation found in his sources, in favour of a mundane, 'common sense' one. A good example of this is the capture of Antioch by the crusaders, on 3 June 1098, after a dreadfully hard siege. His source, Fulcher of Chartres, interpreted the capture as miraculous, but for William it was due to Bohemond's bribery of an unscrupulous defender. The traitor, 'to cover the scandal of his treachery by an excuse that none could overlook, had given his son to Bohemond as a hostage, declaring that he did so by the express command of Christ given him in a dream'.[18] What was miraculous for Fulcher was for William the outcome of a cynical ploy.

---

[14] *Comm. Lam.* I, 2826–7: 'Quocirca, si fas est dicere, nesciens quo nos modo tractares fortunae populandos exposuisti'. Translated in *Lam.*, p. 147.

[15] S. Bagge, 'Ethics, politics and Providence in William of Malmesbury's *Historia Novella*', *Viator* 41 (2010), 113–32.

[16] *HN* prol. (p. 2): 'Nunc ea quae moderno tempore magno miraculo Dei acciderunt in Anglia, ut mandentur posteris, desiderat animus uestrae serenitatis.... Quid enim plus ad honestatis spectat commodum, quid magis conducit aequitati, quam diuinam agnoscere circa bonos indulgentiam, et erga peruersos uindicta?'

[17] *HN* iii. prol. (p. 80): 'inextricabilem laberinthum rerum et negotiorum quae acciderunt in Anglia aggredior euoluere; ea causa, ne per nostram incuriam lateat posteros, cum sit opere pretium cognoscere uolubilitatem fortunae statusque humani mutabilitatem, Deo dumtaxat permittente uel iubente'.

[18] *GR* 363. 1: 'Ille quoque, ut infamiam traditionis insigni excusatione palliaret, Boamundo filium in obsidatum dedit, Christi edicto, quod per somnium didicisset, id se facere professus'.

Rome

William was a historian of 'civilisation'. His notion of it corresponded roughly to our own, even though he did not have, or use, a single noun that covered the full range of its meaning for us. Mostly he defined it in terms of its opposite: 'barbarous', 'barbarian', 'barbarity'.[19] Among the Latin words he used for these terms the most significant is 'inciuiliter'. The positive words he used to denote civilisation were ones that described components or manifestations of it, such as 'cultior/cultius', 'comitas morum', 'affabilitas', 'curialitas'. I give just a few examples. David I of Scotland is described as 'a young man of more courtly disposition ("curalior") than the rest, (who) had from boyhood been polished by familiar intercourse with the English, and rubbed off all the barbarian gaucherie of Scottish manners'.[20] And of the French William states: 'both in martial exercises and in polish of manners ("comitate morum") the men of France are easily first among the nations of the West',[21] able therefore to teach the art of governance to King Ecgberht of Wessex.

Civilisation was for William pre-eminently a Roman phenomenon.[22] This becomes most explicit around the mid-point of the *Gesta Regum*, when he is about to deal with the degenerate Rome of Pope Urban II's day. Here he breaks into an evocation of ancient Rome, quoting Virgil on its inhabitants, 'dominators of the world, those who the toga wore', followed by the near-contemporary elegiac poem by Hildebert of Le Mans, *Par tibi Roma nihil*.[23] With this viewpoint we may connect William's interest in Roman building in stone, of which he correctly identified remains at York, Carlisle[24] and Hexham: 'People coming from Rome nowadays ..., when they see the manner in which Hexham is built, ... swear it gives them a mental picture of the best Roman work'.[25] Such building was typically found in towns, and for William civilisation was literally 'citification'. Thus, the district around Wearmouth and Jarrow was 'brilliant with many cities of the Romans' building',[26] and he remarked upon the Roman origins and remnants of Chester and Bath.[27] He gave attention to the physical layout of ancient Christian Rome (summarising an ancient Itinerary and listing inscriptions) and Constantinople.[28] Once again, William's ideal is further clarified by reference to its opposites. The

---

[19] For instance, 'barbarus' GR 134. 1; 'inciuiliter' GR 97. 6; 'immanis barbaries' GP 259. 1.
[20] GR 400. 2: 'iuuenis ceteris curialior et qui, nostrorum conuictu et familiaritate limatus a puero, omnem rubiginem Scotticae barbariei deterserat'.
[21] GR 106. 2: 'Est enim gens illa et exercitatione uirium et comitate morum cunctarum occidentalium facile princeps'.
[22] GR 351. 1. And see the essay in this volume by W. Kynan-Wilson (pp. 81–91).
[23] GR 351. 2–4.
[24] GP 99.
[25] GP 117. 1–2: 'Nunc quia Roma ueniunt idem allegant, ut qui Haugustaldensem fabricam uident ambitionem Romanam se imaginari iurent'.
[26] GR 54. 2: 'urbium a Romanis edificatarum frequentia renidens'.
[27] GP 172. 4.
[28] GR 353, 354–6.

Celts and Scandinavians were for William barbarians, uncivilised.[29] Of Ireland and the Irish he says 'The soil lacks all advantages, and so poor, or rather unskilful, are its cultivators that it can produce only a ragged mob of rustic Irishmen outside the towns; the English and French, with their more civilised way of life ("cultiori genere uitae"), live in the towns, and carry on trade and commerce.'[30] And of the Scots (or perhaps the Irish again): 'For the *Scotti* ... were more used to lurking obscurely in bogs than living in high cities.'[31] As for the Scandinavians, one of William's statements will stand for many: 'The Danes, once determined on an invasion of England, called in the Norwegians to share their successes. Both peoples are hideous barbarians, but the Norwegians display the more grasping greed and the more dangerous lust.'[32]

Buildings and towns were just the most visible part of Rome's imperial legacy in Europe, a topic that absorbed William. We see this highlighted in the 'Selden Collection', as I have chosen to call it: an assemblage of chronicles and laws compiled and edited by William, found in Bodl. Libr. Arch. Seld. B. 16, written at Malmesbury Abbey by himself and assistants.[33] It begins with a series of edited and excerpted chronicles, covering the Greco-Roman world and its successors, from the Trojan War and foundation of Rome to the Greek and German emperors of his own day, followed by a copy of the *Breviarium Alaricum*, a shortened version of the Theodosian Code. William's introduction to the latter shows that he also knew, or knew of, Justinian's Code, rightly saying that copying it out would be a huge enterprise.[34] The collection speaks to his notion of Empire and its importance. The emphasis is on continuity; even the rise of Christianity, or the hiatus in the imperial line between the last emperors of the West and Charlemagne are not seen as marking major changes. He knew of Charlemagne's importance, though he does not comment on the 'Carolingian renaissance' – this despite the fact that he had read Einhard's *Vita Karoli* with attention and seems to have seen at first hand Charlemagne's palace chapel at Aachen.[35]

---

[29] On William and the Celts, see J. Gillingham, 'Conquering the barbarians: war and chivalry in twelfth-century Britain', *Haskins Society Journal* 4 (1992), 67–84, and 'Civilizing the English? The English histories of William of Malmesbury and David Hume', *Historical Research* 84 (2000), 1–18. On William and the Scandinavians, see R. M. Thomson, 'William of Malmesbury and the Scandinavians', in *History and Intellectual Culture in the Long Twelfth Century: The Scandinavian Connection*, ed. T. Heebøll-Holm, M. Münster-Swendsen, and S. Sønnesyn (Toronto, 2016), pp. 91–103.

[30] *GR* 409. 1: 'Ita pro penuria, immo pro inscientia cultorum ieiunum omnium bonorum solum agrestem et squalidam multitudinem Hibernensium extra urbes producit; Angli uero et Franci cultiori genere uitae urbes nundinarum commertio inhabitant'.

[31] *GP* 72. 6: 'Nam et Scotti ... magis in paludibus inglorii delitescere quam in excelsis urbibus consuerant habitare'.

[32] *GP* 259. 1: 'Dani cum in Angliam uenire offirmassent propositum, ad sotietatem uictoriae Norreganos asciuere. Vtrorumque immanis barbaries, sed Norreganorum cupiditas rapatior, libido infestior.' Thomson, 'William of Malmesbury and the Scandinavians', pp. 93–4, 96–7.

[33] Thomson, *William of Malmesbury*, esp. pp. 28, 66–7, 90–3.

[34] Ibid., p. 63.

[35] Ibid., pp. 139, 141, 144–5; *GP* II, pp. 213–15.

But more important than the ruins or the politics in constituting an enduring legacy of Roman civilisation was writing. Written Latin was for William the fundamental index of this.[36] For his part of the world, Western Europe, he used words such as 'Latinitas' and 'orbis Latinus'.[37] But not just any Latin would do: he clearly had little time for the so-called 'hermeneutic' Latin written in England from the tenth century until the Conquest,[38] commenting sarcastically on what he thought to be the bad Latin of such as Æthelweard and Frithegod, and the anonymous verse epitaph for Bede.[39] 'Exarata barbarice Romano sale condire' ('To season with Roman salt') was one way he described his writing up of English history from Bede to his own day.[40] William was careful to write something akin to 'classical' Latin and he had a good idea of what that meant. Unavoidably using the unclassical word 'firmarius', meaning a lessee, he commented 'ut uerbo parum Latino utar' ('if I may use a word which is hardly Latin').[41] But 'Roman salt' meant more than just an acceptable sort of Latin; it meant Latin sprinkled with quotations and reminiscences from the *auctores*. Probably no twelfth-century writer did this more than William.[42] To take an example from what must prima facie be the most unpromising of his works for this purpose, the *Commentary on Lamentations*: in it we find about 130 quotations or echoes from thirty ancient authors. As in his other works, Virgil is way out in front, but also, less expectedly, he includes a long unacknowledged quotation from Apuleius, *De Deo Socratis*.[43] 'Salty' also implied sharpness: William saw the historian as, in some degree, a satirist, who viewed history as a 'farrago', in which can be met people acting foolishly, irrationally, absurdly, in which events occur which are amazing, miraculous, risible, weird, unaccountable. Written history that recorded such things, mixing the lighthearted with the didactic, the unaccountable with the explicable, was intended as civilised entertainment.[44]

England

But what William actually wrote was 'national' history – secular and ecclesiastical histories of England on a grand scale, Lives of English saints – though it was

---

[36] M. Winterbottom, 'The language of William of Malmesbury', in *Rhetoric and Renewal*, pp. 129–47.
[37] GR 267. 2; GP 65. 5.
[38] On which see M. Lapidge, 'The hermeneutic style in tenth-century England', *ASE* 4 (1975), 67–111, repr. in his *Anglo-Latin Literature 900–1066* (London, 1993), pp. 105–49.
[39] GR bk 1 prol. 2; GP 15; GR 62.
[40] GR bk 1 prol. 4.
[41] GR 314. 3.
[42] R. M. Thomson, 'William of Malmesbury and the Latin Classics revisited', in *Aspects*, pp. 383–93; idem, 'William of Malmesbury and the Latin Classics: new research', in *Writing the Classics*, ed. E. Kwakkel (Studies in Medieval and Renaissance Book Culture 3: Leiden, 2015), pp. 169–85.
[43] *Comm. Lam.* I, 1951–7; *Lam.*, pp. 113–14.
[44] R. M. Thomson, 'Satire, irony and humour in William of Malmesbury', in *Rhetoric and Renewal*, pp. 115–27.

impregnated with his ideas about the actions of Providence and the afterlife of Roman civilisation. These define William's exemplification of piety, correct morals, discipline, good manners and *latinitas*, but within the framework of English history. William's intention was to encourage a restoration of these values in contemporary English society by memorialising their achievement in the English past. He saw the English as a 'chosen people' whose fortunes paralleled those of ancient Israel; this comes to the fore especially in his *Commentary on Lamentations*.[45] Their periodic falls from grace, which William is not chary of describing, had much to do with the invasions and settlement among them of 'barbarians', who were at once (and paradoxically) their corruptors and punishers. William gradually came to see the Normans in this dual role: at first as instruments of God's judgement, later as corrupters, particularly of the English Church of his day.[46]

What returned the English, periodically, to a state of grace was the quality of their leadership,[47] at its best and most effective when there was a harmonious relationship of Church and monarch: peace and stability, learning and piety hang together and flourish when this partnership works. The outstanding examples of this, treated at length, are the ninth- and tenth-century kings Alfred, Edgar and Æthelstan, each of them twinned with great churchmen: with Alfred Grimbald, Asser and John the Scot; with Edgar Dunstan, Oswald and Æthelwold, with Æthelstan Archbishop Oda.[48] He was unable to locate and describe this sort of happy partnership in his own day. In the earliest draft of the *Gesta Pontificum* he drew a highly ambivalent portrait of Archbishop Lanfranc, able and learned indeed, but rather too pliant and subservient to William I; later he literally tore the leaf out of his autograph copy and rewrote the portrait to show that Lanfranc was adroit of necessity rather than merely self-serving in his handling of the king. In the case of Lanfranc's successor, Anselm, William's spiritual hero and the occasion for an extensive intrusion of hagiography into the *Gesta Pontificum*, William could not even be ambivalent: the archbishop's relations with two kings were disastrous, and William, devout Benedictine and friend of Eadmer, could hardly avoid siding with him.[49] After Anselm's death (in 1107) we hear no more of relations between monarchs and archbishops of Canterbury.

At the bottom of all this is a personal element: in the *Gesta Regum* William characterises himself as an 'objective' reporter of the Norman Conquest because

---

[45] e.g. *Lam.*, pp. 122–4, 311–12.

[46] Thomson, 'William of Malmesbury's anti-Norman diatribe', in *The Long Twelfth-Century View*, pp. 113–21.

[47] There is now an extensive literature on William's view of kingship and of individual kings: B. Weiler, 'William of Malmesbury on kingship', *History* 90 (2005), 3–22; idem, 'William of Malmesbury, King Henry I, and the *Gesta Regum Anglorum*', ANS 31 (2009), 157–76; idem, 'Royal justice and royal virtue in William of Malmesbury's *Historia nouella* and Walter Map's *De nugis curialium*', in *Virtue and Ethics in the Twelfth Century*, ed. I. Bejczy and R. Newhauser (Leiden-Boston, 2005), pp. 317–39. See also the essay by Ryan Kemp in this volume, pp. 65–79.

[48] GR 149. 1–6, 122. 3–6, GP 14.

[49] GP 45–66.

of his mixed ancestry, yet even in this work his Englishness is to the fore, the more so as he grew older.[50] It is instructive to observe his attitude toward the English language and its literature. On the one hand, as we have seen, he thought it important to turn the rough annals in a barbaric tongue into Latin (he himself translated Coleman's Life of Bishop Wulfstan of Worcester from English into Latin),[51] and he never actually praises any piece of English writing; on the other, Bede and Alfred are commended for translating key Christian texts from Latin into the mother tongue.[52] And Old English had its own standards; the Celtic inhabitants of the British Isles influence the speech of the neighbouring northern English for the worse: 'the whole language of the Northumbrians, particularly in York, is so inharmonious and uncouth that we southerners can make nothing of it. This is the result of the barbarians being so near, and the kings, once English, now Norman, so far away'.[53]

I have argued that the complex interplay between these three elements, the perceived actions of God, the *Nachlass* of Roman civilisation, and the great but fragile heritage of the English people, form the basis of William of Malmesbury's vision of history. Some may reasonably question whether 'complexity' is a euphemism for lack of unity and self-consistency. What is certain is that writing history according to this sort of sophisticated 'vision' had not been done since the ancient Romans, and would not be done again for a long time, even by William's many admirers and plunderers.[54]

---

[50] Thomson, 'William of Malmesbury's anti-Norman diatribe', pp. 113–21.
[51] *Saints' Lives*, pp. xv–xvii, 8–11.
[52] GR 60. 1, 122. 4, 123. 1–3.
[53] GP 99. 4: 'Sane tota lingua Nordanhimbrorum, et maxime in Eboraco, ita inconditum stridet ut nichil nos australes intelligere possimus. Quod propter uiciniam barbararum gentium et propter remotionem regum quondam Anglorum modo Normannorum contigit.'
[54] This paper was first delivered to a conference of the Centre for Medieval Studies at the University of Bergen in 2014. I have to thank the audience on that occasion for many helpful comments and, for reading and commenting on subsequent drafts, Sverre Bagge, John Gillingham and Michael Winterbottom.

15

Verax historicus Beda:
William of Malmesbury, Bede and *historia*

Emily Joan Ward

WILLIAM OF MALMESBURY saw himself as a successor to Bede. He stated this in the prologue to the *Gesta Regum Anglorum*, acknowledging his debt to the eighth-century monk.[1] In many respects their historical writing reflects comparable outlooks. Combining educative and moralising purposes, both Bede and William presented historical narratives that provided exemplars as mirrors and models for their readers.[2] Yet, while it is often recognised that William used and imitated Bede's writings, few scholars have explored the relationship in detail.[3] This paper will explore William's understanding of Bede's

---

This paper was based on findings from my AHRC-funded thesis, 'Anglo-Norman Perceptions of Bede as a Historical Writer', unpublished MA thesis, University of East Anglia (2011). Thanks must go to Dr Tom Licence, firstly for supervising the initial thesis and, secondly, for providing his thoughts on an initial draft of this paper. Valuable comments and suggestions were also made by Prof. Liesbeth van Houts, to whom I am eminently grateful, and by the speakers and those attending the 'William of Malmesbury and his Legacy' conference.

[1] GR bk 1 prol. 1: 'post eum non facile, ut arbitror, reperies qui historiis illius gentis Latina oratione texendis animum dederit . . . . Unde michi cum propter patriae caritatem, tum propter adhortantium auctoritatem uoluntati fuit interruptam temporum seriem sarcire' ('After Bede you will not easily, I think, find anyone who has devoted himself to writing English history in Latin . . . . It was therefore my design, in part moved by love of my country and in part encouraged by influential friends, to mend the broken chain of our history').

[2] That this aim was held by both Bede and William can be seen clearly from the preface to the *HE* and the prologue to the *GP*. 'Siue enim historia de bonis bona referat, ad imitandum bonum auditor sollicitis instigator; seu mala commemoret de prauis, nihilominus religiosus ac pius auditor siue lector deuitando quod noxium est ac peruersum, ipse sollertius ad exsequenda ea quae bona ac Deo digna esse cognouerit, accenditur': *HE* pref. (p. 2). 'Quid enim dultius quam maiorum recensere gratiam, ut eorum acta cognoscas a quibus acceperis et rudimenta fidei et incitamenta bene uiuendi?': *GP* prol. 3 (p. 3). For a summary of Bede's approach to writing history see A. Thacker, 'Bede and history', in *The Cambridge Companion to Bede*, ed. S. DeGregorio (Cambridge, 2010), pp. 170–89.

[3] For discussions of the relationship between William and Bede see, in particular: Gransden, *Historical Writing in England*, p. 169, and D. H. Farmer, 'William of Malmesbury's life and work', *JEH* 13 (1962), 40.

concept of historical writing, as set out in his *Historia Gentis Anglorum Ecclesiastica*, William's subsequent use of Bede's model in his own work, and how he moved beyond this model. The comparison between these two historians will centre particularly on their use of the term 'historicus', a word with classical origins, used by Pliny, Cicero and Augustine, amongst others.[4] A philological analysis demonstrates that William differed from his contemporaries in the way in which he viewed and used Bede, and that this affected his self-perception of the historian's role. Although the *Historia Ecclesiastica* was by no means William's only model of historical writing, it was one for which he had considerable admiration. Yet the way in which he shaped this admiration in the *Gesta Pontificum* was not the same as in the *Gesta Regum*.

Working from the dual monastery of Wearmouth-Jarrow in the early eighth century, Bede completed the *Historia Ecclesiastica* in 731, four years before his death. In it he used the word 'historicus' only twice, in both instances as a noun. First, he described the fifth- or sixth-century writer Gildas, author of Bede's main source for the coming of the Saxons and the early Anglo-Saxon Church, as the historian of the Britons ('historicus eorum Gildas').[5] The title of Bede's work reflects the fact that he too wanted to be seen as the historian of a people, the English. Later in the *Historia*, Bede referred to himself as a truthful historian ('uerax historicus'), suggesting that he may have viewed his own standards of historical enquiry as higher than those of Gildas.[6] Bede's self-description follows a passage on Bishop Aidan of Lindisfarne, a man whom he much admired in all respects except one: Aidan observed the date of Easter according to the Irish system of reckoning rather than the Roman system which, for Bede, was the true and catholic one.[7] Although criticism of a saint may have been controversial, Bede explained that his role as historian was to record plainly Aidan's deeds ('gesta'), regardless of his personal feelings about Aidan's beliefs.[8] Two later manuscripts of the Anglo-Saxon version of the *Historia Ecclesiastica* omitted Bede's treatment of Aidan, suggesting that some audiences considered such criticism inappropriate.[9] Nevertheless, in his depiction of Aidan, Bede was attempting to observe the true law of history ('uera lex historiae'), a much-debated phrase, taken verbatim

---

[4] Lewis and Short, p. 858.

[5] *HE* i. 22.

[6] *HE* iii. 17: 'Scripsi autem haec de persona et operibus uiri praefati, nequaquam in eo laudans aut eligens hoc, quod de obseruatione paschae minus perfecte sapiebat; immo hoc multum detestans, sicut in libro quem de Temporibus conposui manifestissime probaui; sed quasi uerax historicus'.

[7] *HE* iii. 25: 'uerum et catholicum pascha'.

[8] *HE* iii. 17: 'sed quasi uerax historicus simpliciter ea, quae de illo siue per illum sunt gesta, describens et quae laude sunt digna in eius actibus laudans, atque ad utilitatem legentium memoriae commendans'. See also J. M. Wallace-Hadrill, *Bede's Ecclesiastical History of the English People: A Historical Commentary* (Oxford, 1988), p. 110.

[9] C. Plummer, *Venerabilis Baedae Opera Historica* (2 vols, Oxford, 1896), I, p. 167. The manuscripts missing this section on Aidan are those called T and B, according to Miller's stemma. See S. M. Rowley, *The Old English Version of Bede's 'Historia Ecclesiastica'* (Woodbridge, 2011), pp. 15–35.

William of Malmesbury, Bede and historia

from Jerome's *Adversus Helvidium*, that he had earlier used in his *Commentary on Luke*.[10] Walter Goffart's claim that Bede used his 'uera lex historiae' to argue for common perception as the remit of history, in contrast to theological truth, does not adequately acknowledge the moral and spiritual aspects of Bede's works.[11] Instead, more emphasis should be put on Bede's desire to communicate the will of God to his audience in a simple way, as Plassmann has convincingly argued.[12] According to Bede, although any historian might record the history of a people, the *truthful* historian does so by writing plainly, 'simpliciter', for the moral benefit of the audience, in accordance with orthodoxy, but also to illuminate deeper spiritual truth and to reveal something of God's purpose.

The level of acclaim for Bede's *Historia Ecclesiastica* in the early twelfth century can in part be assessed from manuscript evidence. Richard Gameson has shown that the period between 1080 and 1130 was the highest point in the circulation of *Historia Ecclesiastica* manuscripts in England.[13] Bede was the second most popular author after Augustine among works written in early Norman England or acquired by English collections during these years, with his work appearing in eighty-four surviving manuscripts.[14] Thirteen of these contain the text of the *Historia* or extracts from it, and one additional copy of the eleventh century was edited substantially between these years.[15] Commonly found alongside the *Historia* is Cuthbert's *Epistola de obitu Bedae*, demonstrating that there was an active interest in Bede's biography and in promoting his possible sanctity.[16] The addition of an archiepiscopal list to an early twelfth-century manuscript of the *Historia Ecclesiastica* made at Canterbury but soon after at Battle (Hereford Cath. P. V. 1) illustrates the work's enduring importance.[17] The list, which names the

---

[10] R. Ray, 'Bede's *uera lex historiae*', *Speculum* 55 (1980), 1. When Bede repeated the phrase in the preface to the *HE*, Ray suggests he may have used it to confer a slightly different meaning to that in the *Commentary on Luke*: Ray, 'Bede's *uera lex historiae*', p. 10. See also W. Goffart, 'Bede's *uera lex historiae* explained', *ASE* 34 (2005), 114, and A. Plassmann, 'Beda Venerabilis – Verax Historicus. Bedas Vera Lex Historiae', in *Wilhelm Levison (1876–1947). Ein jüdisches Forscherleben zwischen wissenschaftlicher Anerkennung und politischem Exil*, ed. M. Becher and Y. Hen (Siegburg, 2010), pp. 123–43. In particular, see pp. 141–2, where Plassmann argues additionally that this passage in the *Historia* needs to be seen in the light of two further works of exegesis by Bede, the *Expositio Actuum Apostolorum* and the *Homeliarum Euangelii*.

[11] Goffart, 'Bede's *uera lex historiae* explained', p. 113.

[12] Plassmann, 'Beda Venerabilis – Verax Historicus', p. 142.

[13] This is also reflected across the rest of Europe where the copying of Bede's works peaked in the twelfth century. See M. L. W. Laistner and H. H. King, *A Hand-list of Bede Manuscripts* (Ithaca NY, 1943), p. 7.

[14] R. Gameson, *The Manuscripts of Early Norman England (c.1066–1130)* (Oxford, 1999), pp. 32, 36.

[15] References to these manuscripts can be found in Gameson, *The Manuscripts of Early Norman England*, nos. 68, 175, 176, 232, 320, 353, 449, 589e, 707e, 711e, 716, 723, 751, 805e.

[16] The account by Cuthbert was found in four of the manuscripts listed by Gameson: Cambridge, Trinity Coll. R. 5. 27; Hereford Cath. P. V. I; BL Harl. 3680; and Bodl. Libr. Fairfax 12. See Gameson, *The Manuscripts of Early Norman England*, pp. 75, 91, 108, 137.

[17] Hereford Cath. P. V. 1, f. 152v.

archbishops of Canterbury to Theobald (1138–61), demonstrates that the monks of Battle viewed Bede's text as valuable for its record of archiepiscopal history but not as a static, distant narrative; they desired to update the *Historia* with information down to the present.[18]

Around the same time, the *Historia* was seen as a major authority for the lives of Anglo-Saxon saints. Extracts were lifted from it for inclusion in collections of hagiographical writing. A Durham manuscript (Bodl. Libr. Digby 20) contains chapters from the *Historia* concerning St Cuthbert, alongside Bede's prose *Vita Sancti Cuthberti*.[19] Another, from the Augustinian house of Lanthony Secunda (Lambeth Palace Libr. 173), dated c.1110 to c.1130, containing the Lives and visions of saints and religious men, includes three chapters from Book Five of the *Historia* in its *Visio Drihthelmi* and other *uisiones*.[20] The English saints mentioned by Bede in his *Historia* were of particular interest to the monks of Rochester who appended a tract on the resting places of English saints to an early twelfth-century copy (BL Harl. 3680).[21] This tract was valuable for readers who may not have been familiar with the current locations of the relics of the saints mentioned by Bede, some of which had been moved or translated since the completion of the *Historia Ecclesiastica*. The presence of accents marking out lections in a number of late eleventh and early twelfth-century manuscripts further demonstrates the authority of Bede's stories of the English saints, for the marks indicate that the *Historia* would have been read aloud.[22] Tessa Webber has shown that at least a third of the extant copies of the *Historia* dating from between the late tenth and late twelfth centuries were marked with Roman numerals for lections to be read throughout the monastic horarium, usually at the night office of matins.[23] Lections for the Office of St Birinus were taken from Book Three of the *Historia* and used in Bodl. Libr. Digby 39, a composite manuscript from Abingdon.[24] Goscelin of Saint-Bertin's life of St Augustine described how Bishop Gundulf of

---

[18] Archiepiscopal succession lists for both York and Canterbury can also be found in Durham Cath. B. II. 35, ff. 144–9, dated pre-1096. See Gameson, *The Manuscripts of Early Norman England*, p. 81.

[19] Bodl. Libr. Digby 20, ff. 194–227. Gameson, *The Manuscripts of Early Norman England*, p. 135.

[20] Lambeth Palace 173, ff. 211–18. The chapters taken from Bede's work are *HE* v. 12–14. See also Gameson, *The Manuscripts of Early Norman England*, p. 123, and M. R. James and C. Jenkins, *A Descriptive Catalogue of the Manuscripts in the Library of Lambeth Palace* (Cambridge, 1930), p. 273.

[21] Gameson, *The Manuscripts of Early Norman England*, p. 108.

[22] A good example of accent marking is found in BL Add. 25014, ff. 2–117.

[23] T. Webber, 'Bede's *Historia Ecclesiastica* as a source of lections in pre- and post-Conquest England', in *The Long Twelfth-Century View*, p. 48. For an example of lection readings being marked in a manuscript see BL Harl. 3680, ff. 20v–23v. These accents mark eight lections on the arrival of Augustine in Kent.

[24] Gameson, *The Manuscripts of Early Norman England*, p. 135. The dating of these lections is discussed in Webber, 'Bede's *Historia Ecclesiastica* as a source of lections', p. 54 n. 28. Webber suggests an earlier dating than Gameson for the lections, arguing for a date in the second half of the eleventh century rather than the early twelfth century.

William of Malmesbury, Bede and historia

Rochester drew on the *Historia* for his liturgical readings for the saint's feast.[25] The *Historia* was also used for non-liturgical purposes, such as refectory readings and personal devotion.[26] In fact, the transmission and usage of the manuscripts confirm that the *Historia* was viewed in this period as authoritative at least as much for its hagiographical as for its historical information, if such a distinction can be made.[27]

We find this same emphasis on the *Historia* as a source of reference for Anglo-Saxon saints in the works of writers contemporary with this proliferation of manuscripts, that is between c. 1080 and c. 1130. The Flemish hagiographer, Goscelin of Saint-Bertin, arrived in England in the late 1060s and, between 1078 and 1099, wrote the lives of approximately twenty Anglo-Saxon saints. Goscelin described Bede's work as a most trustworthy account ('historia fidelissima') in his record of the translation of Augustine of Canterbury, written c. 1098 as part of a compilation of new liturgical and hagiographical works to commemorate the translation of Augustine's relics in 1091.[28] Goscelin saw Bede as an authority on Augustine, evident from his heavy reliance on the *Historia Ecclesiastica*, and his instructions to readers that they should consult the original for further information.[29] Goscelin made direct references to Bede's place as the writer of the history of the English people throughout the *Translatio*, calling him 'historiographus' and 'historiae Anglorum scriptor'.[30] For Goscelin, however, the historical and hagiographical significances of Bede's *Historia* were intertwined: the references to Bede as a historian all appear in passages concerning saintly persons such as King Æthelberht or the archbishops of Canterbury, Justus, Honorius and Deusdedit.

Like Goscelin, Symeon of Durham, in his *Libellus de Exordio ... Dunhelmensis Ecclesie*, a local history of the church of Durham written between 1104 and 1115, relied heavily on the *Historia*, primarily as an authoritative source in his discussion of saints.[31] For Symeon, Bede was the 'distinguished author' who had written two Lives of Saint Cuthbert, the dominating figure of the *Libellus*.[32] Symeon also

---

[25] Goscelin of Saint-Bertin, *Historia, Miracula et Translatio S. Augustini*, in *Acta Sanctorum: Maii VI* (Antwerp, 1688), col. 423F.

[26] Webber, 'Bede's *Historia Ecclesiastica* as a source of lections', pp. 67–8.

[27] See the paper by Anne Bailey in this volume, pp. 13–26.

[28] Goscelin, *Historia, Miracula et Translatio S. Augustini*, col. 416A. For a discussion of the dating see R. Sharpe, 'Goscelin's St Augustine and St Mildreth: hagiography and liturgy in context', *Journal of Theological Studies* 41 (1990), 502–16, esp. p. 516. Sharpe suggests that to discuss Goscelin's hagiographical output for St Augustine's Abbey throughout the 1090s as individual texts is misleading. Instead, he suggests that the output should be viewed collectively as a series.

[29] F. Gameson, 'Goscelin's *Life* of Augustine of Canterbury', in *St Augustine and the Conversion of England*, ed. R. Gameson (Stroud, 1999), p. 392.

[30] Goscelin, *Historia, Miracula et Translatio S. Augustini*, cols 419F and 417D.

[31] 'Everything concerning the origin and progress of this church of Durham which could be found in Bede's *History* and in other little works should, in order to preserve its memory for posterity, be assembled and arranged to form the substance of this tract': Symeon of Durham, *LDE* i. 1 (p. 19). Cc. 4–6 and 9 (pp. 28–36) provide an example of verbatim quotations from *HE*.

[32] *LDE* i. 8 (p. 43). Symeon had a personal connection to Cuthbert as a saint, since he had

Discovering William of Malmesbury

demonstrated his biographical interest in Bede by including the whole of Bede's autobiographical endnote and quoting the *Epistola de Obitu Bedae* verbatim.[33] This interest complements that shown in the early Anglo-Norman manuscripts which included the *Epistola* alongside the *Historia Ecclesiastica*.[34] Symeon's biographical interest in Bede was a particularly personal one, since Bede's relics were located at Durham. Symeon mentions this fact on three separate occasions throughout the *Libellus* to connect the eighth-century historian with the Durham community.[35] Symeon further emphasised Bede's monastic connection by describing him repeatedly as a venerable priest and monk.[36] He attributed the eleventh-century revival of monasticism in the north to Bede, claiming that the monk Aldwin chose to found monastic houses again in Northumbria after reading the *Historia Ecclesiastica*, from which he learnt that the kingdom had 'once been full of numerous choirs of monks and many hosts of saints'.[37] Symeon's presentation of Bede as a monastic authority on English saints tied to a cult at Durham supported one of the major purposes of the *Libellus*: to legitimise William of Saint-Calais's expulsion of clerks from Durham in favour of Benedictine monks.[38]

This monastic portrayal of Bede is not characteristic of the *Historia Anglorum*, which the secular cleric Henry, archdeacon of Huntingdon, began writing in the late 1120s. Henry was certainly interested in Bede's autobiographical account, which he too quoted verbatim. Henry viewed Bede as an unquestioned authority on the history of the English saints and relied on the *Historia Ecclesiastica* unequivocally, occasionally even at the expense of what he had written himself, as Diana Greenway has pointed out.[39] Although Henry was aware of Bede's 'uera lex historiae' and copied more extensively from the *Historia Ecclesiastica* than either Symeon or Goscelin, he did not praise Bede primarily for his skill as a historian,[40] but for his spiritual authority as a philosopher of Christ, a man of God and, above all, a venerable individual.[41] 'Uenerabilis' was an epithet probably first applied to

been at the translation of his body in 1104. See *LDE* i. 10 (p. 53).

[33] See *LDE* i. 14 (pp. 64–9) and i. 15 (p. 71).

[34] For example, Cambridge, Trinity Coll. R. 5. 27, Hereford Cath. P. V. I, BL Harl. 3680, and Bodl. Libr., Fairfax 12.

[35] *LDE* i. 11 (p. 57); i. 14 (p. 69) and iii. 7 (pp. 165–7).

[36] 'uenerabilis presbiter et monachus', *LDE* i. 6 (p. 34), i. 14 (p. 64) and appendix A (p. 258).

[37] *LDE* iii. 21 (p. 201).

[38] This expulsion of the clerks from Durham has even been described as the 'climax' of Symeon's work. See Gransden, *Historical Writing in England*, p. 116.

[39] 'I have added none, or nearly none, to the miracles which that man of the Lord, the venerable Bede, whose authority is completely secure, has written in his *History*': Henry of Huntingdon, *Historia Anglorum* ix. 1 (p. 623). Webber, 'Bede's *Historia Ecclesiastica* as a source of lections', p. 69. For Diana Greenway's critique of Henry's use of Bede see *Historia Anglorum* i. 9 (pp. 26–7).

[40] See *Historia Anglorum* iv. 14 (p. 234) for the mention of Bede's 'uera lex historiae'. The only place where someone was referred to as a historian was in Book Two of the *Historia Anglorum*, when the author of the *Historia Brittonum* was called 'quidam historiographus': *Historia Anglorum* ii. 18 (p. 100).

[41] Bede is described as a philosopher of Christ at *Historia Anglorum* iv. 11 (p. 230) and iv. 33 (p. 268). Archbishop Anselm is referred to in the same way at vii. 27 (p. 456). For 'uir domini' see

Bede in the ninth century when a cult began to be fostered around his relics.[42] William of Malmesbury's near-contemporaries, Goscelin, Symeon and Henry, show throughout their works that they saw Bede as the venerable writer of the lives of the Anglo-Saxon saints, using 'uenerabilis' as a mark of their respect for Bede and to emphasise his authority, holiness and possibly even sanctity. Like the manuscript evidence, historical and hagiographical writings from this period emphasised the liturgical authority of the *Historia Ecclesiastica*, the spiritual authority of Bede himself, or both of these. Significantly, none of the three writers discussed so far used the word 'historicus'. Even when Goscelin called Bede a historian, using the word 'historiographus', it was with reference to the liturgical authority of the *Historia* and did not allude to Bede's historical methodology or his standard of historical truth.

At first glance, William of Malmesbury's use of the *Historia* fits into much the same pattern as his contemporaries – he used the text as a starting point, directed his audience to Bede's work and elaborated on the text where needed. Yet William did more than this: he critically engaged with the *Historia* to correct it when he felt it was in error, to differ when he had additional evidence and even to consult variant manuscripts of it, as in his treatment of the story of Oswald, king and martyr.[43] William did not feel compelled to stick as closely to the text of the *Historia* as did his contemporaries. This can be seen by comparing the way in which he and Eadmer of Canterbury used Bede's passages on St Wilfrid of Ripon.[44] Paul Hayward's idea that William was concerned less with hagiographical ideals and more with the principles of writing ecclesiastical history is borne out by William's distinctive use of historical terminology, which departs completely from that used by other contemporary writers.[45] Etymologically, the word 'historicus', like 'historia', is derived from the Greek 'historein', which means 'to see and comprehend'.[46] Isidore of Seville's definition emphasised this etymology. He saw history as the narration of things that had happened, although his description also asserted the role of the historian as eyewitness.[47] Neither Bede nor William could claim to be

---

Historia Anglorum ix. 1 (p. 622). For 'uenerabilis' see *Historia Anglorum*, prol. (p. 6); i. 11 (p. 28); iii. 30 (p. 180); iv. 11 (p. 230); iv. 12 (p. 230); iv. 14 (p. 234); iv. 33 (p. 268).

[42] For a discussion of the title 'uenerabilis' and Bede's legacy see B. Colgrave, 'Historical introduction' to *Bede's Ecclesiastical History of the English People*, ed. B. Colgrave and R. A. B. Mynors (Oxford, 1969), pp. xxii–xxiii.

[43] GR 208. 1: 'In laudibus beatissimi Oswaldi regis et martiris in superiori libro aliquandiu uersata est oratio. Cuius sanctitatis fuere inditia cum cetera, tum illud quod secundum quaedam exemplaria in Gestis Anglorum asseritur'.

[44] P. Hayward, 'St Wilfrid of Ripon and the northern Church in Anglo-Norman historiography', *Northern History* 49 (2012), 12. I would like to thank Paul Hayward for drawing my attention to this article.

[45] Hayward, 'St Wilfrid of Ripon and the northern Church', p. 23.

[46] Ray, 'Bede's *uera lex historiae*', p. 15. See also R. M. Stein, 'Signs and things: The "Vita Heinrici IV. Imperatoris" and the crisis of interpretation in twelfth-century history', *Traditio* 43 (1987), 111.

[47] Isidore of Seville, *Etymologiae*, 1. 44. 5: 'Item inter historiam et argumentum et fabulam interesse. Nam historiae sunt res verae quae factae sunt, argumenta sunt quae etsi facta non sunt,

witnesses to most of the events they record in their historical works. Both men were more reserved about writing contemporaneous history than they were for events in the distant past, perhaps owing to their desire to emphasise the truthfulness of their accounts by maintaining distance from their narrative. Yet Bede's and William's reticence about discussing the historical present could also be one of deliberate caution: to avoid any political ramifications which could affect their monastic communities. Roger Ray has emphasised that restraint must be used when discussing Bede's use of, and regard for, Isidore's works. Over Bede's life, the monk became progressively more disillusioned with Isidore's teachings.[48] Since William, like Bede, was similarly concerned with ideas of truth and historical verisimilitude and had engaged with Bede's conception of 'uera lex historiae',[49] it is possible that he picked up on Bede's critique of Isidore.[50]

In the *Gesta Regum*, William used 'historicus' to describe five men and, as in the *Historia Ecclesiastica*, he used the word as a noun rather than an adjective. Bede is the only person to whom William applied the title more than once and the only individual to receive the title of 'truthful historian' ('uerax historicus').[51] In Book Two William refers to Bede's 'unquestioned authority' ('indubitata historici auctoritas').[52] He describes Gildas as 'a historian not without style and insight', although this appears only in the additions to the B and C redactions of the *Gesta Regum*.[53] These uses of the word fit neatly with Bede's perception of what it meant to be 'historicus'. In addition, Bede's perception of both truth and history is evident in William's writings.[54] Sigbjørn Sønnesyn, placing William's view of the writing of history and historical truth in the context of ethics, has argued persuasively that William found moral instruction and historical truth compatible.[55] From the outset of the *Gesta Regum*, therefore, William based his conception of historical writing and its relation to truth on Bede's own interpretation in the *Historia Ecclesiastica*.

fieri tamen possunt; fabulae vero sunt quae nec factae sunt nec fieri possunt, quia contra naturam sunt.'

[48] Ray, 'Bede's *uera lex historiae*', p. 16.

[49] GR 445. 5: 'ego enim, ueram legem secutus historiae, nichil umquam posui nisi quod a fidelibus relatoribus uel scriptoribus addidici'.

[50] Ray, 'Bede's *uera lex historiae*', p. 21.

[51] Of Oswald, GR 49. 7: 'brachia uero cum manibus auctore Deo, teste ueraci historico, inuiolata durant'. Of Ceolwulf, GR 54. 1: 'Cuius anno quarto idem historicus, post multos in sancta aecclesia libros elaboratos, caelestem patriam quam die suspirauerat ingressus est'.

[52] GR 208. 3: 'Ne autem haec uideantur friuola prohibet indubitata historici auctoritas, simulque beatus episcopus Acca relatoris simmistes'.

[53] GR 20. 1: 'Gildas neque insulsus neque infacetus historicus'. So also in AG c. 7 (pp. 54–5): 'Nam, sicut a majoribus accepimus, Gildas neque insulsus neque infacetus historicus, cui Britanni debent, si quid notitiae inter caeteras gentes habent, multum annorum ibi exegit loci sanctitudine captus'.

[54] For example, Kirsten Fenton has claimed that William saw 'the need to ally the "truth" with what makes a good story': K. A. Fenton, *Gender, Nation and Conquest in the Works of William of Malmesbury* (Woodbridge, 2008), p. 20.

[55] Sønnesyn, *Ethics*, esp. ch. 4, pp. 70–95 and also pp. 263–5.

Unlike Bede, however, who did not describe any of his contemporaries as historians, William found a contemporary of his worthy of the title. In the *Gesta Regum*, William called Eadmer a historian of his own time whose writings exhibited a 'praiseworthy standard of truth'.[56] Although this was not as fervent an acclamation as that which William gave Bede (to whom he dedicated nine chapters of eulogy), this may have been simply because Eadmer was a contemporary whilst Bede's reputation rested on centuries of esteem. William's reference to Eadmer as 'historicus', however, clearly associates him with the tradition of men such as Gildas and Bede. Elsewhere in the *Gesta Regum*, William recorded his appreciation of Eadmer's works, called him lord or master ('domnus'), and praised his writing style in similar terms to Bede's.[57]

The next historian to whom William gave the title of 'historicus' in the *Gesta Regum* was Paul the Deacon, the historian of the Lombards.[58] This was because William, following Bede, envisioned a historian as someone concerned above all with writing the history of a people or nation. Paul the Deacon wrote the *Historia Langobardorum* in the late eighth century and, although left unfinished, it covered the history of the Lombards from the mid-sixth century to the death of King Liutprand in 744. While Bede wrote the history of one people, the English, William extended his own idea of a historian beyond Bede's to include the history of peoples besides those occupying the island of Britain. William stated that he had built up 'a library of foreign historians' to consult whilst writing the *Gesta Regum*.[59] Two of these he also described as 'historiographus': Jordanes, the historian of the Goths, and Josephus, best known for his historical works on the Jews.[60] Walter Goffart has shown that William's nation-based view of history was not unusual at the time. French manuscripts from the eleventh century on contained a range of what Goffart described as 'national' histories, for instance Milan, Bibl. Ambros. C. 72 inf., in which Bede's *Historia* is bound with copies of Jordanes' *De Origine Actibusque Getarum*, Paul the Deacon's *Historia Romana* and

---

[56] GR 332. 1: 'Edmerus, nostrorum temporum historicus, sinceritate ueritatis laudandus'.

[57] GR 315: 'simul et supersedendum est in historia quam reuerentissimi Edmeri preoccupauit facundia'. 'domnus Eadmerus': 413. 2. William praised Bede's writing style at 57: 'Deficit hic ingenium, succumbit eloquium nescientis quid plus laudem, librorum numerositatem an sermonum sobrietatem'. Eadmer's style receives similar praise from William at bk 1 prol. 3: 'Nec uero nostram effugit conscientiam domni Edmeri sobria sermonis festiuitate elucubratum opus'.

[58] GR 410. 2: 'historicus Longobardorum'.

[59] GR bk 2 prol. 2.

[60] GR 116. 2: 'Iordanes historiographus Gothorum'. GR 169. 5: 'ut idem historiographus testatur'. Bede had not used the word 'historiographus' in the *HE*, but it did appear in a number of his other works such as *De Temporibus* and his *Commentary on Luke*. The word 'historiographus' may have had specific links to world histories and to the writing of history in chronicle form for some writers; see: *Mediae Latinitatis Lexicon Minus*, ed. J. F. Niermeyer and C. Van de Kieft (2nd edn, Leiden, 2002), p. 640. This was not the case for William, however, who did not introduce any differentiation between 'historiographus' and 'historicus' in the *Gesta Regum*. The word 'historiographus' is also found in William's *Commentary on Lamentations*, where he alludes to Hegesippus: *Comm. Lam.* II. 21 (p. 131). My thanks go to Michael Winterbottom for pointing out this reference.

Historia Langobardorum, and Dictys's *Ephemeris Belli Troiani*.[61] William applied the words 'historicus' and 'historiographus' only to writers of this sort of history; even Goscelin, whom he lauded as second only to Bede in his celebration of English saints, did not receive either title.[62]

William implicitly rated himself as a 'uerax historicus' who bore comparison with Bede, stating that 'to trust in all respects to partial reports, and trade upon the credulity of one's hearers, ought to be outside the province of the honest historian'.[63] Ray noted that William's use of the term 'uerax historicus' in both the *Historia Nouella* and *Gesta Regum* was entirely true to the sense of the phrase in Bede's *Historia Ecclesiastica*.[64] Not that William imitated Bede blindly. Rather, he presented himself and his *Gesta Regum* overtly as the equal of Bede and his *Historia*, using virtually identical titles for his own work and for Bede's, identified as 'Gesta Anglorum' in William's *Gesta Regum*. On only two occasions did William choose not to use the title *Gesta Anglorum* for Bede's work; in both cases William paraphrased Bede's own words.[65] In the letter to Earl Robert that accompanied William's text, he gave his own work the similar title 'Gesta Regum Anglorum'.[66] Rodney Thomson has noted that the literal translation of William's title should be 'The Deeds of the Kings of the English People', making the point that William, whilst narrowing his purpose from Bede's to focus on the deeds of the kings, was concerned above all with the English context.[67] Although William admitted that his narrative extended outside England, the English aspect of his 'gesta' was especially important to him because it maintained the unmistakeable and explicit connection to Bede's historical writing.[68]

William did not use the words 'gesta' and 'historia' interchangeably; on the contrary he made a clear distinction between them. Thus, in the *Gesta Pontificum* he pointedly chose the title 'Historia Anglorum', not 'Gesta Anglorum', when referring to Bede's work.[69] William's precision in choosing his titles has been

---

[61] W. Goffart, *The Narrators of Barbarian History (A.D. 550–800)* (Princeton, 1988), p. 4.

[62] *GR* 342. 1: 'in laudibus sanctorum Angliae nulli post Bedam secundus'.

[63] When talking of Baldwin and how he subdued Tiberias, Sidon and Acre, *GR* 382. 1: 'Ingentes operas eiusmodi desideret oratio hominis qui ampullato eloquio et curioso habundet otio. Nobis utrumque deest, et, quod maxime obest, rerum expedita scientia; omnia uero indulgenti famae credere, et facilitatem auditorum fallere, ueracis historici non debet esse.'

[64] Ray, 'Bede's *uera lex historiae*', p. 21.

[65] William once gave an expanded title *Aecclesiastica Anglorum Historia* when introducing the passage on Bede's life and once called it *Anglorum Historia* when discussing Bede's dedication to King Ceolwulf. See *GR* 54. 6 and 53. 2.

[66] *GR* Ep. iii. 3: 'uolo enim hoc opus esse multarum historiarum breuiarium, quanuis a maiori parte uocauerim Gesta Regum Anglorum'.

[67] *GR* II, p. 4.

[68] Much has been written on William of Malmesbury's approach to the English. For a recent commentary on the role of nation for William of Malmesbury and the place that England and the English held in his historical writing, see: Fenton, *Gender, Nation and Conquest in the Works of William of Malmesbury*, especially pp. 12–14.

[69] The full title *Aecclesiastica Gentis Anglorum Historia* is only used once in *GP* in an inserted letter from Archbishop Lanfranc to Pope Alexander which was not William's own words: *GP* 29.

noted in the critical discourse on his works, but the focus has previously been on the way he differentiated the chronicle form from the writing of history.[70] In distinguishing between the genres of 'gesta' and 'historia', William reveals the different ways he used Bede as an authority. Initially, in the *Gesta Regum*, Bede was an authority for the secular deeds ('gesta') of the rulers of the English. By the time William came to write the *Gesta Pontificum*, he had chosen the word 'historia' as a more appropriate descriptor for the way he was now using Bede's work. The word 'historia' was used in the liturgy to describe a short account of a saint, so the repetition of the changed title throughout the *Gesta Pontificum* can be read as acknowledgement of the liturgical influence of Bede's *Historia*. William and his readers would have been familiar with this terminology from their experience of monastic life. William would have been more acquainted than most with the liturgical application of passages from the *Historia* since, like Goscelin, his role as cantor included the upkeep and maintenance of local liturgical books.[71] He may even have been responsible for choosing extracts from Bede's work for the night offices and refectory readings. The cantor's role, combined in William's case with that of librarian, meant that he was responsible for what was read or sung within the monastic community.[72] Current scholarship maintains that William's role as cantor and his knowledge of, and engagement with, the liturgy constitute a framework within which can be understood his view of history and historical writing.[73] This is particularly helpful in clarifying William's presentation of Bede and the *Historia Ecclesiastica* in the *Gesta Pontificum*.

This change in presentation is further accentuated by a distinct change in his use of the terms 'historicus' and 'historiographus', interchangeably.[74] William

---

1. *Historia Anglorum* was also preferred as a title for Bede's work by Henry of Huntingdon. See *Historia Anglorum*, p. lxxxvi.

[70] J. O. Ward suggests that William used the word 'gesta' to represent the raw material of annalistic entries, which had been expanded and manipulated to achieve a rhetorical purpose. For this, see Ward, '"Chronicle" and "History": the medieval origins of postmodern historiographical practice', *Parergon* 14 (1997), 120.

[71] GP II, p. xxxv.

[72] M. Fassler, 'The office of the cantor in early western monastic rules and customaries: a preliminary investigation', *Early Music History* 5 (1985), 46–7.

[73] I would like to thank Sigbjørn Sønnesyn for providing me with an advance copy of his article on '*Lex orandi, lex scribendi*? The role of historiography in the liturgical life of William of Malmesbury', forthcoming in the volume *Medieval Cantors and their Craft: Music, Liturgy and the Shaping of History, 800–1500*, ed. K. Bugyis, A. Kraebel and M. Fassler (Woodbridge, 2017).

[74] GP 91. 8: 'Hildam, abbatissam cenobii quod olim Strenesalh nunc Witebi nuncupatur, tunc sanctimonialium modo monachorum, cuius quanti penderit merita, uerax historicus Beda promptum fatiet historia'; GP 107. 1: 'nisi Beda uenerabilis historicus dignus pro sermonum sobrietate cui debeat credi, narrationem preuertisset. Nos ab ipso omissa scripturae perstricte inserimus'; GP 3: 'Nothelmus; quem ferunt illum esse quem in prologo Historiae Anglorum dicit idem historicus aecclesiae Lundoniensis presbiterum multo sibi emolumento fuisse ad gesta compaginanda, ex Romano scrinio allatis epistolis quae essent illi necessariae operi'; GP 160. 1: 'De quo quid miraculi sit quod Beda tacuerit, nondum per me potui aduertere uel per alios addiscere: presertim quod cum Kenredo rege Mertiorum et Offa rege Orientalium Anglorum Romam iuerit,

valued his other sources and he bestowed the title of 'auctoritas' on other men, yet Bede was the only 'historicus' to whom William could turn for anything like a full picture of the deeds of the bishops of England.[75] Other models were certainly available to provide a template for episcopal history. Texts such as Eusebius, the *Liber Pontificalis* and Bede's *Historia Abbatum* have all been credited with influencing the structure of the *Gesta Pontificum*.[76] Thomson has shown that William compiled an edition of the *Liber Pontificalis* around 1119, well before he began the *Gesta Pontificum*, and almost certainly an important influence upon it.[77] Yet William stated in the prologue to Book One that he had few sources to rely on and no lantern of history to guide his path, as compared with the *Gesta Regum*.[78] It is therefore particularly interesting that, in stressing the unique features of the *Gesta Pontificum*, William did not claim parity with Bede as 'historicus'. This omission perhaps suggests a change, or development, in William's definition of a historian, and thus that he conceived his role as author of the *Gesta Pontificum* differently from his role as author of the *Gesta Regum*.

Several reasons can be suggested for William's change of heart. Firstly, the work was unique, as he himself stated. In discussing each bishopric consecutively, William had to structure his work entirely differently from Bede's, which was arranged chronologically. Secondly, the *Gesta Pontificum*'s predominantly monastic audience would have understood the importance of the *Historia Ecclesiastica* as part of the monastic life and liturgy, and this may have made William less comfortable about comparing himself to Bede as he had done, implicitly, in the *Gesta Regum*.

The final reason relates to William's changing perception of his historical work. We know that at a later date William criticised his earlier concentration on historical matters and announced his intention henceforth to write works devoted to God.[79] This change in attitude is first made explicit in his *Commentary on Lamentations*, which was probably written between 1130 and 1135.[80] But the change may have

quorum profectionem historicus non siluit'; *GP* 91. 9: 'Nam quod partem Colmanus Scottiam eodem historiographo teste asportauerit notius est quam ut dubitari debeat'; *GP* 126. 3: 'Haec Beda in uita beati Cuthberti latissime exsequitur. Edfridus, cuius iussu et rogatu idem historiographus felicem Cuthbertum tam oratione rethorica quam dulcedine metrica extulit'.

[75] S. Sønnesyn, 'Obedient creativity and idiosyncratic copying: tradition and individuality in the works of William of Malmesbury and John of Salisbury', in *Modes of Authorship in the Middle Ages*, ed. S. Ranković (Toronto, 2012), p. 130.

[76] *GP* II, p. xxxiii.

[77] R. M. Thomson, 'William's edition of the *Liber Pontificalis*', *Archivum Historiae Pontificiae* 17 (1978), 93–112, rev. version in his *William of Malmesbury*, pp. 119–36.

[78] *GP* bk 1 prol. 4: 'Hic autem, pene omni destitutus solatio, crassas ignorantiae tenebras palpo, nec ulla lucerna historiae preuia semitam dirigo'.

[79] *Comm. Lam.*, prol. 7–11 (p. 3): 'Olim enim cum historias lusi, uiridioribus annis rerumque laetitiae congruebat rerum iocunditas. Nunc aetas progressior et fortuna deterior aliud dicendi genus expostulant. Id erit precipuum quod nos dehortari a seculo, quod ad Deum possit accendere.' See also D. H. Farmer, 'William of Malmesbury's Commentary on Lamentations', *Studia Monastica* 4 (1962), 288.

[80] Michael Winterbottom discusses the problems of dating the composition of the *Commentary* and goes into some detail on the passage in which William discusses his desire to turn from the

begun to develop earlier, even in the course of writing the *Gesta Pontificum*. This too could account for the way he perceived and portrayed Bede and the *Historia Ecclesiastica*.

In both the *Gesta Regum* and the *Gesta Pontificum*, William was doing something different from his contemporaries. Goscelin of Saint-Bertin, Symeon of Durham and Henry of Huntingdon perceived the *Historia Ecclesiastica* as authoritative, primarily because of its presentation of English saints. Their view of Bede as an authority was couched in terms of liturgical, spiritual or biographical interest; a view that fits with the manuscript evidence from this period. To all of them Bede was unmistakably venerable and a man of God. Since both terms ('uenerabilis' and 'uir domini') were regularly applied to saints, it is possible that these characterisations were partially due to their personal views of Bede's sanctity. Henry of Huntingdon, indeed, referred unequivocally to Bede as a saint.[81] The depictions of Bede by Goscelin, Symeon and Henry shadow the image Bede left of himself in his historical writing, as a monk and servant of Christ, 'famulus Christi'.[82] William, while certainly picking up on these aspects, uniquely engaged with Bede as a writer of history and drew out Bede's portrayal of himself as the truthful historian. The term 'historicus' undoubtedly had a precise meaning for William. This meaning, however, evolved over time, from its conception in the *Gesta Regum*, where it was based on and directly comparable with what William saw as Bede's own definition, to its use in the *Gesta Pontificum*, where to be 'historicus' was to have the additional authority of the liturgy, something William was hesitant to claim for himself. These two images were not incompatible, however, since they were bound together by the idea that, for William alone among his contemporaries, the Northumbrian monk was consistently 'uerax historicus'.

---

histories he had written in the past. See *Lam.*, pp. 9–12. This is also discussed in the Introduction to *Comm. Lam.*, pp. x–xi.

[81] *Historia Anglorum* ix. 4 (p. 626): 'Beda sanctus'.

[82] Goffart sees Bede deliberately choosing this portrayal of himself as monk and Christian scholar. See Goffart, *The Narrators of Barbarian History*, pp. 240–1.

⇥ 16 ⇤

William of Malmesbury and the Britons

Emily A. Winkler

WILLIAM OF MALMESBURY wrote his *Gesta Regum* 'out of love for his homeland' ('propter patriae caritatem'). But what was William's *patria*? It was not England alone, as James Campbell has suggested – that English polity with clear territorial boundaries, formed of the united Anglo-Saxon kingdoms.[1] Rather, it was a far greater thing: the continuum of British, Roman, English and Norman history on the island of Britain. What he loved was the history of that island's people, including those who lived prior to the advent of the English kingdoms.

It was in many ways a challenging affection to sustain, because Britain's history of contest and conflict had tested the endurance of the island's peoples, their memory and their honour. William admired the Roman past, and he emulated its style and its attitudes towards history.[2] He valued the continued legacy of the Roman past in Britain – the survival not only of Roman buildings, but also of Roman values and practices.[3] He wanted to praise both the ancient Britons and the Romans in the *Gesta Regum*, but in doing so, he had to admit that the Romans decisively defeated the Britons. Or did he?

It was for love of his *patria* that William sought 'to redeem the broken chain of our history' ('uoluntati fuit interruptam temporum seriem sarcire').[4] The

---

[1] Cf. J. Campbell, 'Some twelfth-century views of the Anglo-Saxon past', in his *Essays in Anglo-Saxon History* (London, 1986), pp. 209–28, at pp. 219–20.

[2] The scholarship on William's erudition and interest in the classical past is extensive: see e.g. Thomson, *William of Malmesbury*; idem, 'William of Malmesbury and the Latin Classics revisited', in *Aspects*, pp. 383–93; J. O. Ward, 'Some principles of rhetorical historiography', in *Classical Rhetoric and Medieval Historiography*, ed. E. Breisach (Kalamazoo, 1985), pp. 103–65; N. Wright, '"Industriae Testimonium": William of Malmesbury and Latin poetry revisited', *RB* 103 (1993), 482–531; idem, 'Twelfth-century receptions of a text: Anglo-Norman historians and Hegesippus', *ANS* 31 (2009), 177–95; idem, 'William of Malmesbury and Latin poetry: further evidence for a Benedictine's reading', *RB* 101 (1993), 122–53; Sønnesyn, *Ethics*; E. A. Winkler, 'England's defending kings in twelfth-century historical writing', *Haskins Society Journal* 25 (2013), 147–63.

[3] For example, *GR* 1–2.

[4] *GR* bk 1 prol. 4. On prologues, see A. Gransden, 'Prologues in the historiography of twelfth-century England', in her *Legends, Traditions and History in Medieval England* (London, 1992), pp.

word 'sarcire' is often rendered as 'to mend' or 'to restore', which can imply a routine or reconstructive task, not a creative one. But the word also means 'to redeem',[5] and this was a central purpose of the *Gesta Regum*. William sought to redeem those people in Britain's distant past who, by many accounts – those of Bede, Gildas, the *Anglo-Saxon Chronicle* and even Caesar himself – surrendered without honour to the Romans, the Irish and the Picts, and the Germanic tribes.

William endeavoured to restore honour to the Britons in Britain's remote past by minimising their subjection to these foreign invaders. He appropriated Roman imperial claims to represent the Britons as a people of strength, pride and authority in their own right, not merely as inhabitants of an oppressed frontier province and victims of invasion. In this respect he shared a renewed interest in the British past with his contemporaries Henry of Huntingdon and Geoffrey of Monmouth.

Throughout his *Gesta Regum*, William entertained the possibility of foreign rule, and was never strictly loyal to those rulers or people of Anglo-Saxon ancestry: not only did he read widely, but he also claimed to have both English and Norman heritage, and lived in an Anglo-Norman world. He applied his open-mindedness – about what comprised the story of English history – not only to the English and the Normans, but also to the Britons and the Romans. In this respect, he moved away from the sentiments of earlier accounts.

John Gillingham has claimed that twelfth-century Englishmen 'undoubtedly' felt superior to 'fellow-islanders, the Celts',[6] but regardless of William's feelings for his present-day neighbours, there is no evidence that he felt this way about the ancient Britons. Nor does Gillingham's premise, that imperial expansion necessitates disparagement of a pre-existing culture,[7] apply to William. William's *Gesta Regum* rather suggests the opposite: William's Anglo-Norman experience gave him the generosity to praise Britain's early history; the story of Roman imperial expansion in Britain as he saw it may have motivated him to contradict earlier chroniclers' disparagement of the Britons.

William and his contemporaries honoured the Britons of England's past: they decisively excised the surrender and shame from the early medieval story. The key point is that William actually helped to restore the Celtic past. He represented Britain and its people as less barbaric, more honourable and more worthy than did his sources. He did so in part by downplaying the sense of providential inevitability and dynastic identity that he found in his sources for the beginning and end of the Roman occupation of Britain.

Scholarship on William's view of Britain's early history has tended to suggest that William's *Gesta Regum* primarily tells a story of improvement from barbarism

---

125–51.

[5] *Oxford Latin Dictionary*, ed. P. G. W. Glare (Oxford, 1996), p. 1691.

[6] J. Gillingham, 'The beginnings of English imperialism', in his *The English in the Twelfth Century* (Woodbridge, 2000), pp. 3–18, at p. 7.

[7] Gillingham is quoting M. Hechter, *Internal Colonialism: The Celtic Fringe in British National Development* (London, 1975), p. 64.

to civilisation.[8] Gillingham's argument about William's interest in progress hinges on an interpretation of William's reaction to the Norman Conquest. He has argued that William narrated a civilising process which began before Æthelberht's conversion in around AD 600, observing: 'As he makes explicit in his reflections on the significance of 1066, William looked upon English history as a progress from barbarism to civilisation – a smug assumption in which he was to be followed by many modern historians of England, from David Hume onwards.'[9] Rees Davies has suggested that William and Henry of Huntingdon wrote a tripartite 'evolutionary' story of English history, of which the first chapter describes how the English became a single people ('unam gentem'). The two subsequent chapters, he claims, describe the political formation of a single English kingdom, and – especially for William – the general improvement in civilisation.[10]

The first problem with this argument is that the first chapters of both William and Henry's histories are not about the English people at all: they are about the Romans and the Britons. This point undermines the validity of the idea that William's narrative is focused on either Englishness or cultural evolution. William's narrative about Britain *before* 'the English' is definitely not a story of progress: instead, the island's moral character regresses with the arrival of the Anglo-Saxons, away from his story of relative mutual respect between the Romans and Britons.

The second problem is with the idea that these early twelfth-century histories advocated the 'English myth' – namely that Hengest and Horsa conquered Britain and inaugurated an era of Anglo-Saxon hegemony and ethnic identity in Britain – and reflected the crystallisation of the English 'gens'.[11] This myth, as it appears in the *Anglo-Saxon Chronicle* and Bede, involved a belief in the superiority of the English, and the sense of an emerging national identity arising from territorial control, political unity and dynastic continuity.[12] But William, Henry and Geoffrey of Monmouth did not tell this story: indeed, they were markedly

---

[8] Gillingham, 'The beginnings of English imperialism'; idem, 'Civilizing the English? The English Histories of William of Malmesbury and David Hume', *Historical Research* 74 (2001), 17–43; idem, 'A historian of the twelfth-century renaissance and the transformation of English society, 1066–ca. 1200', in *European Transformations: The Long Twelfth Century*, ed. T. F. X. Noble and J. van Engen (Notre Dame, 2012), pp. 45–74, at p. 47; cf. B. Weiler, 'William of Malmesbury, King Henry I, and the *Gesta Regum Anglorum*', ANS 31 (2008), 157–76.

[9] Gillingham, 'The beginnings of English imperialism', 5.

[10] R. R. Davies, *The Matter of Britain and the Matter of England* (Oxford, 1996), esp. at pp. 14–15. On the idea of 'formation' rather than 'unification', see now G. Molyneaux, *The Formation of the English Kingdom in the Tenth Century* (Oxford, 2015).

[11] R. R. Davies claims that 'the astonishing success of their particular historical mythology... is one of the clearest expressions of the growing English domination of Britain.' 'The peoples of Britain and Ireland, 1100–1400. 4: language and historical mythology', *TRHS*, 6th ser. 7 (1997), 1–24, esp. at pp. 18–20.

[12] Discussed below; see also R. Bartlett, 'Medieval and modern concepts of race and ethnicity', *Journal of Medieval and Early Modern Studies* 31 (2001), 39–56, esp. at pp. 42–4, 53; R. R. Davies, 'The peoples of Britain and Ireland, 1100–1400. I: identities', *TRHS*, 6th ser. 4 (1994), 1–20; H. E. J. Cowdrey, 'Bede and the "English People"', *JRH* 11 (1981), 501–23, esp. at pp. 504–9.

indifferent towards Hengest and Horsa, unlike their sources. The early twelfth-century historians actually put to rest this very English myth nascent in their sources – at least for a while.[13]

I shall treat these two problems in turn, examining William's portrayals first of the Roman invasions, and then of the Angles, Saxons and Jutes. As moments of conquest, these narratives reveal clearly that William did not find the ruptures caused by invasions as momentous as did his sources. Instead, he rewrote these moments of change to improve the honour of the Britons, thereby reducing the sense that Britain's history was pockmarked by crises. He thus brought continuity to the island's history, as well as giving England a worthy past which predated the arrival of the Anglo-Saxons and the formation of English kingdoms. In doing so, he positioned England itself as a natural descendant of – and heir to – the British past.

From surrender to association: the Britons and the Romans

William and his contemporaries rewrote Bede's account of the Britons' surrenders to the Romans as a story with more emphasis on association, alliance and mutual respect. To understand the significance of the changes they made, we need to examine briefly the Latin model Bede employed in writing about the Britons' surrender.

In ancient Rome, there was a historical and panegyric tradition according to which Roman treaties were presented as Roman initiatives and Roman conquests. In the standard model for reporting them in imperial Rome, as Peter Heather has demonstrated, the Romans accepted the surrender (*deditio*) of a foreign people, then restored legal status to them in order to enter into a treaty (*foedus*). Sixth-century writers like Jordanes and Procopius described treaties of equality; but from imperial Rome through to the fourth century, *deditio* and *foedus* generally implied a legal dissolution and complete submission of the conquered realm.[14] Regardless of whether the Empire's interactions with its frontiers actually resulted in such a clear assertion of superiority and power, it was important for Roman writers to convey to their readership the impression of eternal military victory.[15] Suetonius, writing during the early days of the Empire, described Claudius's conquest of Britain as motivated purely by his determination to have 'the honour of a proper triumph' ('iusti triumphi decus'). After his victory, Claudius brought the spoils of war back to Rome and conducted an impressive triumphal procession.[16]

---

[13] But cf. e.g. Davies, who does not distinguish between the early and late twelfth century in this regard: 'The peoples of Britain and Ireland', 4, 19.

[14] P. J. Heather, '*Foedera* and *foederati* of the fourth century', in *From Roman Provinces to Medieval Kingdoms*, ed. T. F. X. Noble (London, 2006), pp. 242–56, repr. from *Kingdoms of the Empire: The Integration of Barbarians in Late Antiquity*, ed. W. Pohl (Leiden, 1997), pp. 57–74.

[15] See, broadly, M. McCormick, *Eternal Victory: Triumphal Rulership in Late Antiquity, Byzantium and the Early Medieval West* (Cambridge, 1990).

[16] Suetonius, *Divus Claudius*, 17.

These narratives give the sense that the frontiers were subjected to Roman rule through military victory, not that Roman leaders were forced into an agreement. In all cases of foreign interaction the Romans appeared to wield superior power.

Bede, in this respect more like ancient imperial writers than his near contemporaries, depicted Britain as a subjected Roman province, making few changes to his sources for the conquest of Britain. Bede described the Britons' surrender to Caesar as a classic Roman *deditio*. The Trinovantes surrendered themselves ('sese dedit') to Caesar. Other cities followed this example of surrender, and then entered into a treaty ('foedus') with the Romans: 'Meanwhile, the strongest city of the Trinovantes with its leader Androgeus surrendered to Caesar and gave him forty hostages. Several other cities followed their example and made a treaty with the Romans.'[17] Bede reinforced the theme of Britain's surrender ('in deditionem recepit') in his account of Claudius's conquest: 'Claudius crossed to the island which no-one either before or after Julius Caesar had dared to invade until then, and without any fighting or bloodshed he received the surrender of the greater part of the island within a very few days.'[18] Whereas Suetonius had only claimed that Claudius conquered part of the island, Bede and Orosius claimed that he conquered most of it ('plurimam'). The Romans, having accepted several such surrenders, clearly had the upper hand.

According to Bede, the Britons fared no better against the Picts and the Scots. Those Britons who remained after the Romans left were impoverished ('pauperculae Bretonum reliquiae').[19] Although some of the Britons trusted in God and resisted the incursions, Bede explained that famine inflicted a worsening trauma on the Britons and a stain on their memory, and that it compelled some of them to surrender ('deditio').[20] Their treaty with the Picts was only temporary,[21] primarily because God brought the invaders as punishment for the Britons' crimes. This time, the remaining Britons were deeply afflicted ('dolentes') and pitiable ('miserandis reliquiis').[22] For Bede, these chapters of British history, for all the Britons' attempts at defence, were characterised by misery and the shame of surrender.[23]

William and his contemporaries, however, conceived of the Britons as a people who could and did enter into diplomatic relations, both with Rome and with

---

[17] Bede, *HE* i. 2: 'Interea Trinouantum firmissima ciuitas cum Androgio duce, datis XL obsidibus, Caesari sese dedit. Quod exemplum secutae, urbes aliae conplures in foedus Romanorum uenerunt'.

[18] Bede, *HE* i. 3: 'transuectus in insulam est, quam neque ante Iulium Caesarem, neque post eum quisquam adire ausus fuerat, ibique sine ullo proelio ac sanguine intra paucissimos dies plurimam insulae partem in deditionem recepit'; this is taken from Orosius, vii. 6. 9; adapted in turn from Suetonius, *Divus Claudius*, 17.

[19] Bede, *HE* i. 13.

[20] Bede, *HE* i. 14.

[21] Bede, *HE* i. 15: 'Tum subito inito ad tempus foedere cum Pictis' ('Then suddenly they made a temporary treaty with the Picts').

[22] Bede, *HE* i. 15.

[23] See also W. T. Foley and N. J. Higham, 'Bede on the Britons', *EME* 17 (2009), 154–85.

other peoples. The relationship between the Britons and the Romans becomes a symbiotic one, surprisingly, as it had previously been rendered as a story of domination. Although Britain was on the imperial frontier, William considered it a distinguished part of the former Empire – and a *patria* in its own right.

William's narrative in the *Gesta Regum* begins with the words 'Romani Britanniam' – subject and object – poetically placed together at the outset. William recounted no story of shameful defeat of the Britons, but rather began with Roman Britain as a coherent entity already created. He completely omitted the sense of *deditio*, or surrender, thereby minimising the rupture in history:

> The Romans, having under Julius Caesar compelled Britain to accept the rule of Rome, held it in high regard, as we can read in the annals and see for ourselves in the remains of ancient buildings. Severus and Constantius, for instance, emperors of the greatest distinction, both died on the island and were buried with the highest honour.[24]

Crucially, William never actually tells the story of conquest: he does not even mention Claudius, Britain's real conqueror, about whom he would certainly have read in the works of Bede, Orosius and Suetonius.[25] Instead, the sentence's main verb is 'colere' – to cherish: the Romans revered Britain ('magna dignatione coluere'). The compulsion – occurring only in a past participle – has already happened, nor is there any sense of shameful victimisation or subservience. Rather, Rome embodies the role of medieval lord: it acted as a lawgiver, and respected its vassals. William's tone expresses pride in Britain, that it should have been the final resting place of two distinguished emperors.

William was not alone at the time in representing the Britons in a more favourable light than did Bede. Henry of Huntingdon's *Historia Anglorum* reveals a keen interest in Britain's remote past – both Roman and British. Indeed, he gave both peoples equality, for he refers to the entire era as 'in the time of the Romans and the Britons' ('tempore Romanorum et Britannorum').[26] In his letter to Warin the Breton, Henry referred to the flourishing kingdoms ('florentissima regna') of the Britons before the time of Caesar, explaining that he had searched repeatedly for information about them and was astounded ('stupens') to find an account at the abbey of Bec.[27] Britain, he thought, was the best of all islands; its native Britons were more splendid in dress and manner than those abroad 'whence they may

---

[24] GR 1. 1: 'Romani Britanniam, per Iulium Cesarem in Latias leges iurare compulsam, magna dignatione coluere, ut et in annalibus legere et in ueterum edifitiorum uestigiis est uidere. Denique Seuerus et Constantius, imperatores amplissimi, ambo apud insulam diem functi et supremo sunt honore funerati'.

[25] On William's classical reading, see e.g. Thomson, 'William of Malmesbury and the Latin Classics revisited', idem, 'William of Malmesbury as historian and man of letters', in his *William of Malmesbury*, pp. 14–39.

[26] Henry of Huntingdon, *Historia Anglorum*, i. 3.

[27] Ibid., *Epistola ad Warinum*, c. 1, pp. 558–9.

be distinguished from all other peoples'.[28] This was not a man who scorned, but rather one who marvelled.

Henry made moral judgments about the Britons' *internal* conflicts: civil conflict earned harsh criticism from him. But Henry wrote that Britain was attacked so frequently not just because of divine punishment, but because other peoples were jealous of the Britons.[29] He made the Britons look significantly less abject and servile in their conflicts with other invading peoples than did Bede. Henry responded to Bede's story of the famine by writing: 'This famine also affected Britain and other provinces. Then the Britons, therefore, seeing that they could get no human aid, called for divine assistance. Almighty God had compassion on them and tested them. He sent strength to their arms and an edge to their swords.'[30] God did not take pity on a wretched people: rather, by testing them, God gave them the opportunity and the autonomy to prove their own worth.

For Henry, the Britons persisted, and in a far less shameful condition than described in the *Historia Ecclesiastica*. He eliminated from Bede the adjective 'impoverished' ('pauperculae') to describe those Britons who remained,[31] and omitted reference to the temporary nature of the Britons' treaty with the Picts.[32] Without the suggestions of wretchedness and inability to maintain a treaty, Henry accorded the Britons a greater degree of honour and influence over their own fate.

Although William and his contemporaries narrated Britain's history of repeated conquest, they also sought to tell Britain's version of the Roman discourse of eternal victory: the continued worthiness of Britain's varied inhabitants throughout the island's history. They cared about what the Britons and Romans gave to the *patria*, not just what these peoples gave way to – the era of the English. For William and his fellow historians, this ancient period of history was not pre-English: it was post-Roman.

From oblivion to legacy: the Britons and the Anglo-Saxons

The fifth-century Anglo-Saxon invaders were not dynastically important to William as the founders of English identity, nor inherently superior for being the ancestors of the English. William and his contemporaries placed more value on the impressive Romano-British history which came before. The continuity in Britain's history, and the worth of its peoples, were a source of pride: these mattered more than conquest, dynastic change, or the concept of progress. This is a significant

---

[28] Ibid. i. 6; i. 11: 'ex hoc unde sint dinosci possint'.
[29] Ibid., i. 10; cf. i. 4; i. 47.
[30] Ibid., i. 4: 'Tunc igitur Britanni uidentes *humanum* deesse, *auxilium* inuocant *diuinum*. Misertusque est eis Dominus omnipotens et temptauit eos. Inmisitque eorum robur brachiis et aciem gladiis.' Cf. e.g. 2 Kings (2 Sam.) 24: 15–16; Gen 22: 1.
[31] Henry of Huntingdon, *Historia Anglorum* i. 46: 'reliquie Britonum'; cf. Bede, *HE* i. 13; *HE* i. 15, discussed above.
[32] Henry of Huntingdon, *Historia Anglorum* ii. 2: 'federe cum Pictis'; but cf. Bede, *HE* i. 15, discussed above.

departure from Bede's and the *Anglo-Saxon Chronicle*'s pride in the Anglo-Saxon invasions, and their identification with the Anglo-Saxon myth.

Bede felt no particular loyalty to the Britons: his story of the 440s was one of progress, which favoured the unified English. He saw the English as a single people ('gens') – whether of the Angles or the Saxons ('Anglorum siue Saxonum') – from the moment of their arrival in Britain at the invitation of Vortigern, king of the Britons.[33] Although the Angles, Saxons and Jutes were different tribes, Bede was already anticipating the story of Christian conversion and the Latin language unifying all peoples of the island under Anglo-Saxon hegemony.

Although they were based on Bede, the *Anglo-Saxon Chronicle*'s entries for the conquest heightened the sense of both the Britons' inferiority and the Anglo-Saxons' discrete identity. In the *Chronicle*, the Britons had no redeeming qualities, nothing in common with the invaders, and no part in dominion over the land. The chronicler put this in no uncertain terms. He claimed that, in seeking to win allies among the Jutes and Saxons, the Angles ordered their messengers to speak of 'the worthlessness of the Britons and of the excellence of the land.'[34] Indeed, the E version of the *Chronicle* saw the Anglo-Saxon conquest as the defining moment in English identity – the year in which 'we', the English people, began. He concluded the 449 annal by detailing Hengest and Horsa's direct patrilineal descent from Woden, concluding: 'From that Woden originated all our royal family, and [that] of the Southumbrians also.'[35] The passage is very nearly a direct translation of Bede,[36] but the key new word is 'our'. The chronicler located the origins of Anglo-Saxon identity – with which he clearly identified – in the invasion of Hengest and Horsa. King Vortigern's son and heir, Vortimer, is not mentioned. In the face of 'our' new dominion, the chronicler did not acknowledge his existence, let alone the possibility of his accession.

William, however, did not follow *Anglo-Saxon Chronicle* in implying that the Britons deserved to be conquered. They were not inherently inferior to the English, nor inevitably their victims, but a meritorious people with a strong leader and the potential for great deeds, despite their eventual defeat. This is evident in two respects: first, he did not disparage the Britons as harshly as Bede, nor did he ignore them as much as the *Chronicle*. Second, he viewed the arrival of the Anglo-Saxons in 449 as an event of no particular moment, not as the birth of the *patria*.

William's description of the Britons' initial diplomatic arrangements with the Anglo-Saxon tribes presented them as a classic *foedus* – except that this time, the Britons are in the role formerly occupied by the Roman Empire: the king offers

---

[33] Ibid., i. 15.

[34] *ASC* (E) anno 449: 'Brytwalana nahtscipe 7 þes landes cysta'.

[35] *ASC* (E) anno 449: 'fram þan Wodne awoc eall ure cynecynn 7 Suðanhymbra eac'.

[36] Cf. Bede, *HE* i. 15: 'Erant autem filii Uictgilsi, cuius pater Uitta, cuius pater Uecta, cuius pater Uoden, de cuius stirpe multarum prouinciarum regium genus originem duxit' ('[Hengest and Horsa] were the sons of Wihtgisl, son of Witta, son of Wecta, son of Woden, from whose stock the royal families of many kingdoms claimed their descent').

favours; oaths of loyalty are exchanged; the Britons offer both residences and security for the foreign armies in return for the Angles' military support for the defence of the *patria* of the Britons.[37] Hengest is the barbarian:[38] the Britons appear to act in a diplomatic manner with echoes of Roman practice, and they are in a position to negotiate. William gave the *patria* more coherence than the disarray and disaster his sources described.

This amounts to a significant divergence from his sources, which maintained that the Anglo-Saxon Conquest was primarily a divine punishment for the sins of the British people and their king, Vortigern. Even in the *Historia Brittonum*, the sins of Vortigern were the root cause of the Anglo-Saxon invasions: in the Life of Saint Germanus, Vortigern was cursed and condemned by Germanus and the council of the Britons ('Brittonum concilio') for fathering a child with his daughter and for deceit.[39] Gildas and Bede suggest that Vortigern summoned aid from the Angles and Saxons, but foolishly permitted himself to be duped. Because of Vortigern's failings, the Anglo-Saxons took the island of Britain from the Britons.[40]

William, however, did not share this perspective. He criticised Vortigern's rulership not because he was a Briton, but because he was a bad king. He measured Vortigern against the same criteria he uses to evaluate the legitimacy of English kings, accusing him of vice in language that strongly foreshadows his critiques of eleventh-century defeated defenders, Æthelred and Harold:[41] 'The king of Britain at the time was Vortigern, unready and unwise, devoted to carnal pleasures and the servant of almost every vice, enslaved by avarice, dominated by pride and distracted by lechery'.[42] But the critique was not absolute. Vortigern was 'excitatus' – roused to action – at last; he was at least attempting to defend his kingdom. William explained that Vortigern made the decision to summon continental mercenaries on the advice of his magnates. The council decided unanimously, and had good reasons for doing so: the Germanic tribes were armed and nomadic.[43] More so than his sources, William conveyed a sense of accord and consideration on the part of the Britons in organising what they hoped would prove a successful defence.

Although the king's son Vortimer was not even present in the *Chronicle*, he was in the *Historia Brittonum*, a text that provided William with evidence for the Britons' power and autonomy. For William, who believed more in the Britons'

---

[37] GR 6.
[38] GR 7. 3.
[39] *Historia Brittonum*, ed. F. Lot (2 vols, Paris, 1934), c. 39 (II, p. 178).
[40] Bede, *HE* i. 14; Gildas c. 23 (p. 97).
[41] GR 165. 7–10, 228. 11.
[42] GR 4. 1: 'Erat eo tempore rex Britanniae Wrtigernus nomine, nec manu promptus nec consilio bonus, immo ad illecebras carnis pronus omniumque fere uitiorum mancipium, quippe quem subiugaret auaritia, inequitaret superbia, inquietaret luxuria'. William's rhythmic wordplay enhances the effect of his censure: 'inequitaret' and 'inquietaret' are anagrams; each is followed by a rhyming four-syllable word, 'superbia' and 'luxuria'. On similar language in *GR* about Æthelred and Harold, cf. Winkler, 'England's defending kings'.
[43] GR 4. 2.

merit than their misery, Vortimer was a prime example of a patriotic, heroic and worthy leader. Vortimer took the initiative in pursuing and engaging the Germanic tribes overseas in an attempt to extend Britain's frontiers. The author of the *Historia* saw the very real possibility of a future in which Vortimer would become a worthy king of the Britons in 449, a hope dashed because his men failed to honour their lord as they should have. Vortimer asked his followers to bury him on the coast, in the port from which the invaders left the island:

> 'I entrust it to you. Wherever else they may hold a British port or may have settled, they will never again live in this land.' But they ignored his command and did not bury him where he had told them ... if they had kept his command, there is no doubt that they would have obtained whatever they wished through the prayers of St Germanus.[44]

Vortimer's patriotic speech exhorted his followers to be Britain's gatekeepers – not by defending a port, but by honouring their lord. Their Britain was worth defending and they were capable of doing so, a theme which appears to have made an impression on William.

William considered Vortimer worthy of being a king and a defender because of his audacity and spirited defence, even though he was a Briton:

> Vortimer, son of Vortigern, seeing himself and his fellow Britons outreached by the crafty English, decided that this could no longer be overlooked, and set himself to drive them out, kindling his father at the same time to the same venture ... Vortimer, the moving spirit of the war, who was far from his father's easy-going temper, *and would have made a good ruler had God permitted*. With his decease the Britons' strength withered away, and their hopes dwindled and ebbed [*emphasis added*].[45]

Although, according to William, Vortimer's rulership was not part of the divine plan, Vortimer was not implicated in any sins of the Britons, nor had his father's corruption condemned him. William rather expresses Christian hopefulness that Vortimer could have redeemed his father and his people, long before the Augustinian mission of 597 which Bede esteemed so highly.[46]

[44] *British History and the Welsh Annals*, ed. J. Morris (London, 1980) c. 44, p. 72: '"in quo vobis commendo: quamvis in alia parte portum Brittaniae teneant et habitaverint, tamen in ista terra in aeternum non manebunt." Illi autem mandatum eius contempserunt et eum in loco in quo imperaverat illis non sepelierunt ... si mandatum eius tenuissent, procul dubio per orationes sancti Germani quicquid pecierant obtinuissent.' Cf. the Second Branch of the Mabinogi, wherein Bendigeidfran orders his men to bury his head in London facing France, thereby protecting against invasion from overseas while it was interred: *Mabinogion*, ed. S. Davies (Oxford, 2007), pp. 32–4.

[45] *GR* 8. 1–2: 'Guortemer filius Wrtigerni, haudquaquam ultra dissimulandum ratus quod se Britonesque suos Anglorum dolo preuerti cerneret, ad expulsionem eorum mentem intendit, simulque patrem ad idem audendum incendit ... incentore belli Guortemer fatali sorte sullato, *qui*, multum a facilitate patris abhorrens, *egregie regnum moderaretur si Deus siuisset*. Sed eo extincto Britonum robur emarcuit, spes imminutae retro fluxere'.

[46] Bede, *HE* i. 23–33.

William of Malmesbury and the Britons

In William's view, the cause of the success of the Anglo-Saxon Conquest was an arbitrary event: Vortimer's death. God's hand did not guide Hengest and Horsa's ultimate victory; indeed, the only intervention William acknowledged was that of Fortune. William specifies that, in the first of four battles over twenty years, the Britons and the invaders were equals in fortune ('aequa … fortuna'), even though the invaders had the upper hand ('superiorem … manum') in the next three. William's reaction to the defeat of the Britons expresses neither providential vengeance, nor Roman imperial language of conquest and *deditio*. His tone is rather one of regret and resignation at the tragedy of a broken agreement. William described the agreement between the Britons and the Anglo-Saxons as 'fedus fedatum' – 'corrupted concord', a wordplay which echoes the language of Roman treaties; even so, the end result, after Vortimer's death, was peace.[47] For William, the key events which had shaped the history of the *patria* were not only conquests and surrenders, but also treaties arranged with foresight by distinguished leaders.

Throughout the *Gesta Regum*, William sustained his interest in resolutions of conflict. He described the agreement between Edmund and Cnut to divide the kingdom in 1016 – another case of potential divisiveness between natives and foreigners – as a successful 'fedus': 'Edmund, overwhelmed by the unanimous and universal shouts of approval, gave in to peace, and made a treaty with Cnut which assigned himself Wessex, and the other Mercia'.[48] And, after the Norman Conquest, he reduced the validity of Edgar the Ætheling's claim to the throne, resolving the question of legitimate kingship in William the Conqueror's favour.[49] Advocating the superiority of one people over another was less important to William than was relating their eventual achievement of peace.

William gives no impression that the *patria* of which he was so proud was either formed by, or even had its roots in, the Anglo-Saxon Conquest of Britain, nor did he think that the invading tribes had unequivocal providential support. He was more interested in the kind of leadership in England's past, like that of Vortimer, than in the origins of the person who took on such a role.

A people restored: the Britons and the early twelfth century

Interestingly, the only contemporary writer who articulated the 'Anglo-Saxon myth' – making the direct claim that Hengest and Horsa conquered the Britons and began the period of Anglo-Saxon hegemony – was Orderic Vitalis, writing from the Norman abbey of Saint-Evroul: 'It is now about six hundred years since the Anglo-Saxons, under Hengest and Horsa, by their courage and guile won dominion over the Britons who are now called Welsh.'[50] Geoffrey of Monmouth

---

[47] GR 8. 1–2.
[48] GR 180. 9: 'Ita Edmundus unanimi clamore omnium superatus concordiae indulsit, fedusque cum Cnutone percussit, sibi Westsaxonum, illi concedens Mertiam'.
[49] See esp. GR 164–5, 251. 3; E. A. Winkler, '1074 in the twelfth century', *ANS* 36 (2014), 241–58.
[50] Orderic II, pp. 276–7: 'Angli Saxones ducibus Hengist et Horsa Britonibus qui nunc Guali

did not actually accord the Anglo-Saxons dominion over Britain until 200 years later, extending British dominion all the way up to the valiant leadership of Cadwaladr – an interpretation that Henry of Huntingdon accepted enthusiastically.[51]

In these respects, there is evidence that the purported divide between twelfth-century history and pseudo-history in England needs to be revisited: Geoffrey of Monmouth, Henry of Huntingdon and William of Malmesbury, although very different historians, adopted a tone towards the Britons which is in some ways strikingly similar, in that they enhanced the Britons' honour as compared to their shared sources.[52] They all minimised the import of divine punishment for the Britons, either having recourse to a wider range of explanations for defeat, or obscuring the sense of defeat altogether. Orderic Vitalis, on the other hand, was more dismissive;[53] writing from Normandy, he had no incentive to include the Britons in a worthy continuum of Britain's history.

In the days of the Roman Empire, the Romans would accept a surrender (*deditio*) and make pacts (*foedera*) with the peoples they conquered. But William and his contemporaries did not want to tell this story about ancient Britain. Instead, their ancient Britons were a people able to make the terms themselves, whether or not God or Fortune always permitted them to be successful. Although their *patria* had not been eternally victorious, early twelfth-century writers in England nevertheless created a continuum that brought greater distinction to their history.

The early twelfth-century Anglo-Norman historians valued loyalty as well as the making and the honouring of agreements across peoples and boundaries in Britain's history. This provides an important counterpoint to interpreting their works as conquest histories. These writers were in fact open-minded towards the many peoples of Britain – not only in the past, but also in the present day. They resented the Welsh and Scottish rebellions of the twelfth century, but this was as much because of their loyalty to Henry I as anything else: they resented English, Norman and mercenary rebellions just as fiercely.[54] John of Worcester thought that the merits of King Malcolm of Scotland outweighed those of William Rufus – not in spite of Malcolm's being Scottish, but because Malcolm valued tradition and good judgment.[55] William was on some occasions scornful of

uocantur, imperium dolis et fortitudine iam fere dc annis abstulerunt'.

[51] Geoffrey of Monmouth, esp. at pp. 278–81; R. W. Leckie, Jr, *The Passage of Dominion: Geoffrey of Monmouth and the Periodization of Insular History in the Twelfth Century* (Toronto, 1981), *passim*; Henry of Huntingdon, *Epistola ad Warinum* (*Historia Anglorum*, pp. 558–83). See also L. B. Mortensen, 'Roman past and Roman language in twelfth-century English historiography', in *Conceptualizing Multilingualism in England, c. 800–c. 1250*, ed. E. M. Tyler (Turnhout, 2011), pp. 309–20, esp. at 312–16.

[52] See e.g. the competitive battle orations between Roman and British leaders: Geoffrey of Monmouth, pp. 68–9.

[53] Orderic II, pp. 276–7; VI, pp. 380–9; E. van Houts, 'Normandy's view of the Anglo-Saxon past in the twelfth century', in *The Long Twelfth-Century View*, pp. 123–40, at 127–31.

[54] See e.g. GR 311, 396; Henry of Huntingdon, *Historia Anglorum* vii. 1 (pp. 412–15); cf. Weiler, 'William of Malmesbury'.

[55] John of Worcester, *Chronicle*, anno 1093 (III, pp. 64–5).

William of Malmesbury and the Britons

British peoples – as he was about Normans, Vikings, the English, Jews, Christians, kings, peasants and many others – but, like the author of the *Historia Brittonum*, he thought that Vortimer, a Briton, would have made a good king.

The sense of English superiority over the so-called 'Celtic' peoples may well have solidified in the mid- and late twelfth century.[56] But in the second quarter of the twelfth century, the history of the *patria* was – if as patriotic as ever – still open to different peoples. This was a key moment in English history, when those writing about the past were personally acquainted with older people who had been involved on both sides of the Norman Conquest, and had learned from both the humility of the victims and the pride of the conquerors in imagining a broad-minded story of the past. It was a time before the new generation imagined that England had always been a kingdom with dependent British and continental lands, an imagined past which inspired the confidence of the Angevins' imperial pretensions.

This early twelfth-century redemption of the Britons suggests that William's narrative of Britain's history in the *Gesta Regum* did not depend on an idea of progress from barbarism to civilisation on the island, as has previously been argued. William thought that the island of Britain was a worthy and, in many respects, a civilised place long before the arrival of the Anglo-Saxons or the Normans. The merit of Britain, he believed, developed in a Roman Britain wherein both Romans and Britons possessed distinguished virtues.

We already know that William's idea of post-Conquest English identity adopted both Anglo-Saxon and Norman values, and for many reasons: his own mixed heritage, the mixed heritage of his patroness, his experience of living in an Anglo-Norman world, his wide reading in Romano-British, Anglo-Saxon and Norman sources, his personal curiosity and his sensitivity to new ideas. What needs to be added is his receptiveness to an expanded idea of identity, not only of the English and Normans in the recent past, but also of the Britons and the Romans in the remote past. His story of the insular past and its people is not primarily one of progress, but of worthiness – and it began in the time of the Britons.

William's *Gesta Regum* did not surrender Britain's distant past either to Roman imperial propaganda or to an Anglo-Saxon myth. He upheld the diplomatic dignity and potential of the people who lived in ancient Britain. In doing so, he honoured his desire to redeem the history of the *patria* he loved so well.

---

[56] For example, Giraldus Cambrensis, *Expugnatio Hibernica: The Conquest of Ireland*, ed. A. B. Scott and F. X. Martin (Dublin, 1978), pp. 232–3; William of Newburgh, *Historia Rerum Anglicarum*, in *Chronicles of the Reigns of Stephen, Henry II and Richard I*, ed. R. Howlett (4 vols, RS 1884–9), I, p. 107; J. Gillingham, 'French culture, twelfth-century English historians and the civilizing process', in *Cinquante années d'études médiévales*, ed. C. Arrignon (Turnhout, 2005), pp. 729–40, at 729–30, but cf. p. 740; R. R. Davies, *Domination and Conquest: The Experience of Ireland, Scotland and Wales, 1100–1300* (Cambridge, 1990), pp. 14–15.

17

Words, Words, Words...

Michael Winterbottom

I SHALL BE DISCUSSING William as a writer of Latin, and as a virtuoso in that language. When he expounds his aims at the start of the *Gesta Regum* (bk 1 prol. 4) he talks of his wish to 'give a Roman polish to the rough annals of our native speech'; and in that same prologue he comments on the styles of Bede, Æthelweard and Eadmer. Every page he himself wrote shows his wish to give his own turn to the material he had so laboriously amassed. It is partly a matter of style. I have written a little on this,[1] but there is much more to be done, not least because William's manner varies from book to book and even from passage to passage. But it is also, it seems to me, a matter of language, and especially of vocabulary. That too I have touched on in the past.[2] More recently, I have embarked on a systematic investigation of William's words, of which these are the first fruits.

Work of this kind on a medieval text would hardly have been possible until quite recently. In a classical Latin author it is commonplace; there have for many years been concordances of the major authors, not to speak of the *Thesaurus Linguae Latinae*, scheduled for completion, after my time, in 2075. William's vocabulary could be worked on properly only after Martin Brett made it his job, more than twenty years ago, to commission a private concordance of William's historical and hagiographical works. The now yellowing and battered print-out has been of inestimable service. It unfortunately came before the full digital age, and the concordance cannot be searched. But as time has gone on I have accumulated searchable texts of most of the major works, with the important exception of *Gesta Regum*, for which I still rely wholly on Brett's concordance.

One further preliminary: to have any validity the work I have been doing requires proper comparative material. But the sort of authors with whom one would want to make a comparison, especially in the twelfth century, themselves

---

For better or worse, I have preserved a good deal of the informality of the original paper, in the hope of making an abstruse topic as attractive as possible. For the same reason, Latin quotations from William, together with much comparative material, are gathered in an appendix.

[1] 'The *Gesta Regum* of William of Malmesbury', *JML* 5 (1995), 158–73.
[2] 'The language of William of Malmesbury', in *Rhetoric and Renewal*, pp. 129–47.

lack concordances. Nothing can be more wonderful than the Brepols Cross Database, and I have made constant use of it. But it does not yet cover the English writers whose practice would be of such interest. The result is a great digital gap. Private reading can only take one a little way in this vast field. Marjorie Chibnall's Index of Words provides some invaluable aid for Orderic.[3] The *Oxford Dictionary of Medieval Latin from British Sources*, now happily complete, only started to treat William properly late in its course. But for my purposes the evidence needs to be surveyed as a whole, and we cannot as yet do that. So what follows is pioneering work, and work in progress.

I start from a word which on investigation proves to shed light on William's procedures in general. He did not know an adjective to correspond to the noun 'scorpio' ('scorpion'). So he seems to have made one up for himself, 'scorpiaceus': not, I think, because he knew the obscure Greek σκορπιακός,[4] but on the analogy of Latin words like the quite common 'gallinaceus' ('of chickens'). He makes use of the word in three passages, always qualifying 'cauda' ('tail') (**1**).[5] In each case Fortune catches up with a victim late in his career, after a long period of favour: King Oswine, Roger bishop of Salisbury and Sæwig of Ratcliffe. William employs varied but related vocabulary for these very different occasions; he is in a highly characteristic way playing variations on a theme. But the point is always the same: the sting was in the scorpion tail (I suppose this is the origin of the English phrase). But it is no less characteristic that William takes his theme from another writer. This was the late antique Sidonius Apollinaris, bishop of Clermont (consecrated 470), mentioned as such in William's *Miracles of the Virgin* (**6. 2**). Sidonius was a difficult and affected writer, and if only for that reason attracted William, who quite often draws upon him. In this new instance of his use of Sidonius's letters, the end of the emperor Petronius Maximus is described: 'after fortune had long flattered him, her treacherous last act bathed him in blood, for like a scorpion she struck the man down with her tail-end.' I italicise four words in the Latin that recur in William's adaptations. He did not draw attention to his borrowings; it is up to us to recognise his erudition.

There is something to add. William occasionally decorates his prose with snatches of verse, some apparently of his own composition. In the *Gesta Pontificum* he turns the scorpion tail motif into verse: 'The sun had lit up Scorpio with its twelfth dawn / When he felled the king with his tail.' This is an obituary notice for King Æthelstan, who lay buried at Malmesbury. As Thomson explains in his

---

[3] Orderic Vitalis, I, pp. 246–386.

[4] I do not know what Isidore means (*Etymologiae* 12. 5. 4) when he tells us that a scorpion is an 'animal armatum aculeo, et ex eo Graece uocatum quod cauda figat et arcuato uulnere [cf. 5. 27. 18] uenena diffundat' ('an animal armed with a sting, and so called in Greek from the fact that it strikes with its tail and spreads poison through a curve-shaped wound'). The fine English word *scorpiac* (attested 1670) is connected by the *Oxford English Dictionary* with the Greek word, but it might be a reminiscence of William.

[5] Bold figures refer to sections in the Appendix to this paper, under which the Latin references are gathered.

commentary, the sun (in William's view) entered Scorpio on October 15; the king died twelve days later, on the 27th. Here William extends his conceit to the Scorpio of the zodiac. But again the point is that death cut short a glorious career, marked not least by the king's generosity to Malmesbury. We are given different ways of interpreting this event. 'His great deeds were broken short by a day hastened by the fates' (this from Lucan); he did not deserve so early a death, but God thought otherwise. God, the fates, the scorpion tail of Fortune: take your pick.[6]

I add another case of William playing variations on a theme. Again the theme has not been recognised, but again it comes from a book we know William had read with care. This is the Latin translation of Josephus, which goes under the name of Hegesippus. In a striking passage from Book 3, Josephus himself appears before Vespasian's son Titus, in danger of being condemned to death. This situation is milked for its pathos. In particular Titus (2) is moved by the fate of one who had been a warrior, but is now in the power of enemies, waiting for their decision, 'shipwrecked on the sea of life, exiled from the world of hope, uncertain of his safety'. William played various games with this sentence. He does not exploit the phrase 'incertum salutis', but the words 'exul', 'spes', and 'naufragus' are deployed on five occasions. Particularly close is the first passage cited, where the words form the climax of a sympathetic speech by Earl Godwine to the future Edward the Confessor, who is in distress and asking for help in returning to Normandy. The other passages are not so close, but undoubtedly derive originally from Hegesippus. They concern a variety of sufferers in need of help: a Christian requiring a loan from a Jew, relatives at their wits' end out of concern for a mad woman from Evesham, and, in two passages of the *Commentary on Lamentations*, the distressed soul of man.

My discussion of the two words investigated so far has happened to throw up new evidence for William's knowledge of texts we already knew he was familiar with. We now come to two words where new sources show themselves.

'uncus' means 'hook'. The very rare adjective 'obuncus' means 'hooked'; Virgil uses it for the beak of a vulture.[7] The verb based on this, 'obuncare', you will not find in Lewis and Short. William, however, knew it, and employed it three times (3). We have first a highly characteristic sentence, describing the mockery that Bishop Wulfstan had to put up with. The verbs are vivid and concrete (something to which I shall return). 'uellicabant': they nipped him (this is a favourite word of our author) with taunts, secretly; 'obuncabant': they drove hooks into him with words, openly. The verbs, nouns and adverbs balance and rhyme. The two other passages, from the *Gesta Regum*, are closely related to each other. In the first, Hildebrand, later Pope Gregory VII, while an archdeacon, shouts abuse ('obuncans') at the abbot of Cluny from a distance; his words are given, and they start with 'Tu'

---

[6] Orderic (iv. 186 and 188, vi. 66) thought of scorpion tails in connection with the pulley-shoes fashionable at the time. Talking of these, William (*GR* 314. 4) speaks of 'calceorum cum *arcuatis aculeis*' (see n. 4 above).

[7] *Aeneid* 6. 597.

repeated. In case we feel inclined to think this a realistic vignette of everyday life in medieval France, we should look at the third passage. Here William Rufus is in a rage with a prisoner, Helias count of Maine. He too speaks 'obuncans'. He too doubles the word 'Tu'. The confrontation also appears in Orderic, and Chibnall speculated about a common oral source. But that source cannot have supplied the introduction given in William to the king's rant. It is not merely that it is so closely paralleled in the story about Hildebrand. Both of these passages, in fact, derive from a fifth-century source, Rufinus's Latin continuation of Eusebius. Here we find a woman 'obuncans Timotheum', and starting her speech with a repeated 'Tu'. It is perhaps worth remarking that the story was also known to Aldhelm, who, unobserved by the wonderful Ehwald, alludes to it in his prose and verse *De Virginitate*, each time using the word 'obuncare'. But there is no doubt that William drew directly on Rufinus. I add too that Rufinus's remark on the 'procacitas', the pertness, of 'such women' would have struck a note in William, who appreciated the beauty of women, but thought their tempers sometimes left something to be desired. I cite (in the Appendix) a typical instance from his Miracle book.

I dwell for a moment longer on William Rufus's taunting speech to Helias. It shows every sign of being William's own invention, expanding certainly on Orderic and on any common source they may have had. The three imperatives 'discede', 'abi', 'fuge', all appear in a single verse by Paulinus of Nola; we did not previously know that William was acquainted with this author (though we knew he had read Rufinus). William three times elsewhere uses the oath by the face of Lucca as a marker of King William II ('sic enim iurabat'); on one of these occasions, during a siege of Mont Saint Michel, the word 'nebulo' (a favourite of our William's) is again put in Rufus's mouth. And the rest of the short speech to Helias is closely modelled on a passage of Lucan (whose name William actually – and unusually – mentions). That is the way that this historian works.

Finally on the topic of William's borrowings, something less spectacular but again introducing a newcomer.[8] In the *Gesta Pontificum* William tells us of the penance undergone by a citizen of Cologne who had killed his brother (4). For seven years he had to go round saints' churches, encased in tightly fitting iron shackles. Indeed, says William, he added further agonising details, 'doing violence to his own body as though it were an enemy', literally: 'bringing force to bear on his own body with a certain hostility'. 'hostilitas' is not a very common word, and it was in investigating William's use of it that I found that this striking phrase about the penitent of Cologne comes with only superficial changes from the popular Life of St Germanus, where Constantius describes the mortifications of the flesh imposed upon himself by the saint after becoming a priest.[9]

---

[8] See also below, pp. 210–12 (on *absoluere*).

[9] It is tempting to think that William noticed in this passage the use of 'induere', on which René Borius commented: 'Germain ... "revêt le supplice", si l'on ose dire, come on "revêt" l'habit monastique.' The penitent from Cologne too had to 'clothe' his body with his penitential gear (*GP* 268. 3 'uestiret').

It is difficult to know in such cases how intertextual William was trying to be.[10] Did he expect us to know that he was drawing a phrase from Constantius? If so, did he wish us to compare, and if we will contrast, a murderer undergoing penance with a blameless saint? Is William showing off, or is he not? Just after reporting Rufus's speech to Helias, William (as we have seen) mentions Lucan, as though in comment on the borrowing he has just made from the poet. But this is not William's normal practice. Usually, as in the case of the loan from Constantius, we are given no hint.

This leads me on to some thoughts about the enormous number of borrowings that William makes from an astonishingly wide range of reading. Of course that reading is of interest in itself, as a sign of what books were available to him in the first half of the twelfth century in England. But I suggest that we need to do more with the borrowings than that. We need to take note of what William does with his borrowed material, how he adapts it, whether it helps him make some point. But we might also ask how he came to find just these passages of interest in the first place. Looking over the instances I have been discussing, we may conjecture that he was attracted by an unusual word, like 'obuncare' or 'hostilitas'; by a striking phrase ('uitae naufragum', 'exulem spei'); by a striking image (the scorpion tail); or by a memorable context, like Josephus's plight before Titus. These could of course combine. How (to give a new example) did he come to use the word 'titubantia' of impediment in speech (5)? Though 'titubare' of speech is common enough from Ovid onwards, the noun 'titubantia' is very rare. William knew it from two passages of Suetonius. I suggest that his interest in the word was increased by the memorable contexts in which they occurred: the description of Vitellius's only son as 'almost mute and tongueless because of his faltering speech'. William borrows the phrase 'titubantia oris' in his description of Hubald archdeacon of Salisbury, who 'had made much progress in the liberal arts, but because of a stammer could not convey them clearly to those who heard him'. And 'titubantia' is also used by Suetonius in the unsparing and unforgettable picture of the stammering, dribbling, giggling Claudius.

What intervened between William reading a text and using a phrase from it for himself? I should like to think that he copied into a series of commonplace books phrases and words that caught his attention, classified under heads and with attached references in case he needed to look them up again.[11] Such books would not resemble the surviving *Polyhistor*, a collection of miscellaneous material with an allegedly moral theme, presented to his friend Guthlac; none of this (I think I am right in saying) was drawn upon by William for use in his extant

---

[10] This is of course a problem that recurs constantly. I give a piquant example. The Hostess's description of the death of Falstaff in *Henry V* appears to draw on Plato's description of the death of Socrates in the *Phaedo*. What should be made of that is sensitively discussed by Emrys Jones, *The Origins of Shakespeare* (Oxford, 1977), pp. 20–1.

[11] Compare Emrys Jones's account (*The Origins of Shakespeare*, pp. 9–13) of educational practice in the time of Shakespeare.

works. That is also true, so far as I have examined it, of the so-called *Defloratio* of excerpts from Gregory the Great. But we might compare the Selden manuscript containing historical excerpts, some of which William did make use of himself.[12] In the absence of such a conjectured commonplace book, it is hard to see how William, however astonishing his memory, could have drawn so lavishly on previous material in writing all his major works. It is not just that he brought together the factual detail masterfully; he wove into it an extraordinary array of borrowed and adapted ornament.

    I have mentioned the way in which William strives for the concrete. I come now to a good solid word for a good solid thing: 'umbo', the boss of a shield. This is of course a perfectly ordinary word from early Latin onwards. It was (typically) Virgil who seems to have pioneered the synecdoche by which it can stand for the shield itself.[13] The shield was adaptable too; it could be used offensively or quasi-offensively as well as defensively: William's usage reflects this duality. More to our point, he boldly extends the range of the word (**6**), in ways that go beyond Virgil, and Statius too, for whom it was also a favourite. He can use it of a person: thus, after the death of Lanfranc, people (according to William) hoped one day to see an archbishop who should be 'spokesman for all, a standard bearer in their van, a shield to protect the public weal ["umbo publicus"]'. And individuals can deploy the 'umbo' not just of their protection, but of their strength or name or authority or virtue to defend their people.

    But William is equally interested in the joining of 'umbones'. I am not sure how clearly he visualised Roman military procedures, but he will have read in Lucan of Pompey's tactics at Pharsalia, when his soldiers, 'closely packed in serried ranks, joined their shields to form an unbroken line'. So William talks of joined shields ('iunctis umbonibus', and variations). This is a game that two saints can play: at the time of the Danish invasion, St Neot was raised from his tomb and transferred to Crowland, there to stand shoulder to shoulder with Guthlac ('iuncto cum Gudlaco umbone') in protecting the locals. Most strikingly William six times speaks of a common shield, 'communis umbo'. This phrase is always used in the ablative. Thus the Normans defended their country with one accord in the early days of Duke William's minority; so too Edwin and Morcar keeping the peace in Northumbria, and magnates uniting with knights in Lanfranc's time to defend the public weal and private fortunes against the Danes. The Danes were the problem again under Æthelwulf, when the royal advisers promoted a common front to exact reprisals for devastation in London and Kent. The verb is 'ulciscerentur', a clear example of aggressiveness. The fact is that 'communi umbone' is used virtually as an adverbial phrase meaning, in William's concrete way, that men made common cause. In a prominent place in the Life of Wulfstan William asserts that after Hastings the English never again tried to 'rise towards liberty with a common *umbo*'. Hence, in

---

[12] For this collection see Thomson, *William of Malmesbury*, p. 66.
[13] S. J. Harrison on *Aeneid* 10. 884.

a military metaphor, William can say even in the *Commentary on Lamentations*: 'Let us then strive, with the grace of God and the common *umbo*, that is the help of God and our own labour, to repel the common enemy.' He means the Devil.

I should emphasise that I know of no other writer who used this phrase. And I proceed to passages where William experiments with the word still further, and sometimes to mysterious effect. He is not an easy author to translate: and this is perhaps the place to say that readers should always look critically at my translations, in any of the books that Rod Thomson and I have produced. The older I get the harder translating seems to become; and the harder William's Latin.

I illustrate this point at once. I have remarked that William often uses 'umbo' with a defining genitive: 'protectionis', most simply, or (giving the grounds for the help the shield gives) 'uirtutis' or 'auctoritatis'. What though are we to make of passage 6d? Here we learn of British sufferings at the hand of Ceawlin, who drove them out of such cities as they still held and into the wildernesses where (says William) they still remain today. The OMT translation is at fault here. Roger Mynors is in my eyes beyond error, so the mistake must be that of Rod Thomson and myself when we revised Roger's work.

Gloecestrae and the other city names are not genitive ('they had escaped the fate of Gloucester') but locative: it was 'at Gloucester' and the rest that the Britons had previously escaped their doom, though now Ceawlin captures them (so the *Anglo-Saxon Chronicle* for 577). This makes sense of the passage, but we are left with the previous clauses. It is clear that the Britons had sheltered behind the city walls ('claustrorum muralium'). But they had also 'put in front of them' the 'umbo deditionis'. We made of this 'a show of surrender', but I suppose that the literal sense must be 'a shield of surrender': the Britons in some way subordinated themselves to the kings of Wessex to avoid being conquered. There is nothing of this in the Chronicle, and William, I take it, is inventing a twin reason why the Britons survived long enough to be driven out by Ceawlin. That tells us something about his historical methods. But the phraseology is equally typical.

I add a second and even odder use of 'umbo' (6e). In both the *Gesta Regum* and *Gesta Pontificum*, and in identical language, William rhapsodises about the number of pilgrims who swarmed to the shrine of St Mildburh at Wenlock, attracted by a miracle that had revealed the presence of her body after the establishment of a Cluniac monastery there. There was scarce room for their columns in the spacious fields; rich and poor were on equal terms, for it was faith that brought them together headlong 'in commune'. The language is odd. Why, quite apart from 'aequis umbonibus', should faith *precipitate* them, rich and poor alike? It all sounds overdone. A previously unrecognised source here comes to our aid. In the *Peristephanon* Prudentius describes the crowds that thronged from Rome to the shrine of St Hippolytus down river. You will see from my italics how much William takes over from the poet. 'aequis umbonibus' is there, no less mysterious (another Thomson translates 'shoulder to shoulder'). But whereas William has faith sending the pilgrims rushing to Wenlock, Prudentius seems (if Thomson is right) to make it 'banish distinctions of birth'. But translating Prudentius is as risky a business as translating William.

Nouns are much less pliant, even in William's hands, than verbs. Let us look at his use of the verb 'absoluere', at the way he teases it and moulds it, taking hints from his reading here and there, but always the master of his material (7). The word can mean 'to free' a person, from things, tangible or metaphorical, felt as restricting: chains, guilt, debt, and, in a Christian world, sin. But it can also mean to 'loose', 'untie' those bonds themselves. Thus William can speak of St Leonard as 'having the power *absoluendorum uinculorum*', such as the silver fetters burdening Bohemond. Transferring this to a metaphor, he has not long before used the phrase 'morarum uinculis absolutis', 'the bonds of delay being unloosed'. In the *Gesta Pontificum* we find 'absolutis morarum nexibus', which we might think to be William's own reworking, were it not that this precise wording is found in Constantius's Life of Germanus. It is on Constantius that William is playing his characteristic variations. These culminate in yet another passage of the *Gesta Regum*, close to those I have just cited: 'moram pugnae absoluit', 'he untied the delay in giving battle'.

In Plautus's *Amphitruo* it is arranged by the gods that Alcumena should give birth to twins, one Jupiter's son, the other her husband's, 'uno ut labore apsoluat aerumnas duas', 'that she may be rid of two troubles by a single labour'.[14] The connection with childbirth persisted over the ages, and, perhaps via various passages in the Church fathers, William still knows of it. At the end of his life William the Conqueror was laid up, and Philip of France joked: 'The king of England lies at Rouen, keeping to his bed like women who have just had a baby', 'more absolutarum partu feminarum'. They are freed of the burdens in their wombs, as is spelt out in a passage of *Gesta Pontificum*, where Wilfrid's mother 'alui pondus absolueret', 'was releasing the burden of her womb', the literal counterpart of the Plautine metaphor. Similarly, William can, at Dunstan's birth, speak of his mother 'releasing her offspring', 'absoluit partum femina'. There are parallels for this in Ambrose, and (of mares) in the agricultural writer Palladius. But it is not a common expression.

There is another intriguing and early offshoot of the basic meaning of 'absoluere'. In a fragment of the Republican tragedian Pacuvius an unknown person 'paucis absoluit, ne moraret diutius', which seems to mean: 'he let him off with a few words, not to delay him longer'. This usage was taken up by the archaising Sallust, who starts the narrative of the *Catiline* with a resounding phrase that employs 'paucis absoluam'. Sallust perhaps meant no more by it than 'give a brief description'. At all events, the verb henceforth takes on the extra meaning 'describe', and that is how William often uses it. He several times qualifies it with 'paucis', bowing to Sallust, whom he admired for his brevity and tone of old-world moralising. But frequently he uses it without 'paucis', as for instance in the sonorous opening

---

[14] So W. B. Sedgwick on *Amphitr.* 488.

words of the *Gesta Regum*: 'res Anglorum gestas Beda ... plano et suaui sermone absoluit' (where the A manuscripts banalise 'absoluit' into 'describit'). There is nothing unusual in such a locution. But the use of this word here helps to establish the tone of grave dignity; and the sentence as a whole, while clearly stating the object of the book and William's claim to follow Bede, also reminds us that style is going to matter in the ensuing work: and style, it may be noted, without use of the rhythms of the cursus.

How the verb 'absoluere' came to mean 'to complete' is not clear. Lewis and Short suggested that it may arise from the detaching of a finished web from the loom. I suppose that this view was influenced by a phrase in Cicero's *De Legibus*, where Marcus says to Atticus: 'I don't find it as easy to weave together things that have been interrupted as to finish them [*absoluo*] when they have been begun.'[15] It does not seem, incidentally, to have been noticed that William purloins this phrase at a point in the *Gesta Regum* where he is apologising for getting things out of chronological order. In any case, he follows classical and medieval usage in using 'absoluere' of the completion, for instance, of a book or a building.

William uses 'absoluere', then, in traditional ways, to mean 'loose', 'describe' and 'complete'. But it is characteristic of him that he presses to the limit the possibilities of a word that appealed to him. In the Life of Dunstan, he describes how the saint travelled post haste to reach Eadred before the king died. But a message from heaven told him he was too late, and the accompanying thunder caused his horse to drop dead. This not unnaturally disquieted his retinue ('turbauit'), but 'absoluit Dunstanus timorem'. The locution is unparalleled, at least before William. What exactly does it mean? Perhaps that he unloosed their fear; or finished it off? This is the sort of thing that frequently puzzles a translator of William. I myself settled for 'calmed', but of course it does not *mean* that. Or again: in the *Miracles of the Blessed Virgin Mary*, the penitent prostitute Mary of Egypt prays to the Virgin to be allowed to enter a church at Jerusalem. Then she approached the door and 'absoluta ingrediendi licentia gauisa', 'rejoiced to find herself granted entry'. Again, the precise nuance is difficult to capture, and again I know no proper parallel ('absoluta' does not here mean 'absolute'). The woman has been given the freedom to enter; but that is not what the Latin really says. Or again: twice over William praises the writings of Prior Godfrey of Winchester, including his epigrams 'quae satirico modo absoluit'. That seems to mean no more than that he *wrote* them. Finally: early in the *Gesta Pontificum* Frederick, newly elected bishop of Utrecht, makes an impassioned speech to Louis the Pious, chiding him for his incestuous marriage. 'Louis did not take this speech (*dictum*) kindly, *modesta tamen taciturnitate absoluit*.' I translated 'but he had the self-control to pass it over without saying anything'. Perhaps the sense is 'dealt with it', 'disposed of it'.[16] One

---

[15] Immediately preceded by 'historia ... nec *institui* potest nisi praeparato otio nec exiguo tempore *absolui*'. 'orsus' too glances at weaving.

[16] *Oxford Latin Dictionary*, s.v. 5c.

might compare a second passage in the *Gesta Pontificum*, where Anselm does on the spot two things asked of him by a dying earl, but has to go off to see the king in order to dispose of a third, 'tertium . . . absoluturus'. But I am not sure.

I conclude my remarks on 'absoluere' by pointing out a different sort of innovation. In his biblical commentary William says that Jeremiah is bound by the rules of metre, and has no choice but to follow the practice of poets. Poets make a sentence run over from one verse to another, because they lack the freedom of prose, 'absolutae dictationis licentia carentes'. The ordinary Latin for 'prose' is 'soluta oratio'. William's persistent desire to surprise and vary transmutes this to 'absoluta dictatio'. Silver Latin prose liked to replace a compound verb with a simple one. William here does the opposite. This locution seems to be unique to him; nor does he elsewhere, to my knowledge, use the infrequent word 'dictatio'.

I end this catalogue with an adjective and an adverb concerned with pleasure and applause (**8**). But I cannot avoid starting from the associated verb 'plaudere' and its relative 'applaudere'. They both mean 'clap', and both were primarily used of applause (though the noun 'applausus' is less common than 'plausus' in Classical Latin). Applause often involves joy, and 'plaudere' came (it is not clear how early) to be able to bear the meaning 'rejoice'. The adjective 'plausibilis', however, for a long time seems to be restricted to meaning 'capable of winning applause'. So in Seneca, so in the Fathers: and often of oratorical display. But it was not a particularly common word. Even less common is its adverb 'plausibiliter', found very occasionally, perhaps always in connection with applause for a speech.

Against this background we may survey William's usage. He is of course well aware of the senses involving applause. Thus Wulfstan did not convey his teaching in a style of speech ('eloquium') that was 'coturnato et plausibili', 'elevated and applause-seeking'; Jerome before him had talked of 'plausibile eloquium'. The girl who at the village sports in Itchington tried to shipwreck Wulfstan's chastity 'plausibilem psaltriam agit' 'played the part of a dancing girl in search of applause': again there is a connotation of performance. Rather differently, in the *Historia Nouella*, the news of the queen's having found refuge in Wallingford is described as 'plausibile nuntium', where the transition towards 'pleasurable' is apparent. William uses the adverb[17] correspondingly in a passage in the *Gesta Regum* where Bohemond, bringing his silver fetters with him, is welcomed by his people: 'exceptus plausibiliter'. We may compare another scene of welcome in the *Aeneid*, where at the Trojan games in Sicily the Dardans greet the nervous performers with applause ('excipiunt plausu') 'and they rejoice to gaze at them' ('gaudentque tuentes').

I shall come back to pleasure. But I must say something of clapping. This could be done with wings as well as hands. Thus in another scene of the Trojan games

---

[17] He also uses 'plausibiliter' of speech at *GR* bk 4 pr. 1 'quippe presentium mala periculose, bona plausibiliter dicuntur', 'to secure a good reception'. At Sidonius, *Ep*. 8. 10. 3 the comparative is used similarly (not 'triumphantly', as Anderson translates).

Virgil introduces a simile of a dove scared from its rocky home: 'plausumque exterrita pennis / dat tecto ingentem', 'and in its fright beats its wings hugely' (the noise is implied here). Similarly, William described how at Wilfrid's death there were heard sweet bird song and the beating of wings flying up to heaven.[18] The verb 'plaudere' is also used of birds, and Statius uses 'applausus' of flapping wings. But it was left to William to introduce the adjective too into this realm. He has a dove circle around Dunstan's head for a long time as he makes sacrifice, 'plausibili uolatu'. That can hardly mean anything but that the bird flapped its wings as it flew. So too in a scene in the *Gesta Pontificum* when the same Dunstan sees a dove alight on the tomb of his predecessor Oda. We may also invoke yet another story of Dunstan, who in William's Life sees 'a dove of flame, its wings flickering with sparks ('scintillanti alarum plausu').

To return now to pleasure: in the *Miracles of the Blessed Virgin Mary* William describes how a monk of Cluny saw the Virgin Mary in his dying moments; his soul, 'cheerful and in haste, broke free of the bonds of the body and departed *gaudiose et plausibiliter*'. 'Gaudiose', 'joyfully', is itself preternaturally rare, and is not cited, any more than the adjective 'gaudiosus', before the thirteenth century. William may well have invented it. In any case, it makes a fitting companion for 'plausibiliter' in what seems to be the apparently unparalleled sense of 'with rejoicing'. There can be no question of applause here, and two parallel passages ensure the connotation of joy. Both are again concerned with the departure of a soul from the body. Dunstan's soul was trying to gain unimpeded passage to heaven, 'and the more its prison cell crumbled the more joyful it was to sally forth' (I hazarded 'anxious' in my translation, not without a question mark). And in another passage of the *Miracles* William speaks of any man's soul as 'darting forth *plaudens et laeta iuuenta*', 'rejoicing and happy in its youth'. The verb in both these passages is 'emicare', a favourite of William's that would yield ample material for another profile.[19] It may be observed that William will have read the passage in Prudentius's *Peristephanon* where Eulalia's soul leaves her mouth in the form of a dove, and then in the aether 'plaudit ouans', translated by Thomson 'claps her wings in triumph', though it might just mean 'rejoices in triumph'. At any rate, this passage happily draws together the dove and the joy we have found in our examination of words cognate with 'plaudere'.

I shall now try to put all this into a wider context. When I edited the *Commentary on Lamentations* for Corpus Christianorum, I collected in a footnote[20] a number of references to places where William was *not* demonstrably using earlier sources for his interpretations of and comments on passages from the Bible. I have added a few more references in my own margin; but it is still not a long list, considering that

---

[18] Noiseless, however, I presume, the eagle circling a city for a long time 'pennarum plausu' (*GP* 75. 36).
[19] And there is more to say about 'applaudere'.
[20] CCCM 244, p. xxxi n. 74.

the commentary runs to 316 large pages. William's avowed object is to abbreviate Paschasius Radbertus, though he supplements Paschasius from other sources. But he usually adapted the *wording* of the material he inherited, and usually he did not avow his sources. The same goes for his frequent drawing upon non-Christian writers of prose and poetry. His aim, it seems, was to produce something that read like the work of one man, and a careful stylist at that. If the researches of a careful reader showed what lay behind what Roger Mynors would have called the whited sepulchre, that was fine. William (I think and hope) was not trying to deceive; he was trying to produce, in some sense, a work of art.

The same, *mutatis mutandis*, is true of some of William's other works. We can hardly doubt that the Life of Wulfstan was meant to improve on the style of its Anglo-Saxon original. The Life of Dunstan had several rivals on which to improve, especially the tortured author we call 'B'. The Miracles adapt and homogenise the wording of the sources we can recognise. The *Gesta Regum* and *Gesta Pontificum* are a mosaic of extracts from countless sources, many of which are preserved, so that we can catch William out giving his own stylistic unity to the diverse material (even to the extent, as Rod Thomson long ago showed,[21] of editing the letters of Alcuin to make his Latin more correct). Only the *Historia Nouella* can give us some faint idea of what the first draft might have been like before William got down to the work of polishing. And only there, perhaps, is he telling us a story of his own: for he had nowhere to turn except to his informants and his own knowledge of events. Elsewhere, to put it very crudely indeed, he is telling us about things anyone could have known. What he gives his readers is not new information but old information in a new and attractive guise.

I should like to float the proposition that, for all their differences, William and Virgil have important things in common. In the *Eclogues*, Virgil made heavy drafts, of content and language, on the Greek bucolic poet Theocritus. In the *Aeneid*, he did the same for Homer. In each poem, what we used (in the good old days of our innocence) to call borrowings were not obvious except to a learned reader. But if they were recognised, they added much to the pleasure given by the poems. They did not affect the originality of the writing: Virgil's productions, pastoral and epic alike, are absolutely different from these 'sources', quite apart from being in a different language. So too with William. He does not usually tell us where his information comes from, and the learned will get pleasure from identifying the sources. His constant adaptation of passages of classical and late antique writings goes in tandem with his use of his historical sources; again, pleasure may be taken in tracking them down, but it is not essential to our understanding that we should do so. Again, we should not cast aspersions on William's originality, any more than on Virgil's. His finished works, too, taken as a whole, are different from anything that preceded them, however derivative they may seem to be. It is up to historians

---

[21] *William of Malmesbury*, pp. 161–3.

to say in what sense William is a historian.[22] He is certainly a *literary* craftsman, who cared about the way he wrote at least as much as about what he wrote.

But there is a further parallel with Virgil, and this take me back to the main topic of this paper. Virgil was an innovator in language. Every page of any good commentary on him has to grapple with the way in which he stretches Latin to its limits, in syntax and in vocabulary. This is what makes him so difficult, or even impossible, to translate in such a way as to bring out more than the surface meaning, if that. So too with William. He knows Latin perfectly, and he plays with it masterfully. I must end with an apology to him, for so often, however unwittingly, getting him wrong.

APPENDIX

1. *a.*   GR 50. 2 fortuna, multis antea illecebris Oswinum adulata, scorpiacea cauda persequebatur [pro- Aac]

    b.   HN 481 (p. 68) fortuna, nimium ante et diu ei blandita, ad extremum scorpiacea crudeliter hominem [Roger bp of Salisbury] cauda percussit

    c.   VW 2. 22. 3 sed enim fortuna, diu homini [Sæwig of Ratcliffe] lenocinata, tunc autem scorpiacea cauda prosecuta inimicos eius superinduxit

Sidonius, *Ep.* 2. 13. 5 (trans. Anderson) quem cruentauit *Fortunae diu lenocinantis* perfidus finis, quae uirum ut scorpios ultima sui parte *percussit*

    d.   GP 246. 5 Sol illustrarat bisseno Scorpion ortu, / cum regem cauda surruit ille sua

Just above: … ingentes actus festinata dies fatis abrupit. immatura ergo morte, et quae animositatem illam, si Deus uoluisset, non deceret … .

2.   Hegisippus 3. 3 Titus prae ceteris mouebatur ingenita animi mansuetudine, illum dudum bellatorem superbum, subito potestati addictum hostium, alieni nutus sortem opperiri, uitae naufragum, exulem spei, incertum salutis

Whence *GR* 196. 6 regem … qui nunc uitae naufragus, exul spei, alterius opem implorat; *MBVM* 1. 5 offitio suo iniuste spoliatus et spei naufragus uestrum implorat auxilium; *VW* 2. 4. 3 inopes ergo spei, exules consilii; *Comm. Lam.* I. 1108 anima ergo cum se uidet inopem auxilii, naufragam spei …; *Comm. Lam.* III. 756 omnis spei naufragam

---

[22] Note R. Bartlett, *The Natural and the Supernatural in the Middle Ages* (Cambridge, 2008): 'Medieval authors are always doing this [i.e. recycling the words of others], presenting modern scholars with the question, is all they have written mere literary pastiche?'

3. *a.* VW 3. 4. 3 nam plerumque quidam eum uel aperte obuncabant uerbis uel occulte uellicabant ludibriis

b. GR 263. 3 archidiaconus … a longe clamans et abbatem obuncans 'Tu, tu' inquit 'male cogitasti …'

c. GR 320. 3 Willelmus, pre furore fere extra se positus, et obuncans Heliam 'Tu', inquit 'nebulo [cf. GR 309. 1], tu quid faceres? Discede, abi, fuge [cf. Paulinus of Nola, *carm.* 31. 189]! Concedo tibi ut fatias quicquid poteris, et per uultum de Luca [GR 309. 2 sic enim iurabat] nichil, si me uiceris, pro hac uenia tecum paciscar.' Orderic V, p. 248 has merely 'Vade et age quicquid michi potes agere'.

Rufinus 10. 18 (p. 984) tunc illa, ut mulierum se talium procacitas habet, obuncans (v. l. obiurgans) Timotheum 'Tu, tu' inquit 'mihi uim fecisti …'. Known to Aldhelm, *De Virg.* prose p. 274, 3 Ehwald (obuncabat) and verse p. 396 line 1023 (obuncat).

MBVM 38. 6 illa … immodeste tulit, clamitareque cepit, familiari peste huiusmodi mulierculis ut libenter in iurgium prodeant

4. GP 268. 4 quadamque hostilitate uim corpori suo ipse consciscens

Constantius, *Vita Germani* 3 (ed. R. Borius [Paris, 1965]) iam uero enarrari non potest qua hostilitate uim sibi ipse consciuerit, quas cruces quaeue supplicia corporis sui persecutor induerit

5. GP 270. 1 uir [Archdeacon Hubald] qui liberalium artium non exiguum experimentum cepisset, sed pro titubantia oris parum eas audientibus expediret

The word is also used at VD 2. 4. 3 (oris uel mentis), GR 265. 2, GP 81. 3.

Suet. *Vit.* 6 liberos utriusque sexus tulit [Vitellius], sed marem titubantia oris prope mutum et elinguem; *Claud.* 30 risus indecens, ira turpior spumante rictu, umentibus naribus, praeterea linguae titubantia caputque … tremulum

6. *a.* GP 47. 4 si quando Cantuariensem archiepiscopum uiderent qui esset os omnium, uexillifer preuius, umbo publicus

b. Lucan 7. 492–3 Pompei densis acies stipata cateruis / iunxerat in seriem nexis umbonibus arma

c. communi umbone: GR 230. 1 (Normans), 252. 1 (Northumbria), VW 3. 16. 2 (Lanfranc), GR 108. 2 (Æthelwulf: ulciscerentur), *Comm. Lam.* I. 97 (God and man), VW 2. 1. 1 (after Hastings). Cf. GP 182. 3 (SS Neot and Guthlac: iuncto cum Gudlaco umbone).

d. GR 17. 1 [of Ceawlin] Britannos, qui temporibus patris et aui uel pretento deditionis umbone uel claustrorum muralium obiectu Gloecestrae et Cirecestrae et Bathoniae exitium effugerant, … persecutus *e.* GR 216 = GP 171. 3 uix patuli campi capiebant populorum [v. l. uiatorum] agmina, dum aequis umbonibus diues et mendicus se agerent, cunctos in commune precipitante fide

Cf. Prudentius, *Peristeph.* 11. 199–202 urbs augusta suos uomit effunditque Quirites, / una et patricios ambitione pari / confundit plebeia phalanx *umbonibus aequis* / discrimen procerum *praecipitante fide.* (211) *uix capiunt patuli* populorum gaudia *campi*...

7. *a.* GR 387. 5 ille sanctus [Leonard] absoluendorum uinculorum potens [Bohemond]; GR 376. 8 morarum uinculis absolutis; GP 56. 1 absolutis morarum nexibus [= Constantius, *Vita Germani* 9]; GR 384. 6 moram pugnae absoluit

b. Plautus, *Amphitruo* 488 uno ut labore apsoluat aerumnas duas; GR 281 more absolutarum partu feminarum [joke by French king]; GP 101. 4 (Wilfrid) cum adhuc genitrix alui pondus absolueret; VD 1. 2. 1 absoluit partum femina

c. Pacuvius 181 (Ribbeck) paucis absoluit, ne moraret diutius; Sall. *Cat.* 4. 4 igitur de Catilinae coniuratione quam uerissume potero paucis absoluam (cf. e.g. GR 227); GR bk 1 prol. 1 res Anglorum gestas Beda... plano et suaui sermone absoluit [v. l. describit]

d. Cic. *Leg.* 1. 9 neque tam facile interrupta contexo quam absoluo instituta; GR 87. 4 difficilius contexo interrupta quam absoluo instituta

e. VD 1. 25. 2 absoluit Dunstanus timorem; MBVM 40. 8 [Mary of Egypt] accessit ad hostium, et absoluta ingrediendi licentia gauisa...; GR 444. 1 = GP 77. 3 epigrammata quae satirico modo absoluit; GP 6. 6 hoc dictum licet Ludouicus egre accepisset, modesta tamen taciturnitate absoluit; GP 48. 2 (Anselm) prima quidem continuo expediit, tertium uero absoluturus curiam contendit

f. *Comm. Lam.* II. 1256 illi quippe, absolutae dictationis licentia carentes, quod residuum est uersui plerumque sequenti conectunt

8. *a.* VW 1. 5. 2 [Wulfstan] doctrinam non suo confingebat ingenio, nec coturnato et plausibili proferebat eloquio (cf. Jerome, *Ep.* 118. 1 puerilis atque plausibilis eloquii uenustatem); VW 1. 1. 7 illa... gestibus impudicis, motibus inuerecundis, plausibilem psaltriam agit. HN 523 plausibile nuntium allatum est. GR 387. 5 [Bohemond] a suis ergo exceptus plausibiliter (Virg. *Aen.* 5. 575 excipiunt plausu pauidos gaudentque tuentes)

b. Virg. *Aen.* 5. 215–6 [columba] plausumque exterrita pennis / dat tecto ingentem. GP 109. 11 (Wilfrid) cantus suauis auium et plausus alarum in caelum reuolantium auditus. Stat. *Theb.* 2. 515 applausu. VD 2. 8. 1 (Dunstan) columba, incertum unde ueniens, sacrificantem diu multumque plausibili uolatu circuiuit (cf. GP 19. 7 [Oda]); also VD 1. 13. 2 columbam scintillanti alarum plausu flammeam

c. MBVM 19. 1 felix anima, quae... laeta et prepes, corporis nodum eluctata, gaudiose et plausibiliter discessit! *VD* 2. 33. 1 quantoque ergastulum erat dissolutius tanto illa [Dunstan's soul] emicabat plausibilius. *MBVM* 28. 8 [anima] emicat plaudens et laeta iuuenta. Prudentius, *Peristeph*. 3. 161–3 emicat inde columba repens / martyris os niue candidior / uisa reliquere et astra sequi; ... (169) flatus in aethere plaudit ouans / templaque celsa petit uolucer

EPILOGUE

The Rediscovery of William of Malmesbury

Rodney M. Thomson

I HAVE BEEN ASKED, by some much younger than myself, to provide a brief narrative of my personal discovery of William of Malmesbury and of how Michael Winterbottom and I came to collaborate in editing and translating his works.[1] This is not a review of William of Malmesbury scholarship over the last forty years; that is for another to undertake. But, in concentrating on myself and Michael, I do not mean to imply that we two have been solely responsible for the increased interest in, and discoveries about, William in recent years.

The beginning of the story is told in the Introduction to my book *William of Malmesbury*.[2] My postgraduate work, at Melbourne and Sydney Universities, and my earliest publications, focused on books and learning at the great East Anglian abbey of Bury St Edmunds. In 1973–4, while 'treading water' between academic jobs – yes, they were hard to get then too – I began to think of studying an individual person rather than the culture of a religious institution. I envisaged such a person as a Benedictine monk of the twelfth century, a scholar and writer, perhaps a historian, certainly someone learned in the literature and ideas of the Ancient World – in other words, a William of Malmesbury-shaped individual. William was certainly a name to me, but I knew of him only as a historian. Then I found M. R. James's Murray Lecture, *Two Ancient English Scholars*,[3] in which he discussed the books and authors read by Aldhelm and William, and the possible connections between them. In a few pages James pulls from the pie plums such as William's great collection of Cicero's works, including the passage in which the monk defends his love of pagan literature, and the *Polyhistor*, which gathers together extracts from this literature, telling of ancient peoples and places, and

---

[1] This is emphatically not an academic paper, but a kind of memoir, which seeks not only to explain how Michael Winterbottom and I came to work together on William, but to evoke some of the memorable Oxfordian characters who were part of the story and who inhabited and exemplified a world now gone from us. It is also not an attempt to evaluate the last forty years of scholarship on William, hence the absence of names such as John Gillingham, Björn Weiler, Nicholas Wright, and Sigbjørn Sønnesyn.
[2] *William of Malmesbury*, p. ix.
[3] M. R. James, *Two Ancient English Scholars* (Glasgow, 1931).

much more. Here was the man I was looking for. An anxious search for more recent scholarship building on James's revelations revealed mercifully little, with the important exception of Leighton Reynolds's monograph on the medieval tradition of Seneca's letters.[4] Reynolds had shown that Seneca's correspondence circulated in two parts from late antiquity until the early twelfth century, when someone in south-western England, very probably William, united them. What was beyond doubt was that William knew both parts of the tradition – the first writer to do so since antiquity. I was now completely hooked, and began a hand-written card-file[5] listing all the authors and works known to William at first hand. The result was well beyond my expectations: here was a man who had read at first hand some four hundred individual works by a couple of hundred authors – surely the best-read European of his age.

In 1975 my findings were published in *Revue Bénédictine* as 'The reading of William of Malmesbury', followed by supplements in 1976 and 1979.[6] In 1975 my friend John O. Ward of Sydney University, expert on the Ciceronian tradition of rhetoric from Antiquity until the Renaissance, was on study leave in Oxford, where he was (justly) lionised. He wrote to me that the legendary Richard Hunt, just retired from the Keepership of Western MSS in the Bodleian, had seen my article and found it interesting; he also advised me to look up Richard Southern, whose writings both of us had been taught to revere when we were undergraduates.[7] On a short visit to Oxford the following year, I met Hunt. He was walking down the aisle of Duke Humfrey, accompanying a friend to lunch, when I sallied out from the bookcases and greeted him with 'Dr Hunt? I'm Rod Thomson'. He reacted as to an electric shock: 'Rod Thomson!' he exclaimed, 'Oh what *fun*!' Grasping the

---

[4] L. D. Reynolds, *The Medieval Tradition of Seneca's Letters* (Oxford, 1965), esp. pp. 117 and n. 2, 120–3.

[5] This was long before the advent of the word-processor.

[6] 'The reading of William of Malmesbury', *RB* 85 (1975), 362–402; 'The reading of William of Malmesbury; addenda et corrigenda, *RB* 86 (1976), 327–35; 'The reading of William of Malmesbury; further additions and reflections', *RB* 89 (1979), 313–24. Also 'William of Malmesbury and some other western writers on Islam', *Mediaevalia et Humanistica*, new ser. 6 (1975), 179–87, 'William of Malmesbury and the *Noctes Atticae*', in *Hommages à André Boutemy*, ed. G. Cambier (Coll. Latomus 145: Bruxelles, 1976), pp. 367–89, 'William of Malmesbury and the letters of Alcuin', *Mediaevalia et Humanistica*, n. s. 8 (1977), 147–61, 'William of Malmesbury as historian and man of Letters', *JEH* 29 (1978), 387–413, 'William of Malmesbury's edition of the *Liber Pontificalis*', *Archivum Historiae Pontificiae* 17 (1978), 93–112, 'William of Malmesbury's Carolingian sources', *JMH* 7 (1981), 321–37, 'Identifiable books from the pre-Conquest library of Malmesbury Abbey', *ASE* 10 (1981), 1–19, 'John of Salisbury and William of Malmesbury; currents in twelfth-century humanism', in *The World of John of Salisbury*, ed. M. Wilks (Studies in Church History Subsidia 3: Oxford, 1984), pp. 117–25 These were eventually combined together in, and in some cases superseded by, chs 1–3, 5–9, 11 of my *William of Malmesbury*. More recently I have returned to the fray: 'William of Malmesbury and the Latin Classics revisited', in *Aspects*, pp. 383–93, and 'William of Malmesbury and the Latin Classics: new research', in *Writing the Classics*, ed. E. Kwakkel (Leiden, 2015), pp. 169–85.

[7] For these men, see the eloquent obituaries in *Proceedings of the British Academy* 67 (1981), 371–97, and 120 (2003), 413–42. The one of Hunt, a particularly evocative and affectionate character-portrait, was written by Southern.

elbow of my jacket and motioning his friend to go on ahead, he towed me down the aisle to Arts End and propped himself against the window-sill. I was, of course, expecting him to tell me how much pleasure my great article had given him. Not a bit of it. 'Now then, your article on William: there are one or two things you didn't get *right*', he vociferated, and proceeded to the detail of my shortcomings ('You hadn't read Millas y Vallicrosa's *Assaig* on the *Mathematica Alhandrei* ...'). I was enthralled. Richard had a knack of telling one things, bluntly and forcefully, that he felt were needed to show the way forward. Instinctively I knew that he was taking me seriously. And indeed the conversation was the beginning of a friendship terminated, alas, all too soon by his death three years later.

Encouraged by this reception, I wrote to (Professor Sir) Richard Southern, then Master of Balliol, who in reply invited me to lunch.[8] This meeting too was memorable, but in a quite different way. Came the day, and I awaited him in the anteroom to his office. He appeared, fixed me with a gimlet gaze from his clear blue eyes, and asked 'What are you working on?' I froze internally; he evidently knew nothing at all about me. I explained that I was working on William of Malmesbury. He frowned alarmingly. 'Oh, I shouldn't do that if I were you', said he, 'all the great men have worked on him; I should think there was scarcely anything more to be found.' 'But Sir Richard', I stammered, 'I've just published an article on his reading in *Revue Bénédictine*.' 'I'm sorry, I haven't read it', he said, distantly, 'Now let's go to lunch.' You may imagine my feelings. What he had said was such evident rubbish that I assumed he must be setting me some kind of test; and so it turned out. After lunch (during which each of us spoke with others) we circumambulated the Fellows' garden. 'So you've written about William's reading; have you found any evidence that he visited Canterbury?' Aha, here was an opening. I got into my stride, talked of William and Eadmer, and Southern listened. Similar questions followed. At the end he bade me farewell, with the admission that I had clearly found some things of interest; I had told him that I was going on to Cambridge, would I call in again on my return? I did so, and his first words were apologetic: 'You see', he said, 'so many young men come to Oxford wanting to work on William of Malmesbury, without adequate preparation', something like that, as exaggerated as his earlier remarks. And so began, in unlikely fashion, another friendship, thankfully longer than the one with Hunt.

Some time in the early 1970s the name of Winterbottom swam into my ken. Michael was by then Fellow and Tutor in Classics at Worcester College; later (1993) he would become Corpus Christi Professor of Latin. He had a formidable reputation as a Latinist, based upon his OCT edition of Quintilian's *Institutes*, in which for the first time sense was made of the manuscript tradition. I'm not sure

---

[8] Our undergraduate teacher at Melbourne was Marian (Molly) Gibbs, author of *Early Charters of St Paul's* and (with Jane Lang), *Bishops and Reform*. She was a long-standing friend of Richard Southern, Beryl Smalley and Michael Wallace-Hadrill. I am happy to pass on to beginners in medieval history her (despairing) advice to all of us – 'Try and write like Dick Southern'. Speaking for myself, I have been trying ever since.

how I got to know of him (though I suspect John Ward played a part), except that he was one of the readers for my edition of the *Vita Gundulfi*, published in the series Toronto Medieval Texts. Someone (again probably John) told me he thought well of my work, so of course I had to like him. In 1978, when I was in Oxford on study leave, we met for the first time, and quickly became friends. Fast-forward to 1986, when Michael sent me a letter that was to prove fateful: he had been casting about for a medieval Latin text to edit and asked me for my opinion, suggesting Matthew Paris's *Gesta Abbatum S. Albani*, among others. I replied that Paris's homespun Latin was not worthy of his steel, but he might like to consider this man William of Malmesbury. I already knew that the *Gesta Regum* and *Gesta Pontificum* had been commissioned for publication, long before, in the series Oxford Medieval Texts (OMT), but I was fairly sure that the projects were becalmed. I had in mind *Gesta Regum* in particular, commissioned from Roger Mynors and – Richard Southern. (Professor Sir) Roger Mynors, one of the greatest Latin scholars of his day, had been Michael's *Doktorvater*.[9] Michael browsed *Gesta Regum* and was excited by it. I was duly told off to find out from Southern and Mynors whether they had really abandoned the project. On a subsequent short research trip to Oxford I tackled the two grand old men. Southern, over morning tea, told me that he'd never done anything at all because of an editorial disagreement with Roger (*GR* II, p. xviii). Southern believed that his account was the correct one and, said he with a chuckle, 'Roger doesn't like to be shown that he's *wrong*.' A little while later I spent a weekend at Treago, the Mynors family seat outside the tiny village of St Weonards, mid-way between Hereford and Monmouth. On a warm evening before dinner, on the terrace with its clipped yews and pond, to the accompaniment of sherry and Bath Olivers, I delicately broached the subject of the *Gesta Regum*. 'Who wants to know?' asked Mynors, looking at me sharply. I told him it was Michael Winterbottom and the sharpness was instantly replaced with benignity. He explained that his new edition of the *Gesta Regum* had languished for decades in his desk drawer, and that he proposed to do no more with it. 'But if Michael Winterbottom – for whose brains I have the greatest respect – is interested in finishing the job, I will hand over my material forthwith, if it's thought to be of the *slightest* use.' A little while later Roger came down to Oxford and handed to Michael his copy of Stubbs's *Gesta Regum*, with Roger's collations written into its margins in his exquisite tiny italic hand.[10] Later still, Roger remembered that he had also translated books 1–4. He at once set to,

---

[9] Mynors was Kennedy Professor of Latin at Cambridge 1944–53, Corpus Christi Professor of Latin Language and Literature at Oxford 1953–70, editor of the OCT Virgil, Catullus, Pliny's letters, and the *Panegyrici Latini*. He was also deeply interested in medieval Latin ('going a-whoring after medieval Latin texts' he once referred to it as), unfashionably editing Cassiodorus's *Institutes*, producing the grand book *Durham Cathedral Manuscripts*, and serving on the editorial board of OMT (as did Michael Winterbottom). An eloquent character portrait, composed by Michael Winterbottom, is in *Proceedings of the British Academy* 80 (1993), 371–401.

[10] While Southern handed over an actual typescript of Roger's edition.

translated book 5, and passed the typescript to Michael. A few weeks later he was killed (aged 86) in a head-on collision, on his way home from a happy day's work in Hereford Cathedral library.

At this point I need to pursue momentarily a tangential course, in order to describe the genesis of the monograph *William of Malmesbury*, first published in 1987. In 1980 I had been introduced to Richard Barber, a director of the newly formed publishing house of Boydell & Brewer. Richard was, and is, a dynamic publisher with a genuine passion to produce books on medieval and renaissance history and culture, especially if they have been spurned by the major academic publishing houses. At some meeting between us – I don't recall the details – I wondered out loud what to do with my articles about William, and how I should proceed to write the monograph that I was sure was needed. Richard suggested that I should use the articles as a framework for the book. Thus was the first edition of *William of Malmesbury* conceived, a collection of papers rather than a monograph; the second edition, of 2013, is more of a coherent entity. It is probably time for a third edition, which ought to be an entirely new book, given how much more we know after editing the *Gesta Pontificum, Commentary on Lamentations* and *Miracles of the Blessed Virgin Mary*, not to speak of the scholarly work of so many others.

In the meantime, Michael had written to me suggesting collaboration, as the task of commenting on and interpreting the *Gesta Regum* clearly required the attention of a historian. I agreed, and the rest, as they say, is history. It is unnecessary to describe in detail our collaboration in editing, translating and commenting on this and William's other works. The only difficulty of any magnitude occurred right at the beginning and the issue was technological. I had just begun to use a word-processor and email was only just invented. Michael used an ancient typewriter, but preferred to correct and annotate by hand. These differences made exchange of information between Hobart and Oxford problematic. The difficulty was resolved in 1995, when I was Visiting Fellow at Corpus. Just before I arrived Michael wrote to me that the University was offering staff heavily discounted computer packages (computer, keyboard, monitor and printer), together with a tuition programme entitled 'Computing for the Terrified': should he buy one and take the other? I said Absolutely, to which he responded that he would do it if I would help him when I came to Corpus. I arrived to find the package in his elegant study, distributed among several cartons. Together we assembled it, and I recall Michael's pleasure and wonderment when he created a file, typed a sentence ('William of Malmesbury rules OK' or similar), saved it and printed it out. We never looked back after that.

Working on the *Gesta Regum* increased our fascination with William: his formidable intelligence, his philological, rhetorical, and historical capability, and the weak points that made him human: occasional haste and carelessness, overuse of his imagination, a mischievous, sometimes spiteful, attitude to others. We learned to pursue all other avenues before concluding that he was simply wrong. So we began to turn our attention to the *Gesta Pontificum*, for which David Farmer and

Benedicta Ward were contracted with OMT. This time the approach was made by the Press; it emerged that little or nothing had been done, and Farmer and Ward were happy to relinquish the project in favour of a more active team. We went to work at once. A little while later, when I was in the library of Worcester Cathedral, an email arrived from Michael telling me that he had discovered hitherto unknown text that William had edited out of his autograph. At first I thought it must be a joke. But it was true, and constituted practically the only oversight of the Rolls Series editor, N. E. S. A. Hamilton, whose scholarship was in general impeccable.[11] By now we had set ourselves the goal of editing all of William's work not already in modern editions, and in late 2015 this was achieved with the appearance of William's *Miracles of the Blessed Virgin Mary*.

Septuagenarius sum hodie,[12] and Michael is *octogenarius*. It is time to pass the torch on. We have enjoyed thirty-five years of collaboration in discovering – or beginning to discover – William of Malmesbury. Of course it has not been merely collaboration but a friendship. Readers will note how important a role in my story has been played by several such. The nexus between scholarship and friendship has been recognised since the Ancient World; it is a nexus unfortunately hard to sustain in the modern academic environment, yet highly desirable. And not only friendships between the living; Michael and I both think that we have in some sense become friends of William. Here the paper by Sigbjørn Sønnesyn (one of our younger friends) in this volume is relevant.[13] While we have found ourselves becoming William's friends through the study of his writings, could it be that, all the time, he was reaching out to *us*?

---

[11] Published in *JML* and of course included in *GP*.
[12] I adapt *Comm. Lam.*, I. prol. 13–14 (p. 3).
[13] Above, pp. 153–63.

INDEX

Aachen 77 n. 80, 170
  Albert of 129, 131, 135 n. 28, 136
Abingdon 178
  Faricius, abt. of 20, 120
Acre 184 n. 63
Adam 95, 102
Adana, Eutychianus of 51
Adhémar, bp. of Le Puy 131
Ælfgar, bp. of Wiltshire 15
Ælfheah, abp. of Canterbury 33–4
Ælfhild 22
Ælfric Bata 86
Æthelberht, k. of Kent 179, 191
Æthelfrith, k. of Bernicia 31
Æthelnoth, abp. of Canterbury 72
Æthelred II, k. 6, 17, 69, 38 n. 11, 39 n. 17, 150, 197
Æthelric 111 n. 21
Æthelstan, k. 29 n. 6, 31, 72, 167, 172, 204
Æthelweard 171, 203
Æthelwine, bp. of Durham 111 n. 21
Æthelwulf, k. of Wessex 73, 208, 216
Agnes, empress 146
Aidan, bp. of Lindisfarne 76, 176
Al-Andalus 53
Alcuin 35, 77 n. 80, 110, 114 n. 37, 126, 142, 214
Alcumena 210
Aldhelm, abt. of Malmesbury 14, 16, 19–22, 24–6, 61, 72–3, 82–3, 90, 107, 113, 118, 119 n. 18, 166 n. 8, 206, 216
Aldwin 180
Alexander the Great 44
Alexander II, Pope 146, 184 n. 69
Alfonsi, Petrus 52
Alfonso VI, k. of Castille 56
Alfred, k. of Wessex 73, 76, 94, 110, 172–3
  Vita Alfredi 142 n. 18
Alps 19, 24–5, 42
Ambrose, St 118 n. 6, 119 n. 15, 210
Amelius, bp. of Toulouse 57
Androgeus 193
Angles 192, 196–7

Anglo-Saxon Chronicle 42, 110–11, 190–1, 196–7, 209
Anglo-Saxons; *see* England, English
Anjou 39
Annales Mettenses Priores 111
Anselm, abp. of Canterbury 38, 47, 58 n. 53, 62 nn. 70–1, 83, 90, 118, 120–7, 153–4, 157, 160–1, 172, 180 n. 41, 212, 217
Anselm, abt. of Bury 49
Antioch 131, 134–5, 168
Antiphonetes 53
Apuleius 171
Arabic 52
Aristotle 133, 160 n. 43
Arius 62 n. 72
Ascalon, Battle of 136
Asia Minor 131
Asser 142 n. 18, 172
Athulf: *see* Æthelwulf
as-Sinnabrah, Battle of 131
Augustine, abp. of Canterbury 18, 179
Augustine, St, bp. of Hippo 14, 33, 119, 139, 154, 155–7, 176–9
Augustodunensis, Honorius 51, 52 n. 25, 60 n. 64, 62 n. 70
Auxerre, Remigius of 119

'B', biographer of Dunstan 214
Babylonians 28
Balkans 131
Barbarossa, Frederick 139–41
Bath 30, 169
Battle Abbey 40, 53 n. 25, 177–8
Bec 120, 194
Bede 1, 2, 6, 15–18, 74, 76, 84, 90, 95–7, 99, 100–2, 104, 110–11, 114–15, 163, 171, 173, 175–87, 191–8, 203, 211
Bernard the Monk 130
Belvoir Priory 113
Birinus, bp. of Dorchester 16 n. 15, 178
Blois, Henry of, bp. of Winchester 86, 88–90
  Stephen, count of 131

Bohemond of Antioch 168, 210, 212, 217
Bouillon, Baldwin of 131
  Godfrey of 131, 134–36, 138
Breviarium Alaricum 170
Bridlington Abbey 113
Britain, Britons 4, 7, 10, 29, 40, 109, 131–2, 176, 189–201, 209
Bury St Edmunds Abbey 49, 60 n. 61, 111 n. 21, 116, 219
Byzantium 137–8
  Constantinople 33 n. 28, 129–31, 136, 138, 142, 169

Cadac-Andreas 114
Cadwaladr, prince of Gwynedd 200
Caerleon 31
Caesar, Claudius 192–4, 207
  Julius 37, 38 n. 10, 40–1, 42, 44, 89–90, 190, 193–4
  Tiberius 100
  Nero 38
Calixtus II, Pope 88, 143
Canossa 149
Canterbury 18, 32–5, 69, 71 n. 42, 72, 77, 108, 111, 115, 120, 121 n. 27, 177–8, 221
  abps. of: *see* Ælfheah, Æthelnoth, Æthelred, Anselm, Augustine, Deusdedit, Dunstan, Eadsige, Justus, Honorius, Lanfranc, Laurence, Oda, Paulinus, Stigand, Theobald, Thomas
  Gervase of 40, 75
  Osbern of 15, 17, 33–4, 82
Carlisle 29 n. 5, 82, 88, 108, 110, 115, 169
Carolingians 67 n. 11, 77–8, 112, 118, 140, 142, 144–5, 148, 170
Cassian, John 119 n. 15, 155–6, 159, 161
Cassian of Forlí, St 114
Ceawlin, k. of Wessex 29, 209, 216
Celts, Celtic 21, 115 n. 44, 170, 173, 190, 201
Ceolfrid, abt. of Wearmouth 114
Ceolwulf, k. of Northumbria 182 n. 51, 184 n. 65
Chaldeans 99
Charlemagne 43, 114 n. 37, 141–3, 147, 151
Charles the Bald 22, 144
Charles the Fat 144–5, 148
Charles Martel 142

Chartres 61 n. 67
  Fulcher of 129–30, 168
Chester 169
Chester-le-Street 111
Cicero 32, 43, 59, 85, 87–90, 154–5, 176, 211, 219–20
Cimbri 108
Cistercians 113, 166
Clare, Osbert of 55 n. 35
Clermont, Council of 130
Cluny 45, 205, 213
Cnut, k. 30, 72, 73–4, 199
Coleman 17, 110, 173
Cologne 206
Comnenus, Alexius 129
Conrad I, k. 140 n. 5
Conrad II, k. and emperor 145–6
Conrad III, emperor 141
Constantine I, emperor 131–2
Constantinople; *see* Byzantium
Constantius, emperor 194,
Constantius 206–7, 210, 216–17
Coutances 61 n. 68
Cricklade, Robert of 159 n. 37
Crowland 18, 208
Crusade
  First 58, 130–1, 133–6, 138, 168
  of 1101 130
  King Sigurd's 129–30, 136–8
Cumberland 39, 115 n. 44
Cumbrians 108
Curthose, Robert 41, 43, 70, 131
Cuthbert, bp. of Lindisfarne 33 n. 27, 73, 110–11, 114, 178–9
Cuthbert. abt. of Wearmouth 76, 177
Cyprian, Pseudo- 76–7

Damasippus 89, 90
Danes, Denmark 30, 69 n. 22, 170
  in England 29–31, 34–5, 110, 208
  See also: Scandinavians
Daniel 105, 146
Dardans 212
David I, k. of Scotland 169
Deusdedit, abp. of Canterbury 179
Devizes, Richard of 40
Dictys Cretensis 184
Dionysius Exiguus 95–7, 99, 100–1

226

Diss, Ralph of 75, 86
Dol, Baudri of 131
Domesday Survey 103
Domitius 41
Dover 21
Dunstan, abp. of Canterbury 17, 20, 33, 66–71, 77, 172, 210–11, 213–14, 217–18
Durham 33 n. 27, 40, 103, 109–116, 178–80
    bps. of: *see* Æthelwine; Eadred; Eanbert; Eardwulf; Ecberht; Edmund; Flambard, Richard; Hathuredus; Saint-Calais, William of; Tilred
Durham, Symeon of 14 n. 3, 75, 93, 103, 110–15, 179–81, 187

Eadbald, k. of Kent 76 n. 77
Eadmer 6, 14 n. 3, 38, 40, 45, 47, 58, 62 n. 70, 66, 71–2, 74, 88, 93, 124–5, 172, 181, 183, 203, 221
Eadred, k. 68, 211
Eadred, bp. of Durham 111 n. 21
Eadsige, abp. of Canterbury 72
Eadwig, k. 17, 69
Ealdred, abp. of York 72
Ealhstan, bp. of Sherborne 73
Eanbert, bp. of Durham 111 n. 21
Earconwald, bp. of London 16, 23
Eardulf, bp. of Durham 111 n. 21
Ecgberht, k. of Wessex 73, 169
Ecgberht, bp. of Durham 111 n. 21
Ecgfrith, k. of Northumbria 72
Ecgwine, bp. of Worcester 19
Edgar, k. 17, 43, 66–8, 70, 73, 112, 172
Edgar, k. of Scotland 44
Edgar the Ætheling 6, 31, 130, 199
Edmund, St 19, 74
Edmund (Ironside), k. 30, 199
Edmund I, k. 68
Edmund, bp. of Lindisfarne/Durham 110
Edward the Confessor, k. 72–3, 101, 112, 144, 205
    Laws of 58
Edward the Elder, k. of Wessex 31
Edwin, brother of Morcar earl of Northumbria 208
Egyptians 99
Einhard 77 n. 80, 170
England, English 1, 3, 6, 7, 14, 24, 26, 28–9, 31, 81–8, 90–1,148, 151, 168, 177, 184, 207–8, 220
English, Old 17, 20, 33 n. 27, 109–10, 173
Ethelwold, bp. of Winchester 172
Eulalia 213
Euphorbus 37
Eusebius 186, 206
Eustace, count of Boulogne 130
Evesham 205
    Dominic, prior of 49, 51, 113
Exeter 29 n. 6, 31

Faricius, abt. of Abingdon 20, 120
FitzOsbern, William 45 n. 57
Flambard, Ranulf, bp. of Durham 111, 115
Fleury, Abbo of 97
Franks, Francia 67 n. 11, 140, 142–5, 151
Frederick, bp. of Utrecht 211
French, France 28, 61, 169–70, 183, 217
Freising, Otto of 74 n. 63, 139–52
Frideswide, St 73
Frithegod 171
Fulk, bp. of Beauvais 125

Gaimar, Geffrei 42, 45
Galen 132 n. 18
Gerbert 52–3
Germanus, St 197- 8, 206, 210
Germany 34, 134, 139, 140, 143 n. 20, 146 n. 39, 147, 149–50, 151–2
Gesta Francorum 130
Gildas 76, 176, 182–3, 190, 197
Glastonbury 2, 68, 72 n. 46, 73, 108
Gloucester 167, 209
    Robert of 40, 42–3, 48, 135 n. 27, 168
Godfrey, abt. of Malmesbury: *see* Jumièges, Godfrey of
Godfrey, prior of Winchester 211
Godwine, earl of Wessex 205
Goscelin of Saint-Bertin 15–16, 66, 84, 178–9, 180–1, 184–5, 187
Goths 56, 183
Greece, Greeks 99, 114, 170, 214
    Language 53, 132, 181, 204
Gregory I, Pope 56, 77 n. 80, 118–19, 155–6, 158–60, 162, 208
    his *Registrum* 56
Gregory VI, Pope 143

Gregory VII, Pope 149, 205
Gregory, Master 89–90
Grimbald, abt. of New Minster 172
Guiscard, Robert 149
Gundulf, bp. of Rochester 178–9, 222
Gunnhild, empress 146, 148
Guthlac, St 87 n. 26, 208, 216
Guthlac, a monk 207
Guy, bp. of Lescar 49 n. 2

Hadrian I, Pope 142–3
Harold, k. 6, 101, 197
Harold Harefoot, k. 30
Hastings, Battle of 30, 208, 216
Hatto, bp. of Mainz 150
Hegesippus 183 n. 60, 205
Helias, count of Maine 41–2, 206–7
Heathuredus, bp. of Durham 111 n. 21
Helperic 99
Hengest 191–2, 196–7, 199
Henry I, k. of Germany 142 n. 11
Henry II, emperor 146
Henry III, emperor 141, 145–8
Henry IV, emperor 135, 141, 148–51
Henry V, emperor 143
Henry I, k. of England 39, 40–1, 43–4, 47–8, 52, 70–1, 88, 125, 151, 200
Herbert Losinga, bp. of Norwich 83, 90
Hereford Cathedral 52, 95, 98, 101, 103, 222–3
 bp. of: *see* Robert
Hersfeld, Lambert of 146 n. 41, 147
Hexham 108, 110, 115, 169
Hildebert, bp. of Le Mans 40 n. 25, 108, 114, 169
Hildebrand: *see* Gregory VII
Hildesheim, bp. of 147
Hincmar, abp. of Reims 77 n. 80
Hippocrates 132
Historia Brittonum 180 n. 40, 197–8, 201
Homer 214
Honorius, abp. of Canterbury 179
Honorius Augustodunensis 51, 53 n. 25, 60 n. 64, 62 n. 70
Horace 89
Horsa 191–2, 196, 199
Hubald, archdcn. of Salisbury 207, 216
Hugh, abt. of Cluny 45

Hugh the Chanter 88
Hume, David 191
Huntingdon, Henry of 45, 48, 75, 112 n. 32, 180–1, 185 n. 69, 187, 190–2, 194–5, 200
Hyginus 99
Hippolytus, St 209

Ine, k. of Wessex 72–3
Innocent II, Pope 86
Investiture Controversy 139, 143, 151
Ireland, Irish 28, 34–5, 67 n. 11, 114 n. 37, 170, 176, 190
Irene, empress 141
Isidore of Seville 99–100, 104, 181–2, 204 n. 4
Israel, Israelites 75–6, 172
Italians 82, 83 n. 9, 137 n. 43
Itchington 212
Itinerarium Urbis Romae 130
Ithamar, bp. of Rochester 82
Ivo, St 107 n. 4

Jarrow 114, 169, 176
Jeremiah 212
Jerome, St 119 n. 15, 177, 212, 217
Jerusalem 28, 131, 134–6, 142 n. 11, 148, 211
Jews, Judaism 10, 49–63, 183, 201
John, k. 39
Johnson, Samuel 165 n. 2
Jordanes 183¬–4, 192
Josephus 183, 205, 207
Judith, empress 144
Julius Valerius 44 n. 50
Jumièges, Godfrey of 1–2, 55, 119 nn. 14, 17
Jumièges, William of 30
Justinian, emperor 170
Justus, abp. of Canterbury 179
Jutes 192, 196

Kalonymides dynasty 56
Kenelm, St 82, 84–8
Kent 178 n. 23, 208
Kunigunde, empress 146

Lanfranc, abp. of Canterbury 44 n. 52, 47, 69–71, 83, 90, 172, 184 n. 69, 208, 216
Lanthony Secunda 178

228

Index

Laurence, abp. of Canterbury 18
Leo, Pope 84
Leo IX, Pope 146
Leonard, St 210, 217
Liber Eliensis 75
Liber Pontificalis 114, 125 n. 38, 186
Lindisfarne 110
  bps. of: *see* Aidan, Cuthbert, Edmund, Tilred
  Gospels 111
Liutprand, k. of the Lombards 183
Livy 87 n. 23
Lombards 183
London 29–31, 34, 58, 198 n. 44, 208
Lothar I 144
Louis the Pious, emperor 141, 143–4, 211
Louis III, k. 140 n. 5
Louis IV, k. 140 n. 5
Louis the German, k. 144
Lucan 41 and n. 27, 41 n. 29, 42 and n. 34, 44 and n. 51, 82 n. 4, 89, 205–8

Magna Carta 79
Maine 39, 41, 44, 206
Mainz 95, 150 n. 66
  abp. of 147
Malcolm III, k. of Scotland 31, 44, 200
Malmesbury Abbey 20–1, 24–5, 47, 61, 112–13, 117, 119, 163, 170
  abts. of: *see* Adhelm; Jumièges, Godfrey of; Warin
Manuscripts
  Brussels, Bibl. Royale 2004–2010 121 n. 31
  Cambridge
    CCC 43 113 n. 34
    CCC 139 112 and n. 31
    CCC 330 118 n. 5, 119
    CCC 332 119 n. 15
    Peterhouse 246 121 n. 31
    St John's Coll. A. 22 (22) 100
    Trinity Coll. O. 2. 44 (1148) 119 n. 15
    Trinity Coll. O. 4. 7 (1238) 119 n. 15
    Trinity Coll. O. 5. 20 (1301) 118 n. 7
    Trinity Coll. R. 5. 27 (722) 177 n. 16, 180 n. 34
    Trinity Coll. R. 7. 13 (751) 113 n. 34
    University Libr. Dd. 9. 5 121 n. 29
    University Libr. Dd. 13. 2 87
    University Libr. Ff. 1. 25 113 n. 34
    University Libr. Ff. 1. 27 109
    University Libr. Ff. 4. 32 119 n. 15
    University Libr. Ii. 3. 20 118 n. 6, 158 n. 34, 159 nn. 38, 39, 162 n. 53
  Chicago University Libr. 147, 56 n. 40
  Copenhagen, Kongelike Bibl. Thott. 26 56 n. 40
    Thott. 128 56 n. 40
  Durham Cathedral B. II. 35 114, 178 n. 18
    C. IV. 15 111
  Eton Coll. 80 119 n. 15
  Hereford Cathedral P. V. 1 177 and n. 17
  London
    BL Add. 25014 178 n. 22
    BL Add. 25112 56 n. 40
    BL Arundel 346 56 n. 40
    BL Burney 310 114 n. 43
    BL Cotton Claudius A. V 113
    BL Cotton Claudius E. I 121 n. 31
    BL Cotton Cleopatra C. X 56 n. 40
    BL Cotton Domitian A. VII 112 n. 28
    BL Cotton Nero A. VII 123 n. 35
    BL Cotton Nero C. V 101 103
    BL Cotton Nero E. I 51 n. 14
    BL Cotton Tiberius B. V 53 n. 25
    BL Cotton Vespasian D. XII 119 n. 15
    BL Cotton Vitellius D. XX 110 n. 15
    BL Harl. 3020 51 n. 14
    BL Harl. 3680 177 n. 16, 173 n. 23, 178, 180 n. 34
    BL Harl. 4719 51 n. 14
    BL Royal 5 B. XI 119 n. 15
    BL Royal 5 C. I 119 n. 15
    BL Royal 5 E. XIV 121 n. 31
    BL Royal 5 F. IV 118 n. 6
    BL Royal 5 F. IX 123
    BL Royal 6 A. IV 119 n. 15
    BL Royal 6 C. IV 119 n. 15
    BL Royal 8 D. VIII 121 n. 31
    BL Royal 8 D. XVI 119 n. 15
    BL Royal 12 C. I 119 n. 15
    BL Royal 13 A. VI 112 n. 32
    BL Royal 15 A. XXII 119 n. 15
    BL Royal App. 85 118 n. 7
    Inner Temple Petyt 511. 2 112 n.32

Lambeth Palace Libr. 76 119 n.15
Lambeth Palace Libr. 173 178 and n. 20
Lambeth Palace Libr. 224 118 n. 7, 121 and n. 2, 123 and n. 33, 126, 153 and n. 1
Milan, Bibl. Ambros. C. 72 inf. 183
Oxford
   All Souls Coll. 36 112 n. 32
   Balliol Coll. 240 56 n. 40
   Bodl. Libr. Arch. Seld. B. 16 118 n. 9, 170
   Bodl. Libr. Auct. F. 3. 14 98, 101–5, 118 n. 10, 153 and n. 3
   Bodl. Libr. Bodl. 134 119 n. 15
   Bodl. Libr. Bodl. 297 111 n. 21
   Bodl. Libr. Digby 20 178 and n. 19
   Bodl. Libr. Digby 39, 178
   Bodl. Libr. Fairfax 12 177 n. 16, 180 n. 34
   Bodl. Libr. Laud. misc. 363 160 n. 42
   Bodl. Libr. Laud. misc. 410 56 n. 40
   Bodl. Libr. Laud. misc. 725 159 n. 37
   Bodl. Libr. Rawl. G. 139 118 n. 5
   Corpus Christi Coll. 157 100, 111 n. 21
   Lincoln Coll. 100 118 n. 5
   Magdalen Coll. lat. 172 113, 118 n. 4
   Merton Coll. 19 121 n. 31
   Merton Coll. 181 118 n.8
   Oriel Coll. 42 118 n. 4
   St John's Coll. 97 112 n. 32
Paris
   BnF lat. 2873 56 n. 40
   BnF lat. 3809A 56 n. 40
   BnF lat. 14463 56 n. 40
   BnF lat. 15694 121 n. 31
   BnF lat. 18168 56 n. 40
Rochester Cathedral Libr. A. 3. 5 (on deposit at Maidstone, Kent Archives, DRc/R1) 119 n. 15
Rome, BAV Pal. lat. 830 101
   Vat. lat. 10611 121 n. 31
   Worcester Cath. F. 41 121 n. 31
Marianus Scotus 95–105, 120
Marius 108
Martianus Capella 119
Martel, Charles 142
Martel, Geoffrey 43

Mary, Virgin 10, 17, 49–63, 213
   in the liturgy 60–1
   miracles of vii, 1, 28, 33 n. 28, 49–63, 99, 114, 166 n. 8, 204, 211, 213, 223–4
Mary of Egypt, St 211, 217
Matilda, empress 43 n. 45, 134 n. 27, 168
Matilda, queen 2, 43 n. 41, 125
Matilda, marchioness of Tuscany 124
Mercia, Mercians 29, 84–5, 142, 199
Metz, 77 n. 80
Mildburh, St 209
Monmouth, Geoffrey of 75, 190–1, 199–200
Mont Saint Michel 206
Morcar, earl of Northumbria 31, 208
Muslim(s) 49, 49 n. 2, 53

Narbonne 56
Nathan 75
Neot, St 208, 216
Nicholas, St 53 and n. 25
Noah, 95, 102
Nogent, Guibert of 58 n. 53, 136
Norman Conquest 7, 9 n. 33, 18, 58 nn. 52 and 54, 166, 171–2, 191, 199, 201
Normandy, Normans 4, 7, 18, 31, 35, 39–40, 55–6, 58 n. 53, 71, 81–3, 88, 90–1, 101, 107, 123, 166–7, 172–3, 177, 189–90, 199–201, 205, 208, 216
Northumbria, Northumbrians 28, 31, 34–5, 72, 109, 142, 173, 180, 187, 208, 216
Norway, Norwegians 129–30, 133, 136–7, 170

Octavian, emperor 53
Oda, abp. of Canterbury 72, 172, 213, 217
Offa, k. of Mercia 142, 185 n. 74
Orontes r. 131
Orosius 2–3, 193–4
Osbern of Canterbury 15, 17, 33–4, 82
Osbern Pinnock 86
Oswald, k. of Bernicia 76, 172, 181, 182 n. 51
Oswald, bp. of Worcester 84
Oswine, k. of Deira 76 n. 77, 204
Ottonians, 140, 142, 145
Ouse, r. 34

Index

Outremer 130
Ovid 37, 156 n. 21, 207
Oxford 30, 219–23

Pacuvius 210, 217
Palladius 210
Paris 139
  Gilo of 131, 136
Paschasius 214
Paul the Deacon 51, 52 n. 17, 183
Paulinus, abp. of Canterbury 28
Paulinus of Nola 206, 216
Peter, St 73, 85–6, 89
Petronius Maximus 204
Pharsalia 208
Philip, k. of France 210
Picts 190, 193–5
Pippin, k. 142
Plautus 210, 217
Pliny 176, 222 n. 9
Poitiers, William of 30 n. 16
Pope, Alexander 9 n. 35
Pompey 208
Procopius 192
Prudentius 209–10, 213, 217–18
Prüm, Regino of 79 n. 87, 111, 145 n. 29
Pythagoras 37

Ralph, bp. of Chichester 38 n. 8
Ralph, abt. of Battle 119 n. 15, 160
Raymond of St Gilles, count of Toulouse 57 n. 46, 131
Reading Abbey 100
Reccared, k. of the Visigoths 56
Regularis Concordia 78
Richmond 115
Rievaulx, Aelred of 156
Ripon 108, 110, 115
  Stephen of 108
Robert, bp. of Hereford 95, 97–105
Rocamadour 61 n. 68
Rochester Cathedral 119–20, 127, 178–9
  bps. of: *see* Gundulf, Ithamar
  See also Textus Roffensis
Roger, bp. of Salisbury 47, 204, 215
Rome, Romans 10, 21, 24–5, 29, 33 n. 28, 34–5, 38, 40–2, 81–91, 96, 99, 108, 115, 118, 119 n. 15, 135, 139, 141–6, 149, 151–2, 154–5, 158, 160, 169–73, 176, 178, 183, 185 n. 74, 189–201, 203, 208–9
Roscelin of Compiègne 125
Rouen 58, 210
Rufinus 206, 216

Sæwig of Ratcliffe 204, 215
Saint-Bertin, Goscelin of 15–16, 66, 84, 178–81, 184–5, 187
Saint-Calais, William of, bp. of Durham 111, 180
Saint-Evroul 199
Saint-Pierre-sur-Dives 61 n. 68
Salians 145–8
Salisbury 112
  John of 5, 42, 89–90, 157 n. 24
Sallust 210
Saracens 134
Saul, k. 75
Saxons (continental) 141, 166, 176, 191–201
Saxons, East 29
Scandinavia, Scandinavians 115 n. 44, 133, 170
Scot, John the 22, 112–14, 172
Scots, Scotland 28, 31, 35, 44 n. 53, 114, 133, 169–70, 193, 200–1
Scotus, David 143 n. 20, 143 n. 22
Seneca 77 n. 80, 84, 114, 166, 212, 220
Sergius, Pope 24, 114
Severus, emperor 194
Sherborne 73, 107
Sicily 212
Sidon 130, 184 n. 63
Sidonius Apollinaris 204, 212 n. 17, 215
Sigurd, k. of Norway 129–30, 136–8
Sir Aldingar, Ballad of 146 n. 39
Solomon, k. 75
Somerset 1
Spain 56
Statius 208, 213
Stephanus, Eddius: *see* Ripon, Stephen of
Stephen, k. 131, 168
Stigand, abp. of Canterbury 73
Stoics 157–8
Suetonius 38 n. 10, 82 n. 4, 192–4, 207
Swein, k., 30, 74
Swithhun, bp. of Winchester 73, 107 n .4
Sylvester II, Pope: *see* Gerbert

231

Syrio, Marcus Aurelius 108

Tancred 134
Telese, Alexander of 74 n. 63
Textus Roffensis 119
Theobald, abp. of Canterbury 178
Theocritus 214
Theodore 49 n. 1, 53–5, 62
Theodosian Code 170
Theodulf of Orleans 114 n. 37
Theophilus 49 nn. 1, 3, 51–3, 61
Thomas II, abp. of York, 125 n. 37
Thomas Becket, abp. of Canterbury 33
Tiber, r. 135
Tiberias, 184 n. 63
Tilred, bp. of Lindisfarne 111 n. 21
Titus, emperor 205, 207, 215
Toledo 49 n. 1, 55–62
   Cathedral 56
Toulouse 41 n. 1, 57, 59, 62
   bp. of: *see* Amelius
   counts of: *see* Raymond of St Gilles, William
Trinovantes 193
Troy, Trojans 118, 170, 212
Tyre 130

Urban II, Pope 83, 133, 169

Vegetius 133
Vespasian, emperor 205
Vikings 22, 29–33, 73, 110, 201
   See also Scandinavians
Visigoths 56–7
Vitalis, Orderic, 31, 40–2, 45, 75, 88, 130 n. 8, 199–200, 204–6, 216
Vitellius, emperor 207, 216
Vortigern 196–8
Vortimer 196–201

Wace 42, 45, 75
Wærburh, St 19, 23, 26
Wærstan, bp. 72 n. 47
Walcher, prior of Malvern 98
Wales, Welsh 28–9, 35, 44, 107, 133, 199, 200

Wales, Gerald of 5, 28, 114 n. 37
Wallingford 212
Waltheof, earl of Northumberland 18, 26, 31
Warin the Breton 194, 200 n. 51
Warin of Lire, abt. of Malmesbury 55
Wear, r. 109
Wecta 196
Wearmouth 114, 169, 176
Wenlock 209
Westminster Abbey 55
Wihtgisl 196
Wilfrid, St 16–17, 83, 90, 108, 181, 210, 213, 217
William I, k. 30–1, 43, 46–7, 55, 58 n. 54, 69–72, 101, 172, 199, 210
William II, k. 37–48, 206
William, count of Mortain 48
William, count of Toulouse 57 n. 46
Wiltshire 1
Winchcombe Abbey 84
Winchester 30, 46 n. 64, 86
   Cathedral 94
   bps. of: *see* Ethelwold; Blois, Henry of; Swithhun
   Hyde Abbey 94
   New Minster 94
Witta 196
Woden, 196
Worcester 17 and n. 20, 60 n. 64, 68, 98–116
   Cathedral, 51–2, 224
   bps. of: *see* Ecgwine, Oswald, Wulfstan
   John of 6, 75, 98–116, 200
   See also Coleman
Worms, Concordat of 143
Wulfstan, abp. of York 77–8
Wulfstan II, bp. of Worcester 17–18, 72 n. 47, 74, 98, 107, 110, 173, 205, 212, 214, 217

York 28, 31, 34–5, 59 n. 55, 113, 115, 169, 173, 178 n. 18
   abps. of: *see* Ealdred, Wulfstan

Zadok 75